Contents

Chapter 1

Computer Graphics, Visualization, and Virtual Reality, 35

Chapter 2

Virtual Worlds and the World Wide Web, 77

VRML
Exploring Virtual Worlds on the Internet

Walter Goralski ■ Matthew Poli
■ Peter Vogel

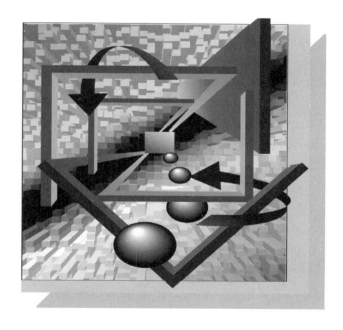

PRENTICE HALL PTR

UPPER SADDLE RIVER, NEW JERSEY 07458

http://www.prenhall.com

Library of Congress Cataloging-in-Publication Data

Goralski, Walter.
    VRML : exploring virtual worlds on the Internet / Walter Goralski,
  Matthew Poli, Peter Vogel.
        p.   cm.
    Includes index.
    ISBN 0–13–486960–5
    1. VRML (Document markup language)   2. Internet (Computer network)
 I. Poli, Matthew.   II. Vogel, Peter.   III. Title.
QA76.76.H94G67   1996
006--dc20

                               96–24170
                                  CIP

Acquisitions editor: Mary Franz
Cover designer: Design Source
Cover design director: Jerry Votta
Manufacturing manager: Alexis R. Heydt
Compositor/Production services: Pine Tree Composition, Inc.

 © 1997 by Prentice Hall PTR
Prentice-Hall, Inc.
A Simon & Schuster Company
Upper Saddle River, New Jersey 07458

The publisher offers discounts on this book when ordered in
bulk quantities. For more information contact:

  Corporate Sales Department
  Prentice Hall PTR
  One Lake Street
  Upper Saddle River, New Jersey 07458

  Phone: 800-382-3419
  Fax: 201-236-7141
  email: corpsales@prenhall.com

Printed in the United States of America
10 9 8 7 6 5 4 3 2 1

ISBN: 0-13-486960-5

Prentice-Hall International (UK) Limited, *London*
Prentice-Hall of Australia Pty. Limited, *Sydney*
Prentice-Hall Canada Inc., *Toronto*
Prentice-Hall Hispanoamericana, S.A., *Mexico*
Prentice-Hall of India Private Limited, *New Delhi*
Prentice-Hall of Japan, Inc., *Tokyo*
Simon & Schuster Asia Pte. Ltd., *Singapore*
Editora Prentice-Hall do Brasil, Ltda., *Rio de Janeiro*

Chapter 5

An Introduction
to the VRML Language, 209

Chapter 6

Creating Simple Virtual Worlds, 261

Chapter 7

The Future of VRML, 325

Appendix A

Internet Browser Fundamentals, 347

Appendix B

The Virtual Reality Modeling Language, 369

Preface

In late 1995, the first version of the Virtual Reality Modeling Language (VRML) was completed. This made it possible for "world builders" to construct realistic, interactive, three dimensional models of reality, and place these worlds on the World Wide Web portion of the Internet. The real world has never quite been the same since, although it may take a while for VRML to become common to other Internet tools like Java or ShockWave. The good news is that no one needs to wait any longer at all. Virtual worlds exist on the Internet now. They are waiting to be explored by the first 3D travelers in cyberspace. This book is about exploring these 3D virtual worlds on the Internet.

After people have seen Internet virtual worlds in 3D with VRML, the effect is similar to walking outside into the park after years of staring at a flat TV screen. Information is no longer presented on a 2D page, as in a book, but by being experienced, as on a nature walk. Instead of looking at pictures of birds and having an annoying "click here" demanding to be pushed to hear a peep, VRML promises a walk through the marsh, with birds rising on either side, calling to each other.

Such a VRML virtual world is still in the future. But there is plenty to see and do in the meantime. This book is a guide for this future.

About the Book

Introduction—The Promise of VRML: The introduction will familiarize you with the potential of VRML and virtual worlds on the Internet. The whole process of Web browsing, world building, and other issues are discussed. The terms used with these activities can be confusing, so they are all introduced here. The relationship of VRML to other Web tools such as Java and ShockWave is also introduced.

Chapter 1—Computer Graphics, Visualization, and Virtual Reality: This chapter outlines the development of computer-based "Virtual Reality." Graphical interfaces have always been crucial for human-machine interactions. The chapter traces the development of computer graphics and graphical interfaces. It also explores the relationship between the graphical visualization of information and the idea of "virtual worlds" where everything is graphical. Virtual Reality is the logical conclusion of information visualization in this context.

Chapter 2—Virtual Worlds and the World Wide Web: This introduces you to the concept of virtual worlds on the World Wide Web. As becomes obvious after tracing the evolution of the Internet and World Wide Web, Virtual Reality is the logical conclusion of information visualization on the Internet. You are now ready to explore this new version of "cyberspace."

Chapter 3—WorldView—A VRML Browser: This chapter introduces you to the publicly available VRML browser. Details of WorldView's installation, configuration, and operation are given fully in simple language. Step-by-step instructions and illustrations make this task easy for even the most inexperienced users.

Chapter 4—Exploring Virtual Worlds: In this chapter you will use the VRML browser installed in the previous chapter. You will explore several example *worlds,* and many possible Internet VRML sites are recommended for independent exploration and study. The whole point is to detail the function and operation of almost every option and button available to you.

Chapter 5—An Introduction to the VRML Language: This chapter introduces you to the intricacies of the VRML language itself. There is added emphasis to the understanding and utility of VRML for even the most unsophisticated potential users. This chapter also points out that VRML is much more complex than HTML and can easily become confusing. You will examine key aspects of the VRML specification with the idea of de-mystifying some of the more accessible components of VRML from a user perspective.

Chapter 6—Creating Simple Virtual Worlds: This chapter will allow you to build some simple, yet complete, virtual worlds of their very own, which can then be accessed and explored with a VRML browser, or even made available to others on the Web itself. Even after exploring the complexities of VRML, you can still feel confident that VRML is useful and useable by novices and non-computer scientist types.

Chapter 7—The Future of VRML: This chapter closes the book with a speculative look at the future of VRML and the whole idea of virtual worlds on the Web. You will become more comfortable with how other new Web tools such as Java and ShockWave fit into the VRML picture. You will be left with the valid impression that you have embarked on an exciting new journey.

Appendices

Appendix A—Internet Browser Fundamentals: This appendix is a "review" for many readers, but an essential part of any introduction for readers not yet familiar with *surfing the Internet*. It fills in the details of operation of a variety of browsers, particularly Netscape. It introduces details of some concepts mentioned earlier, but at a higher level. Such concepts explored more fully include HTML itself and the key idea of "Helper Applications" for URL formats that are not HTML (which has direct relevance to VRML).

Appendix B—The VRML Specification: This appendix contains the latest version of the VRML 1.1 specification.

Appendix C—Guide to the WorldView Browser: This appendix takes all of the options and commands for the WorldView VRML browser and reproduces them in one convenient place.

Appendix D—VRML Resources and Web Sites: Some places to look for more information on VRML and related products.

Appendix E—Other Sources of Information, Products and Services: More places to look for VRML information.

Appendix F—The CD-ROM contains all examples and several tools for using VRML.

About the Authors

Walter Goralski has spent more than 25 years in the data communications field, including 14 years with AT&T. He is currently a Senior Member of the Technical Staff at Hill Associates of Burlington, Vermont, and a professor of computer science at Pace University Graduate School in New York. He is the author of several books on ATM and TCP/IP, courses on APPN and SNA, and articles on data communications and other issues.

Matthew Poli has a BS in Physics and an MS in Computer Science. He is currently a technical consultant at the Pace Computer Learning Center in New York. He has served as managing editor for many books from the *Getting Started* software series and is currently working on several Internet related projects at Pace University.

Peter Vogel has a BA from Pace University. He is currently the PC Applications and System Support Analyst for Pace University's School of Computer Science and Information Systems. His current activities include implementation of a University-wide network and administration of the World Wide Web server at the university.

Introduction

The Promise of VRML

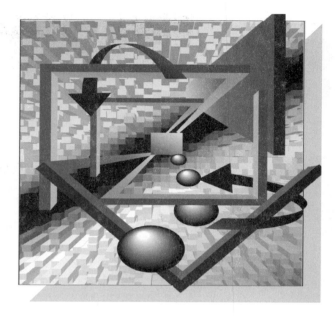

What Are Internet Virtual Worlds?

Virtual Reality on the Web portion of the Internet is a new way to experience and encounter information. It is no more but no less than this. Some still use terms like World Wide Web, or WWW, to describe this portion of the Internet, but just *Web* is enough today. The Virtual Reality Modeling Language (VRML) is a type of programming language for creating "virtual worlds" on the Web for those with VRML-enabled browsers such as Netscape or Mosaic to navigate. The use of the word *navigate* is intentional and fitting. There are real spaces to maneuver in. Scrolling becomes strolling. Instead of merely reading the text of a book found in a Web site library, virtual worlds on the Web allow for the experiencing of content of the book itself.

Consider the following scenario. A person with a personal computer and access to the Internet and Web today can easily find a book about almost any topic with only a few minutes searching. But a book is only a book. Suppose that the object of the search was a book about the Great Pyramid. The seeker could be a high school or university student, a specialist with considerable knowledge in the field of Egyptology, or just an interested private citizen on a lunch break. The Internet access could be provided by the school, by a corporation, or by any Internet service provider on a dial-up basis from the comfort of one's own home.

A book on the Great Pyramid today would contain many pictures of the Great Pyramid. A flat, static representation of this wonder of the world. A VRML book on the

Great Pyramid on the Web today would *contain the Great Pyramid*. The Great Pyramid would be there in all its glory, to be not only looked at, but walked around, flown over, and clambered up. The interior passages could be squeezed into and crawled through. The central burial chamber could be experienced in bright light or semi-darkness. The shafts pointing to the stars could be peered through, while the stars rotated into view in their season and time. The great empty stone box in the King's Chamber can be explored both inside and out.

This is not to say that the Great Pyramid VRML book has no text. On the contrary, the text available at the Great Pyramid virtual world site on the Web could be many times the amount of text accessible in a book. This is because books have to be made to be portable and affordable. A truly large book containing all of the accepted knowledge and information on even a small topic could not be carried. Multiple volumes are possible, of course, but only at a considerable increase in price. And portability of the set becomes a new problem.

The text for the Great Pyramid VRML book need not be written on pages of paper, either. The text could appear when needed with a point and click of a mouse button. A point at an object and a click on the right mouse button could bring up a whole "what's this?" query answer, cross-indexed from various sources of information scattered all over the world on the Internet and presented in the virtual world itself. A point at something else and a click on the left mouse button could bring up a background material audio presentation, the audio portion just being spoken text, of course. This additional audio material, and even animated video, could be programmed in the Java programming language and embedded in the VRML world.

It should be emphasized that few of these activities involving the Great Pyramid of Giza would be possible even with a trip to Egypt. Various restrictions limit access to the more interesting aspects of the Great Pyramid to a select few, if at all. The student or specialist or citizen has capabilities undreamed of without the existence of virtual worlds on the Internet.

Virtual worlds on the Internet do not allow for the experience of the Web "as never before." They allow for the experience of *experience itself* as never before. The Great Pyramid has not yet appeared on the Internet. But there is no reason why it cannot and should not.

Magic Words of Power

The Internet. The Web. Netscape. Mosaic. Java. VRML. The words used in the preceding section appear constantly and insistently in many books, magazine articles, financial and business newspaper pages, on radio shows, and on television programs. The repeated use and appearance of these words seems to embody them with a certain kind of power. These words have come to possess an almost magical potency and to have attained a level of meaning far beyond that of mere definition.

The Internet has become not merely a worldwide network linking computers and networks all over the world, but has come to represent a nearly mystical land where all the people of the world gather on equal terms to discuss important concepts like peace and hunger in a free-flowing environment beyond the reach of the forces of repression. The Web has become not merely a subset of this Internet with point-and-click links to other information, but has come to represent a kind of ideal marketplace where goods and money change hands, movies are advertised and previewed, and any worthwhile product must be marketed.

Netscape and Mosaic began as words and names to represent browser programs, which are user application tools to explore the Web and other portions of the Internet in a more user-friendly manner, and have ended up representing brilliant stock market investments (in the case of Netscape) or the promise and fulfillment of the Internet (in the case of Mosaic). Java threatens to follow along this same path to icon-hood, having come from representing a new kind of object-oriented programming language for the Web to representing a whole new wave of ideas and software that will transform the Internet.

VRML has also begun the transition from concrete term to abstract promise. Magazines can now splash cover blurbs claiming that VRML "means you'll experience the Web as you never have before" without even considering how the difference is meaningful or significant, or even why such a change might be desired. But what is the problem? Why should anyone care whether a word like Web is a real place or a wonderland? Because once any word like *Internet* or *VRML* has made the transition from concrete to abstract, from term to promise, from object to symbol, it becomes that much more difficult to *understand* the meaning and purpose of the concept behind the word in the first place. The process of understanding is even more difficult in this case for the amateur, who now feels like an intruder treading on holy ground.

There are many reasons why Virtual Reality seems to have exploded overnight. One is the decrease in price of sophisticated virtual reality hardware. A head-mounted VR goggle has come down in price from about $6,000 two years ago into the $500 to $1,000 range. Specialized VR trackballs with six degrees of freedom (up/down, left/right, in/out, and pitch, roll, and yaw) have come down from about $1,000 to about $200.

Another reason is the increased availability and power of software capable of creating and exploring virtual worlds. More and more games are using either full VR or at least full 3D designs, including Nintendo's Virtual Boy game product. Several commercial software products are available and affordable for creating 3D and VR worlds based on VRML. Several of these products even work in Windows, whereas earlier VR products usually needed a powerful UNIX workstation to function at all. Microsoft's commitment to VR products and the whole virtual world concept lends instant credibility to VR.

The third reason is the tremendous increase in processing power available on even home computers. An even modestly fast Pentium processor running at 75 MHz can create and display dazzling worlds of light and motion. Astonishingly, PCs from only a few years ago will not even run much of the advanced software available today intended for modern processing platforms. And when the advances of truly sophisticated UNIX workstations are thrown in, the possibilities are even more staggering.

The combination of all three factors means that virtual reality is no longer a promise and a dream, as it was for decades. Virtual reality is no longer a plaything for science fiction buffs only. Virtual reality is as close as the Internet.

What is the meaning and purpose of VRML in this context of virtual reality in general? That is what this book is about. It is one thing to say that VRML lets people experience the Web as they "never have before." It is quite another to point out exactly what is different and why anyone should care. That is also a goal of this book.

Virtual Reality and Real Reality

Virtual reality is sometimes called *cyberspace,* but this term has been misused and misapplied so frequently in the recent past that it has become essentially meaningless. This fact has not prevented anyone at all from using it, in contexts from "colonizing cyberspace" to "civilizing cyberspace" to "controlling cyberspace." In this book, the term *cyberspace* will just mean those portions of the Internet and Web that have begun to implement VRML. Whether cyberspace needs colonization, civilizing, control, or even tidying up a bit will not be considered further. But the truth is that the term cyberspace is probably better for describing the intent and content of VRML than virtual reality. Here is why.

The word *virtual* itself needs some explaining. The use of the word virtual indicates that the term after it is not used in the same sense as the original term, but it looks just like the real thing. Virtual memory in a computer is not real memory, but it works just like real computer memory. In fact, virtual memory works so much like real memory that no one could possibly make a distinction based on its operation.

It also has often been pointed out that the term *virtual* in combination with anything else means that the second term is a lie. For instance, virtual money means that the term *money* is a lie. There is no real money involved in virtual money. Substitute the word *fake* for *virtual* to get a feel for the implications of this definition. *Fake money* has none of the magic of the term *virtual money,* but the use of this term would evoke many protests from financial visionaries. Virtual money is not the same as counterfeit, they would claim. After all, virtual money works so much like real money that no one could possibly make a distinction based on its operation. But no one wants to get paid in *virtual money.*

So virtual reality would seem to work so much like real reality that no one could possibly make a distinction based on its operation. Of course this cannot be true. The virtual worlds created with VRML are not that good—yet. And while some cyberspace visionaries cannot seem to wait for the day when immersion in a virtual world on the Web will be indistinguishable from walking down the street, many will find this thought rather disconcerting.

This only points out that virtual reality has a number of levels of meaning. The term *virtual reality* has been used to apply to everything from PC-based games like Doom II, allowing a mouse-maneuvering game player to stalk and be stalked in dark corridors and passageways shredding everything in sight with astonishingly effective weaponry, to expensive and sophisticated head-movement tracking helmets and goggles that are used for some government training exercises that seem to rival Doom II itself. The difference is mainly in the degree of immersion in the scene itself.

Virtual Reality can be experienced at arm's length, on a computer screen or series of video monitors that present a nearly 360 degree field of view to the participant. It is most common to explore virtual worlds with this degree of involvement. But with the investment in additional hardware and software, the experience of virtual worlds can be made more immediate and personal.

For example, goggles can be added to a PC in order to feed an image of the monitor screen directly into each eye of the participant. These goggles are no longer an expensive luxury, but a viable option. A step beyond goggles is a complete head-motion tracking unit. These "helmets" can track the motion of the user's head and adjust the view in real time to reflect the changes on scenery. A glance up shows the ceiling of the virtual room. A look down examines the floor. And adding a glove-like device (a "data glove" to some) to track arm motions and hand movements instead of controlling a mouse is not that much more difficult or costly than the simple goggles. Usually, pointing ahead means moving ahead, down means stop, and so on. But it seems to be only a matter of time before footgear for virtual walking becomes common. Some may find this possibility of total immersion in a virtual world fascinating, others may find it spooky, and still others may find it dangerous.

Virtual Worlds on the Internet are usually explored with nothing more sophisticated than a PC, mouse, and Internet connection to the World Wide Web, dial-up or direct connection through a LAN.

Virtual Reality and the Internet

Until the 1990s, few people had even heard of the Internet. Those that had were usually university students, government employees, or U.S. military contractors. There were few signs that this network would suddenly grow into the worldwide community and storehouse of knowledge that the Internet has become.

One of the problems that the Internet had to overcome was the incredibly dense and awkward user interface needed to maneuver around the Internet. This interface was inherited from the UNIX world of a command-line driven interface of typed command and terse response. Usually a command executed without a problem gave no response at all! But an interface that could be used only by programmers and "techies" was not a problem in a world where the only people using the Internet were programmers and techies.

Things changed in the 1990s when the rest of the world discovered the Internet. The proliferation of PCs in offices and homes led to the development of on-line services such as CompuServe and Prodigy. These users were less sophisticated than UNIX wizards and, at the same time, more or less expecting the simpler interfaces of a commercial service.

The change to the old Internet interfaces came slowly at first, but with increased pace in the 1990s. A good part of the recent explosion in Internet use, and probably the actual cause of it, has been the drastic change in the way that ordinary people can access the treasure troves of Internet information. New Internet access service providers, such as America Online, have created Internet interfaces that anyone who knows how to use a computer with a mouse can handle with ease. These new interfaces hide the cryptic Internet commands behind an enormously easy to use interface. The new interfaces have combined with the new Internet popularity to make it possible for a whole generation of users, both corporate and private, to take the Internet where it has never gone before.

The most sweeping and most recent change to the Internet interface came only a few years ago. With the advent of the Web, or World Wide Web, it was possible to tie all of the available Internet computers and resources together into a rich fabric of text, graphics, images, movies, and sounds. The Web has even created for itself a brand-new kind of "publishing," a publishing without paper and one that could not even exist on paper. This was the *Web page*.

The Web page made it possible for ordinary citizens to have a presence and personality on the Web portion of the Internet. Usually, when a Web page is used to represent an individual's interests and career, the Web page is called a "home page." But it is good to keep in mind that not all Web pages are necessarily home pages. A home page could reflect a person's interests, hobbies, job, or family. Sounds could be mixed in with pictures of the children, or a movie combined with a master's thesis. Home pages could be linked to other home pages. The other Web pages could belong to another family member, a close friend, a favorite rock band, or even a senator. The Web today has ended up looking more like a familiar family album than a library or even a shopping mall. The Web page has given the Internet a personality, and a warm, friendly, and human one at that.

But what was missing from this vast collection of Web pages was a sense of *location*, or place. People need places to occupy and live in. The places can be as simple and natural as a cave, or as architecturally complex as a cathedral. Either one could end up being equally awe-inspiring and sacred (think of the various painted caves of early human culture). These early architectures became sacred spaces in the form of temples. Whole civilizations came to define themselves through the structure of their sacred places, from the Temple of Jerusalem to the Acropolis in Greece. The sacred places became gathering places that grew into cities. And the development of cities led to the beginning of this marvelous journey humanity still finds itself embarked upon.

So location and place are an essential part of the human experience and civilization. This being the case, it seems only natural that the Internet should be as concerned and involved with architecture as it is with text. The question is one of how to best create and build the "sacred" spaces and eventual cities of the Internet? The answer is VRML.

Users must do several things before they are able to explore Internet virtual worlds with VRML. First, the user has to obtain a tool that understands and "speaks" the VRML language. These are the VRML browsers. There are freely available and downloadable versions of several browser products. Some examples are Caligari worldSpace, Intervista WorldView, Paper Software's WebFX and TGS WebSpace. Most browsers allow users just to browse in 3D. Other related software tools allow for various levels of 3D world creation with VRML authoring. Since most people browse before they build, and a lot of people only browse, this book will focus on browsing first and discuss aspects of the creation of VRML worlds later.

After a user has installed and configured the VRML browser, a VRML file can be loaded the same way a user would access an HTML file. This is usually accomplished either by clicking a mouse button on a link or typing in a URL and hitting the return key. Based on the speed of the connection and the size of the VRML file, loading times can vary from as little as a few seconds to as much as a few minutes (and sometimes even beyond). The more well-structured VRML worlds will allow the VRML browser to load the file, representing the virtual world, in pieces. The advantage is that a user can start exploring the virtual world immediately while the browser is fetching more detailed objects and those that are not in view from the present user perspective.

Objects in a VRML virtual world on the Internet are linked in the same way that HTML pages on the Web have links elsewhere. If a user points and clicks on these links, the user jumps either to another VRML world or to even another media type like a 2D HTML page. This is an effective method for traveling from place to place on the Web, but it also leads to the same problem as jumping from link to link in HTML. The problem is that a user can jump from a document on one topic on a server in one place to another document on a different topic in a completely different place. This can be disorienting, to say the least.

There are some ways to offset this feeling of disorientation. When people walk through a room, a town, or a city, they look around constantly and build up a mental map of the environment. If someone gives directions to turn left at the next intersection, people can visualize this information and get where they want to go easily. There is a sense of flow, of continuity, and people use this sense to see how quickly they are progressing toward the goal. People do sometimes get lost, but this is part of the whole experience, and often that is how people discover new places or meet new people. In either case, there is a sense of going somewhere. Merely typing in a URL and watching the byte counters roll as the information at the destination loads into the computer is just not the same.

Of course, many programmers and experts have no trouble with this jumping around the Internet and Web. Experts can use the Internet just by typing UNIX commands like "ftp" and "telnet". But the vast majority of people will only get on-line and explore the Internet if it works just like the real world. URLs can be very abstract and difficult to understand and remember. And of course jumping from one page fragment to another is not something that people do on a daily basis (consider the feeling of mild annoyance when a "continued on page . . ." is encountered in a magazine article).

Once the Web allows normal, everyday users to navigate using spatial perception and conforms to the way real people work instead of forcing users to adapt to the way that computers work, the Web will become just another place to go. On this new and improved Web, people can accomplish what they set out to do, meet with friends old and new, and even learn new skills.

HTML and VRML

HTML is much more restrictive than VRML when it comes to navigating the Web. When viewing two-dimensional home pages, options are essentially limited to jumping from page to page and looking at images from a fixed, pre-determined perspective. However, when exploring VRML worlds on the Internet, people can freely choose the perspective from which to experience the VRML world. Moreover, users can wander unencumbered through dazzling 3D worlds, the contents of which are only limited by the imaginations of the world creator. VRML worlds are very inexpensive to build, and normal rules, like gravity, can be suspended for the object within a VRML world and often are. Users can walk or fly through these virtual worlds and pick up objects, turn them over, and inspect them from all sides.

Creators of VRML worlds have even more capabilities. With simple authoring techniques, anyone can create and modify 3D objects to inhabit a VRML world of their very own. If a creator does not like the color of an object like a car or house, a few clicks of the mouse can repaint the object in a different color. VRML allows 2D home pages to expand into a realm of 3D home worlds.

The Internet is growing in leaps and bounds. Whole libraries are being made available on the Internet. The text of most older works from earlier centuries are accessible in a number of places. More and more commercial sites are being added to the Web each day.

The increasing pace of this avalanche of available information should not be underestimated. In the book *Multimedia and Hypertext: The Internet and Beyond,* by Jakob Nielson, the author reports some statistics on Internet and Web growth that applied to the beginning of 1995 (see Table I-1). The numbers have only increased since then.

Table I-1

Internet and Web Growth in	Annual Growth Rate (percent)	Doubling Time (days)
Number of Internet hosts	85	411
Amount of Internet traffic	121	320
Amount of Web traffic	2,136	81
Number of Web servers	679	123

The numbers illustrate the explosive growth of the Internet and Web and the information available through these means. A doubling time of 123 days for Web sites means than if the number of Web sites today is 50,000 then only 123 days from now (a little over four months), the number of Web sites will double. Web site information availability in the form of URLs is now popping up all over the place, from TV automobile advertisements (http://www.toyota.com) to motion picture timetables in daily newspapers (http://www.paramount.com).

Companies with commercial sites see the Internet and Web as a way to do business, of course. Whether the goal is to make marketing information available through the Web or to make actual sales, the whole point is to get people (potential customers) to visit. Traditional commercial Web sites can draw in new visitors by adding three-dimensional worlds that are fun to explore and by providing a natural way to navigate through the information available at the site. Eventually, visitors will be able to collaborate with others in rich 3D worlds rather than typing away at the command prompt in a text-based "chat room".

Networking VRML

All experienced Web server and site administrators must be concerned about the bandwidth required for VRML enhancements. Many early Web enthusiasts, quickly implementing high-resolution images, sound, and video to attract visitors to a site, found out just as quickly that these additions made the site very slow or even inaccessible to the millions of ordinary people who connect to the Internet by means of a common 14.4k modem. But since more and more HTML browsers have added the necessary support for the incremental loading of images (rather than attempting to load the images all at once), many Web server administrators have changed the images at the site so that the images can be loaded in pieces. This practice has made even the most graphic-intensive Web site much more accessible to the average modem user.

If a user accesses such a site, where images may be loaded progressively and the user has a browser that supports this increasingly common feature, users may start reading text and clicking on links before the images have completely arrived and been displayed on the monitor. Often these users will see an image that is very fuzzy or only shows every other line. While it is true that VRML files are usually more compact than Web video files and often even smaller than high-resolution graphic images, the better VRML browsers and add-on tools will allow users to access 3D virtual worlds in pieces. This process is known as "in-lining". With in-lining, a VRML world designer can break up large VRML worlds into a collection of smaller files that can be loaded incrementally, piece by piece.

An HTML browser has no idea what image or what part of an image is of most interest to a user. On the other hand, a VRML browser *knows* where a user actually is within a VRML world, and in what direction the user is facing. The VRML browser can use this user-perspective information to give the highest priority to loading the objects that are in the user's current field of view. All remaining objects are loaded in the background or as the user's point of view changes.

Many VRML files are surprisingly small and may not even require any in-lining. In contrast, images, audio, and video files tend to be somewhat large because these file types must store every piece of information that appears on the monitor bit by bit. Because a similar bit by bit approach would get very complex very quickly in a virtual world, VRML files just store sets of coordinates for each object and some simple instructions to the VRML browser on how to connect the "dots" and how to display the resulting surfaces. Since the VRML browser still has to generate the 3D world from this information, the real bottleneck for large-scale VRML environments is the power of the video card and the CPU, and, to a lesser extent, the bandwidth of the Internet connection.

VRML also includes a feature that has been used quite successfully by game developers for a number of years: the concept of *levels of detail* (*LOD*). Through levels of detail, the VRML browser can take some shortcuts and display a rough approximation of an object in the background before displaying the object in full detail. Since the user always has a first-person perspective in VRML, the browser always *knows* what the user is looking at. For instance, if the user's point of view is still quite far away from an object, the VRML browser can merely display the approximation, which is the same object at a lower level of detail.

As the user moves closer to the approximated object, the VRML browser will dynamically display higher and higher resolutions of the same object. Once the user gets close enough to the object to examine it in some detail, the object is displayed in full detail. If the designer of the virtual world has chosen the correct "switch points" for levels of detail, the user will not even notice any abrupt transitions in detail. Far-away objects are usually so small that users cannot see more detailed features in any case.

Levels of detail exist in VRML to help the video card and CPU maintain acceptable movement rates. This is because levels of detail keep down the number of objects that have to be displayed in full detail in real time. Displaying the full details of all objects in a world, even the most remote ones, of course, will only slow down the entire process. With levels of detail, moving closer to an object will increase the detail for that particular object, but the total number of objects that have to displayed in a VRML world may actually go down. This is because other objects may move out of the field of view and no longer need to be displayed at all. Levels of detail enable an experienced VRML world designer to keep the total number of objects in view fairly constant and allow the VRML browser to maintain a decent speed of movement as a user moves through the VRML world.

At first, the levels of detail may seem counter-productive. After all, the VRML browser will only have to download several versions of every object that contain multiple levels of detail. This can only slow down the entire process anyway. But this is exactly the situation where in-lining comes into play. One of the best features of VRML is that a VRML world designer can combine levels of detail and in-lining of objects. This means that a user can display a world with little initial delay and only load the more detailed versions of an object as the user moves closer to it. So levels of detail and in-lining are two key features of VRML that can be used together to make it possible to build very large virtual worlds on the Internet that are easily accessible to the greatest number of average users.

Web Sites and VRML

VRML worlds will be a critical part of each Web site that is intended to snare users and keep them coming back for more. Eventually, all Web sites will include some degree of 3D content. There is an important role to play for virtual 3D worlds in almost every Web site. A possible exception might be sites where the content is highly symbolic and therefore difficult to visualize effectively, or where the potential visitors are used to accessing information through the older command-line interfaces and are comfortable with these methods. But even in the case where Web site content is primarily symbolic, a good VRML world designer can use 3D to help any less symbolically inclined visitors to visualize the information. An example might be a mathematician who has just published an important paper on an important new theorem or problem. The paper could concern fluid flow or a tricky aspect of fractals. The mathematician's Web site could employ VRML to let people visually explore the dynamics of such a symbolic system. The visitors need not even understand the subject matter in detail, or have any comprehension of the underlying equations or mathematical principles involved. Through simple exploration, these casual but interested visitors could gain an understanding of the subject matter that would be impossible without VRML visualization techniques in a virtual world.

Admittedly, this day may be some way off. For the time being, VRML world creators will have to consider the potential audience of a Web site. The goals and nature of the Web site content have to be considered carefully as well. Web sites specializing in entertainment will probably attract visitors that expect the site to be on the *bleeding* edge (one step beyond leading edge) of technology and interactivity. To do so, it will be more or less necessary to spruce up the site with new technologies such as VRML and Java. Of course, designers must still be conscious of both the bandwidth and the equipment commonly used by potential visitors to the site, so that the end result is not a stunning VRML virtual world that is almost impossible to navigate.

Even for Web sites that do not have a special theme like entertainment, but are still trying to reach a more broad and general audience, VRML is an obvious choice because 3D is so comfortable and familiar to everyone. Very young children who have previously only piled up stacks of building blocks and have not yet even learned to read are often quite good at navigating through 3D environments. The endless hours that children spend engaged in playing 3D video games gives them a built-in ability to navigate almost flawlessly through 3D VRML worlds and spaces.

Another interesting factor that makes VRML worlds attractive content for Web sites is the utter lack of a language barrier. The use of almost any form of text is frowned upon among VRML world designers for this very reason. This lack of the need to deal with a new or unknown language in VRML is another aspect of VRML that makes Web sites more attractive to a general audience, even foreign audiences. Although the Internet is now truly international in scope, and most Europeans, Japanese, and others who currently use the Internet have some command of the English language, international communities do tend to appreciate content that is not culturally biased with regard to language. There are exceptions, of course, and there are international users that actively seek out American cultural content on the Internet. But because the VRML architecture can easily go beyond the mere replication of reality (and sometimes even approaches the bizarre and grotesque), VRML worlds still tend to be equally accessible or inaccessible to people of widely varying cultural backgrounds and heritage.

Spaces are an effective form of communication, in and of themselves. When spaces are used to communicate, the spaces affect very fundamental cause and effect relationships. People from other cultures often have difficulties encountering text-based Web pages bristling with typical droll American humor or even endless text debates over passionately held political or moral viewpoints. However, a well planned and designed VRML world is understood and appreciated across cultures. When visitors from cultures as diverse as Japan or China enter a monument to Western culture like the Vatican, the visitors know instinctively that this is a sacred space and hallowed ground and they act accordingly. There is no need for signs to reinforce this message or drive it home. All eyes instinctively fall upon the ceilings and the altar. While the religion expressed may be foreign to such visitors, the feeling is universal and grasped immediately. As the Internet reaches more and more cultures and diverse populations, such non-cultural content will become more common and even a requirement.

World Building

The potential problem with using VRML at a particular Web site is that someone needs to create a lot of content from literally nothing. Whole worlds need creators. Some will need to hire the necessary expertise that is lacking within the organization. Not every graphics wizard makes a good VRML world builder. Designing a convincing and captivating VRML world requires visualization skills that even experienced 2D, text and graphics page layout artists often lack. Even many accomplished architects may not make the transition to VRML world designer because the virtual world medium offers challenges (and real opportunities) that are very different from those encountered in the physical world of everyday reality.

Fortunately, there are a number of tools that can help. Some tools are appropriate for building simple "home worlds" for everyday users. Others can be used for commercial implementation on a corporate Web site. A heavy-duty site requires heavy-duty virtual reality modeling tools. While the modeling features of any tools are of primary importance, usability is also an aspect to consider. Some tools may be relatively easy to learn, but may be neither easy nor fast to use. The best tools have been developed over many years, even before VRML was dreamed of. These tools usually incorporate the feedback and numerous suggestions from previous users on how to work more productively and effectively in a 3D environment.

While simple text editors offer more than enough to convey the most complex ideas that could be expressed in HTML, serious users of VRML will need to invest in good 3D creation and VRML authoring tools to design worlds that go far beyond a simple collection of just spheres and cubes. Even though it is theoretically possible to sit down with a text editor software package, such as pico or even notepad, and type up a VRML file that describes the objects, geometry, and all the surface attributes (shiny, dull, etc.) of a complex world, this process really does not work in actual practice. Text is more than adequate for reasoning, even complex symbolic reasoning, but text does not help at visualization. A text description of a car will invariably cause the reader to vividly picture a car in the mind's eye, but even the simple word "red" will produce imaginary cars of every shade of red possible, from a bright scarlet to a metallic crimson. Detailed enough descriptions are nearly impossible to conjure up identical images. But VRML makes the task easy and quick.

Tools of the VRML Trade

Most VRML tools today fall into one of two categories. First, there are VRML browsers. Then there are the VRML authoring packages, also simply known as 3D creation tools. Because the whole market for these tools is still quite young, all the tools not only vary widely by features, but also by more fundamental aspects such as navigation techniques and manipulation methods. Of course, all of the available tools differ considerably in terms of ease of use, ease of learning, system requirements, price, and even reliability and stability.

Most of the VRML authoring packages and 3D creation tools have been developed by established companies in the modeling arena. This is not true of most of the VRML browsers and add-ons available today. The difference between a full VRML browser and an add-on is that a full VRML browser includes full HTML capabilities along with the VRML browsing function. A VRML add-on (or add-in, as some insist) simply adds VRML world browsing capabilities to an existing and previously installed HTML browser such as Netscape. Add-ons tend to be more painless to obtain and use, but both approaches have merits.

Most VRML browsers and add-ons were developed by companies that were started after the first VRML specification was drafted in late 1994. There is nothing wrong with this, of course, and many of these companies exist because of VRML. Most of these companies come from a networking rather than a 3D graphics background. However, these young companies were able to beat much larger and more established competitors to the market with VRML browsers and add-ons because they realized the importance and potential of VRML very early on.

Some VRML browsers, such as WebSpace, need an HTML browser to access VRML worlds. Others, such as WorldView and worldSpace have built-in networking support and only need to communicate with HTML browsers when these browsers encounter an HTML document on the Web. On the other hand, VRML add-ons such as WebF/X integrate seamlessly with HTML browsers like Qmosaic or Netscape to preserve the familiar HTML interface for the user.

Some tools attempt to combine both the VRML browsing and authoring functions. Caligari worldSpace is the only VRML browser that also includes 3D creation tools and VRML authoring.

Although VRML is relatively new, 3D creation tools have been around for a while. Many CAD (Computer Assisted Design) packages allow for 3D design, although some of the least expensive still merely do 2D projections of 3D objects. But the preferred tools for game designers and multimedia producers have been modeling and animation packages such as Softimage, 3D Studio, Strata Studio, and Caligari trueSpace. It is true that VRML currently does not support animation, but it will in the near future, especially as the more widespread use of such networked animation tools as Java become more common. It is always a good idea to purchase a 3D creation tool (hopefully with VRML capabilities built in) from a source that is committed to and will be able to add functionality as VRML evolves into a language for describing animated, interactive, multi-participant virtual worlds.

Some of the available 3D creation tools already allow spaces and models to be saved in VRML. But others require the user to download or purchase separate translation utilities that convert from the package's native or internal format to VRML. Built-in, direct VRML output is always preferable to converters. Just as with conversion programs for going from bitmaps images to "metafiles" and the like, something always seems to get lost in the translation process. Another good idea is to make sure that the tool under consideration not only can write VRML files but can also read or import them. Otherwise, a saved world may end up not being accessible even from the editing tool that created it!

There are other things to watch out for as well. For instance, some elements of a VRML world may be lost when a world or space is saved in VRML instead of the software's native format. It is not unusual to wind up with a totally unrecognizable world because the software package supports such features as light attenuation, while VRML does not. Because there are various levels of VRML support, a tool must be fully examined to determine exactly the extent of the VRML support promised. Most modeling packages still cannot write out all VRML primitives.

For pure VRML authoring, Virtus Walkthrough, WebSpace Author, Home Space Builder, and Caligari worldSpace are the most popular authoring tools. While all of these products allow for the addition of hyperlinks, only WebSpace Author and Caligari worldSpace support in-lining and levels of detail at the present time. WebSpace Author runs on very fast but very expensive SGI machines and includes some very sophisticated technology. However, unlike Caligari worldSpace, WebSpace Author does not include any 3D creation tools, which may or may not be a consideration. The biggest advantage of Caligari worldSpace is that it runs on Windows 3.1 and Windows 95 and is freely downloadable for non-commercial use.

Which Authoring Tool Is Best?

Because the available products differ so widely, each needs to be evaluated in terms of which features are absolutely essential and which ones are just nice to have. For instance, if a company or university already has certain 3D models developed that would be appropriate for use on a Web site virtual world, the company or university would need to make sure that the prospective VRML authoring tool can import objects in that particular format. Naturally, the tool should be able to import VRML objects. Not only does this ensure that the resulting world will be readily modifiable, but the users of the tool would be able to take advantage of importing for their own purposes all the objects that are accessible on the various VRML sites on the Web.

Even if a site relies quite heavily on pre-built and pre-existing models downloaded from other VRML Web sites, it is likely that the site will want to create a few objects all their own or simply modify a few of the others found on the Web. If the site already has a 3D modeling tool with VRML import and export capabilities and the developer (or artist) knows how to use it, a separate VRML tool is probably not necessary.

However, it is always good to remember that many of the traditional 3D modeling packages were built for photorealistic output and may be overly complicated or even lack the features essential for interactive 3D graphics. While most 3D modeling packages still force designers to work with what are known as "wireframe" models, the latest generation of tools allows a designer to manipulate "texture-mapped" objects in real time. But this level of sophistication may not be necessary in all instances. There are older and more traditional 3D modeling tools available such as lathing (rotating a curve about an axis to form a solid object) or extruding (dragging a 2D object such as a letter of the alphabet through a third dimension to achieve a 3D effect) that can be very cost effective and just as adequate for creating stunning 3D virtual worlds.

Before spending a large amount of money on a texture-mapping high-end tool, it may be acceptable to use lathing and extrusions. In other cases, such advanced features and functions as organic deformations (bending and shaping objects with a variety of methods) and 3D Boolean operations ("ANDing" or "ORing" one object with another related object) may be necessary to accomplish what the designer had in mind. While deformations and the like can bring an eye-popping object to a virtual world, the routine employment of such techniques can also have the undesirable side effect of increasing the resulting VRML file size into uncomfortable ranges and place a heavy burden on the networks links and even the computers of visitors. Always remember that visitors need to view and wander through the virtual world in real time.

Not everyone that wishes to develop or explore a VRML world has a high-end SGI computer at their fingertips. It is always a good idea to keep the average network speed and desktop configuration of the target audience in mind. Of course, whatever the platform used to develop and deliver the virtual world to users, care is needed to choose authoring tools that run on the available platform and the amount of memory and other system resources these packages require. For those that are lucky enough to have machinery like an SGI computer accessible, some of the best modeling tools in the industry are available.

Of course, the software that runs or such heavy-duty hardware will be more costly than more modest tools. And somewhat ironically, the selection of VRML authoring tools will be much more limited than on a PC platform. There just are not that many vendors in the high-end market. Costs for the Macintosh are similar to prices for the PC, but again the software selection is much more limited. This is also somewhat ironic, since the Mac has traditionally had much better graphic capabilities than the PC architecture. Most VRML browsers do not even work on the Mac yet. The best selection of browsers and tools will be on the familiar PC platform. Also, the stiff and often cut-throat competition for market share in the PC industry will continue to keep both hardware and software prices lower than for any other platform.

However, this is not to say that the PC is a perfect virtual world building tool. Some of the authoring tools, and even the browsing tools, may require the purchase of more memory. There may be system freeze-ups and outright crashes to deal with (Windows 95 users may fair better in this regard). But just because most of a Web site's visitors will explore the VRML virtual world with a Windows' browser, this does not automatically mean that a PC platform should be used as the primary development platform for the target VRML virtual world.

Larger VRML Web sites may choose to purchase and employ several VRML tools and use each for its most appropriate role rather than settling for and focusing on only one VRML tool exclusively. In all multiple tool cases, however, the developers need to make certain that all of the tools inter-operate quite well and there are no unexpected surprises in the resulting virtual world when transferring models and scenes from one tool to another.

There are a few other simple guidelines for these more elaborate VRML world creation shops. If there are existing 2D sources, make sure that the VRML tools can take advantage of these sources and assets. If there is a need to employ 2D graphic illustrations, make sure that the VRML tools can at least import PostScript files, the most common format for these sources. Most existing Web image maps can be converted to JPEG (Joint Photographic Experts Group) format, but it is a good idea to find out exactly which bitmap formats are supported by both the VRML authoring and browsing tools. If an integrated tool that can do practically any VRML operation from creation to browsing is chosen, compatibility problems are minimized, of course. However, unless there is a desire to optimize the VRML virtual world for a particular browser, there is still a need to check on how the world will look when visited by the most common browsers.

Further Considerations

A couple of other points should be made. Right now, VRML is *hot!* Many packages claim to do VRML authoring. But it is always good to remember that a VRML world at heart is just an ASCII format and that therefore any text editor can technically claim to be a VRML authoring tool. However, unless a developer enjoys working directly with the straight ASCII file (not a pleasant task), make sure that such VRML features as levels of detail and in-line objects can be created by the authoring tool without having to perform any editing by hand. If the designer doing the virtual world modeling is not comfortable with the task, select a tool that includes a feature known as "polygon reduction" so that levels of detail do not have to be modeled separately.

There are other convenient features that authoring tools may have but are seldom absolutely essential. It all depends on the goals of the virtual world designer. Almost any powerful enough 3D creation tool will generate the objects and spaces needed. In VRML tools, a capability known as "material editing" will end up determining just how the objects and spaces will look. For maximum flexibility in material editing, there are tools that allow a developer to assign material attributes not only for entire objects but also for each side, or face, of the object. Such flexibility can be helpful for created objects with wood trim, for example. Since the use of many texture maps increases the amount of data that has to be transferred, look for advanced paint tools in the modeling package such as "vertex painting". The vertex painting technique allows for the creation of multiple color gradients (gradual changes in color) across surfaces. Used in the proper situations, vertex painting often eliminates the need for texture maps altogether.

The best way to evaluate VRML tools is by the available options for reducing the VRML file size. There are several ways to do this. VRML files are formatted with new line characters, tabs, and the like to make them easier for developers to read. But VRML browsers do not need them. VRML files frequently include *normal* information. Normals are perpendiculars that give the VRML browser clues as to the orientation of objects and surfaces (is the four-sided object shorter at the rear because it is tilted or because it is meant to be a trapezoid viewed head-on?). But VRML browsers can determine normals at the cost of added processing time. The VRML specification lists default values for all parameters now otherwise given explicit values. These default values need not be included in the VRML file, but often are.

By stripping out things like ASCII formatting, normal information, and default values, a good VRML tool can reduce total world file sizes by as much as 50 percent. Many VRML files can be reduced even more by advanced techniques such as reducing precision, collapsing hierarchies, using VRML primitives, and including only one "instance" of an object that appears in various places in a world. The details of how these techniques work are not necessary, but an appreciation of their existence is still desirable.

Common compression techniques can also be used to further pare down the size of a VRML file. For example, the common UNIX compression method known as GZIP is widely used for this purpose. If a

VRML world file is GZIP'd after having trimmed the VRML file to the bare bones with the other methods mentioned, the VRML world file may end up at only about 5 percent of its original size. This will dramatically speed up loading times for visitors, and allow a VRML Web site to serve up worlds to more users without adding disk space or bandwidth.

The techniques used to reduce a VRML file size must be used with care. This is especially true if a world must be created to accommodate the widest range of available VRML browsers and add-ons possible. For example, not all VRML browsers, especially those designed for the Windows environment, do not yet accept GZIP'd VRML files. This can require a lot of switching back and forth between the authoring tool and various browsers to make sure that the VRML world is accessible, all the intended links work, and all the objects look right. VRML virtual world creators should also check to see if any in-lines load as intended and if objects that contain levels of detail are displayed properly on as many different browsers as possible.

Recommending VRML Browsers

This brings up the whole issue of whether or not it is a good idea to recommend a VRML browser to Web site visitors or not. The issue is not one to be approached lightly.

Before recommending a browser for the visitors to a specific VRML site, see how each of them performs on a similar (if not the same) system configuration. The differences in speed can be quite startling and dramatic. Some VRML browsers have already been set up to take advantage of the newer 3D acceleration chips being built in to newer video cards. Other factors that need to be considered are ease of use and, of course, stability. Many of the newer browsers, especially from individual developers working more or less on their own, have not been tested adequately. It is much better to recommend a browser for visitors to a VRML world that has been thoroughly debugged. A current joke has it that an army of monkeys pounding away at keyboards at random may produce *Hamlet* in a million years, but could produce a passable VRML browser in about a week and a half.

The overworked term *ease of use* is to a large extent a subjective matter. Some people will always prefer to use extensive navigation controls like joysticks and even head-mounted gear while others will feel just as comfortable using the mouse and buttons. A really good browser will give the user a lot of choices for navigating.

If a site does choose to recommend a specific VRML tool for browsing, check with the developer of the tool to see if it can be made available for downloading from the VRML Web site itself. This can save users a lot of time and effort better spent on exploring the target site. Many developers are quite approachable and may even feel somewhat honored that their tool has been so chosen and will allow the browser to be distributed free of charge. Not all developers are as cooperative, however. If the VRML tool chosen to be distributed also includes some authoring capabilities, visitors may even want to add to the VRML site or make what they perceive as definite improvements. In this case, the VRML Web site should make it abundantly clear ahead of time exactly what the site policy is regarding VRML scenes uploaded to the server.

Virtual Worlds on the Internet

No other aspect of the Internet, except perhaps E-mail, has invaded the public consciousness as much as the World Wide Web. From rather humble beginnings at CERN (the European Center for Nuclear Research: initials in French) in Geneva, Switzerland, in the early 1990s, the number of World Wide Web servers on the Internet has grown astronomically. Today Web servers dish all kinds of Web sites for colleges and universities, corporations, movie and TV studios, and even rock bands and fan clubs.

The idea of a Web server and the associated browser software arose at CERN from a researcher familiar with the concept of *hypertext* and *hypertext links*. Even users unfamiliar with the concept of hypertext links have frequently used help files included with many Windows and OS/2 applications. These help files include various words and phrases that appear in a distinctive color and are underlined. With a simple point and click of the mouse, the user will "hyper-link" to some additional text or other information that will add to the user's understanding of the term accessed in the original help file text. Of course, the linked text resides on the same computer, and usually within the same file, as the original help information.

The breakthrough with the Web and browser software was just to extend the concept of hypertext link support from a single computer to literally *any* computer in the world meeting three relatively simple requirements. First, the computer had to be running TCP/IP and attached to the Internet. Second, the computer had to be running some Graphical User Interface package such as Windows for DOS-based machines or X Windows for UNIX platforms. Third, the computer had to be running either Web server or browser software, or even both.

Most of the applications discussed in the TCP/IP network protocol environment have come in two distinct *flavors*. They have been called *client* and *server* process versions. Usually, the same term has been used to describe both in a specific application, such as FTP. The context of the sentence or some additional information has been required to distinguish the client and server FTP process. For example, it is common to say "the FTP client process is run on the user's workstation to attach to an FTP server process running on a remote computer across the TCP/IP network." It is necessary to refer to the "FTP client process" and the "FTP server process" because just using the term "FTP process" would frequently be ambiguous.

The Web servers and browsers are built along these same client-server TCP/IP lines, of course. However, there is no ambiguity when it comes to discussing Web servers and clients. World Wide Web servers by definition run the Web server software and are referred to as "Web sites" or, less often, "Web servers." The client software packages used to access these sites are called "browsers" or "Web browsers" instead of "Web clients," but the concept is exactly the same. So a Web site always runs the WWW server software and the browser is always the Web client software that accesses the WWW server software at any Web site. The method of access is always TCP/IP.

Many organizations have somehow reached the conclusion that establishing and maintaining a Web server is a way to make money. But few organizations have figured out exactly how to offset the cost of Internet connectivity and hardware and software and technical staff with revenues from Web servers. The few that have are organizations that typically sell goods through other channels such as franchises or catalogs and see the Web as a high-tech way of reaching a new community of potential customers. However, most other kinds of organizations, especially in the service or valued-added sectors, just see a Web site as an extension of marketing and advertising efforts, made necessary by the business pressures of having a competitor appear on the Web with a very eye-popping graphical "welcome screen" known as a *Web page.*

A *home* Web page is what a user typically sees when the user accesses a Web site with a browser. The home Web page universally consists of a mixture of graphics (as distinctive as possible) and text, with the text kept to an absolute minimum. Other Web pages are accessed through this initial *home* Web page. Some graphics may be outlined in a color (blue is usually the default, but it depends on the browser software) and some words or phrases in the text appear in the same color and are underlined (in some browsers, underlining is also a configurable parameter). These colored pictures and text are the hypertext links. A typical home Web page is shown Figure I-1.

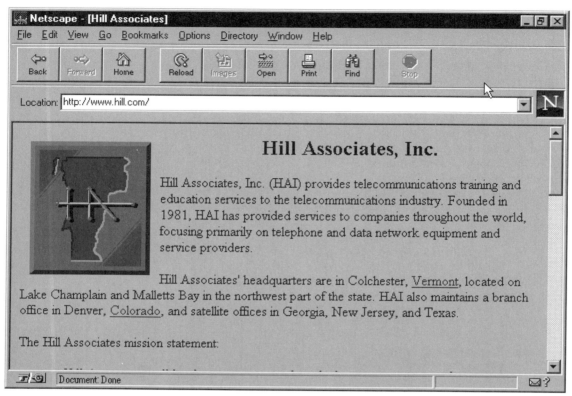

Figure I-1
A Typical Web
Page

The appearance of a home page is determined by a special Hyper-Text Mark-up Language (HTML). This HTML (frequently seen in lower case as well: html) is a standard set of features that Web browsers interpret to use the correct format for placing HTML text and graphics on a computer screen. An *author* of an HTML home page (or any other pages linked-to from the home page) on a Web server (pages normally reside on the Web server, but client-resident pages are not unheard of) inserts special control character sequences into an otherwise unremarkable text file. These special character sequences (<b> to produce **bold** text, for instance) control the browser software when the page is delivered across the Internet from the Web server.

The hypertext links on a home page may not only link to another HTML page on the same Web server. The links may point to a computer located halfway around the world and display a page from a Web server that the end user has never even heard of before. This is the wonderful aspect of hypertext links in general and the

Web in particular. And the resource pointed to by a hypertext link need not be just another page of prettily formatted text and graphics. Almost any TCP/IP application (FTP, Telnet, even E-mail and others) or information format (audio, video, VRML, MIME content-types, etc.) can be linked to, run, and the results displayed by a Web browser.

The HTML formatted pages are sent from a Web server to a browser inside IP datagrams. The protocol for the Web applications (server and browser) is known as HyperText Transport Protocol (HTTP) and has the same relation to TCP/IP and Web servers and browsers as SMTP (Simple Mail Transfer Protocol) has to TCP/IP and E-mail. That is, HTTP (also frequently seen in lower case: http) is the vehicle for transferring information from a Web server to a Web client (browser) over a TCP/IP network (in this case, the Internet).

Web server software has been developed to run on Apple, DOS, and UNIX platforms. Web browser software has been developed to run on these same platforms (or, technically, a *windowed* interface on these platforms) and OS/2 as well. Strangely, the server software is usually available for free from a variety of sources (but all over the Internet, of course), while the browser software has begun to be commercialized and available only at a price, even if the cost is supposed to be for "registration". Many excellent Web browsers are still freely available at no cost, however.

Of course, there must be a way for all of the numerous implementations of Web servers and clients to know whether the "linked-to" resource or information is an application like FTP, an audio or video clip, or another HTML formatted page on a Web server. And many video, audio, and graphical coding formats are possible. The trick is to allow the browser to determine "what's coming if the user clicks the mouse button on this link" and interpret the resulting bit stream correctly.

The method for designating all these services and formats is known as the "URL." The term itself is somewhat controversial. Many sources insist URL stands for "Universal Resource Locator" and just as many insist that URL *really* stands for "Uniform Resource Locator," which is gaining in popularity. Also, most Web users will pronounce it as "U-R-L" with each letter pronounced (as in "T-C-P-I-P"), but others say "earl" as if it were a noble title. The irony is that there are several ways of referring to the accepted way of referring to everything on the Web!

All URLs have a common format: the resource type, followed by the string ":// " (full colon, two *forward* slashes, for those used to DOS back slashes), followed by what is known as the "fully qualified Internet domain name," and ending with some optional information such as port number or resource file name. The whole is harder to describe than to understand if illustrated by a series of examples. The following list interprets several forms of URLs.

Sample URLs

1.   http://www.w3.org
        "Use http to get the default WWW home page from host www.w3.org"

2.   http://www.wol.pace.edu/csis/csis.html
        "Use http to get a WWW page called csis.html from host www.wol.pace.edu in the sub-directory csis"

3.   http://stwing.resnet.upenn.edu:8001/~jruspini/starwars.html
        "Use http to get a WWW home page called starwars.html from host stwing.resnet.upenn.edu. Use port 8001 instead of the default port 80, and use the parameters setup up in the jruspini login file to find the page"

4.   ftp://ftp.microsoft.com/pub
        "Use ftp to contact the host ftp.microsoft.com, login as 'anonymous', and go to the pub sub-directory"

5.   telnet://rs.internic.net
        "Use telnet to contact the host rs.internic.net"

Returning to the positioning of the World Wide Web as a multimedia platform, most Web browsers will transfer the entirety of a video or audio clip to the destination and then connect to and run a "helper application" on the computer that actually displays the video or pipes the audio to the speakers. Due to the many formats of Web resources, these various helper applications (known on the Web as *viewers*, even for audio resources), are not always bundled with the browser itself.

Depending on the speed of the Internet connection shared by the users and the instantaneous load on the link (mid-afternoons are notoriously slow), a 2-second video clip of about 100 Kbytes of digitized video may take up to 3 minutes or more to load and ready itself for playing. A similar 2-second audio-only clip of about 33 Kbytes of digitized audio may take up to 2 minutes. Again, performance is dependent on load and raw bandwidth available.

Although the Web is strictly an Internet construct and concept, many organizations have adapted the Web server and browser software for use on private TCP/IP networks. The resulting "private Web" ("intranet") is used internally for training, marketing, and other purposes as well, without the performance penalties imposed by the Internet Web connections. Of course, connectivity in this case is not worldwide, but limited to local resources. But this is also a good security feature.

Browsing Virtual Worlds on the Internet

It is all well and good to talk about the visual delights of virtual worlds on the Internet. But it is much more instructive to actually see the *real* virtual thing. As a preview of some of the sights that will be discussed much more fully in later chapters, this section will attempt to convey some of the feel that browsing virtual worlds can offer to an explorer.

The first and foremost requirement is, of course, a VRML browser. This can be a stand-alone application or, more likely, an add-in to a well-known Web browser such as Netscape. A company called Paper Inc. makes a VRML browser "plug-in" for Netscape 2.0. When the VRML plug-in is downloaded from the Paper Inc. Web site and installed, the Netscape browser looks like Figure I-2.

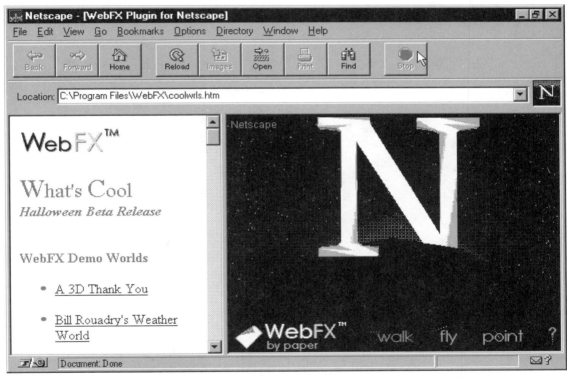

Figure I-2
WebFX Plugin
for Netscape

The Paper Inc. browser is known as WebFX and is one of the more capable VRML browsers around. WebFX is quickly learned and easy to use, a must for exploring VRML worlds. The Netscape *N* in the WebFX viewer window is in VRML, of course, and users can zoom around in a variety of ways to view the big *N* astride the earth.

At all points when using most VRML browsers, help is available on just what navigational techniques are available. For example, when visiting the textured globe at http://jaka.eecs.uic.edu/dave/vrml /JASON/TexWorld.wrl, clicking on the "?" at the bottom of the WebFX window brings up a list of possible navigation actions available in the *walk* mode superimposed on the screen (see Figure I-3).

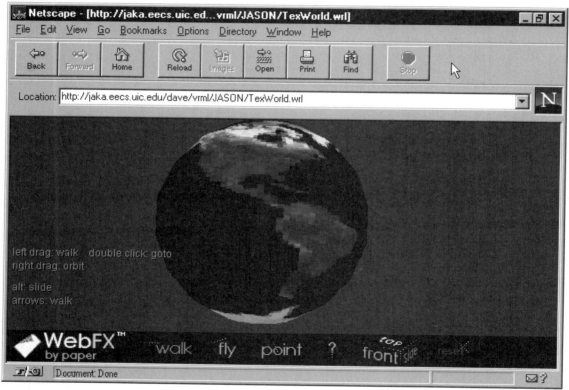

Figure I-3
The WebFX Globe

The whole point of VRML is to make a Web site as friendly and inviting as possible. Nothing is more inviting and more friendly than the building encountered when visiting http://www.ncsa.uiuc.edu/General/VRML/ncsaApps.wrl. This site is at the University of Illinois at Urbana/Champaign (uiuc) at the National Center for Supercomputing Applications (ncsa). This location is famous as the site that gave birth to the Mosaic Web browser a few years ago. The same site now plays host to a number of VRML worlds (/General/VRML) and offers access to a representative sample of possible applications for VRML virtual worlds developed at the NCSA (ncsaApps.wrl).

To explore the sample VRML virtual worlds, it is only necessary to enter into the inviting red building with the little trees. The whole scene says "Come on in!" A push of the mouse approaches the building and the user is quickly inside. Once inside, the interior is almost like a gallery. White squares hang in space, again inviting the exploratory probe of the user's mouse. As the cursor moves over the squares, a green banner appears in the window. These are embedding hyperlinks just like the links on HTML Web pages, but much more impressive than a blue "click here."

Figure I-4 shows that the second square on the right will transport the user to http://jean-luc.ncsa.uiuc.edu/Viz/VRML/HOLE.wrl. This virtual world is a scientific visualization (basically a set of numbers rendered visually) of a black hole. This world may be explored in detail as well, again with a flick of the wrist.

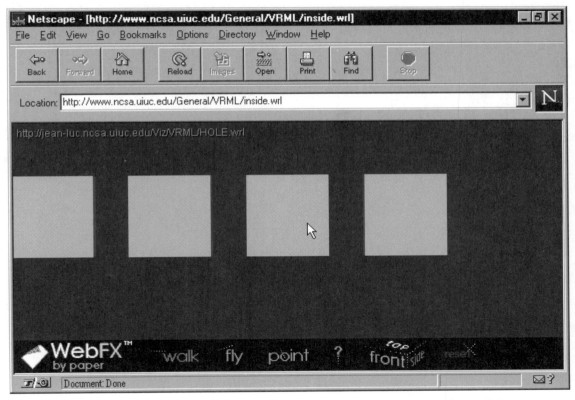

Figure I-4
URL Associated with
a Virtual World

Not all virtual worlds on the Internet are as serious in intent and content as the worlds at the NCSA. After all, what does one expect from a bunch of supercomputing geniuses? There are plenty of lighthearted worlds to explore also. For example, a recent British Wallace and Grommit animated film called *The Wrong Trousers* featured a penguin, Feathers McGraw, disguised as a chicken. The penguin has found its way into a virtual world, in full chicken, at http://www.dcs.qmw.ac.uk/~steed/WandG/chicken.wrl.gz. The chicken/penguin (see Figure I-5) appears in full 3D, and users can soar overhead to view the splendid red comb or glide behind to view the fake tail feathers.

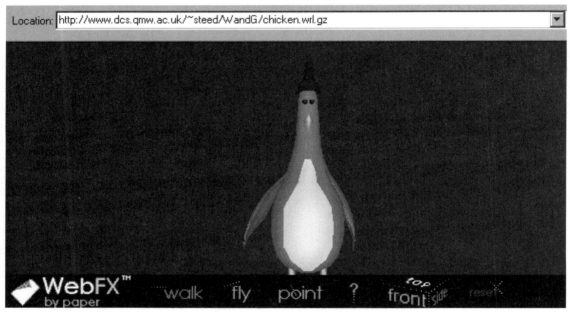

Figure I-5
The VIRTUAL
Chicken/Penguin

This is only a sampling of the possible worlds that currently inhabit the Internet. Some are serious attempts to represent the latest scientific findings in a more realistic and accessible fashion. Some are architectural delights such as cathedrals and other famous structures. Some are cities and towns. And some are just penguins disguised as chickens. But they are all 3D virtual worlds built with VRML.

Exploring Internet Virtual Worlds with VRML

There are few attempts to go beyond the endless hype and give non-computer programmer and expert types a real feel for what is and is not possible in this new networked environment of the Internet; Web, browser, and VRML. This is not to downplay the crucial role that visionaries have played in the development of all of these key areas. There would be no Web or browsers or VRML without them. But the meaning behind the vision, the purpose behind the plan, must be conveyed in a clear and concise fashion to those who would follow.

This book will give easy to follow and step-by-step instructions for exploring the new virtual worlds available on the Web portion of the Internet and built with the VRML language. Once the exploration has begun, it is relatively easy for the explorer to form his or her own opinions as to the significance of the newly discovered lands. There is really no need for more hype and more claims for the promise of "cyberspace".

Chapter

1

Computer Graphics, Visualization, and Virtual Reality

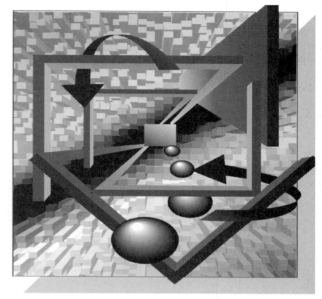

T he entire concept of virtual reality on the Internet has sprung from three parallel developments in the field of computing in the recent past. The three lines of development are in the fields of graphics, visualization, and the World Wide Web portion of the Internet. This chapter will explore the developments in the fields of graphics and visualization. The next chapter will examine the related developments on the Internet and World Wide Web in more detail.

All three fields were necessary before virtual worlds on the Internet became available for exploration. This is because computerized graphics techniques had to become sophisticated enough to enable the illusion of reality to be effective and affordable. Also, separate techniques had to become mature enough to enable the information content to be visualized in 3D to be created and maintained. And of course the Web had to become accessible enough to allow access to the widest possible audience. All three of these things have happened in the 1990s.

The three fields have become key pieces in the puzzle that has been assembled to reveal a picture of virtual worlds on the Internet, all created with VRML. Here is a look at the first two pieces, computer graphics and visualization.

The First Piece: Computer Graphics

Everyone is used to the idea that computers can manipulate large volumes of information. In fact, the whole procedure of using a computer to handle information is known as *data processing*, but the term is not as widely used as it once was. Most organizations would be lost without using computers to process the large amounts of information they generate daily and could not possibly be handled today by pencil and paper. One of the reasons that the term data processing has fallen into disuse is because computers are increasingly used today for *image processing*. The information manipulated in this instance is an image. However, since the term *image* implies the processing of a single picture, the more general term *computer graphics* is preferred. Computer graphics is simply the use of a computer to create or change still and motion pictures.

Another term for this process is *computer-generated imagery*, or just CGI. Computers have proven to be perfect tools for dealing with large amounts of information, whether the information represented is text or graphics or even human speech. Computers never get bored, never call in sick, never ask for a raise, and always do exactly what they are told to do. While a whole generation of computer scientists are busily trying to make computers act more like people, a whole generation of average users like computers just the way they are, thank you very much.

For a long time, computers were only adequate for processing text-based information (the original data) because of severe limitations in processing power and the expense of computing equipment. Storing graphics takes up much more space in computer memory and on disk drives than mere words. For example a typical full-page glossy magazine ad might take up the same amount of storage space in a computer as about 20 copies of the entire Bible, which contains about 775,000 words. Modern desktop platforms have more than enough power and storage to handle these amounts of information with ease.

Only within the last 10 years or so have desktop computers been equal to the task of graphics processing. Before that, customized systems had to handle graphics tasks. Today, most consumer outlet stores that sell computers have systems that not only can handle digitized desktop video, but also support newer graphics formats like Kodak's Photo CD. The CD-ROM release of Microsoft's Windows 95 included the entire MTV video of Weezer's *Just Like Buddy Holly*. All of the new, low-cost, high-powered PCs allow everyone to capture, view, play, and even modify pictures. The results are revolutionizing the photography and motion picture industries.

A Brief History of Computer Graphics

There have been computers with at least some modest graphics capabilities for almost as long as there have been computers. Jay Forrester at MIT led a research team to look into using the newly invented computer for air traffic use. The ultimate result, called Whirlwind, was linked to radar towers and mapped detected aircraft on a monitor screen as moving points of light. The demonstration of Whirlwind on April 20, 1951, led directly to the modern air traffic control systems in use today (contrary to the opinion of some modern air travelers, the computer at their airport is *not* the original Whirlwind).

In 1961, MIT student Ivan Sutherland created a computer drawing program called Sketchpad. Sketchpad used a lightpen to actually draw shapes directly on the monitor screen. These shapes could be saved and displayed later, a real revolution. Sutherland's Sketchpad pioneered many of the computer graphics techniques taken for granted today, such as viewing an image as a collection of objects rather than a single image. Sketchpad could expand a circle in a scene, for example, without affecting an overlapping square.

By 1964, IBM and General Motors had created the DAC-1 (Design Augmentation by Computer). This was the first real computerized drawing system. It enabled car designers to input a 3D description of an automobile and rotate the image to view the car from different angles. The entire design effort took a full five years. Most CAD products owe their existence to the DAC-1.

These early systems used simple line drawings known as *wireframe* models. There were no real surfaces, and colors were usually out of the question. Even with such primitive graphics, however, some arresting images could result. In the early 1960s, another MIT student named Steve Russell created the world's first video game, Spacewar. Written to run on a DEC PDP-1 minicomputer, the game became so popular, in spite of the simple points of light and lines display, that DEC technicians used it as a diagnostic program on every PDP-1 that was shipped to a customer. The customers, needless to say, played Spacewar endlessly as their own diagnostic when the boss was not around.

By the mid 1960s, computer graphics really caught on. Smaller computer vendors such as TRW, General Electric, and Sperry Rand all released products with graphics capabilities. But things really took off when IBM released the IBM 2250 Graphics Terminal, the first commercially available graphics terminal (it still required a mainframe computer to provide the processing power, of course). The invention of the mouse helped with the awkward task of trying to draw with only a keyboard.

All these products yielded graphics that were hardly realistic at all. One problem was the presence of *hidden surfaces*. The drawing of a cube, for example, could be looked right through to the supposedly hidden back surface. This was a problem for wireframe models in general. By the late 1960s, computer graphics objects took on color and no longer displayed hidden surfaces, as shown in Figure 1-1. At the

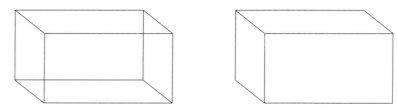

Figure 1-1
The Hidden
Surface Problem

same time, graphics images began to be represented bit-by-bit rather than line-by-line, allowing more realistic shading and coloring of surfaces. A real advance was the use of mathematical techniques to adjust to the amount of light reflected from a tilted surface. This formed the basis for *flat shading* in the 3D worlds of today. Each surface changed tint slightly when tilted, but over the whole surface, not point-by-point.

The 1970s was the period in which computer graphics began to move beyond the world of computer scientists into the everyday world. For example, television began to use computer graphics at this time. A company called Computer Image Corporation (CIC) developed customized hardware and software packages with names like CEASAR and ANIMAC. These packages allowed for the scanning of existing artwork, the manipulation of it, and then for the inclusion of these squashed and stretched images into a television videotape. Companies like the Bell Telephone system and CBS Sports made use of these video graphic sequences in their logos and advertisements.

The first use of computer graphics in a Hollywood motion picture was in the 1973 film *Westworld*. A technique called *pixelization* was employed to break up a film frame into color blocks called pixels. If the pixels are small enough, they cannot be detected. Larger pixels, which were used in the film, created a blocky patchwork approximation of the scene. The technique was used to represent the berserk robot's view of the world.

Curved surfaces were especially challenging to computer artists. Straight horizontal or vertical line segments were no trouble at all, but curved segments appeared jagged and hardly realistic. This effect was different than the jagged edges caused by monitor pixels. Also, the bland smoothness of colored surfaces was a dead giveaway that the viewer was looking at computer-generated images and not the real thing. And the whole screen and the scene displayed on it remained flat. Figure 1-2 illustrates this effect.

Figure 1-2
The "Jaggies" on
the Right

All three of these problems were addressed by one person. In 1974, Ed Catmull covered three major topics in his computer science Ph.D. thesis. Curved surfaces were represented more convincingly by *rendering*. Rendering processes images before they are displayed, instead are just blasting graphics images from memory to screen as quickly as possible. The bland colors were addressed by the concept of a *texture map*. A texture map merely "wrapped" a 2D picture around a 3D graphic. A photo of a brick wall, for instance, could be wrapped around a cube to make a fairly convincing building. The texture could be repeated, saving space in the computer for the 2D texture. Windows background "wallpaper" uses exactly the same technique. Finally, the "Z-buffer" stored information not only about the X and Y vertical and horizontal location of a point on the computer monitor, but also its "distance" from the front of the screen (the Z axis).

Color came to computers in a big way in the 1970s and color also came to computer graphics in an equally big way at the same time. The new Dr. Ed Catmull installed himself at the New York Institute of Technology (NYIT) with two colleagues and came up with a paint program that handled *true 24-bit color*, which is even more color capability than many computers have today. The NYIT Computer Graphics Lab continued to work on programs to assist with 2D animation for films and television, eventually growing to 60 people who developed tools later used by Disney. 3D graphics techniques were also pioneered by this group.

In 1979, IBM introduced the 3279 color terminal. Although the terminal could do little more than display text in a limited number of different colors like blue and red, the difference from traditional monochrome models featuring green phosphors on a black background was so arresting that IBM quickly sold 10,000 units in a mere 9 months. The importance of the 3279 was to make ordinary people aware that computers could do more than scroll monochrome text. At the close of the 1970s, the computer graphics market worldwide was a billion dollar industry.

But the market was closed to all but the richest companies and individuals who could afford the expensive custom hardware and software needed to run graphics applications or those lucky enough to attend universities and colleges that specialized in computer graphics research. The 1980s opened the graphics market to the people with one key development: the PC.

The personal computer exposed many people to the power of computers and the possibilities of computer graphics for the first time. Virtually every science fiction movie made since *Star Wars*, and even some mainstream Hollywood releases, employed computer graphics to enhance visuals in a variety of ways. The technique of *morphing,* changing one image into another smoothly and continuously, was first used in the movie *Willow.* A few years later, the same effects could be duplicated on a simple PC with the proper software. This was the power that the PC brought to the field of computer graphics.

If the PC was the big event of the 1980s that helped shape the whole industry of computer graphics, the big event of the next decade in this regard was the release of Windows 3.0 by Microsoft in May of 1990. Previously, the vast majority of PCs based on the original IBM architecture had featured an interface not much different from the teletype machine and color capabilities not much different from the 3279 color terminal. Borrowing from the Graphical User Interface (GUI) concepts pioneered by Apple Computer, Windows brought the benefits of graphics to the desktop and grew in popularity in leaps and bounds. Pointing and clicking became common. In 1990, only two of the top ten PC applications ran on Windows. By 1991, the figure was nine out of ten.

Also in 1990, Autodesk released its first 3D computer animation program, called 3D Studio. Although pricey, 3D Studio quickly became the standard in 3D animation software. In the 1990s, films like *Beauty and the Beast* and *Terminator 2* made the creation of Hollywood films *without* the inclusion of 3D computerized graphics unthinkable. The hit of 1995 and 1996, *Toy Story*, began in 1991. Disney and Pixar, whose mind-bending Lifesaver, Listerine, and Tropicana commercials raised the general public's awareness of 3D video computer graphics a few more notches, came together to create a motion picture that was *entirely* composed of 3D video computer graphics.

Toy Story is a good place to end this section. The promise of VRML is that almost any Web site can become as visually arresting as the scenes in *Toy Story.*

The Use of Computerized Graphics

Today, on the edge of a new century and a new millennium, the use of computerized graphics has become so common that it might be a good idea just to run through some of the more important applications for computerized graphics. Given the visual nature of graphics images themselves, these applications tend to fall into one of two categories: those for entertainment and those for everything else.

In the entertainment field, virtually all television broadcasts include computerized graphics, especially the opening and closing credits. But even more common is the use of computerized graphics for commercials and promotional spots. A single 30-second promo or commercial shows 30 frames per second on the television screen. These 900 images, from dancing credit cards to cola-guzzling polar bears, usually exist on a computer hard drive somewhere before they make their way to videotape.

Cartoons are another field that has been transformed by the employment of computerized graphics. Instead of the usual *cel animation* that involves the pains-taking individual hand painting of each frame, computers enable the cartoonist to scan in backgrounds, layer on separate images, and even generate the action between "key frames" automatically. Colors are changed at the click of a mouse, and glass surfaces are illustrated with convincing detail.

Motion pictures have employed many forms of computerized graphics for many years. Their use is so common that it is no longer remarkable. For instance, few people wondered how Arnold Schwarzenegger maneuvered a Harrier jet through the streets of downtown Miami in the film *True Lies*. He didn't! There was no plane, no helicopters, no rockets fired through skyscrapers. Those scenes only existed in the heavily processed final film images.

Morphing is a relatively new technique added to the film makers' bag of tricks. For example, given a starting image, a person, and a final image, a tiger, morphing can automatically generate the computer images to realistically transform one image to the other in as many steps as the programmer desires. Software packages that allow morphing and computer animation are now affordable to almost any dabbler in computerized graphics.

Although not usually considered entertainment, computerized graphics have invaded every aspect of print magazine graphics and the fine arts themselves. Processing in print media used to be limited to the practice of "airbrushing" shadows and streaks from photographs. Now, convincing photos can be generated by computer to make it seem that Albert Einstein is entertaining Madonna at the Super Bowl when, in fact, all three images have been brought together for the first time in a computer. The ethical issues involved with such processed or "manufactured" images have yet to be thrashed out when the guarantees of the First Amendment right of free expression are factored in. Even if restricted to pure text, the swoops and whirls of lead articles in magazines such as *Wired* have raised the graphic arts to the borderland of chaos. Finally, many artists who would have been content to put paint on canvas are exploring the possibilities of cursor and monitor in a variety of ways.

Art and entertainment is not the only fertile ground for computer graphics to grow in today. Other applications for these advanced techniques are almost everywhere. Architects employ both 2D and 3D graphics to illustrate and experience how new buildings will look and feel on the actual site intended.

Mapping and Geographic Information Systems (GIS) are two areas that have also profited immensely from computerized graphics. Land surveying satellites began to examine the surface of the earth in 1972 with the launch of the original LandSat. The images yielded by this family of satellites help geologists, cartographers, conservationists, and other scientists learn a great deal about the earth. It came as a shock, for example, when early satellite images revealed that up to 80 percent of the earth was covered by clouds at any one time and that numerous thunderstorms are raging continuously all over the earth. It is not unusual for oil companies and diamond miners to begin a search for new resources with satellite images. Planetary science was advanced immensely by the Voyager and Mariner space probes. Their images could be processed in a number of ways to enhance hitherto unimagined features on distant planets.

The field of medical science is quite dependent on computerized image processing today. The familiar CAT scan is an acronym for Computer Assisted Tomography, in which X-ray machines create thin "sliced" images of the human body. Putting the images back together to reveal a hidden tumor or other condition would be impossible without computerized graphics to display and analyze the resulting images. All of the newer methods used for diagnosis and exploration use computerized graphics. Techniques such as MRI (Magnetic Resonance Imaging), PET (Positron Emission Tomography) and MSI (Magnetic Source Imaging) would all produce numerous slides of shapeless grays without the computer to process the images. Computer graphics saves lives, a strange, and yet true, thing to say.

Computerized graphics have even invaded the courtroom. What angle was the fatal bullet fired from? Given the position of the body, how could it have fallen? Or was the body moved? Suicide? Could someone reach around to fire a gun in that position? How did blood splatter all the way over there? All of these questions could be and have been addressed with computerized graphics sequences. The whole field is known as *forensic graphics*. Once limited to crude sketches from eyewitness accounts, computerized forensic graphics can cut to the core of a police case or a defense strategy. And the judge and jury can see with their own eyes a sequence of events that may have remained cloudy if based solely upon purely verbal descriptions and information.

The point to be made is that all of these applications, and more, will find their way onto the Web and into VRML worlds. As the information used in generating computerized graphics finds its way onto the Internet and Web, so to will the visitors who wish to use and experience it. And the easiest way to do so is through VRML virtual worlds.

Pictures as Numbers

Representing letters of the alphabet inside a computer as bits (binary digits: 0s and 1s) is easy and simple. The letter *A* is just represented by the number 65 (in the American Standard Code for Information Interchange: ASCII) which is the string 01100101 in bits. One letter, eight bits. Two letters, sixteen bits, and so on. But graphics are different.

The most common way to get text into a computer is (still) to type it in from the keyboard. The most common way to get a graphic into the computer in the first place is with a piece of equipment called a scanner. Scanners are close relatives to ordinary copy machines. But instead of outputting the image on the glass onto a piece of paper, a scanner outputs the image electronically to the computer. There are many different kinds of scanners. Scanners range from small hand-held units that are only a little larger than a mouse to large sheet-fed devices than fill up a desktop.

Most scanners first expose the image to a very bright light. Then electronic receptors known as charge-coupled devices (CCD) sensors detect the reflected light from the image and convert the signal to electrical pulses. The pulses are translated to a string of bits: numbers. Scanners come in monochrome or color models. Resolutions for different scanner models can range from about 100 dots per inch to 2,000 dots per inch or even beyond.

A scanner knows exactly where it gets every sample of information from the scanned image. A scanner's *optical resolution* determines the number of colors a scanner can detect in one square inch. The output resolution of the image may differ from the actual optical resolution of the scanner. The output resolution may actually be higher than the optical resolution of the scanner. This seems impossible, but the scanner can increase resolution by *interpolation*. Interpolation can add an "average" piece of information between two scanned pieces of information, and so increase output resolution beyond optical resolution.

The word "resolution" is somewhat overworked in the field of computer graphics. The meaning can often change from one use to the next, and the context is often the only clue as to which shade of meaning is meant. Most people use the term "resolution" in the general sense of image quality, and there is nothing wrong with this. A more precise definition will be given later.

To store a graphic, the computer must first break up the image into little squares. The effect is the same as looking out a screened window. The world outside is broken up into an array of little squares. The image can still be seen, of course, but it is overlayed with the screen grid pattern. The computer does the exact same thing, and breaks up the image to be stored into tiny squares of color. The computer distinguishes one square from another by assigning them all numbers, or coordinates. If the image is ten squares long and ten squares wide, the computer assigns all 100 squares two numbers to indicate the row and column coordinates of each square. Most imaging software will start the row and column numbering in the upper left corner of the image, but some will start with the lower left. Every square is referenced by the two numbers.

Each square is called a *pixel*. Some graphics processing equipment vendors have used the term *pel* in the past (both stand for *picture element*, "pix" being a common industry abbreviation for pictures), but the use of term pixel is now nearly universal. Pixels obey one very important rule in computer graphics: they may have only one color. This leads to an interesting situation. If there are not enough pixels, which is another way of saying that the pixels are too large, a source image can look very grainy or distorted. The image must be represented by enough small pixels to allow for the viewing of the image realistically. The more pixels an image has, the better it looks.

For example, consider the three images in Figure 1-3. The first was created with 15 pixels per inch. It looks pretty bad. The second was created with 30 pixels per inch. It is better, but not good enough to see much detail. Only at 150 pixels per inch does the image become recognizable as a cat.

Figure 1-3
A cat at different
resolutions

The computer assigns colors by number, of course. To store the color of each individual pixel, all the computer has to do is store the number representing the color at the correct row and column coordinate location of the pixel in the overall array. That seems easy enough, but storing color numbers is harder that it looks. How many colors are there? As it turns out, there are a lot. To vision scientists, color is *analog*. This means that each tint or shade of color blends seamlessly into another to the human eye. The total number of colors, therefore, turns out to be infinite. Now, computers can handle large amounts of numbers, but an infinite amount is still beyond any computer's power and always will be.

But these same vision scientists have also found that the human eye is far from perfect. The eye does not see an infinity of colors. The human eye can only perceive about 16.7 million colors. Interestingly, it was not until computers could *generate* so many different colors that scientists even found this out. After all, vision scientists did not have 16 million different color crayons on hand. Blending paint pigments by hand initially led researches to believe that the human eye could only distinguish about 50,000 colors of all hues. It was something of a surprise, especially for house paint manufacturers, that the eye was much more acute than that. Matching paint samples became *much* tougher.

More shades and hues can be represented. Just add more numbers. But the effort is wasted because the human eye cannot see the subtle differences. Now 16 million may seem like a lot, but the computer can handle a mere 16 million different possible colors quite easily. This is because bits can be used in combination to represent large numbers, whether the numbers represent colors, dollars, or people. And if the colors used in an image need not be all of the colors possible, fewer bits are needed. Fewer colors meant fewer numbers, and fewer numbers meant less storage and processing power needed.

Various generations of PC color monitors have used increased numbers of bits to improve the color images displayed on a monitor. Table 1-1 shows the number of bits per pixel for color, the total num-

Table 1-1
Some Common Color Standards

Number of Bits Used	Total Number of Colors	Common Name
1	2	Monochrome, "black and white"
2	4	CGA (Computer Graphics Adapter)
4	16	EGA (Enhanced Graphics Adapter)
8	256	SVGA (Standard Video Graphics Adapter)
16	64,000	Advanced VGA, or "high color"
24	16,700,000	True Color, or "24-bit color"

ber of colors possible, and the common name for these generations of computer monitor capabilities.

Consider a true color picture of the letter A, photographed in natural light, partly shaded, splattered with paint, and using a 200 by 200 pixel array, which is a fraction of the total screen area on a typical PC monitor. The number of bits used to represent the graphical A is not 8 bits, but almost 1 million bits ($200 \times 200 \times 24 = 960,000$). Of course, since files are measured in bytes, or octets, of eight bits each, the letter A would take up 120 KB of space in memory or in a file or disk, all for one letter. Small wonder that more storage and processing power were needed on PCs to process images routinely.

Because the total number of colors that can be represented depends on the number of bits used to represent each color, images are often referred to by their *bit depth* or *color depth*. Although a 24-bit color image has all the colors anyone can see, the image size can be kept down by using only 256 colors and using an 8-bit color depth.

The point has already been made that the appearance of an image is dependent on not only the number of colors but also the number of pixels. The term *resolution* in this context describes how many pixels make up an image. If a picture is represented by a 200 by 200 array, then the resolution is 200 by 200. A typical 3-inch by 5-inch newspaper photo is represented by about 3600 pixels by 6000 pixels. On the other hand, the same size picture in a glossy magazine may have a resolution as great as 7200 by 12,000. The size of the image in terms of inches is exactly the same, but the size of the glossy magazine image in terms of resolution is twice as great, so the magazine image looks much better. The number of pixels, or *dots per inch* (dpi), is much greater in the magazine.

In the case of the newspaper photo, the image size stored in the computer is about 28,800,000 bits, or about 3.6 Megabytes (MB). In the case of the glossy magazine version, the image size stored in the computer is about 86,400,000 bits, or about 10.8 MB. The size differential is a result of the differences in resolution and number of colors (256 versus 16.7 million). These sizes are one of the most important reasons that desktop computer graphics is a relatively new field.

The previous example only considered still images. If successive images must be displayed to achieve full-motion video, the images must be processed and displayed at 30 frames per second. And if a sound track is to be added, this takes even more power. The computer has to process huge amounts of information to display full-motion video with stereo sound. Even with the fastest PC platforms, in many cases video playback is limited to a small window, usually one-fourth or even one-eighth total monitor size. Newer computers have begun to overcome this limitation, but it will still be a while before such capabilities can be assumed.

For routine computer use, the desktop monitor need not display thousands of pixels and millions of colors all the time. Print resolutions are one thing, windowed applications are another. The average desktop PC can display images up to a maximum resolution a 1024 pixels across and 768 pixels high with 256 colors. Higher resolution images can be displayed, of course, but they must be scrolled if they do not fit on the default 1024 by 768 monitor. Even at the 1028 by 768 resolution and 256 colors, each screen requires about 2.5 MB to store the display monitor image.

If the eye can see 16.7 million colors, representing computer graphics images with only 256 colors may not seem to be a very good idea at all. But these 256 colors can yield very good graphics quality unless the image has an unusually large number of shades and hues of color. And using only 256 colors has the added benefit of considerably reducing the size of the images and the processing time needed to manipulate them. Less memory is used, less disk space is needed, and less computer processing power is required when dealing with a smaller number of colors.

A technique known as *dithering* can help to reduce the number of colors needed to display a graphics image of good quality. Dithering allows for the simulation of more colors than are really there. The technique has been used for many years in all forms of graphic representation. For example, a black and white newspaper photo consists of pixels that are either all black or all white. But when viewed from a normal reading distance, the image seems to include many shades of gray, from just dirty white all the way to not quite black. But when examined closely, the newspaper photo image can be seen to consist of an array of tiny black dots separated by white spaces. Where the black dots are farther apart, the shade of gray is lighter. Where the black dots are closer together, the shade of gray is darker. When viewed at a normal distance, the dots blur and merge together and the image appears to consist of a rich mixture of grays, blacks, and whites.

The same dithering methods work for colors as well. Color television sets, for instance, have only three colors: red, green, and blue. These three colors are usually abbreviated as RGB. The combination of these three colors electronically makes it appear that the television set can display an almost unlimited array of colors. But this is only an illusion. Looking closely at a television set (for brief glimpses) will reveal tiny clusters of the three colors. The illusion is quite effective, as shown in Figure 1-4.

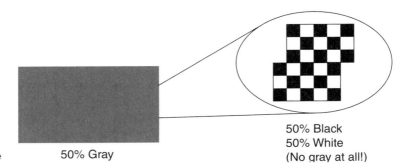

Figure 1-4
Dithering with
Black and White

50% Gray

50% Black
50% White
(No gray at all!)

Computer display monitors work exactly the same way. There are only three colors: the RGB colors of the television set. However, the three colors are displayed more densely on a computer screen than on a television screen. This higher density, or higher resolution, makes computer monitor images more clear and text easier to read. Text displayed on a standard television set has to be fairly large to be easily legible.

In fact, this low text resolution on a television screen has had an interesting effect on motion pictures, of all things. Motion picture credits have become much larger on theater screens in recent years. Hollywood has realized that most movies will eventually be seen on television screens, either on broadcast or cable channels, or as pre-recorded video tapes. The text credits from older films were so small that they were pretty much unreadable when transferred to video and shown on a television set. Extra-large text in movie houses means readable text later, at home.

When computer graphics people talk about the number of colors a computer can display, they really mean the number of colors that the computer can display *at the same time*. With color dithering, even if a computer monitor is set up to display only 256 solid colors simultaneously, the eye will still see a dazzling array of colors. Dithering the 256 colors together can create a tremendous variety. Moreover, the 256 colors chosen can be varied as well. Usually, the 256 colors for a particular image can be chosen by the computer to best represent the image from a total set of 256,000 colors. The 256 color sub-set is known as the *palette* for the image. The process is the same employed by a human artist who might mix paints smoothly on the artist's palette and, then, select only those variations that best match what the artist's eye perceives.

Graphics Formats and Compression

Once scanned into a computer, the image must be stored in memory, and probably ultimately on disk, as a file. For storage purposes, images fall into one of a small number of main image classes. There are six main categories: raster, vector, image, metafile, 3D, and video (also used for animation).

Raster images simply create files with every pixel of the image in a sequential format. Usually starting with the upper-left pixel, the raster file stores all of the pixel color information row by row to the bottom-right of the image. Vector images are made up of lines, not individual pixels. Formulas that describe the image are stored instead of each pixel. When displayed, the computer must determine which pixels along a line must be set to display the image. Vector images work best for typeface like TrueType fonts and technical drawings and illustrations. Vector images do not represent "continuous tone" images very well at all. Continuous tone images have gradual changes in tones or hues from one color to another. Raster formats handle continuous tone images well but have other drawbacks. Vector images scale well, from smaller to larger, which is why their use for typefaces is so common. The lines are just re-calculated and re-drawn, and the quality remains the same. But raster images do not scale well, and blow-ups can reveal the individual square pixels making up the image.

Metafiles are part raster and part vector. That is, pixel information as well as line formulas are stored in the image file. But although metafiles contain both types of information, in most respects metafiles are most like vector images. 3D file formats are most relevant to VRML. 3D files store formatted 3D scenes with object, lighting, and camera (point-of-view) information. This may also include animation or video information as well. 3D file formats can be very complex, as in the case of VRML. Some of the formats are text-based description languages, as is VRML, while others are binary (just a very long series of 0s and 1s). Text-based 3D files contain ASCII text to describe the 3D scene and can be read by people (although an understanding of the 3D language is also necessary). Binary 3D file formats require a program to decipher.

Video files (also used for animation) store a sequence of images for play back. The video is played back directly from the file to video memory. The difference between just what is a video file and just what is an animation file is a subject matter of great debate. Some experts consider video to be animation plus a sound track. This definition is probably too rigid to be of much use. The best description of the difference is probably the number of frames per second the file play back causes the monitor to display. Any video file played back at 24 or 30 frames per second, as in television and motion pictures, may be considered video whether it includes a sound track or not. Video files played back at 16, 12, or even 6 frames per second may be considered animation. This description applies whether the content of the video file is a live-action subject or a cartoon.

An image file that has been stored in a specific format in one of the major classes takes up a certain amount of space. Compression techniques can be applied to the files to reduce their overall size. Compression effectiveness is measured by the ratio of the uncompressed to compressed file size. A compression ratio of 10:1 would mean that the compressed image file takes up only one-tenth the space that the uncompressed source image file occupied. This usually applies to the *average* reduction in file size when the compression technique is performed on a number of different image files. Actual file size reductions may vary greatly, depending on the image itself. A 10:1 compression technique applied to the letter "A" image example (960,000 bits or 120 KB) might yield a compressed file of only 12 KB. This can be an enormous savings in disk space, but not memory. The file must be uncompressed in main computer memory and sent to video memory for display anyway.

Some image formats lend themselves to even higher compression ratios with advanced compression techniques. These can be as high as 22:1 or above. Unfortunately, there is a trade-off in these compression techniques. Often, to achieve these very high compression ratios, the images must be processed longer by the computer, both to compress the images and to decompress them for display. More powerful processors can do the job more quickly, but only at higher initial hardware costs.

Compression processing load is not even all of the problem. Very high compression ratios usually require that some details of the image be discarded. Compression techniques that do this are known as "lossy" compression techniques, because these techniques "lose" some of the information in the original, uncompressed image. The original, detailed image is now "lost" also if not saved in an uncompressed state, defeating the whole purpose. Some loss of detail may be permissible, but it all depends on the image and application. Medical X-ray images are not good candidates for lossy compression methods.

Many compression techniques are quite simple in nature. A common technique called Run Length Encoding (RLE), used in many imaging file formats, simply detects long strings of consecutive 0s and 1s and replaces them with special RLE "code words." Compression is quick and simple, but RLE does not yield very impressive compression ratios, especially with complex color images.

Better compression ratios are achieved in modern graphic file formats using more elaborate compression techniques. Two of the more effective are Huffman encoding and Lempel-Ziv-Welch (LZW) encoding. Huffman encoding was invented in 1952 by David Huffman and is now an international standard. It is similar to the way Morse code works. Samuel Morse gave the shortest codes to the most common letters (. for *e*, - for *t*, and so on). Longer codes went to more uncommon letters (. . .- for *v*, --.. for *z*, and so on). Huffman took the most common patterns in a file and assigned a small code word to them. The assigned words could vary from file and file, and usually did. The file was always scanned for patterns first and then compressed in a second pass. Huffman encoding is known as a statisitical compression method. Huffman encoding must also store the meaning of the code words with the file so that it can be uncompressed properly. Typically, Huffman compression ratios are about 8:1, which is not bad at all.

LZW compression was invented in 1977 by Abraham Lempel and Jacob Ziv and expanded in 1984 by Terry Welch. LZW was specifically intended to overcome some of the shortcomings of Huffman encoding. To do so, LZW compression builds a "dictionary" and compresses the file as it is scanned. The dictionary codes are inserted in the file as it is compressed, overcoming the two-pass and separate table limitations of Huffman encoding. Typically, LZW compression ratios are about 10:1 and much faster to create and process than pure Huffman techniques.

One of the problems of applying techniques like RLE and LZW to images is that they are both generic compression techniques. That is, neither was or is specifically intended to work with image files. But another advanced compression technique was intended from the start to work well with the particular structure of image files. This is known as JPEG compression.

JPEG (Joint Photographic Experts Group) compression is very sophisticated. JPEG achieves the highest compression ratios by fooling the eye. This means that JPEG will attempt to discard details that the human eye cannot possibly see. JPEG compression is thus a "lossy" compression technique. But the lossy method is not perfect. Some JPEG-compressed images can suffer from two problems known as blocking and smearing. Blocking occurs when the eye picks up groups of pixels in the decompressed JPEG image in places where too much detail has been discarded in the interests of compression. Smearing occurs when the edges of an object in a decompressed JPEG image are blurred, for the same reasons.

Lossy compression is still impressive. Compression ratios of 100:1 are achievable if some blocking and smearing is deemed acceptable. This is the equivalent of making an entire 100 yard football field only 3 feet long. Even newer lossy compression techniques, called *fractal image compression* methods, can give compression ratios of up to 600:1. The football field would now be only six inches long!

Table 1-2 contains some common image file formats that fall into these six main classes, along with some other attributes. The list is admittedly biased toward PC and Windows formats and support. The "owner" refers to the developer of the file format. These are all 2D image formats.

Table 1-2
Common Image File Formats

Format	Type	Owner	Features	Strengths	Weaknesses
BMP	Raster	Microsoft	1 to 24-bit color	Windows support	Little or no compression
EPS	Metafile	Adobe	1 to 24-bit color	Good print quality	Little or no compression
GIF	Raster	CompuServe	1 to 24-bit color	LZW compression	Becoming aged
JPEG (Joint Photographic Experts Group)	Raster	ANSI	8-bit grayscale to 24-bit color	High JPEG compression	lossy compression
PCD (Photo CD)	Raster	Kodak	24-bit color	Excellent color	Only Kodak creates files
PCX	Raster	ZSoft Corp.	1 to 24-bit color	Very popular	Little or no compression
PSD (Photoshop)	Raster	Adobe	8 to 24-bit color	RLE compression	Elaborate
TGA (Targa)	Raster	Truevision, Inc.	16 to 24-bit color	Alpha channel RLE comp.	Many different formats
TIFF (Tagged Image File Format)	Raster	Aldus Corp. and Microsoft	1 to 24-bit color	Many compression schemes	Many incompatible versions
DXF (Autocad)	Vector	Autodesk	16 to 24-bit color	Very common	Elaborate

A few words may be in order about some of the table entries. The term "little or no compression" next to some items means that even though a compression scheme like RLE is allowed in some formats, many of these formats do not allow any compression at all for truly large files based on 24-bit color depths. RLE is seldom very effective for 24-bit color in any case. The "Alpha channel" is a concept pioneered by Truevision for the Targa format and includes no only color information, but *transparency* information about objects in an image. With an Alpha channel, a window can be made as transparent as desired, from nearly invisible to downright grimy, and yet other objects can be seen "through" the window. An entry of "elaborate" is purely a subjective one and simply means that the format is quite complex to understand and write application programs to manipulate easily.

Table 1-3 shows common graphic file formats used for 3D graphics applications. All are capable of true color.

Table 1-3
3D Graphics File Formats

Format	Type	Owner	Features	Strengths	Weaknesses
3DS (3D Studio)	3D	Autodesk	Video support	Very popular	Elaborate
Alias	3D	Alias	Video support	Wide range of features	Not as common as others
COB	3D	Caligari	Video support	Wide range of features	Elaborate
DXF (Autocad)	3D	Autodesk	CAD tool	Nearly standard	No video support
Lightwave	3D	NewTek, Inc.	Video support	Good features	Not as common
OBJ	3D	Wavefront	Flexible formats	Open structure for text format	Proprietary binary format
POV	3D	Drew Wells	Video support	Shareware	Elaborate
RIB	3D	Pixar	Video support	Excellent package	Elaborate
SoftImage	3D	Thomson Digital Image	Video support	Good features	Not as common

All of the 3D formats include such features as lighting, camera information, and so on. Most include a video or animation method, but the quality can vary. The POV format is actually shareware and can be very cost effective to use as a result. Strangely, Wavefront's OBJ format is similar to VRML when stored as a text description, in the sense that it is "open" (as is VRML) and so can be used by anyone freely.

But the OBJ binary format is strictly proprietary and can only be controlled by Wavefront. Many VRML virtual world authoring packages allow for the importing of OBJ and DXF file formats, and some allow for even others.

Table 1-4 contains some common video and animation file formats.

Table 1-4
Common Video Animation Formats

Format	Type	Owner	Features	Strengths	Weaknesses
FLI	Video	Autodesk	8-bit color, no audio, 320x200	Very popular	Low resolution, no audio
FLC	Video	Autodesk	8-bit color, no audio, 1280x1024	Very popular	No audio
AVI	Video	Microsoft	8 to 24-bit color	Windows support, compression	Low quality
QT (QuickTime)	Video	Apple	8 to 24-bit color	Windows support, compression	Compression not so good
MPEG (Motion Pictures Experts Group)	Video	ANSI (American National Standards Institute)	8 to 24-bit color	Best there is: highest quality, best compression	Very elaborate, compression requires special equipment to create

The FLI and FLC formats differ mainly in resolution. As time goes by, MPEG will become the format of choice for playback purposes. However, an annoying MPEG limitation is that it requires special hardware to perform the very complex processing that MPEG compression needs. Also, MPEG comes is a variety of different standard types (MPEG-1, MPEG-2, etc.). On the other hand, the video quality is unsurpassed.

Processing Computer Graphics

Once an image has been scanned into a computer and stored as an array of color bits, the computer can process the image in a variety of ways. For instance, the computer may do something as simple as displaying the image on the computer monitor. The monitor board that handles the display graphics has a fixed amount of what is known as *video memory*, or VRAM (Video RAM), which is separate from the main processing unit memory. The computer is constantly displaying the contents of the video memory (sometimes called the *frame buffer*) on the monitor screen. When the central processor in the computer needs to display a graphic or image on the monitor, all that needs to be done is to write the information bits to the correct video memory address space. Then the image is more or less automatically displayed on the screen.

Monitor boards are often 32 or 64-bit graphics cards, with regard to their color depth. It should be kept in mind that most marketing literature from vendors about 32/64/128 bit video cards usually refers *not* to the color depth of the card, but to the width of the card's internal data transfer bus. Faster video cards can take advantage of fast internal data transfers to accelerate the most common graphics operations, which gives much better performance in GUI environments. So a "32-bit graphics card" may have "24-bit color depth." There is no hard and fast relationship to follow.

In any case, if the maximum useful color depth is 24-bit color, what are the extra bits used for? A 32-bit graphics card can use the other 8 bits per pixel to specify transparency, using the Alpha channel information if available in the file format. A 64-bit graphics card uses the extra bits available to help speed up video and functions such as zooming. Some high-end computers even make use of 128-bit graphics cards, but this is overkill for even the most elaborate virtual world viewing.

Monitor boards today are being marketed specifically for displaying 3D file formats more efficiently, including the 3D virtual worlds in the VRML language found on the Internet. Products such as Matrox' Millennium board and Creative Labs' (makers of the popular SoundBlaster audio product line) 3D Blaster are especially made for handling 3D file formats, text-based or binary.

This is important for another reason. 3D image files must be displayed in a fundamentally different fashion than 2D image files. 3D graphics consist of a set of 3D objects that are created by a process called 3D modeling. 3D images and virtual worlds are not so much displayed by the computer, as *rendered*.

The constant mapping of a monitor board's video memory to monitor for a 2D image is essentially a passive operation. The image is just read from a file, transferred to video memory, and displayed. But 3D images are not just bit-by-bit loadings of pixel information to screen location. A 3D image file must be heavily processed on its way from file to video memory. The rendering process takes the 3D image file and mathematically turns it into a collection of 3D objects, adjusted to allow for the user's perspective. Rendering consists of a number of complex steps.

The computer must determine just where the lights shining on the 3D objects are located, the exact shape of the objects, the camera information (field of view, focal length, etc.), and other details. The computer then sets up a "virtual screen" in memory and projects the 3D scene onto the virtual screen. It is this set of projected bits, and not the 3D image itself, that is transferred to video memory and displayed on the monitor. As the 3D world is shifted, the whole scene must be re-computed, re-projected, and re-displayed. The nice thing about the newer special 3D monitor boards is that they can perform these operations on the board itself, rather than take up the main processor's time and memory to perform exactly the same tasks.

3D rendering is a vast and complex process. Details such as textures (2D images wrapped around 3D objects), reflection maps (reflected images seen on shiny objects), and shading (coloring of surfaces) must be rendered as well. Even such a simple operation as shading may have several ways of being rendered. Flat shading is simple and fast, coloring a basic wireframe with bland swatches of unvarying shades. Gourand shading (developed by Henri Gourand in 1971) varies the color more realistically with little more processing power. Finally, Phong shading developed by Phong Bui-Toung in 1974) varies color most realistically, but can be up to 100 times slower than Gourand shading.

Finally, the size of the monitor screen, whether 14, 15, 17, or even 20 inch, has no relationship to the quality of the images produced on it, no matter what the sales person says, although small screens yield small images. As long as the monitor is *noninterlaced* (to reduce flicker), has a *dot pitch* (a measure of how close together the points of light on the screen are) below .28 mm, and has a *vertical refresh rate* of at least 72 Hz (Hertz; and forget about the *horizontal* refresh rate: all are adequate), the monitor should have no trouble displaying detailed virtual worlds. If changes in resolution are desired, for instance from 800 by 600 to 1280 by 1024, a *multi-sync* monitor rather than a *fixed-frequency* monitor is almost a necessity.

The revolution in computer graphics techniques and capabilities has been matched by a revolution in the *contents* of the graphics images. This leads to a discussion of the second piece of the virtual reality puzzle: visualization.

The Second Piece: Visualization

It may be that when virtual worlds on the Internet become common and routine places to visit and explore, the images and graphics may be as complex as a Hollywood motion picture. Certainly there are

Web sites that approach this level of sophistication now. But the vast majority of Web sites, like the Internet it is based on, excel at serving up information. The second piece of the virtual world puzzle in the revolution is how information is presented: visually instead of exclusively textually.

Human beings are distinguished by their ability to use binocular vision to observe a world in three dimensions; a world having depth as well as height and width. Human eyes are set forward and apart to accomplish this. The binocular feature is almost exclusively a feature of predators in the animal world, and its presence in humans has been a subject for much debate among anthropologists. The image of humans as hunters has long been one of considerable attraction or repulsion, depending on school of thought and sometimes even political persuasion. This debate need not be rehashed here, merely noted. The fact remains that human eyes are not set on the sides of the head to scan nervously for potential enemies, but peer straight into a world of three-dimensional vividness.

Mathematical Visualization

Perhaps the first application of human binocular vision to a field of human effort other than hunting or scavenging was in the field of mathematics. This development was painfully slow in coming. The great Greek geometers such as Euclid seem to have produced texts utterly devoid of any graphical representations at all, even something as simple as a cube. The earliest surviving manuscripts are simply page after page of text uninterrupted by even the most trivial illustration. The study of geometry and other mathematical fields is inconceivable today without graphical representations or demonstrations, but the idea of illustrating texts seems to have occurred to none of the ancient Greeks at all.

Not until the 1200s do mathematical manuscripts begin to include diagrams to allow the reader to more easily visualize the concepts the words refer to in a text. Strangely, the diagrams in many of these medieval manuscripts are un-enlightening, or just wrong. For instance, a thirteenth-century copy of a work known as *The Division of the Canon*, attributed to Euclid but not authored by him, discusses proportions. In the section discussing the proportion 8:4:2, the medieval commentator thoughtfully refers the reader to a diagram, supposedly meant to help the reader grasp the concept. But the graphic consists of three evenly spaced vertical lines, labeled simply 1, 2, and 3. The lines are all exactly the same height.

Fortunately, things got better as the use of graphical representations to help in the visualization of mathematical concepts became more common. In fact, the whole process of representing complex mathematical information as pictures—graphics or diagrams—is referred to today as *visualization*.

Visualization is a way of showing the properties of a collection of items through graphics. Usually the collection of items is very large and the very abundance of this information would make it difficult for a person to comprehend the relationship among and between individual items at a glance. This is a perfect place to illustrate the principle with a simple example.

Suppose an ice cream company wanted to figure out which age group should be the target of a considerable marketing campaign for a new flavor. Call the flavor *Vanilla Dream*. Marketing campaigns are expensive, so the ice cream company wants to make sure the money is spent where the chances of success for the new flavor are the best. A market research firm hired to perform a study has surveyed 892 people and have delivered their results to the ice cream company. Consider this short list of items in Table 1-5 containing information on the preference of different age groups for Vanilla Dream.

Table 1-5
Vanilla Dream Taste Test

Age Group	Number preferring flavor
0–10	100
11–20	101
21–30	98
31–40	97
41–50	199
51–60	101
61–70	96
70+	100

Which age group has the best chance of success for the new flavor? The eye flicks down the list and after some initial processing settles on the fact that the new flavor has the highest number of favorable responses to the survey in the age group from 41 to 50. But what if the list had a hundred items instead of eight? A thousand? The eye would quickly be overwhelmed by the amount of textual information that needed to be analyzed before a conclusion was reached. And is their anything else about the information contained in the list that might be of interest to the ice cream company?

Now consider the graph below, made from the information in the list. This is just a simple graphic to help visualize the information but makes the point. Other, more elaborate forms are possible for the list of information (see Figure 1-5).

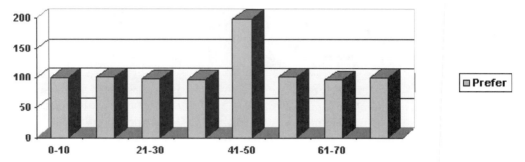

Figure 1.5
Visualization of
Vanilla Dream Data

The advantages of visualization for analyzing information are now obvious. The Vanilla Dream-loving age group leaps off the page. In fact, other, more subtle aspects of the information that were obscured when the information was presented as a mere list of numbers now become apparent as well. For example, not only is the new flavor most popular with the 41 through 50-year olds, the new flavor is almost more popular in that age group than in any two of the other age groups combined! This fact is of obvious interest to marketeers and perhaps even others. "What is it about the 41 to 50 age group that leads them to like vanilla so much?" sociologists might wonder.

The first glimmering that graphs and diagrams could be useful in a mathematical environment came from the 1600s when the French mathematician René Descartes began to invent and use the concepts of coordinate geometry to plot and present data and information. In his work *The World, or A Treatise on Light*, Descartes wrote, "For a short time, therefore, allow your thoughts to leave this world in order to come to see a wholly new one, which I shall cause to be born in the presence of your thought in imaginary spaces." There is certainly little difference between what is meant today by the term "virtual reality" and Descartes's intentions for his imaginary spaces.

The design and use of modern graphical aids for visualization requires at least as great a degree of imagination as Descartes possessed. And the results will be far more wide-reaching and accessible. The utilization of visualization to illustrate the relationship among multiple items and objects may be a foregone conclusion, but the packaging is not. The graphical method to be used is not determined by the information to be portrayed. The ice cream graphic, for instance, could have been presented as a pie chart or line chart just as readily as the 3D bar graph chosen.

All researchers dealing with statistical graphics in pre-computer days were aware of this situation. The seriousness of the issue has only been heightened by the enormous power of computing available today. The issue goes beyond mere packaging to the root of just how a tool may be used by individuals. Individuals have their own perception of the world that embody particular cultures and lines of reasoning.

The methods of visualization have burst the bounds of the mathematical elite and entered the realm of everyday experience. Why not visualize catalog prices or words in a play? Would that not make the most affordable item or most common phrase leap out at the viewer? Very likely. New types of visualization must handle new information environments and the users that access the information. This will more than likely be everyone quite soon.

Thinking and Seeing

The entire process of thinking is wrapped up in visual metaphors. People talk about having an *insight,* getting a different *point of view,* gaining a *better perspective,* and so on. These ways of thinking, including *seeing clearly* and *looking at things this way,* are not arbitrary, but reveal something profound about the preferred sense (vision) for experiencing the real world and all phenomena in it.

In spite of Plato's distrust of sight and sight's main information tool, writing, most ancients valued sight above the other senses. Aristotle differed with Plato, his teacher, and elevated vision to the position that seeing, and the visual center of the brain, holds today. To Aristotle, and even Leonardo DaVinci, the vision center of the brain was where all senses came together into one great *common sense.* Today, even with vast amounts of research into neurons and dendrites, exactly what happens in the brain during the whole process of having a mental image remains a mystery.

One of the most profound aspects of visualization carried out by computer is that it builds upon these vision-based metaphors of thought.

Many visualization packages enable the user to rotate an object on the computer monitor screen in three dimensions. In actual fact, the display monitor is really just projecting a 3D image onto a 2D screen, but the process is so convincing to the brain's visual center that no one even talks about this process in any detail. The whole point is that visual information is so natural that this projection is taken for granted and rarely taken as a topic for further discussion.

The linking of visualization to vision would seem to be obvious. But visualization has grown beyond the bounds of the strictly visual sense when applied to virtual reality. Virtual reality gear can be hooked up to the computer to enable walking through the graphs of data, especially when the amount becomes overwhelming even visually. Chemists can now handle a molecule rather than just look at it. This tactile experience gives a better feel for the structure than looking alone.

The addition of taste and smell may not be far behind. The issues are identical no matter what sense is discussed. Of course, vision will always remain in the forefront, if for no other reason than computers are basically looked at. Other senses will not be as efficient as others in analyzing some information. For example, would the number of vanilla fanciers in the 41 to 50 age group have a more powerful sense of smell? Perhaps not.

But other methods may be appropriate. Electric current is defined as a *flow*. An appropriate visualization technique for comparing electrical currents may be touch and feel. Why not represent various currents under study as a river on the computer and dip a virtually real finger into each, feeling the tug of current? Currency transactions flow as well. Why not detect the most powerful by feel? Not only power could be represented by touch, but other information as well. Cold flows would be outgoing cash flow, warm would be revenue *streams*. An impending bankruptcy would be as obvious as a dip in an icy stream. Desirable stocks might reveal themselves as a hot Jacuzzi. The possibilities are endless and limited only by the imagination.

The whole point of this visualization exercise is that people *see* things more easily when information is presented in a graphical format than as a series of numbers. The examples presented numerical information, but the whole idea is that *any* information at all is more useful when presented with some form of visualization.

Visualization and the Computer

Computers are sometimes thought to deal solely with numbers. After all, the very term *computer* came from a U.S. Army job description that the mechanical device replaced. As the vacuum-tube computer took on more and more of the routine mathematical manipulations human computer clerks had performed, more and more computer clerks were freed from their pencils and sent off to the front. So the impact of the advent of the computer on human activity was felt immediately.

But it would be a mistake to think that the modern computer is concerned with numbers alone. This is not to say that all information inside the computer is not represented numerically: it must be. All of the letter *A*s in computers everywhere are no more than a string of 0s and 1s at heart. However, people must deal with *A*s in a word-processing document, and not the numeric context that represents the letter *A* within the computer itself.

Contemporary computers deal in *information*, pure and simple. Information must be prepared for human consumption in four separate stages, although people seldom stop and think about what they are doing when they prepare their own information. Consider a trip to the library to research a paper on some topic. The information must be *found* in the card catalog (probably electronic itself!). The information must next be *accessed*, usually by walking the library stacks. Accessed information must next be *evaluated* for relevance or appropriateness, usually by a weighing of detail, but sometimes just by a weighing of weight (this book is *too* heavy!). Finally, the information must be *understood* if it is to be utilized in an intelligent fashion. These four steps: finding, accessing, evaluating, and understanding are followed whenever information is used.

The task of making sense of information is made that much more difficult given the huge amounts of information available in a variety of formats today. The difficulty of dealing with a large variety of different media increases proportionately. Literally millions of sites are now linked together on the Internet, each with potentially millions of facts, documents, and other pieces of information in formats as varied as video and audio. Complete texts of nearly every world-class author are available, as well as newspaper archives, news broadcasts, and current stock market quotations.

Information is basically a set of facts gathered without regard to relevance, significance, or relationship to each other. Information must be evaluated to yield knowledge, and knowledge must be used effectively to yield wisdom. Visualization and such methods as virtual reality can help transform information into knowledge. Help with turning knowledge into wisdom remains beyond the scope of any computer technology or current tool, however.

Unless information can be evaluated quickly and easily, the potential for the torrent of information being made available through the Internet and Web to transform business, science, medicine, education, and all other aspects of daily life will remain unrealized. Reading will not only fail to provide a means for evaluation of this flood of information, it will become impossible. No one person can even attempt to read all that is currently published on a monthly basis in such reading-intensive fields as medicine, science, and law, to name just a few. And when the need to research past publications for information on successful medical treatments, experimental procedures, and legal precedent is added, the task becomes overwhelming. Information analysis by means of computerized techniques of visualization and virtual reality is one of the more viable approaches to the problem.

The entire process of visualization enables people to use their most obvious sense—sight—as a natural tool for exploring the relevance, significance, and relationship that one fact has with another. The eyes as well as the brain can be used to extract knowledge from separate pieces of information. And this may be done in a more efficient and effective manner than ever before.

Visual Information

Spatial metaphors for information are everywhere. The challenge is to translate these spatial metaphors into visual representations in a consistent and sensible manner. People speak of *low* temperatures, of *high* priority documents, of *top* secret messages, just to name a few examples. The graphical representation of these terms is entirely arbitrary. It might make the most sense to map *high* priorities to height representations, but the choice is individual. The final goal must be clarity.

The practice of representing information in a virtual world is relatively new and not well understood. No one knows what all the ramifications are. But the same is true of all new technologies. The telephone was not invented so that people could make telephone calls. People wrote letters before the telephone. The telephone was envisioned by Alexander Graham Bell as a business tool so that doctors could call pharmacists, manufacturers could call suppliers, and so on. It came as a shock to everyone that people would actually want or need a telephone in their homes, to the extent that mail deliveries dwindled from twice a day, six days a week (people went calling in person on Sunday afternoon) to the current service levels.

The crucial factor in the development of the telephone and voice as the preferred method of communication between people was a firm understanding of the strengths and weaknesses of the two media of voice and written expression. Once these differences were finally worked out, each one, writing and talking, could be used more effectively. And one need not suffer at the hands of the other. Abraham Lincoln once debated a political opponent for a full seven hours before a live audience. Today he would issue a written position paper. In the same way, some of the things that visualization and virtual reality can do best are known now, but others will take a number of years before a full understanding of their potential will develop.

For instance, early users of visualization and virtual reality still struggle with the twin problems of rapid change and motion. The information upon which the graphical representation is based may change quite quickly, as when the current price of a stock is represented by the height of wall, for example. Color and other display characteristics may change with disconcerting unpredictability in a virtual world.

The motion problem is concerned with things like animation (getting lost), hyperlinks (sudden jumps to...where?), and interactivity (through such tools as Java). Walking through a visual representation without becoming lost requires the addition of signposts or other orientation features that are sadly lacking in many virtual reality worlds today. The use of hyperlinks may be effective and even absolutely necessary to relate data items, but can also be enormously disruptive to any feeling of *place*. Finally, interaction with the information source can be so complex that even simple tasks like highlighting important parts of a virtual world or activating close-ups can become very disorienting as well.

There are also limitations in the current state of display devices. It is difficult to jam much detail onto even the most expensive display monitors. Also, many users cannot stare into a screen for long stretches of time. Goggles and headsets currently only intensify and draw attention to these problems, they do not overcome them.

Simple Visualizations: Trees

Early research and development efforts into visualization tended to concentrate on a broad but still limited set of information types. Most of these information types naturally lent themselves to computerized sources of data. These information types (or *spaces,* as they are sometimes called) include disk drive file and directory trees and structures, networks, and graphs. All were and are well-suited for representation as objects with multiple interrelationships. Other information spaces later included text, database queries, and even statistics about the Internet itself.

As an example of what these early forms of visualization were capable of, consider the simple case of the Windows 3.1 File Manager graphical representation of the directory and file structure of a hard disk drive (see Figure 1-6). The visualization is simple, effective, and neat. Yet it embodies many of the concepts discussed up to this point. However, there is much to be desired in the way of evaluating the information visualized. Even a few simple changes to the uniform icons employed could make the visualization more effective and useful. For instance, the size of the icon could vary with the size of the files within a given directory. The color of the icon could change with the contents of the individual files themselves, for example, a blue icon for text, green for executables, and so on. Even more information could be loaded into the visual representation that would be practical by other means. A file that had not been backed up for many months could have a red border, and files duplicated elsewhere could be outlined in black.

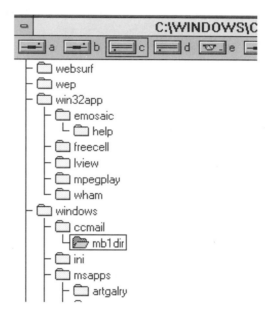

Figure 1-6
Windows 3.1 File Manager "Visualization"

The tree-like link and node diagrams like those used in Windows quickly become cluttered and too large to be of much use. One alternative, developed at Xerox's Palo Alto Research Center (PARC), is known as the *cone tree*. PARC is justly famous in the computer industry for its pioneering efforts in such critical computer developments as the PC itself, the mouse, the LAN, and the laser printer. And of course this pioneering spirit extends to computer visualization also.

The cone tree is one of the earliest applications of visualization to general information, rather than strictly numerical data. A cone tree is a true 3D representation of hierarchical information such as disk drive directories and files. Any node on the cone tree is located at the upper point (apex) of the cone and all of the node's *children* (information dependent on the upper node) are arrayed about the circular base of another cone. The cone tree makes the largest amount of information visible at one time (see Figure 1-7).

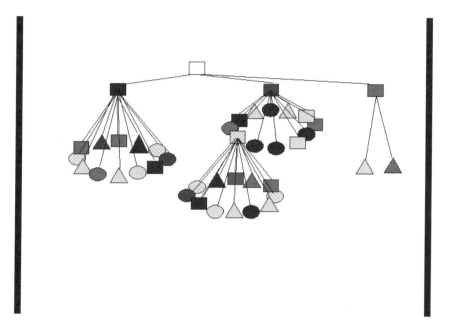

Figure 1-7
Cone Tree
Directory and File
Representation

Any node in the cone tree can be rotated to the front of the display by clicking a mouse on it. The tree smoothly rotates to overcome the motion problems mentioned above, but the cone tree reaches its new orientation fairly rapidly.

There are various variations on the simple cone tree. One is called the *tree map,* which just fills in the available 2D screen space in a meaningful way. Usually, the information is displayed as a series of rectangular boxes, each of which may recursively be divided to represent such things as the relative sizes of files, contents, and so on. For example, the total disk space in use may be represented as a large rectangle on the screen. The rectangle would be divided into strips representing sub-directories, with the width of each strip indicating the percentage of total disk use in the sub-directory. This process repeats within each box, with further partitionings for each sub-directory and file. The strips and rectangles can be color coded to indicate various attributes, such as file creation date or file contents.

Visualizing Networks

Networks have been created to link computers for a number of years. Whether private networks or the public Internet, all networks consist of a number of common features. All networks consist of network nodes and the links between them. This is true for local area networks within a building and wide area networks linking computers across the country. The network nodes may be hubs, routers, or packet switches. The links may be twisted pair copper wire, coaxial cable, or fiber optic cable. Each node has a physical location associated with it and each link connects two or possibly even more nodes.

There are other properties associated with network nodes and links besides the obvious ones of location and type. Statistical information can be associated with the node or link as well. A count of packet traffic between routers on the Internet is an example. Packets are small units of information used by the Internet protocol to exchange information between network nodes (routers) on the Internet. Packet counts can change rapidly with time of day and other activities such as new sites and links. Other properties may be more static than traffic counts. The node's manufacturer, model, and port speeds would be examples of these properties.

The usual way to represent a network visually is with simple color coded lines and boxes (see Figure 1-8). Colors and forms indicate one property or another. Icons or other graphical symbols are typically used to indicate the network nodes. The nodes are also usually laid out spatially to indicate the geographical relationships between the network nodes. This sometimes even extends to using a background map of a state or country to make the relationship obvious.

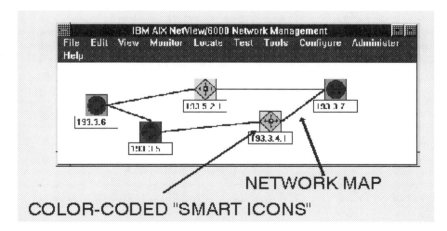

Figure 1-8
Visualizing a Network

The technique works extremely well with small networks. In fact, this is the basis for a number of commercial network management software packages sold today. However, the node and link relationships quickly become much too cluttered to use for any reasonably large network.

For larger, global networks, the visualization is typically a 3D globe of the world. Color coded arcs connect major nodes in this representation. There is no line crossing as on a 2D projection and the end result is an uncluttered view of changing traffic conditions and patterns. The globe may be rotated, of course, and zoomed to a particular area of interest. Cities are identified by geographical position on the globe alone.

Network visualizations for non-geographical information are possible as well. A deeper understanding of relationships is still possible without reference to actual, physical space. For example, this type of visualization could be helpful in enabling a manufacturer to keep better track of the parts and subassemblies that go into a finished product. Each node in the network would not represent a location, but a specific part. The color and size of each node would indicate the number of parts on hand. Small red nodes might mean that a part is in short supply, for instance. Each part, down to the tiniest screw, would be linked by lines to all assemblies that require it. The thickness of the lines connecting the nodes might encode the number of individual parts used in the assembly process. There could be a pair of parts used very frequently, three-way assemblies that appear less often, and so on.

A cluster in such a network visualization, such as big screws, metal plates, and wiring, would indicate the subassemblies necessary in the manufacturing process. Clicking on a specific node would call up details like supplier, warehouse location, and reordering information. The product manager could filter out node information based on a number of criteria, or rotate the display to focus in a specific area of concern without losing the overall picture. Tens of thousands of items have been successfully related using this method of network visualization, Figure 1-9 shows a simple example. In the near future, a logical next step would be to represent the entire manufacturing process as a virtual world for the product manager to wander through. Hyperlinks would enable warehouse visits, or even supplier home office visits, as part of the tour.

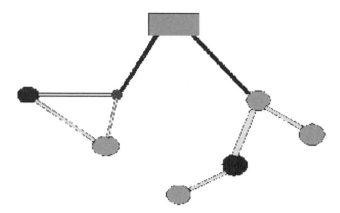

Figure 1-9
Network Visualization
for a Manufacturing
Process

The Information City

So far there has been little discussion of true virtual reality visualizations. This has been intentional, the purpose being to illustrate the development of computerized visualization techniques. The natural end of the process is the development of full virtual world visualizations, whether the information represented is numerical, textual, or some other form entirely.

The information city technique works well for both hierarchical (such as the directory-file structure) and network (such as the manufacturing process) visualizations. The visual metaphor used in this case is the *cityscape,* which resembles a city skyline in three dimensions with streets showing the relationships between the buildings. The cityscape usually is built to resemble an array of city skyscrapers intentionally. The whole idea is to extend the familiar 3D bar chart type information into a 3D virtual world.

Information is recorded in the individual 3D building icons, again represented as differences in a building's height, color, and shape. These coded differences may even extend to architectural styles such as spires or arches.

Users can view the parts of the city interactively with a virtual reality interface. A simple mouse movement can maneuver around a large building to view a small house located behind it. A zoom feature can then expand the house to workable proportions. The user can enter the dwelling and wander through the information storehouse revealed within. Users enjoy the cityscape virtual world because of its intuitive ease of use and gain instant insights because of the human ability to grasp 3D space quickly.

Information that has been presented in the cityscape format include financial data and document relationships. For instance, the relative standings of a group of companies competing within the same business field, such as high-speed modems, could be represented by a cluster of buildings. The buildings would be linked by joint marketing ventures and the companies distinguished in terms of employee numbers, profits, revenue, and long-term debt by various architectural details such as building size, color, shape, and roof. A large, low-rising, red building with a flat roof could be an over-staffed company with little revenue, a crushing long-term debt, and in Chapter 11 bankruptcy. A better investment might be the sleek, tall, green structure with the sweeping spire next door.

Documents can be mapped by this method as well. In many university libraries, the central computerized card catalog has entries not only for the main building's holding, but also for numerous annexes and special collection areas as well. A query on the topic First Punic War to a library database could yield an information cityscape with results that are easy to interpret at once as shown in Figure 1-10. The big buildings (books on this topic) are in the main part of town (the main library), small houses (journal articles) are on the back streets (in the journals area), the old churches (rare books) are apart some distance (in the annex across town), and the central glass tower (the book most relevant and desperately needed) is isolated on a dead end street (it's at the book repair service being re-bound).

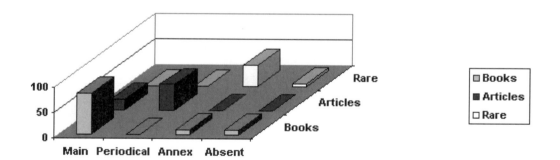

Figure 1-10
Library Cityscape
Search Results

What Are Words for?

Visualization, whether delivered as a simple 2D projection or a fully interactive 3D virtual world, has little presence on the Internet of Web today. This state of affairs is rapidly changing, of course, but for the time being the vast amount of information accessible through the Internet and on Web pages is just scrollable text. The fonts may change, and the colors as well, and some impressive pictures may even appear, but the textual aspect of information on the Internet is a fact of life. They are not called Web *pages* for nothing.

Individual Web sites may hold many millions of words of text, and huge collections of these words may be available for research and analysis. But even large collections of textual information may be candidates for visualization and virtual reality exploration.

In most word processing software packages, there is the ability to turn on *revision marks*. Revision marks give an editor or writer the capability of determining more precisely where changes to text document have taken place. A deletion of a word, sentence, or paragraph may be indicated by a strikethrough, or line passing through the center of the deleted text: ~~This is strikethrough of strikeout text.~~ Any additions may be color or font coded in any one of a number of distinct styles: This text has been *added*. A problem often arises when deletions and additions are made by many authors or editors at different times. It becomes extremely difficult to sort out exactly which deletions and additions were made by whom and exactly when. The history of a document in terms of additions and deletions may often be just as important as the final text.

Visualization can make it easier to detect and understand the creative process of producing text. Each author or editor may use a distinctive color or style for strikethroughs and additions. Alternatively, or even in addition, each successive revision (first, second, third. . .) may have distinctive markups as well. The changes to a text may then be applied successively and selectively by viewers of the text (see Figure 1-11).

Visualization can make it ~~less difficult and~~ easier to detect and understand the creative process of producing ~~material~~ text. Each author ~~or editor~~ may use a distinctive color or style for ~~strikeouts and~~ strikethroughs and additions. Alternatively, or even in addition, each successive revision (first, second, third...) may have distinctive markups as well. The changes to a text may then be applied successively and selectively by viewers of the text.

Figure 1-11
Visualizing Revisions
to Textual Information

Changes to other types of text than pure prose may be visualized in the same fashion. For example, a huge task in the software industry today is keeping track of the change history of software programs that may be comprised of literally millions of lines of computer code. Several commercial products exist to visualize these revision levels, often using simple 2D colored columns and rows. The visualization is added on top of the files of code lines themselves. The actual computer source code still has the traditional formatting of indentations, line lengths, paragraphs, comments, and so on. But the visualization layer adds such features as color coded modification dates to the source code itself. Using typical virtual reality motion techniques of mouse movements and button clicks, a software developer can zoom out to see which modules of the lengthy source code have had the most and most recent modifications, or zoom in to see the detailed structure of a particularly volatile section of code.

At these higher levels of abstraction, the program seems to be transformed into a number of color bars. The task of finding heavily modified code sections would be nearly impossible with text-based revision dates next to individual lines, as has been done in the past. The virtual world of program source code enables software developers to take in such information at a glance.

So far, the discussion of textual visualization has centered on the words within a single document. But other possibilities exist as well. The relationships among and within the content of a complex set of documents is another aspect of textual analysis that can be aided with visualization techniques. When dealing with large collections of text documents, a visualization method known as the *themescape* in some virtual world applications has been developed in several forms. A themescape is an abstract, 3D landscape of information constructed by the relationships between documents, rather than within each individual text document.

As an example, consider the text of all news broadcasts during a specific time period. The text may be analyzed visually to illustrate the concentration of themes and their relationships across the textual database. For instance, the textual database may be queried for items mentioning the *federal budget* and other related phrases such as *congress* or the *president*. Figure 1-12 illustrates this process. The closer the documents appear in the resulting landscape is an indication of the proximity of these terms to each other in the text document of the news broadcast. The elevation could indicate the number of times the terms are mentioned. On the outskirts of the landscape, single mentions of the target terms form isolated bumps on the horizon. The broadcasts of most interest will form mountain ranges with a central peak for the source with the most mentions. A quick inspection of the landscape could show that most broadcasts mentioned congress and were broadcast on CNBC, for example.

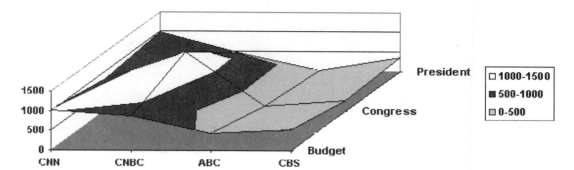

Figure 1-12
A Landscape of Document Collection Text Terms

Other topological features of the landscape, such as cliffs and valleys, represent details about the interrelationships between the documents and target terms. It is important to point out, however, that the landscape may change drastically with other target terms or even a simple reordering of the news broadcast source. Visualization is not a substitute for the wise choice of analysis topics. The result of an ill-formed question will be an ill-formed answer.

Text analysis with visualization techniques can also be extended to the relationships and correlation words within a single document. For example, if the words *congress* and *president* occur within some pre-defined distance in a document, they may be said to be correlated. The distance may be within a word or two (The President and congress today...) or within the same sentence (Congress today passed . . . and sent it to the President.), or within the same paragraph. A high correlation within a document would indicate that the document would be more relevant for the study of the relationship between congress and the President.

The visualization would involve the graphical representation of correlations. A simple visualization would just be a table of one-to-one correlations where each row and column are labeled with the words in the entire document. The cells of the table would contain the number of correlations in the document between each pair of words. The two words would give the x-axis and y-axis coordinates of the cell. The problem is that such a table would be much too large to be of any use, since the interesting correlations would be scattered all over the table.

These large tables are difficult to use, let alone analyze. But of course the order and even inclusion of any two words on either axis may be arbitrary and flexible, so the entries can be manipulated, also with a virtual reality method, to isolate the desired correlations of interest.

For example, consider an analysis of the text of this chapter so far. Instead of making a table with each of the 6000 or so words written up to this point, the table can focus on a number of terms of interest (see Table 1-6). The table contains only four entries to be manageable and

Table 1-6
Textual Information in Tabular Form

Words	Visualization	Reality	Hardware	Text
Virtual	7	13	0	3
Visual	1	1	0	2
Software	0	1	0	0
Computer	5	2	0	0

yet forms a good example of the visualization process. One axis contains the words *virtual, visual, computer,* and *software.* The other consists of the words *visualization, reality, hardware,* and *text.* For the purposes of this analysis, a correlation was defined to be when each pair of words indicating a cell were mentioned in the same sentence. A 3D visualization of Table 1-6 results has been added below the table itself (see Figure 1-13).

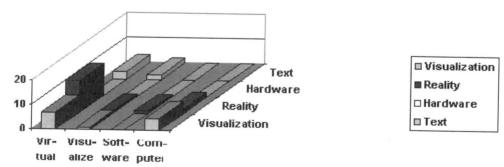

Figure 1-13
World Correlation
Visualization

A glance at the visualization chart instantly shows the high degree of correlation between *virtual* and *reality,* as might be expected. The use of this information is not obvious, but possible applications of textual analysis of this type might include literary style, content, and even authorship determination. These three aspects of a text are highly dependent on word correlations of one type or another.

Naturally, the cityscape, tree structures, or any other means of visualization can form the basis for a virtual world containing the information desired. All databases consisting of textual documents can benefit from some form of visualization. It is still necessary, however, to perform query operations, analyze the results, and deal with potentially very large amounts of data. The advantage of a virtual world representation is that alternate visualizations can be visited as a series of virtual worlds until the one form is found that best presents the query result in an intuitive manner. The visiting of these alternate visualization realities is made much easier by the embedding of hyperlinks into the virtual reality world that the visualization has constructed.

The whole concept of hyperlinks has gained popularity with the rise of the World Wide Web portion of the Internet. Hyperlinks are also known as hypertext links, but the term hyperlink is preferred since the links are no longer restricted to text.

Computer Graphics and Visualization

This chapter has traced the development of computerized graphics and the visualization of information. But why? What has all this to do with VRML and virtual worlds on the Internet? The point is simply that the vast amounts of information available on the Internet are more easily accessed and understood when computerized graphics and visualization techniques are combined with virtual reality concepts to build 3D virtual worlds on the Internet.

This chapter has covered the computer graphics and visualization part of the whole picture. The next chapter will look at the development of the Internet, World Wide Web, and virtual reality itself.

Chapter

2

Virtual Worlds and the World Wide Web

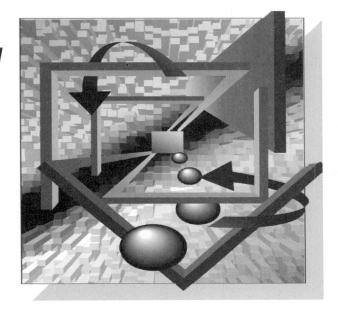

The Birth of the Internet

The Internet is hot stuff. A growing portion of it, the World Wide Web, has invaded both universities and corporations to the point that credibility is won for institutions and products by having a "dot edu" or "dot com" to call one's own. The information superhighway and cyberspace are somehow tied up with the Internet and Web, it seems, but no one is quite sure just how. But the Internet has a full and even colorful history, one that is well worth reviewing as the Web and VRML worlds are poised to move even further into the mainstream.

The Internet, today's symbol of international cooperation and commerce, owes its very existence to three things: allied battle plans during World War II, the Cold War, and the threat of thermonuclear destruction to the United States. This is not an ancestry many computer enthusiasts dwell on. Official and casual Internet histories usually mention U.S. military involvement, but quickly slide over the reasons that led the Pentagon to fund the development of the Internet in the first place.

Early in World War II, military planners and civilian technologists conceived of an analytical system that came to be called *operations research,* or just O.R. (so old is the O.R. idea that the acronym still had the dots after the letters. O.R. attempted to apply sound scientific modeling principles to military planning ad operations. For instance, an early O.R. effort generated statistics showing that by setting depth charges to explode at varying depths, instead of uniformly, more enemy submarines could be destroyed. Other O.R. research showed how anti-aircraft fire could be coordinated with allied fighter flight paths to avoid shooting down friendly fighters with enemy bombers. Numbers backed up decisions that no longer had to depend on a key individual's gut feeling or isolated experiences. For example, Hitler blundered repeatedly during World War II by drawing on his experiences in the trenches during the First World War to make key decisions.

Early computers like Howard Aiken's Harvard Mark I in 1944 and the Moore School of Engineering at the University of Pennsylvania's ENIAC (Electronic Numerical Integrator and Computer) in 1945 (just *after* the war ended) were needed to process the complex calculations needed in O.R. After the war, the three major military branches all pursued individual O.R. work by private contracts with universities and non-profit organizations. The Navy had the Center for Naval Analysis, run by the Franklin Institute in Philadelphia. The Army had the Operation Research Office, run by Johns Hopkins University. But the most famous of all these "think tanks" was the Air Force's use of the RAND Corporation.

Starting out as a technical branch of the Douglas Aircraft Company in Santa Monica, California, RAND was spun-off in 1948 and incorporated as a non-profit organization. The name was an acronym for Research ANd Development (by 1948, obviously, all acronyms had lost their dots). RAND's relationship with the Air Force was significant. The Army Air Corps was only separated from the Army after World War II, and there were still some in the Army that wanted it back. As the newest of the three services, the Air Force was faster, looser, not bound by tradition, and in fact looked for ways to distinguish itself from Army and Navy flight operations research.

The world turned upside down on October 4, 1957, when the Russians launched Sputnik, the first earth-orbiting satellite. The rival Russians, thought to be so ravaged by the effects of World War II that it would take years to recover even basic industrial capacity, had actually done something better and faster than the United States—and dangerous. What was to stop a Soviet satellite from dropping an atomic bomb on Washington? (Many stories along those lines actually appear in many newspapers.)

Cries to close the perceived science gap fell on eager ears. Overnight, it seemed, advanced science and math programs popped up in high schools and colleges all across America. The president of Harvard, James B. Conant, atom bomb advisor, told parents that children's homework needed to be done "for your own sake and for the sake of the nation." And the Defense Department created the ultimate O.R. group, the Advanced Research Project Agency (ARPA). Plenty of money was budgeted for scientific research, and all the dollars were channeled through ARPA.

The first problem that ARPA had to address was the limitations of the computers used in O.R. in the late 1950s. The Pentagon wanted to extend the use of computers right onto the battlefield to support what was known to war planners as C3: command, control, and communications. But the mainframe computers then in use were anything but portable. No networks as such existed. Remote computer access was accomplished by punch cards or even paper tapes that were sent for processing to the nearest computer. The results were encoded on more cards or paper tapes.

The problem of using mainframes remotely tied in to America's nuclear war contingency plans. In the name of nuclear survivability, NORAD burrowed into Cheyenne Mountain in Colorado to secure the air defense headquarters. The president and other important staff members were to seek shelter at secret locations in the Maryland mountains. All 535 U.S. Congress members were to be stuffed into a missile-hardened complex under the grounds of the Greenbrier Hotel in White Sulpher Springs, West Virginia. The problem of communicating between these sites after a nuclear war, and with forces organizing a counter-attack, was deemed too important to trust to connections over phones lines that, if broken, had to be re-routed before communications could resume.

RAND's solution to the problem involved creating a network that would dynamically route around failures. No connections could be broken because there were no real connections to break. The network was connectionless. In addition, the scheme had no centralized network control or management center. RAND had invented connectionless packet switching.

ARPA embraced the concept immediately. ARPA had continued to fund research into all of the areas of computer science many people today perceive as new. But by the mid 1960s, ARPA had funded research into software and hardware for computer graphics, visualization, parallel processing, head-mounted virtual reality displays, artificial intelligence, and produced the world's first real supercomputer, the University of Illinois' ILLIAC IV. ARPA immediately saw the RAND proposal as a way to solve the problem of remote computer access between organizations needing to collaborate on agency projects. ARPA wanted a network to enable users to exchange E-mail, transfer files, and remotely access computers without necessarily having connections between them, or having to buy one for everybody working on a project.

So ARPA agreed to fund the RAND idea and create an experimental computer network. In 1968, ARPA requested bids to link four sites with an expandable network. The sites were heavily involved in ARPA work at the time: the University of California at Los Angeles (UCLA) and Santa Barbara, the Stanford Research Institute (SRI), and the University of Utah. Representatives of these four "ARPAnet" nodes came together to form the Network Working Group.

The Cambridge firm of Bolt, Baranek, and Newman (BBN) won the bid and used their ties with nearby MIT to develop the communications gear and software needed. While Woodstock raged in upstate New York, BBN shipped the software to UCLA in August of 1969 and to SRI in October. In November of 1969 the two sites exchanged packets for the first time. All four nodes were linked by the end of the year.

The first results were pretty dismal. The network crashed all the time and hardly lived up to its billing. But by learning from mistakes and finding out what worked and what did not, an enterprising computer scientist named Vinton Cerf had come up with TCP/IP by 1973. By that time, ARPA had added a *D* for Defense in 1972 and realized the improvements that TCP/IP offered. At the time, people worried about whether sending messages via E-mail might violate government monopolies and regulations on postal service. Times have changed.

By the early 1980s, two other elements of the ARPAnet had become common. The TCP/IP protocol suite was standardized and officially adopted to allow users to perform the three main tasks of E-mail, remote login, and file transfer in a standard and uniform fashion. And the University of California at Berkeley began to distribute AT&T's UNIX operating system as BSD (Berkeley Systems Distribution). BSD came with the TCP/IP protocols and applications built-in, and was essentially available for free from the mid 1980s on.

It was mainly universities in the United States that wanted it. These universities usually had a very diverse range of computing equipment rather than the uniform environment corporations preferred. This situation was mostly the twin result of low bid purchasing and tax deductible corporate donations. The universities needed a common operating system and network protocol to link these computers together for the use of students, staff, and alumni.

The easy availability of UNIX and TCP/IP led to a period of explosive growth. From a handful of hosts, as large and small computers running TCP/IP are called, the network grew into an international network of tens of thousands of hosts. The original ARPAnet backbone became the backbone network for this collection of LANs and routers linked together and known at first as the ARPA-Internet and then globally as the *Internet*. By 1988, DARPA decided to turn the Internet over to the National Science Foundation, where the ARPAnet backbone became known as the NSFnet.

Today, of course, the Internet connects hundreds of thousands, and perhaps even a million, hosts to LANs at universities and companies around the world. Even non-LAN connected PCs can easily obtain dial-in access to the Internet for a variety of reasons. These reasons extend to obtaining corporate marketing and product information on the portion of the Internet known as the World Wide Web, sending and receiving E-mail, and even doing research. Millions of corporate employees, private individuals, and students around the world access the Internet for these reasons every day.

All of this Internet history may be nice to know. But what has all of this to do with the Web and virtual reality? The simple answer is that corporations have discovered the Internet.

Companies that always thought of networks for corporate use exclusively in terms of private lines have found that the Internet can be used in a variety of ways to reduce the enormous costs involved with setting up the required meshed private lines. For example, companies have found that instead of attempting to cost-justify a link to Europe to connect European sales offices to the corporate network in the United States, an Internet connection will serve the same purpose at a fraction of the cost. After all, users will just be using the corporate network link for the same applications that the Internet can provide: remote login, E-mail, and file transfer. But the Web adds more to the equation, much more.

The Birth of the World Wide Web

Almost as soon as Mosaic, the first Internet graphical browser, was introduced and transformed the Internet from a realm of mysterious ether, where strange professors in the basements of many a university endlessly typed cryptic UNIX commands cackling wildly, to today's surfers who sit at home or office cackling wildly as they endlessly point and click from site to site, there was a common belief among the Internet community that Mosaic was but the first step in the Internet's transformation. While home pages and hypertext have simplified navigation around the Internet, it still remains in the realm where information is presented in a form more for a computer than a human. The next step needed to be taken was the transformation of the computers 2-dimensional world to a more human perspective as a 3-dimensional environment.

From the beginning, two computer scientists, Mark Pesce and Tony Parisi, who would become the founding fathers of VRML, realized that the Internet could be something more. The information that the Internet offered was so immense that if it was to be valuable to the regular user it needed to be presented in a more realistic fashion or rather in a more understandable format and environment. One great problem of the Internet is that it is flat, it can only offer you a single point of view. While links can offer the opportunity to jump to related views and objects, they remain only pieces of the whole. VRML is the first building block in allowing someone to create a 3D environment and through the Internet allow another user to navigate around in that 3D space. It is a much more intuitive way to navigate the Internet. There are not any hypertext links or buttons to represent things, rather you have the actual objects to interact with. The objects themselves have substance in the VRML world and can even be the link to other worlds or objects. The difference between the worlds created with HTML and VRML is analogous to the difference between shopping by leafing through a catalog and actually going to the store and walking around. Everything suddenly has depth and shape where before it was flat.

Perhaps one of the great misconceptions of the Internet is in the concept of its relationship to cyberspace. The word *cyberspace* has become a common vocabulary word for any who venture onto the Internet. It was first coined by William Gibson in a science fiction book in 1984 called *Neuromancer*. He defined *cyberspace* as "A consensual hallucination experienced daily by billions of legitimate operators, in every nation, by children being taught mathematical concepts. . . . A graphic representation of data abstracted from the banks of every computer in the human system. Unthinkable complexity. Lines of light ranged in the nonspace of the mind, clusters and constellations of data. Like city lights, receding." While cyberspace today may not be exactly as Gibson portrayed, it has become the collective envisionment of cyberspace in the Internet community. Additionally though, it is eerily becoming prophetic as the Internet continues to develop and expand upon its boundaries, and users are beginning to truly navigate through cyberspace. The information superhighway, as the Internet is sometimes called, exists in cyberspace but the 2D home pages of the present HTML Internet worlds are but billboards posted along the way. Most users, for their part, only pass through cyberspace on their way between these "billboards" and use cyberspace just to transfer E-mail and files. Cyberspace, until the development of VRML, therefore was only a medium with little or no true form. But with VRML's ability to create a 3D environment, cyberspace has begun to develop substance. VRML has become the tool that has allowed the construction of actual places that exist "in" cyberspace as opposed to "just passing through" to get and transfer information or resources. The Internet, as the information superhighway, finally has real exits for places to visit and explore. Gibson's cyberspace has begun to truly exist in a place that does not really exist.

Vehicles on the Information Superhighway: Creation and Development of the Internet Browser

The best way to understand the rapid growth of the Internet and its transformation from just a giant computer network to Gibson's cyberspace is to track the development of the graphical browsers and their resulting impact that makes the Internet what it is today.

In the 1970s the Internet, which at that time was still only called the ARPAnet, continued to grow and expand as it added on computers from many universities. While this giant network was a great way for computers to communicate between themselves, with no tools designed for navigating on this network, it was a rather poor environment for the users themselves to communicate and exchange information on the net through their various interfaces. But difficult as it was, by the later half of the 1980s, ARPAnet had grown so big that to better oversee its development it was split into two domains between the military networks (MILnet) and the academic networks, which was overseen by the National Science Foundation and was aptly named the NFSnet. But even with this continued growth and progress the greatest use of the Internet was primarily for E-mail. With so many rich resources and data available as each university joined the NFSnet, it still remained mostly an untapped gold mine unless a user was very familiar with their sites system, knew specifically where to go, how to get there, and what to do once there. The problems of the early Internet can be referred to as "the messy room syndrome". There may be valuable resources buried somewhere under that pile of clothes, or then again it might not even be close to what you want. Where to start and just trying to find anything may be more a matter of luck than skill, and finding one sock does not always guarantee that you will find the other one.

The Internet was a prime candidate for some organization and perhaps some kind of cyberspace compass. There existed two opposing organizational methods, hierarchical versus hypertext, that have been developed, debated, and implemented in trying to bring some idea of order to the Internet's messy room. The Internet Gopher, developed by the University of Minnesota and released in late 1991, took the hierarchical approach. Named for the school's mascot (the gopher, of course) and for every construction worker who at one time had to "go fer" coffee, it was designed to allow servers to be setup as information providers and offer files with readable lists, organized hierarchically, containing locations and resources across the Internet that allowed users to "go fer" it simply by pointing and clicking. By 1992 and early 1993 graphical Gopher clients were available on both the Macintosh and Windows platforms (see Figure 2-1). Because of its ease of use, in-

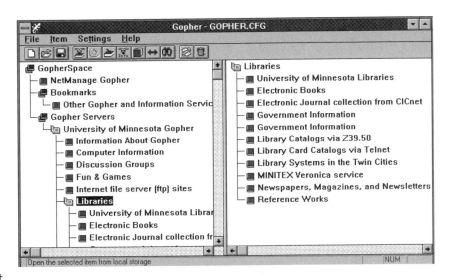

Figure 2-1
Gopher Client

stallation, and availability across multiple platforms, Gopher quickly caught on, became, and still is a popular tool for navigating the Internet. But apart from its popularity Gopher would not be the tool that would be the catalyst for the explosive growth of the Internet.

In the shadows of Gopher's popularity was a piece of the Internet using a different method of data connecting. In opposition to the hierarchical approach of Gopher it was designed on the use of hypertext for navigation and linking of data. The actual term *hypertext* was invented in 1981 by a Computer Scientist named Ted Nelson in his book called *Literary Machines.* Hypertext is based upon the idea of following a non-linear path through data and documents through a series of linked nodes of information.

The concept of hypertext can trace itself back to 1945 when its methods were proposed by a man named Vannevar Bush who wanted to design a computer information database called a memex. A user of a memex computer would be able to read data on a subject and from that document be able to link to related information throughout the database. In essence following a "trail" throughout the database that was not limited to a specific topic but allowed for connections across boundaries of classification. Just as any good scientist knows, for example, that while Biology, Chemistry, and Physics are all separate fields of study they are in reality so interrelated that to truly understand one field a scientist must have an understanding of the others. Bush therefore surmised that knowledge, in any field, needed to be explored, accessed, and found by users taking different pathways and/or on different journeys in their pursuit of information.

In summing up the basic approach of the two systems of Internet organization it is important to realize that neither method is right or wrong, but only two different ways that we, as the end-user, think and conceptualize information gathering. Hierarchical is based primarily on organization and classification; a place for everything and everything in its place. To counter the messy room syndrome hierarchical cleans up the room and puts everything in a drawer. If you need socks, they're in one drawer (with a nice selection), pants in another, shirts in the closet, and so on. It is easy to get dressed if you know what you need.

Hypertext views the relationship of data as the guiding factor because it believes that data and information need the ability to cross boundaries and classifications to be useful to the end-user. This method leaves the messy room messy but finding a pair of socks can lead you to finding a pair of jeans, leading you to a pile of shirts (ones that actually go with the jeans); and even though you were not planning on needing anything else, it leads you to some ties that you decide would make the outfit perfect. Of course both hierarchical's and hypertext's strengths are the weaknesses of their counterparts. In a hierarchical system a user needs to climb up and down the hierarchical tree before they can get to a different but related subject.

For example, in the original messy but now hierarchically clean room once someone finds the sock drawer, all there is within the drawer is socks, nothing else. If one needs a shirt, they must return to the room's door and follow the path to the closet to find the shirts. Unfortunately with this method it is improbable that anyone will ever think of wearing a tie (which would make the outfit perfect) because the ties are neither socks, shirts, or pants. On the other hand, returning to the hypertext's messy room and finding a pair of socks does not guarantee that anyone can then find pants or shirts. As a matter of fact, the socks that were found could be white and we may need blue socks.

But the worries do not end there: following links can be a confusing thing. Take the earlier example of picking out clothes to get dressed. Finding socks led a person to pants then to shirts, but in with the shirts is the disco shirt last worn for a seventies party that led to our collection of disco records that led to the entertainment cabinet where the manual for programming the VCR just happens to be located. What does the VCR have to do with getting dressed? Maybe nothing, maybe something. But perhaps that is the important point that has led to the success of hypertext as the navigation of choice for many Internet users.

Through hypertext a user has the flexibility to organize and link information anyway they see fit (even hierarchical) and also link information together in a way so the user can go from one concept to another without limitations. Life does not always fit into nice categories nor can human beings be expected to think in a completely linear fashion.

Hypertext in a very real sense is the information organization idea that just would not go away, even while experts both praised and condemned its methods and implementation. While many associate hypertext with the Internet, it would eventually have its first productive application outside of the Internet. In 1987 Apple Computers released a software package called HyperCard that came bundled free with the Macintosh and its operating system. Not only did it allow the linking of documents it was also able to create links to sounds and images within those documents. While it was limited to restricting its links to the same system, its popularity would go a long way in setting the stage for users to adopt its methodology on the Internet.

The foundations of bringing hypertext to the Internet began in the late 1980s when a man by the name of Tim Berners-Lee was employed as a software engineer at CERN, the European Particle Physics Institute in Geneva, Switzerland. The problem facing Berners-Lee was that the high-energy physics community was spread throughout various universities and industries in Europe. Information and results of various experiments and the research data it produced was spread over many computers and LANs. It was believed that there was great potential to accelerate research if a way could be found to correlate and share all this information electronically.

In March of 1989 Berners-Lee proposed a way of linking text documents with other documents using "networked hypertext." Working with colleague Robert Cailliau, they produced a design document and published it in November of 1990 as a proposal for developing a system based on this idea of networked hypertext. "Hypertext is a way to link and access information of various kinds as a web of nodes in which the user can browse at will," the document stated. "Potentially, hypertext provides a single, user-interface to many large classes of stored information such as reports, notes, databases, computer documents and on-line systems help."

The term *World Wide Web* was introduced in this document, although without the capitals. It proved to be a name that would stick. After passing documents between computers they knew there needed to be a format to the documents that could be interpreted by each computer and still convey the information contained within it. With this in mind they developed a language called the *Hypertext Markup Language* (HTML) modeled after, and basically becoming, a subset of a powerful but much more complex formatting language called *Standard Generalized Markup Language* (SGML). SGML has been around for about 20 years, which is somewhat surprising.

The resulting Web software would be a mixture of "Web servers" and "Web browsers". The browser is software that runs on the user's *client* computer and *talks* to the software running on the Web *server* to request certain files. These files could be any type representing the various resources a user wants. If written in HTML, the files can contain information the browser can display in addition to the names of files of related resources and their locations (the hypertext links). By May of 1991 the World Wide Web was successfully in use at CERN. The first browser developed was a *line-mode* browser that really was just an advanced version of a telnet session (Figure 2-2). Line-mode refers

```
        Welcome to the World Wide Web
        THE WORLD WIDE WEB


        For more information, select by number:
        A list of available W3 client programs (1)
        Everything about the W3 project (2)
        Places to start exploring (3)
        The first International WWW Conference (4)


        This telnet service is provided by the WWW team
        at CERN (5)
        1-5 Up, Quit, or Help
```

Figure 2-2
Line-mode Browser

to the line-by-line output of this first browser. Berners-Lee then presented the World Wide Web in December of 1991 to the Hypertext '91 conference in San Antonio, Texas. In January of 1992 the line-mode browser was available to anyone on the Internet.

In true Internet fashion the ideas of the World Wide Web spread and were developed through Internet discussion groups on many newsgroups and conferences. In July of 1992, the University of California at Berkeley became the birthplace of the first *modern* looking browser. This browser was developed by an associate named Pei Wei. The browser, which he named Viola, was available on UNIX systems using X-Windows[1]. It was the first browser to distinguish hypertext links by colors and underscoring. Viola's other great feature was the ability to allow simple mouse point and click to activate those hyper-

---

1.   *X-Windows* : The original implementations of TCP/IP were all intended for simple, command based, ASCII display terminals with white (or green) letters on a black background. A user typed in a command at a prompt and pressed the "enter" key. TCP/IP did its job and the output was displayed, line by line, on the screen. If the response was long enough, the beginning scrolled off the top of the screen. DOS still functions in exactly this way.

However, newer computers today offer Graphical User Interfaces (GUI) that display many colors and different lettered fonts. GUIs can display the output from several programs running simultaneously in "windows" and will accept not only from keyboard entered commands but from pointing and clicking with a mouse. Microsoft Windows is a perfect example of a GUI, windows-based user interface.

X-Windows was developed at the Massachusetts Institute of Technology (MIT) to bring GUI capabilities to a TCP/IP and UNIX environment. X-Windows includes specifications and tools so that developers can write their own X-Windows interfaces for TCP/IP. With X-Windows, a user may be running FTP, Telnet, and editing E-mail simultaneously, each in a different window. This accounts for X-Windows' popularity, of course.

X-Windows is not particularly notable as a TCP/IP application, but it is very common and useful as a TCP/IP interface and frequently distributed on UNIX-based operating systems using TCP/IP. In fact, X-Windows is rapidly becoming as common on UNIX systems as Microsoft Windows is on PC systems.

X-Windows is noteworthy in one other regard. The developers of X-Windows actually *reversed* the usual interpretation of "clients" and "servers" in TCP/IP. While most documentation about TCP/IP defines a "server" as "listener" issuing a "passive open" and a "client" as a "talker" issuing an "active open", X-Windows reverses these definitions. To X-Windows, the server is the user's workstation and the client is the remote process being accessed, by definition. This peculiar terminology is often referred to as "X servers" and "X clients" to distinguish these terms from "normal" TCP/IP meanings. But it may still be confusing.

A special device known as an "X Terminal" has no native applications of its own, but only accesses remote systems and applications and displays the results on a built-in X-Windows GUI. All "X" implementations use TCP/IP as a network protocol and was therefore a prime interface for the developers of Internet applications and browsers to use.

text links. Unfortunately, Viola remained only an interesting experiment because it was never further developed or utilized.

By early 1993 the World Wide Web had a solid , yet small, foundation of interest throughout the Internet community. But Gopher remained king as it was generating most of the Internet community interest. Gopher in its hierarchical approach had more Internet traffic, more servers, more interest, but fewer features than the Web. So in discussions with the Web community to try and figure out how to compete with Gopher, Berners-Lee and his group of developers at CERN detailed out the major limitations of the fledgling Web.

The two major points that resulted from these discussions were based on two fundamentals of the Web itself: the Web server and the Web browser. In the case of the Web server, the installation and maintenance of the server software was quite difficult even for very experienced system administrators. As for the browsers, many users who accessed the Internet were going through a terminal, such as the popular VT-100, on their company's or university's mainframe computer. The problem was, there didn't really even exist a reliable text-mode VT-100[2] based browser that could deal with the many limitations of the full screen features that a VT-100 client offered. But more importantly, for a PC market that was already growing in leaps and bounds, a simple, full screen, color, point and click browser was needed to compete with the already successful Gopher browsers.

The first point about improving the Web server software was immediately set upon by Berners-Lee and his group of developers at CERN as well as others around the Web and resulted in much improvement over the next year. Along the lines of improving the browsers, once again in true Internet fashion, a VT-100 text-mode browser called Lynx was modified from an existing client software project. The Lynx parent software had been developed a year before, in 1992, by Lou

---

2.   *VT-100 Display* : A "line-mode" display device used with many DEC mini-computers. Not an intelligent device, the VT-100 family of devices consisted of a keyboard and green-on-black monitor. The monitor was incapable of displaying anything except ASCII text, one line of 80 characters at a time. The screen was usually 25 lines long. If a line scrolled off the top of the VT-100, it was lost, because the VT-100 had no memory to store information from the central computer.

DEC later extended the product line to include the VT-102, the VT-200, and so on. All differed in support for color and number of rows and columns of the screen. But all remained "dumb terminal" devices.

Today, many PC's run software that makes the intelligent and powerful PC behave as a VT-100 dumb ASCII terminal. These "terminal emulation" packages are popular methods for accessing the Internet, especially in older situations where Web support is not critical.

Montulli for a campus information system for the University of Kansas. Lynx would develop into the standard for text-mode Web client software.

As for the development of a graphical browser, and quite strangely in a community such as the Internet where there existed an environment of sharing, borrowing and modifying, Viola existed but remained an unknown, undeveloped browser. Fortunately, events were unfolding that would not only meet the requirement of providing a graphical browser, but would also transform the Web from a little-known corner of the Internet into being THE dominant presence on the Net. This browser would also be the major catalyst resulting in truly opening the Internet and cyberspace to the public.

In February of 1993, a new Web browser called Mosaic (Figure 2-3) was announced for release by the National Center for Supercomputing Applications (NCSA), part of the University of Illinois at Urbana/Champaign. The NCSA is subsidized by the United States government to develop tools and software that provide the means for researchers to be able to work collectively and share data and resources. Berners-Lee's project at CERN and the resulting development of the World Wide Web utilizing HTML on the Internet had caught the interest of many of the researchers at NCSA as a promising medium for the interchange of information on a national, if not global, scale.

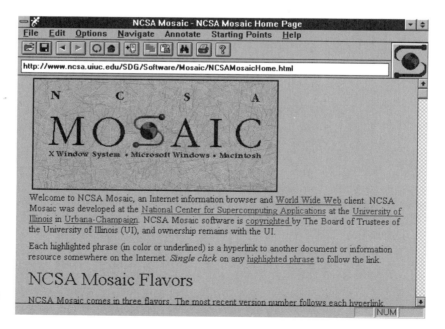

Figure 2-3
Mosiac Internet
Browser

Marc Andreesen, a graduate student at the University of Illinois at Urbana/Champaign where NCSA is located, with the help of Eric Bina, a programmer at the NCSA, developed the new Web browser that was originally designed to run in a UNIX environment with X-Windows. Because of its popularity, although still limited as only a UNIX browser, MS Windows and Macintosh versions of Mosaic were released by the Fall of 1993.

Although the Web community had specified a GUI browser as important to the further development of the World Wide Web, the initial success of Mosaic was based primarily on the fact that Mosaic was easy to obtain, install, and use. Of course, this would not make any true difference if a software package was terrible, easy to use or not. Many powerful and productive software packages have failed because no one wanted to expend the effort in obtaining, learning, or just plain using it. Mosaic was not only easy but also flexible. It was designed as more than just an HTML browser and could handle links to other Internet services such as FTP and gopher.

On top of that, Mosaic could *learn.* If Mosaic met a file it did not know how to handle, it allowed the user, within Mosaic itself, to set a link to an application (referred to as a *Helper Application)* that could handle the file at once and in the future. But Mosaic did not stop there. Marc Andreessen wanted to expand the graphical browser and HTML beyond just text and hypertext. Mosaic was designed with the ability to display in-line images and pictures within the same document as the hypertext. Furthermore, images were taken another developmental step to exist as *image maps.* Image maps allow for different sections of the picture to operate just like a hypertext link and access another source. A user can click anywhere on the image and the browser interprets its corresponding link.

With all its new features and flexibility, Mosaic was not just a innovative Internet application, it was the tool that opened the portal to the Internet for the regular person. Once there, many realized that HTML was not a terrible, scientific, complicated computer language, but rather a relatively simple format that even those who had previously only used a word processor could master in a short time. Today many word processors allow users to build pages within them and will generate the HTML code so that the users never even have to learn any of the HTML code. The users just keep using the word processor as they have been all along. With its initial success, Mosaic would be the first of many Internet browsers to come. Marc Andreesen, the creator of Mosaic, left the NCSA and helped form a company called Mosaic Communications, which eventually became Netscape Communications Corporation with the release of their

Netscape browser (Figure 2-4), a souped-up redesign of Mosaic from scratch. Andreesen jokingly called Netscape a "combination of Godzilla and Mosaic," and the merged code-name of *Mozilla* has crept into the Netscape world in a variety of forms.

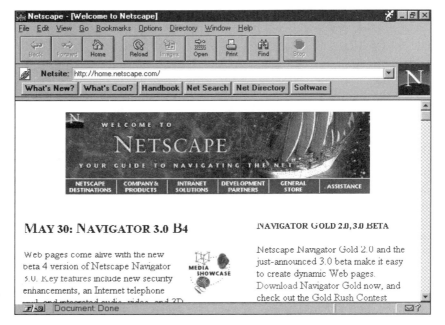

Figure 2-4
Netscape Internet
Browser

It has been estimated that 75–90 percent of those who travel the Internet do so with Netscape. And Netscape has been maintaining this edge even while the number of other browsers available and in use has skyrocketed. Microsoft even held off the release of its much anticipated *Windows95* operating software so that it could incorporate its *Internet Explorer* Web browser into the package. To keep ahead of the pack, Netscape has continued to offer extensions to the HTML standards to enhance the interaction and function of its Web browser. The constant race is to continue to offer a more creative, simpler, interactive medium through the browser.

Behind the explosion of the World Wide Web and what it has to offer has been the belief that the 2D interfaces will only be able to offer the end-user so much. The problem is that 2D computer interfaces are still to far away from the human experience to be completely intuitive. Therefore, in the background of all the hype that has been built around the Web, many in the Internet community have been developing the 3D language interface known as *Virtual Reality Markup Language* (VRML). Various browsers continue to be developed for viewing VRML files, but they have the unique property of being created in parallel with the creation of the standard language they are supposed to be interpreting. So they are at once completely up to date and completely obsolete. But the goal of VRML is to transform browsing the Web from a passive activity to an interactive one.

Virtual Reality: Life in Cyberspace

What VRML is setting the stage for, or better yet, *building* the stage for, is the creation of an interface that more closely resembles an environment that a user can feel more comfortable in and that will make sense in a conceptual way. Computer-to-user interaction is a two step process of *translation*. The first step belongs to the computers in their attempts to *translate* the data they have, which in its most basic form is really just a bunch of zeros and ones, into a form that the end user can understand. The second step is for the user to further *translate* what they see on the computer screen into information that their brain can process. The continual quest for all computer scientists is to make the computer do more of the translating, and therefore more of the work, than the user needs to do.

For example, as noted above, computers at their most basic level deal in zeros and ones. To better visualize the following discussion, imagine a fictional computer that will contain the data for a major brokerage firm. For the computer to display its data as zeros and ones requires the computer to do very little translating.. The user, a very dedicated broker, on the other hand, hoping that he or she is very comfortable with calculating in binary, will need to do huge amounts of translating in order to make those zeros and ones into data that can be understood.

So while the computer can do a wonderful job of number crunching, it falls short in this instance in translating that information to the user. What if the computer could translate the binary into decimal and ASCII, or better yet, into actual text? The computer now has a much greater job and hence it needs more processing power, but the end result is the user has information that can be more quickly interpreted and understood. But while text and numbers are a big step up from binary, it is difficult to see relationships to other data, the proportions, percentages, data flux, trends, and what ever else our broker is going to need. Thus the user is therefore spending valuable resources in translating data all over again.

Once again the computer may be required to do a greater job of translation. The computer is asked now to represent the data graphically in line graphs, bar charts, or pie charts. Human eyesight is in itself one of the brain's (the real and actual ultimate end-user) greatest tools for translating data into information that the brain can use and understand. Graphical representation of data appeals to the most basic of human skills of pattern recognition, evaluating, and comparison in which the eyes, trained for years from the instant a baby opens them, begin the association and translation process.

To go even further, data could be transformed into 3D objects to better approximate that which the data is representing, whether as a multi-relational data graph for the broker or a picture of a building newly designed by an architect. The translation load has now transferred much of the work to the computer and away from the end user. But this is not without cost. The computing power that is required to generate graphics would literally overwhelm the early computers of the computing age.

The core element of any computer is its CPU (the Central Processing Unit), which in every current PC can only perform *one* operation at a time. The first computers could pass through the CPU hundreds of operations per second. Designed originally only as number crunchers, spitting out data in binary, this was quite an accomplishment in automating data calculations. But today's CPUs need to not only number crunch, but also translate and present that data graphically. These CPUs require, and can process, millions of instructions per second (MIPS). The Intel Pentium CPU chip can process at around 100 MIPS. The next generation P6 chip that follows the Pentium (the Pentium Pro) is capable of processing over 250 MIPS. It is this power that will allow PC computers to begin taking the next step in converting the translation burden between a computer and a user.

While graphical representation of data has eased the process of information transfer and conceptualization it still remains an artificial symbolization of the data. On the computer, 2D and 3D objects are limited in the aspect of only being viewed through the 2D interface of the PC. To break that barrier it is necessary to cross over into the world of virtual reality (VR). This is the computer's next translation step.

Two of the primary foundations of VR are the concepts of *immersion* and of *navigation*. The idea of immersion is that the computer can create an environment for the user that will represent the illusion of existing within a 3D world. It is not just displaying 3D representation of objects, but rather creating a world where a user can navigate within it and explore objects at various perspectives. Virtual reality also means that the generated 3D world is not limited in its existence to that of only a *visual* environment, but that it can and will reflect the tenants of immersion and navigation through the other human senses (touch, sound, taste, and smell). The brain uses all of these senses as input devices to translate and interpret data.

Human senses in relation to the brain are analogous to what the zeros and ones are to the computer. The closer a computer can simulate sensual data, the easier and more quickly the user will be able to operate and interface with the computer. The balance of the translation process has now become more weighted on the computer side than for the human user.

This process of past and future development of computer-user interfaces has not, is not, and should not be interpreted as limited to only the computer's output. The word *interface* reflects that users need to interact with a computer through both output and input. Therefore the development of "reappropriating" the burden of the translation process of computers to users has always reflected this.

From switches to punch cards to keyboards, plotters to mice, input/output devices have continued to develop with eventual creation of the VR tools such as the data glove and the VR helmet. It would surprise many to know that many of these have been around since the sixties and seventies. While crude, expensive, and awkward, they were in many cases tools that did not have anything that could yet tap their true potential.

One question immediately suggests itself; "Why create tools that have no real definitive or immediate use?" The answer is simple. Above all else, the guiding principle in shaping computer interfaces continues to be that the user in the computer-user relationship is the *human being*. Therefore the user interfaces need to be designed to reflect human needs and abilities, rather than forcing human behavior to adapt and fit the demands of computer technology. It is the irony of computer science that many times the tools exist before the jobs they will be used for exist themselves, or a tool developed to meet the needs of a distinctly different project becomes the key tool for another. Once the jobs for, and the potential for, a tool begin to be explored, the tools can be modified and refined or even be developed to spawn others.

Many times this process is not only limited to the discipline of Computer Science. Ideas and tools can come from various sources and people. Scientists, researchers, and inventors working in concert or on totally separate projects can contribute pieces that another will perhaps use to develop something never envisioned. A wonderful example is the Internet itself. Remember that the Internet and the TCP/IP protocol was developed merely as a way to link the computing power of the few supercomputers in the United States and to meet the needs of how to get around routing problems in case of nuclear war. Who could have envisioned the development of the present day Internet community when scientists made the first supercomputers talk to each other in October of 1969? It is within these principles that VR and cyberspace has taken root and continues to grow as the computer science community explore the boundaries of what can be.

Virtual reality is not a new concept. The ideas and products that make up the wide range of applications of VR have been around for decades. In truth VR has been a concept that is almost as old as the first computers, but in many cases scientists' ideas and visions needed to wait for computer technology to catch up to their ideas and visions before they could even begin to try and develop VR technology. It is most likely that many people have some concept of what virtual reality is whether it is through the basic level of 3D games, such as DOOM, to that of full immersion virtual reality simulators such as the ones the military and major airlines use to train pilots.

Hollywood has continued to develop the publics image of VR through many of its movies. The movies *The Lawn Mower Man* and *Johnny Mnemonic,* based on the book by William Gibson (who is said to have coined the word *cyberspace*), are great examples of what computer VR can offer; and not only because of the vision of technology created in these movies, but more for the reason that the special effects were already the product of computer generated scenes.

Perhaps the best way that most people interpret the word *Virtual Reality* is from the airplane simulators noted above. Any good military officer worth their salt knows the value of training. The idea is that the closer the training can simulate reality, the better. It is should therefore not be a surprise that VR technology has been greatly developed by heavy military investment over the years. The U.S. Air Force had developed many years ago a head mounted display system that was extremely sophisticated to be used in training their pilots in a flight simulator. The millions of dollars invested was considered to be justified in relation to the training it could offer pilots before they stepped into a $50 or $100 million dollar aircraft.

This idea has also transferred to the commercial market where airlines, using more financially conservative systems, have developed simulators as well. A pilot sitting in a training cockpit has replica controls and a windshield that is actually a computer graphics display screen. The cockpit is even mounted on a hydraulic lift that will rotate the cabin in response to the pilot's actions and the simulator's programming. Today's airline simulators are actually cheaper to use to train pilots than real hands-on training in small jets. The common argument for the use of flight simulators is while there may be no substitute for flying the real thing, there are some things that cannot be tried safely in the sky. So this is where one of the great strengths of VR shows through.

The origins of the development of the first virtual reality tools and components arguably can be claimed to be started in the 1960s by Dr. Ivan Sutherland. Perhaps the word *development* is not as appropriate as *transformation*. For example, the light pen was created as a new input device with the development of the cathode-ray tube (CRT) screens developed in the 1950s. The pens are used to select screen positions by detecting the light coming from the points on the CRT screen. The pens are sensitive to the short bursts of light emitted from the phosphor coating the instant the electron beam strikes a particular point. The computer can then detect where on the screen the light pen is and records its coordinate position in relation to the screen.

While tools such as the light pen and graphical computer screens had existed for years, Sutherland's work would transform these tools into the very first building blocks of the vision of converting computers as mere data processors to that of interactive computing. First working as a graduate student in 1963 at the Massachusetts Institute of Technology, Sutherland developed an interactive graphics program called SketchPad. His work was done on the MIT Lincoln Laboratory's TX-2 supercomputer called Whirlwind. Weighing in at around 250 tons, filling up the space of a two story house with about 12,500 vacuum tubes, it had the computing power of only about one twentieth of a Macintosh II.

While ridiculously slow by today's standards, Whirlwind's great advantage among the supercomputers of its day was in its having more than twice the memory of other computers. And, more important for SketchPad, it offered various input systems that included a keyboard, a point plotting display, and a light pen. Sutherland's SketchPad could manipulate and modify drawn objects, as well as edit them with the light pen, all as a real time interaction. It could recall previously drawn and saved basic figures, such as squares and circles, and manipulate these as well.

This was a conceptual breakthrough in which the user could create images simply by drawing them with the light pen. The idea was that the user did not have to be an expert programmer to utilize the power of a computer effectively. This idea would not only impact the use of interactive graphics, but could also arguably be one of the inspirations well before its time for the development of computers for the non-professional user. SketchPad in its simplicity would become the catalyst that would inspire both the government and private industry to heavily invest in research and development of interactive computer graphics. SketchPad was not a single isolated development, rather it was a new way of viewing the computer that inspired a new methodology. One direct result of SketchPad's influence was being the first of the computer aided design (CAD) software programs. This simple program would inspire and launch an industry that is worth over $1.6 billion today and is still growing.

Interactive graphics with SketchPad was only the first step for Sutherland. The concept of virtual 3-dimensional space was not enough. He wanted to develop true interactive graphics, graphics where a user could actually move around in a 3D environment, as opposed to merely viewing it through a 2D flat computer screen, and manipulate objects in a virtual world just as one does in a physical world. To reach this end, Sutherland began research on what would become the first head mounted display (HMD). The goal of the HMD would be to create the illusion of immersing a user into a computer generated 3D world. Then 3D graphic processors would update the images and body tracking would determine at what and where the user was looking in the computer generated virtual world.

As noted previously, it is the irony of computer science that many times the tools exist before the jobs they will be used for exist themselves, or a tool developed to meet the needs of a distinctly different project becomes the key tool for another. Sutherland, being a good scientist, envisioned what the HMD would do and then either assembled the existing technology or built what was needed (and probably did not even exist in concept before) to integrate it all together. The first HMD was an unwieldy giant of a machine that locked the users head into a large helmet suspended from the ceiling, unlike today's modern HMDs (see Figure 2-5).

Figure 2-5
Modern Head
Mounted Display

But on January 1, 1970, the threshold of cyberspace was breached for the first time when one of Sutherland's assistants, Daniel Vickers produced and viewed a 2-inch cube in cyberspace. Daniel Vickers was responsible for creating the software that integrated all of the various systems Sutherland conceived. Many of these components created in relation to the first HMD would lay the foundation for the development of full immersion virtual reality at a level where they exist today. These are used in many varied products as flight simulators, CAD systems, and even as VR games in public arcades.

The first HMD, though a monster of a piece of equipment, showed the potential that VR had to offer as an exciting new interface. While Sutherland may have been the first with his HMD, there were many others who developed various HMDs that achieved their success using a multitude of different methods and equipment, nor would HMDs be the only VR tools developed. The important overall factor is that there is no right or wrong way to enter cyberspace, just different doorways.

While HMDs allowed a user to look into cyberspace it was still impossible to actually *touch* or manipulate objects within cyberspace except through the usual tools of a light pen or keyboard. The next great development was the *data glove* (Figure 2-6). Once again various approaches have yielded an assortment of products. The first approach was to attach the hand onto an exoskeleton hand (though obviously not specifically a *glove* it still performs the desired function). Ultrahigh frequency sound emitters attached to sensors on the glove and sensors placed around the user can mathematically map the position of the glove.

Figure 2-6
Typical Modern Data
Glove

With the exoskeleton system strapped to a hand, this was an extremely accurate way to calculate finger movement. But the early exoskeletons tended to be large, uncomfortable, and unwieldy. By the early 1980s at least two other different designs existed to counter the cumbersome exoskeleton. While most still used the method of using ultra-high frequency sound to map the position of the glove, the method of monitoring finger and hand motion varied. One glove developed used small mechanical switches in each finger joint to calculate movement. The other used optical tubing, eventually replaced with fiber optics, placed along the fingers with scratches placed at the knuckles to allow light to "leak" out. Following the basic laws of optics, light transmitted through the tubing would diminish, based on the bend in the tubing and the scratches at the bends leaking light, as a result of bending a finger.

Though these gloves were not as specifically accurate as an exoskeleton, they were much lighter, flexible, and thus easier for a user to perform more natural movements. Today, modern material technology and miniaturization has helped bring the exoskeleton method back into competition with these other methods. While it remains a little more bulky and unwieldy than a glove it still offers a much more accurate position monitoring method. It is important to remember that hardware is only as good as the software that allows it to integrate itself into a successfully working VR tool, and many times it is the deciding factor between success and failure.

As with many components in the consumer market, it is the need that usually determines the tool. And because VR can potentially touch so many different aspects of the consumer market it is perhaps why there is plenty of room for the various approaches to the data glove. From the VR community alone, another reason for the continuing varied approach to the data glove is the possibly that it is one of the steps along the evolution process in designing a tool that will one day allow a user to don a VR body suit. The idea of allowing a user to have the capability of full immersion into cyberspace is certainly enticing.

Interestingly enough, there have been developers who in trying to reach this goal have taken the approach of trying to avoid burdening the user with VR tools. Rather, they create a VR immersion room in which a user would be surrounded with full screen displays and be monitored by the system through *gaze-trackers* and allow voice recognition for commands and input. Like many projects in the VR business, many, if not all, of these components exist.

For example IBM has a voice recognition system that is capable of a impressive 98.7 percent accuracy. However, the key is to be able to tie everything into a successfully integrated system. The NCSA in collaboration with the Electronic Visualization Lab at the University of Illinois at Chicago has developed a virtual reality theater called the CAVE (Cave Automatic Virtual Environment). It was first premiered at the ACM SIGGRAPH 92 conference resulting in instant excitement and interest throughout the international VR community. The CAVE is a surround-screen, surround-sound VR application that exists in a 10 by 10 by 10 cube. A CAVE dweller is immersed into cyberspace as images are projected on the walls and even the floor. The dweller is computer tracked by sensors on both the head and hands while the images and surround sounds are constantly updated to create the proper perspective. For now interaction in the cyberspace of the CAVE is limited only through a three button "wand" that lets users *grab* virtual objects, but other VR tools are being integrated into the system to continue to enhance the immersion factor of the CAVE.

Tip

For information about current projects at the NCSA visit their Web site at *http://www.ncsa.uiuc.edu.* For an overview of the CAVE project go directly to *http://ncsa.uiuc.edu/EVL/docs/html/ CAVE.overview.html.*

The concept of the CAVE can perhaps help people understand some of the capabilities offered by having a VR room located in universities, labs, offices, or best of all, in homes. The CAVE offers a VR container that has great potential for immersion. Imagine being able to visit the beach while a blizzard howls outside. Within the "home-cave" a heat lamp is producing the feeling of the sun on the skin while the computerized climate control raises the temperature and even offers a refreshing movement of air to simulate a breeze. A smell of salt is laced within the breeze thanks to an "odorizer" and the cry of a gull over the sound of crashing waves can be heard thanks to the surround-sound audio equipment. And best of all, no crowds!

The trip to a virtual beach may appear as a selfish and non-productive goal of VR, but it shows that with the exception of the "odorizer", all of the features of the home-cave exist in present day technology. It is not only just tying it all together, but VR can offer to generate worlds and environments that we as end-users could never visit, nor could many of them even exist outside of the boundaries of cyberspace. There have been various space probes and scientific research into the study of Mars. The potential of VR offers the ability to take the data collected and create a virtual Martian world. What would it be like to walk on another world of the solar system? Or walk through the *Titanic* as it lays on the bottom of the Atlantic Ocean? A scientist in cyberspace holding a molecule in one hand and trying to fit various pieces of other molecules into it, is perhaps getting a better insight to its structure. Cyberspace is a realm where human imagination, intelligence, and creativity can be augmented because it allows us to exceed our human limitations exponentially.

VRML: What It Is . . . And What It Is Not

It should come as no surprise that real VR does not exist on the Internet. Then again it depends upon what one defines as *real VR*. No one is strapping on an HMD and a pair of data gloves or "jacking in" like users did in entering into William Gibson's cyberspace. What is being offered is the creation of virtual 3D worlds and the ability to enter and navigate through them. While virtual reality on the Internet is certainly a limited excursion, it is these virtual worlds that begin to support the promise that VRML has to offer in perhaps one day bringing *real VR* to the Internet.

Detailed discussion of the history, development, and structure of VRML will be investigated in later chapters but it is important to understand the foundation of what the VRML language is designed for. To begin with, in breaking down the VRML acronym (Virtual Reality Modeling Language) the M which represents Modeling is intrinsic to the essence of VRML itself.

Originally the name proposed was *Virtual Reality Markup Language* as it was planned a direct extension of HTML (Hypertext Markup Language). "Markup" was changed to "Modeling" because the creators of VRML didn't want it to be only interpreted as an editor's "markup" of a page, but rather reflect the fact that VRML was rendering objects and environments in 3D. Of course the real world is a very complex place with such unlimited inputs that it is presently impossible to create a true *virtual world*. VRML was not and is not designed to create that perfect virtual world. But as the saying goes "The journey of a thousand leagues begins with the first step." With that in mind, the creators of VRML knew that to bring VR to the Internet the very first thing needed was a "place", some corner of cyberspace that has been given structure and form, before it can be appropriately decorated with links, images, sound, and so forth.

So above all else, VRML is the very first step in rendering a model of 3D space for use across the Internet. It is not as simple as merely having the shapes and proportions representative of objects and dimensions of a room. Rather, VRML takes into consideration distance, spatial relationships, special lighting, and camera angles. To a human, this is the world we live in, but for a computer, the implementation was, and is, no easy task.

The difficulty lies first in generating a language that would produce scene descriptions that can be platform independent. In other words, it could be understood by different computers over various systems and produce a uniform 3D world whether the end user was in a UNIX, Macintosh, or Windows environment (or any other operating system tomorrow may bring). This alone would not really pose a great inconvenience to the developers of VRML, as there already exist many 3D rendering tools that could meet this requirement.

The second half of the problem, and the true catch, derives from having the Internet as the transportation medium. Like HTML files, VRML files needed to have the ability to work well over low-bandwidth connections that result in data-throughput bottlenecks. Whenever a network carries a block of information from one souce to a destination, the amount of data that can be passed to the destination per second is defined as the bandwidth of the connection. Anything under 64 K, such as a 28.8 Modem (which is 28.8 K per second) is considered low bandwidth. To demonstrate the limitations that the majority of users who access the Internet via a modem have with data-throughput is best done by example. Ten seconds of CD quality sound takes up about 1.76 MB of space. Across a 28.8 Kbps modem the transmission will take roughly 600 seconds (10 minutes). And so the massive files generated by the existing 3D design tools, which would have met the needs of the first requirement, are their fatal failings when considering using them across the Internet.

Therefore the original design requirements of VRML 1.0 was primarily focused on the interdependent goals of platform independence and transmission portability. Additionally, to be a viable Internet environment that would be considered an advancement of present Internet worlds, VRML needed to retain the functionality of HTML in which the objects can be linked with sound, video, images, and other Internet sites.

While VRML is by no means capable of granting full immersion now or in the near future, it is the first step in building a bridge between the Internet and the virtual reality which present day software designers can offer. By creating an interactive 3D environment, VRML is literally building the stage from where it can hopefully expand some day to generate a true virtual reality experience and environment. The next generation VRML 2.0 specifications are already being designed with the concept of interactivity among objects within a 3D VRML world. Users will no longer be limited to only looking and linking. Instead they will be able to interact with objects, as well as perhaps with others, all within the 3D virtual worlds that exists only in cyberspace.

Stepping into a Virtual World

One of the very first sites proposed to simulate a real world environment in the ether of cyberspace with the help of VRML was and is being created by the residents of the San Francisco South Market District (SOMA) where many Internet software and animation developers work. The project is aptly named VIRTUAL SOMA.

A description of VIRTUAL SOMA is located at http://www.hyperion.com/planet9/vrsoma.htm. This is a work in progress but its potential is high. Figure 2-7 shows the model of what the virtual world designers are working towards. Their goal is that each building will be a link to worlds of their own and Internet surfers can visit, stroll, and interact in a virtual representative of the real neighborhood.

Figure 2-7
Virtual SOMA

Of course, this virtual SOMA world cannot be visited by buying a ticket aboard a plane, boat, or train. The ticket needed to enter a virtual world is the VRML browser. Many exist already, with many more to come. One of the first will be discussed in the next chapter.

Chapter

3

WorldView—A VRML Browser

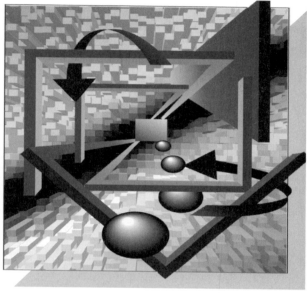

The *passport* needed to explore virtual worlds on the Internet is, of course, a VRML browser. This chapter will help you to learn how to install and use WorldView, a typical VRML browser.

This chapter will help you to determine whether you have the required system specifications, both for Windows 95 and Windows 3.1. For Windows 3.1 users, the installation of the WIN32S software is detailed. Next, the installation of WorldView itself is covered for both Windows 3.1 and Windows 95. Configuration of World-View for use with the popular Netscape 2.0 browser will be discussed as well.

This chapter will also guide you in becoming familiar with all of the WorldView features used in exploring VRML worlds. Finally, other VRML browsers besides WorldView are examined and a brief summary presented.

Required System Specifications

To run the WorldView VRML browser for Windows 3.1 effectively, you will at least need the following minimum hardware and software requirements.

A 486DX processor running at 66 MegaHertz (MHz).

8 Megabytes of Random Access Memory (RAM).

10 Megabytes of free hard disk space.

A 1.4 Megabyte 3.5 inch Floppy Disk Drive

256 color display driver or better and compatible graphics card.

Windows 3.1 or Windows for Workgroup 3.11.

While this configuration will at least get you up and running, the recommended system specifications follows.

A 486DX4 100MegaHertz or Pentium system.

16 Megabytes of Random Access Memory.

A Double or Quadruple Speed CD-ROM drive.

Of course, the above says nothing about the network requirements that are also essential. If you are planning to surf the World Wide Web and access Virtual Worlds on the Internet, you will need the following items.

A 14,400 or 28,800 baud modem.

A SLIP (Serial Link Interface Protocol) or PPP (Point to Point Protocol) account with an Internet Provider (for more information, consult Appendix A: Internet Browser Fundamentals, for a complete list of Internet Providers).

TCP/IP Dial-up Software.

Netscape version 2.0 WWW Browser.

If you plan on surfing the World Wide Web and the Internet but are not yet familiar with its concepts and theory or how to gain access to the Internet, you should see Appendix A: Internet Browser Fundamentals. In Appendix A, you will be able to familiarize yourself with the Internet concept, using the Netscape World Wide Web Browser, the fundamentals of URL (Uniform Resource Locator), and consult a list of Local Internet Access providers.

Installing the WIN32S Software (Windows 3.1 only)

WIN32S is Microsoft Corporation's 32-bit program for use with Windows 3.1 and Windows for Workgroup 3.11. Originally, Windows 3.1 was a 16-bit Graphical User Interface (GUI), which means that it will allow you to run programs written as 16-bit applications only. Many new software applications are running as 32-bit applications (especially Internet applications such as Netscape and Java). The WIN32S software will allow 32-bit applications to run in a 16-bit environment. WorldView is a 32-bit application that, therefore, needs WIN32S in order to run in your Windows 3.1 environment.

If you are running Windows 95, you will not need to install WIN32S. Windows 95 is a 32-bit GUI.

You can always download the latest release from the Internet itself at the following addresses:

> http://www.webmaster.com/vrml/wvwin

> http://www.microsoft.com

Follow these instructions for Installing WIN32S.

1. Save the WIN32S program to a temporary directory on your hard drive. In Windows, go to the Program Manager and click on `File` and choose **Run** (see Figure 3-1).

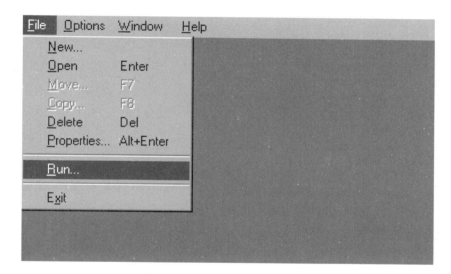

Figure 3-1
Program Manager's
File Menu

2. In the **Run** dialogue box, type the following: `C:\TEMP\SETUP.EXE` (see Figure 3-2).

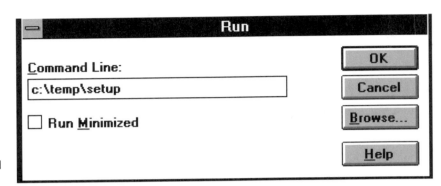

Figure 3-2
Windows' RUN
Dialogue Box

Once you press **OK** the WIN32S setup program will start and the 32-bit files will be installed in the default directory of **C:\WINDOWS\ SYSTEM.** You can, of course, specify an alternative directory. However, it is recommended that you use the default directory.

You can keep track of the installation procedure by viewing the percentage bar during the installation process.

Do not interrupt the WIN32S installation procedure. WIN32S is making changes to your Windows' system files. Your computer may not function correctly if the installation is interrupted.

Once WIN32S has been installed in Windows, the setup program will ask you if you want to install FreeCell, a 32-bit enhanced card game. If you like card games, you can press **OK** to install the game. If you are concerned about space on your computer's hard drive, you can simply **Cancel** the installation at this point.

After the WIN32S software has been installed on your computer system, Windows will restart itself. You are now ready to run 32-bit enhanced applications under Windows 3.1.

Installing Intervista Software's WorldView 0.9f for Windows 3.1 and Windows for Workgroup 3.11

WorldView is a VRML browser. It allows you to explore virtual worlds on the Internet as well as the virtual worlds you created yourself. There are two ways in which you can install WorldView to your hard drive: you can install WorldView from the CD-ROM, or, if you feel adventurous, download it from InterVista's World Wide Web homepage.

If you are not yet familiar with the Internet and World Wide Web, we recommend that you use the CD-ROM provided with this book to install WorldView on your hard drive. However, if you are familiar with the Internet and World Wide Web and you have a SLIP or PPP account with a local Internet access provider and TCP/IP and a World Wide Web browser running on your computer, you can http to the following address: http://www.intervista.com.

InterVista has many useful suggestions and a large database of information pertaining to VRML and their VRML browser. Another useful advantage is that the most recent version of WorldView will be available for downloading at this location.

Installing WorldView from the CD-ROM

Before attempting to install WorldView on your PC, you should consider the following questions:

1. Do I have enough space on the hard disk I am installing to?

2. Do I want WorldView to install to the default directory or a different directory?

3. Do I want WorldView to make a backup copy of my files during installation?

4. Is Windows running in 256 color mode?

These are the suggested answers to these questions:

1. I have 10 megabyte of free hard disk space.

2. I want WorldView to use C:\WRLDVIEW as the default directory.

3. I want WorldView to make backup copies of my files because I do not intend to use WorldView forever and I might want to uninstall WorldView in the future.

4. My Windows is running in 256 color mode (not 16 colors).

Now you are ready to install WorldView. Follow these simple steps to guide you through the procedure.

1. Insert the CD-ROM provided with this book in your CD-ROM drive. In Windows go to Program Manager and click on **File** and choose **Run** (Figure 3-3).

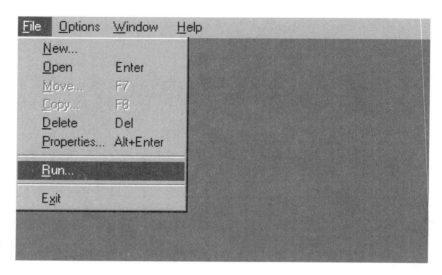

Figure 3-3
Program Manager's
File Menu

2. In the **Run** dialogue box type the following: $x: \backslash$**WRLDVIEW**$\backslash$**IN-STALL**, where $x: \backslash$ is the letter of your CD-ROM drive (Figure 3-4).

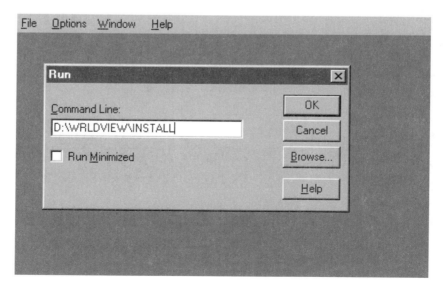

Figure 3-4
The Run Dialogue Box

Once you press OK, the WorldView installation program will start and you will be asked to make some decisions about the installation procedure (refer to the previous questionnaire).

When the WorldView installation program starts, press **OK** at the first dialogue box. The second dialogue box will ask you where you want WorldView installed (Figure 3-5).

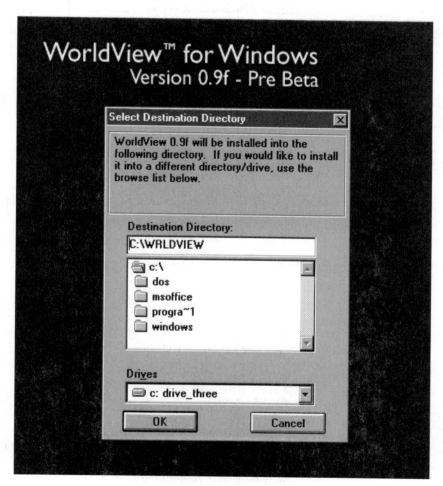

Figure 3-5
WorldView Version 0.9f Main Installation Menu

You can specify in the **Destination Directory** where you want WorldView installed. The default directory is **WRLDVIEW**. However, you can specify any name up to eight characters. You can also specify a different drive in the **Drives** option if you have multiple hard drives or multiple partitions installed in your computer.

Do not specify the CD-ROM drive or floppy disk drive. The installation will fail when these are specified.

Once you have made your decision and you have pressed **OK**, WorldView will ask you if you want backup copies made of the files that will be replaced during the installation (see Figure 3-6). It is recommended that you allow the program to create these backups in case you intend to uninstall WorldView in the future. Press **OK** if you want backup copies made of the replaced files.

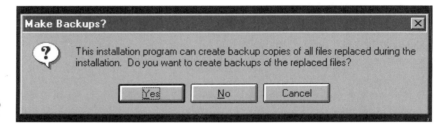

Figure 3-6
WorldView's Backup
Option

WorldView will not replace any of your own data files or other programs. It will replace certain system files in the Windows System directory.

Once you have pressed **OK** another dialogue box will appear to specify the directory where you want the backup copies of the files saved. WorldView recommends the directory **c:\wrldview\backup**. We recommend the same directory. However, you may specify another directory or drive if you want. Once you have made your decision and have clicked on **OK**, the actual installation process will begin. You can monitor the installation progress by watching the percentage bar (Figure 3-7).

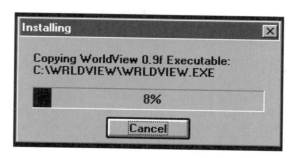

Figure 3-7
WorldView Installation
Percentage Bar

Do not press Cancel unless you really have too, the installation process will fail and WorldView will not be installed correctly.

---

3. Once the program has been installed, WorldView will prompt if you want a Program Group and Icons added to your Program Manager. You should press **OK** since it will allow you to find the WorldView browser easily in your Program Manager.

If you press Cancel at this point, WorldView will not be added to your Program Manager and the Icons will not be installed. If you do that you might not be able to find WorldView in Windows.

---

4. Once you have pressed **OK**, WorldView will prompt you for a Program Group name (Figure 3-8).

Figure 3-8
WorldView's
Program
Manager's Group

WorldView recommends the name **WorldView 0.9f**. You can, of course, specify a different name or add WorldView to an existing group. Press **OK** to finish the WorldView installation.

5. Once WorldView has been installed, the installation process for WorldView will terminate. However, the complete installation process is not over yet. Immediately following the WorldView installation will be the Microsoft Reality Labs 3D software setup program. This rendering software is used by WorldView to display the 3D worlds you want to display or create with WorldView. It is recommended that you install this software (Figure 3-9).

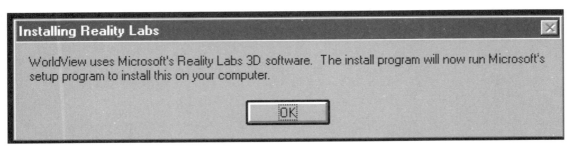

Figure 3-9
Reality Labs 3D
Utility Install   In the dialogue box, press **OK**.

The next dialogue box will tell you that Setup is installing the Install-SHIELD Wizard. This is a new Microsoft feature widely used with Microsoft software and other products. At this point the installation will no longer require user input. The **InstallSHIELD Wizard** will make decisions on how to best install the product on your computer.

The installation of Microsoft's Reality Lab 3D will self-terminate once it has finished installing its files. Once the installation program terminates you can see the WorldView icons in the Program Group (Figure 3-10).

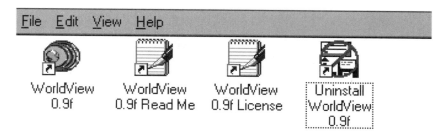

Figure 3-10
The WorldView Icons

6. There are four icons created at this point inside the WorldView program group.

WorldView 0.9f   →   Program Executable

WorldView 0.9f Read Me   →   Release Note

WorldView 0.9f License   →   Shareware License Agreement

Uninstall WorldView 0.9f   →   WorldView Uninstall Program

It is now recommended that you restart Windows in order for the changes to your system to take effect.

Installing Intervista's Worldview Version 1.0, Beta 3 for Windows 95

The installation for WorldView for Windows 95 does not differ much from the installation for Windows 3.1 or Windows for Workgroup 3.11. In fact, the installation for Windows 95 is relatively simple and straightforward. If you are installing WorldView 1.0, Beta 3 for Windows 95, you do *not* need to install the **Win32s** 32-bit program. To install WorldView for Windows 95 you do need to consider the following hardware requirements:

486DX4 100Mhz or Pentium Processor.

8 Mbytes of Random Access Memory (16 Megabytes highly recommended).

A graphics board able to display 256 colors or higher (e.g., 16 Million colors).

At least 10 Megabytes of free hard disk space.

A CD-ROM drive and sound card (optional).

If you plan on exploring virtual worlds on the Internet you must make sure you have a modem and access to a local Internet Provider. Please refer to the "recommended system requirements" in the previous section.

To install WorldView for Windows 95 follow these simple instructions.

1. From the Start ▐▐Start button choose the **Run** option (Figure 3-11).

Figure 3-11
Windows 95 Start Menu

2. In the **Run** dialogue box click or type out the location of the WorldView Installation program. This would typically be your CD-ROM drive if you are installing from the CD-ROM (Figure 3-12).

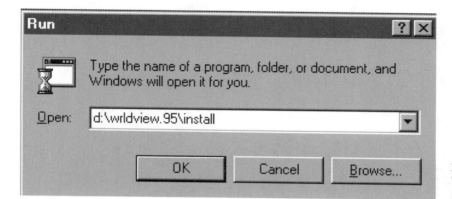

Figure 3-12
Windows 95 Run
Dialogue Box

If the RUN program cannot find the WorldView Installation program your CD-ROM drive may have a different drive letter assigned to it. You can use the BROWSE option to locate your CD-ROM and search for the install program.

4. Once you have located the desired installation program you can click on the **OK** button on the **RUN** dialogue box and the WorldView Installation program will start. A screen similar to the one below will appear (Figure 3-13).

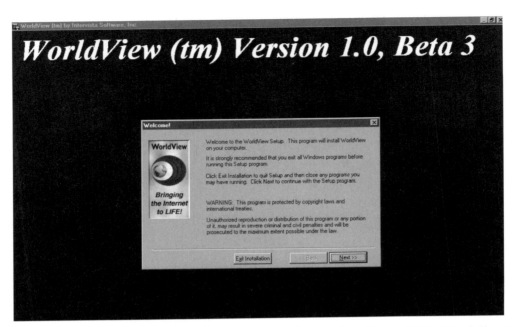

Figure 3-13
WorldView Version
1.0, Beta 3 Install
Menu

5. To install click the **Next** button (see Figure 3-13). The following screen will ask you where the WorldView program should be installed. You can take the default **WorldView** directory or type in an alternative directory or drive if you have multiple drives or partitions in your computer (see Figure 3-14).

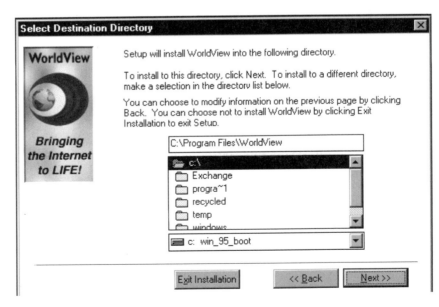

Figure 3-14
WorldView's
Directory Install
Menu

Since Windows 95 is a 32-bit operating system, filenames and directories can be up to 255 characters. The 16-bit operating systems can only assign 8 characters to a given directory or filename. Please note that if you go to a DOS prompt the worldview (9 characters) directory will look something like this: *C:\WORLDV~1*. This will not cause any instability to your system but it may confuse certain people to think this is a corrupt directory. Do not erase this directory and its sub-directories.

6. To continue the installation click **Next**. A dialogue box will appear asking if you want to make backup copies of replaced files during installation. This is highly recommended since you may want to uninstall WorldView at a later date. To backup the replaced files click the **Yes** box, to *not* backup the replaced files click **No**. Once you have made your selection you can click **Next** (see Figure 3-15).

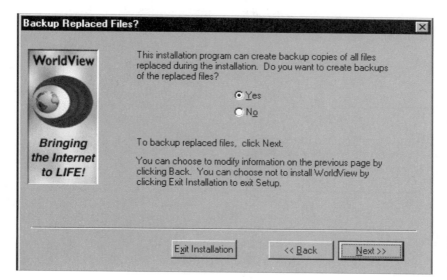

Figure 3-15
WorldView's Backup Option

7. Next, WorldView install will ask you to assign a directory for the backup files. Typically this directory will be located as a sub-directory under WorldView (Figure 3-16).

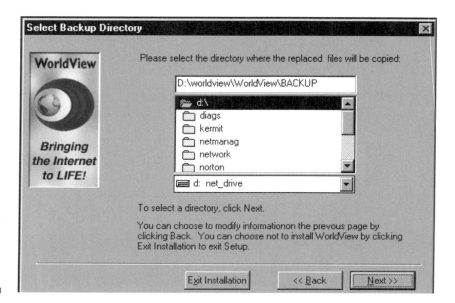

Figure 3-16
WorldView's
Backup Option

It is recommended that you make the backup directory beneath WorldView simply because the WorldView uninstall program can easily find it there. If you make the directory something else in another location, the uninstall program may fail.

8.   Next, the install program will ask you if you want to add World-
View to the **Start** ![Start]🔲 Menu. You should choose **Yes** so you
can find the program quickly instead of searching for it. Click **Next** to
continue (Figure 3-17).

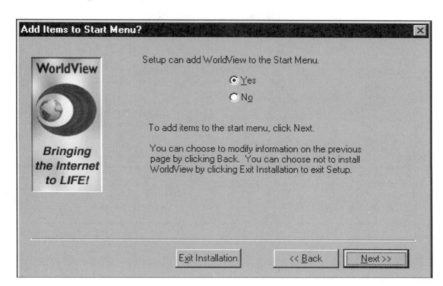

Figure 3-17
Option to add
WorldView to the
Start Menu

9.   Now you will be prompted to actually install WorldView. At this
point, simply click on **Start Install** (Figure 3-18).

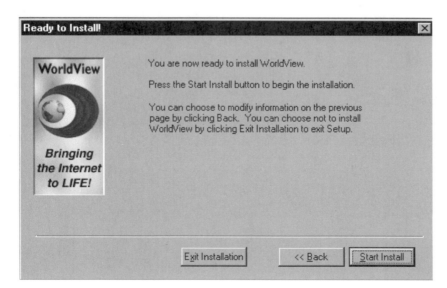

Figure 3-18
Ready to Install!

10. You can keep track of the installation process by observing the percentage bar (Figure 3-19).

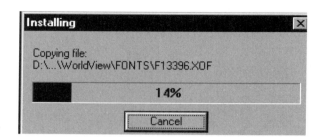

Figure 3-19
WorldView
Installation
Percentage Bar

The installation can take from one minute to three minutes depending on the speed of your computer.

11. Once the installation is complete, WorldView will launch the **3D Reality Lab** installation that will install the 3-dimensional drivers to display VRML worlds in WorldView. Setup will launch the Install-SHIELD Wizard that will automatically install the neccesary files. InstallSHIELD Wizard will not require you to input any additional information (Figure 3-20).

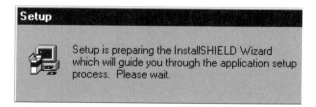

Figure 3-20
WorldView's
InstallSHIELD Wizard
Utility

You can keep track of the installation by observing the percentage bar (Figure 3-21).

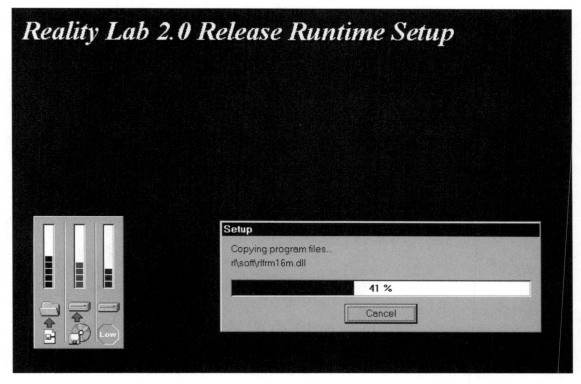

Figure 3-21
Installation of Reality Lab 2.0

12. The **3D Reality Lab** installation will take about 2 to 3 minutes. Once the installation is complete, InstallSHIELD Wizard will terminate the installation and WorldView will be succesfully installed on your computer.

13. You can start the WorldView program from the **Start** menu bar (Figure 3-22).

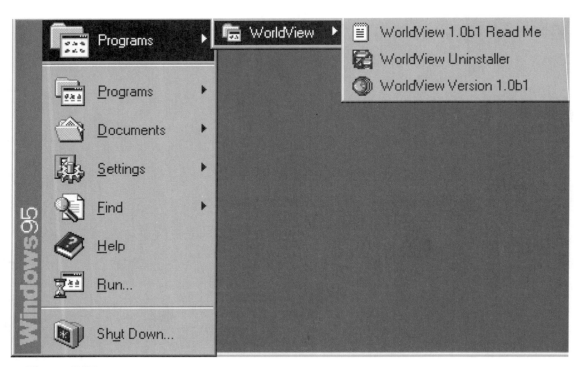

Figure 3-22
The Windows 95
"Start" Menu

Becoming Familiar with WorldView Features

As soon as you run the WorldView VRML browser, the first virtual world to explore is automatically displayed on the main screen.

Figures 3-23 and 3-24 will show you what WorldView 0.9f looks like
in comparison to WorldView 1.0, Beta 1.

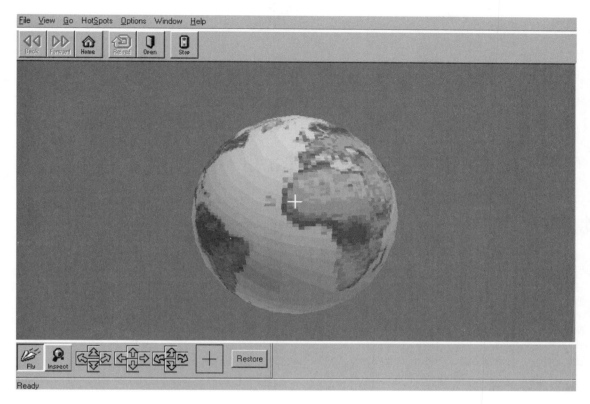

Figure 3-23
WorldView 0.9f
Main Screen

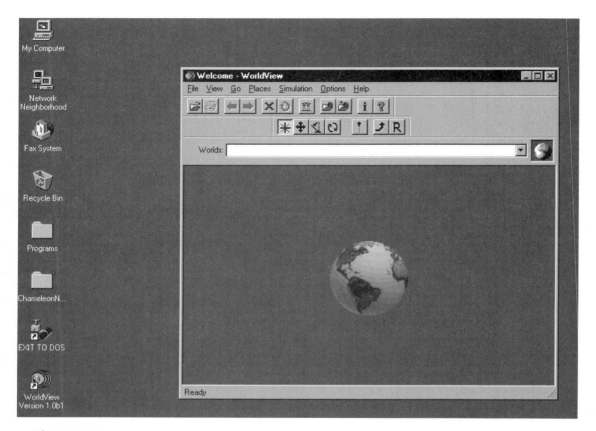

Figure 3-24
WorldView 1.0,
Beta 3
Main Screen

The fundamental differences between the two versions are the toolbars that are used for navigating through the virtual worlds. The Windows 95 version of WorldView has more enhanced features compared to the Windows 3.1 version. However, the fundamental principal for navigating in a virtual world remains practically the same.

There is a lot of information besides the beautiful globe, so we will first start with identification of the features of WorldView for Windows 3.1. WorldView has many features installed for the user to explore the virtual world. Although you will probably enjoy figuring out what all the features can do by yourself, we will assume that a small explanation would suffice to send you on your way exploring virtual reality on the Internet and World Wide Web.

.9f for Windows 3.1 Menu Bar

HotSpots   Options   Window   Help

on where location is an Internet address.

here File is a file locally stored on your hard drive.

where you can save a file you have retrieved from t.

/iew.

:an:

orld that you recently loaded, as well as a world on iet.

wpoint of an object in a world or a entire world.

. **Viewpoint** that you recently saved with **Save int.**

a **Scene** that you created.

current loading of a world, or **Stop** the animation of a

w.... **ame, Flat, Gouraud, Phong,** and **Dither** the world you want to manipulate. These four features allow you to add special effects to your world.

3. In **Go** you can:

Go Forward to another homepage on the Internet that you recently loaded.

Go Backward to another homepage on the Internet that you recently loaded.

Go **Home** to InterVista's homepage on the Internet.

View History of the homepages you recently visited.

4. In **HotSpots** you can:

Add HotSpot of a Internet homepage that you would like to access more often.

View HotSpots that you created with **Add HotSpot**.

5. In **Options** you can:

Load **Preferences** that will allow you to save some decisions on how you want certain Virtual Worlds to load while you are connected to the Internet.

Load **In Line Objects** that are not automatically loaded when a VRML world is first accessed.

Hide Crosshair that will hide the Crosshair from the current Virtual World you have loaded.

Save Options of the current changes you have made in **Preferences.**

6.   In **Window** you can:

Hide or show the **Navigator,** a bar that is shown on the bottom of the page. Hiding this bar will prevent you from moving around an object in the Virtual World.

Show **Parser Warnings** that are syntax errors that may arise when WorldView reads some VRML files.

7.   **Help** is not available in this version of WorldView.

The WorldView 1.0, Beta 3 for Windows 95 Menu Bar

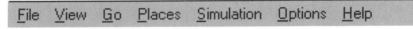

1.   In **File** you can:

Open an Internet location by use of an internet address, or you can open local WRL files that are stored on your hard drive.

Save As... allows you to save files you have retrieved from the Internet as well as files you have built yourself.

Print allows you to print a world on your printer.

Edit Source allows you to edit the source code of a particular world. Please refer to chapters 5 and 6 on how to build and edit worlds.

Exit will terminate WorldView.

2.   In **View** you can:

Reload a world you recently loaded from the Internet as well as a world that you have saved locally on your hard drive. This allows the image to refresh itself.

Zoom Out or **Zoom Into** a particular world for closer observation and analysis.

Add Camera, allowing you to add different viewpoints to your world so you can look at it from different angles.

Default Camera, allowing you to reset WorldView to use the default camera, not the camera's added with **Add Camera**.

3. In **Go** you can:

Go **Back** to a previously viewed homepage or world that you loaded from the Internet.

Go **Forward** will jump you to the next homepage or world that you loaded from the Internet.

Go to the **Home World** that will connect you to InterVista Software's Internet homepage at `http://www.intervista.com`.

Stop Loading, interrupting the loading of a homepage or world from the Internet. This is especially helpful when the loading process becomes slow or has stopped loading.

View History of the homepages or worlds that you recently visited.

4. In **Places** you can:

Add a **favorite place**, allowing you to save a particular homepage or world that you have found on the Internet and wish to revisit at a later time.

View a **favorite place**, allowing you to retrieve the homepages and/or worlds that you have saved with the **Add favorite place** feature.

5. In **Simulation** you can:

Animation allows you to animate your world to perform certain functions that you can then replay later. The following features are combined with animation:

A.   **Start All** will start the animation recording process.

B.   **Stop All** will stop the animation recording process.

C.   **Reset** will reset the animation to its original settings.

D.   **Next** will jump you to the next animation.

E.   **Previous** will jump you back to the previous animation.

In **Quality** you can adjust the quality of your world. This is helpful if your world is rendering very slowly or if you need to see specific details of a world. The following quality controls are available:

A. **Best (smooth shading)** Most detailed display of the world (slow rendering).

B. **Good (flat shading)** Less detail, but still pretty good (fast rendering).

C. **Poor (WireFrame)** Wire frame details of your world, allows you to see how the world was made (very fast rendering).

In **Speed** you can set the rendering speeds of your world. Typically this is set at **Very Fast** although sometimes you may need to decrease the speed because of loading and/or downloading problems. **Speed** has 5 different speed settings: **Very Slow, Slow, Medium, Fast**, and **Very Fast**.

Load Textures when checked will load all detailed textures of the world you are looking at. When not checked, the world will display in less detail.

Prevent Collisions when checked will allow you to navigate through a world without walking straight through objects in that world. It prevents you from colliding with a specific object (e.g., a wall, door, floor, etc.).

6. In **Options** you can:

Set **Preferences** on how you want worldview to behave and operate. Preferences has four major features that we will discuss at this point in detail. It is important to know what these features are because they direct how WorldView operates (Figure 3-25).

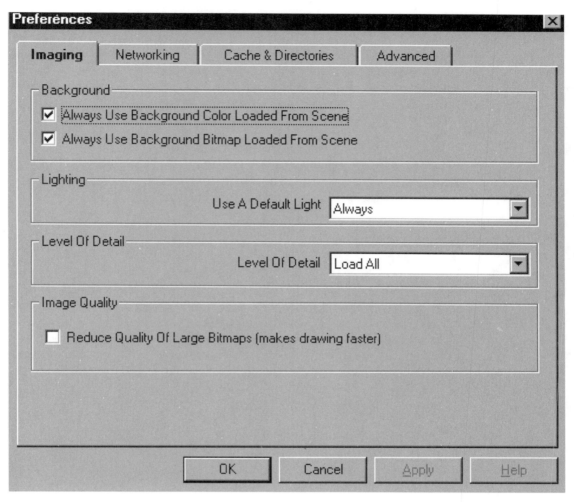

Figure 3-25
Preferences "Imaging" Options

A. **Imaging** allows you to set the way WorldView will load **background** colors and images, which type of **lighting** it will use, what type of **detail** you want displayed, and what type of image **quality** you want to use for all worlds you are going to load. The keyword for selecting these features is speed. If you have a slow machine with 8Mbyte of RAM and/or a slow Internet connection. It is recommended that you *not* load all details at once or *not* load specific backgrounds. Not checking these features will increase your speed but will take away from the image quality.

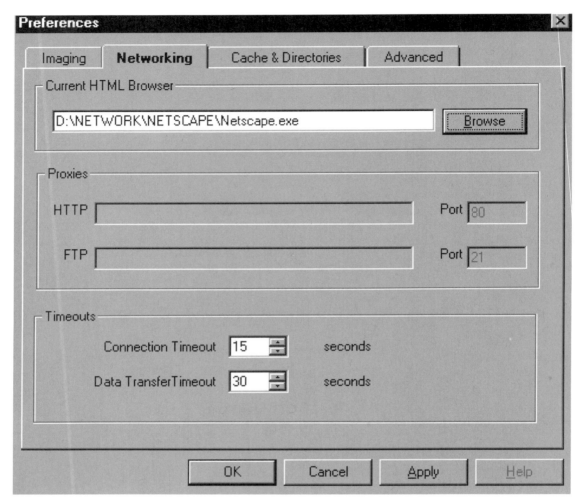

Figure 3-26
Preferences
"Networking"
Options

B. **Networking** allows you to set Internet preferences (Figure 3-26). You can set the default **HTML browser** to view HTML pages on the World Wide Web. We have selected Netscape in this section; however, you can use whichever browser you are comfortable with (e.g., Spry Mosaic, Netmanage's WebSurfer, Webcrawler, etc.). **Proxies** allows you to set helper applications, which WorldView will invoke when necessary. **Timeouts** allows you to set up the timeout delay in seconds before WorldView will stop trying to retrieve a world or homepage. For slower machines or slower modem users, the higher the timeout rate the better the chance of retrieving the world from the internet. Users with fast machines and fast modems or direct internet connections do not need to change these options.

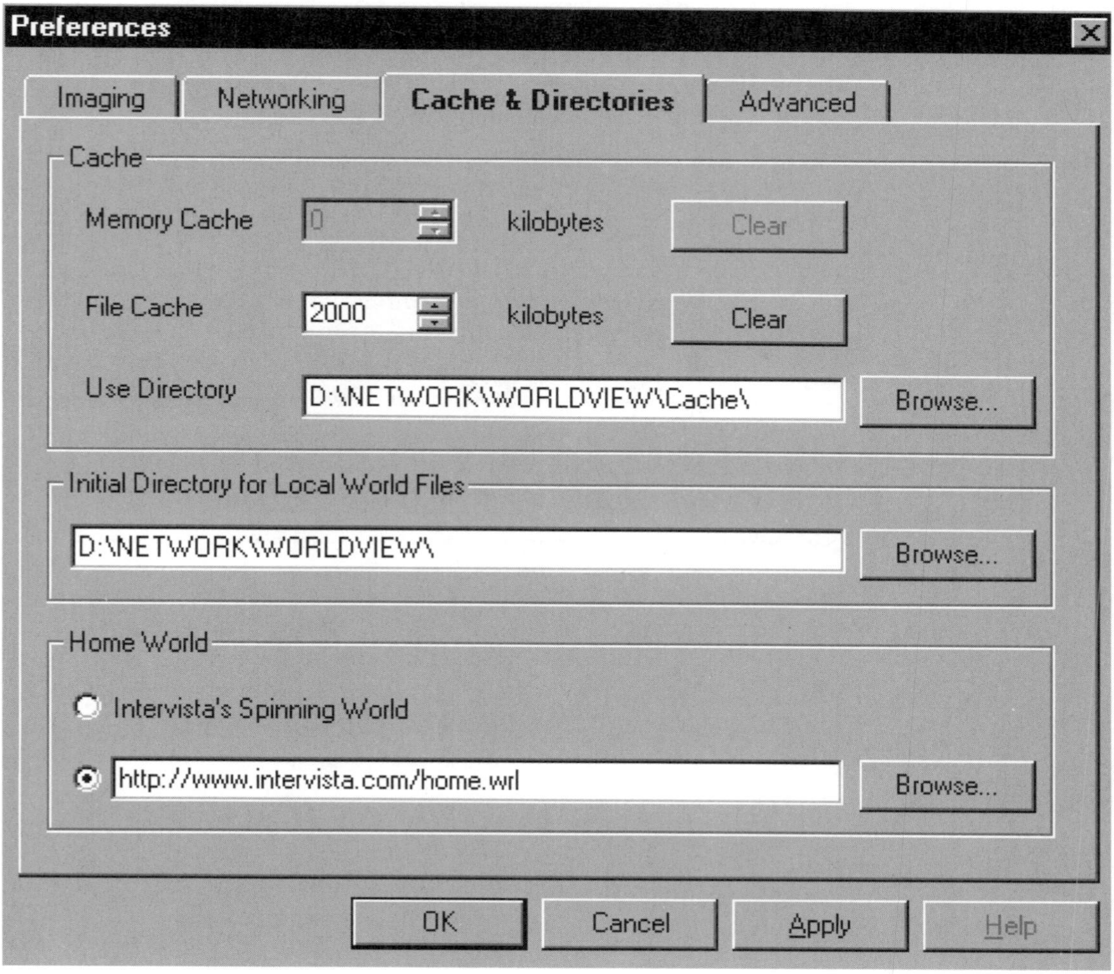

Figure 3-27
Preferences "Cache of Directories" Options

C. In **Cache and Directories** you can set the **Memory Cache** and **File Cache** sizes as well as the directory in which to load the cache files (Figure 3-27). Cache memory and files uses a portion of your hard drive to temporarily store temporary files in order to increase the performance of WorldView—this is especially important for users who have slow computers. The temporary cache files are stored in the directory given in the following paragraph. The default directory is a sub-directory below WorldView called cache.

When you install WorldView, the program installs a view sample world file on your computer to play with. The default directory is **X:\worldview\worlds**, where **X:** is the drive you installed WorldView on.

Home World is the default page you can specify for WorldView to load when loading WorldView.

Intervista's Spinning World is the Globe that loads automatically when WorldView is loaded.

Http://www.intervista.com/home.wrl is the world that is loaded automatically from the internet.

If you choose the last option, make sure you have an Internet connection active before loading WorldView. WorldView will not load properly when it cannot find the Intervista internet site.

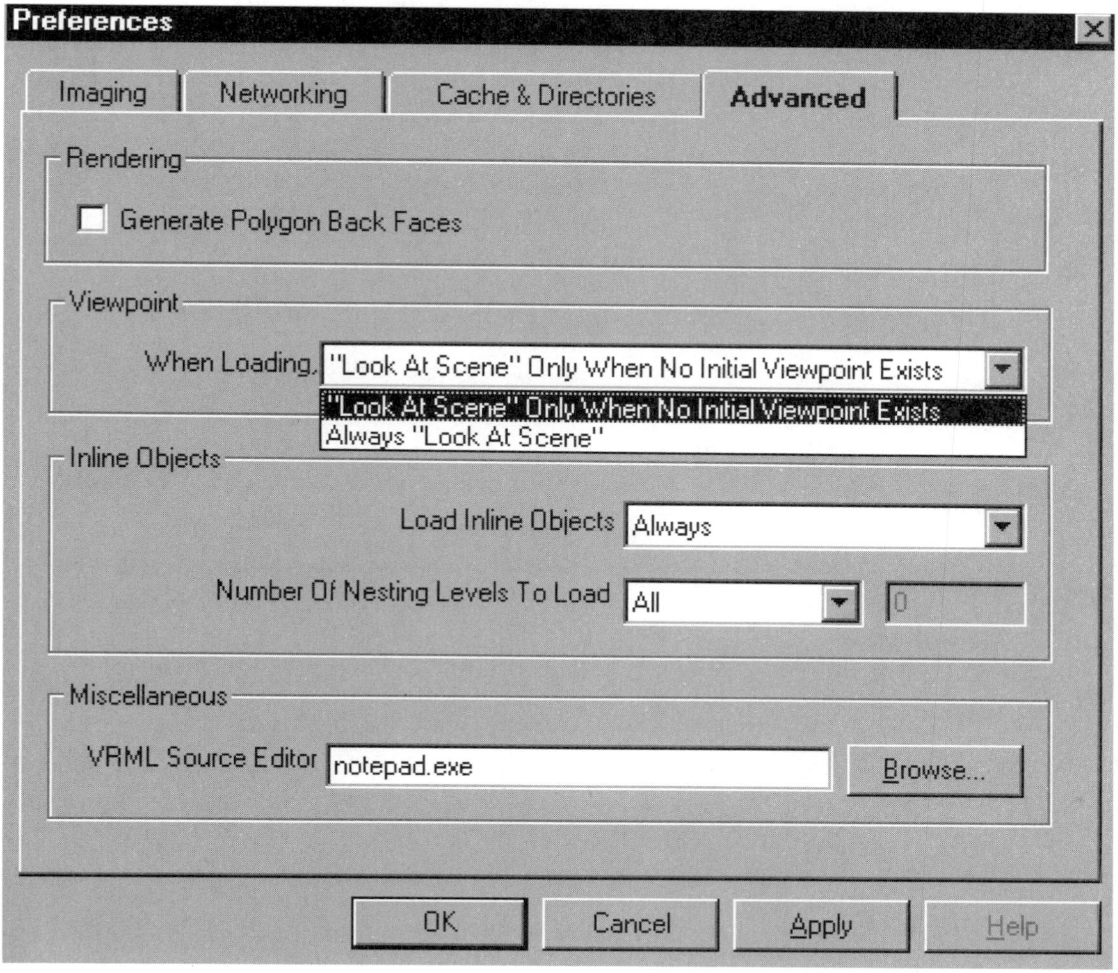

Figure 3-28
Preferences
"Advanced" Options

D. The **Advanced** options allow you to specify the rendering of a loading world (Figure 3-28). Depending on how you choose the following options, your speed will be either optimized or decreased. If you have a slow machine, do not mark **Generate Polygon Back Faces**. The **Viewpoint** option allows you to either load one object in the world at a time, or load all objects at once. **Inline Objects** allows you to load objects that are not automatically loaded when a VRML world is first accessed. The **VRML Source Editor** allows you to set up an external program that will be used to edit VRML code. (Please note that a VRML Editor must be a *text* editor, *not* a Word Processor.)

Show Navigator Tools allows you to load the Navigator toolbar when WorldView is loaded.

Show Toolbar allows you to load the Toolbar when WorldView is loaded.

Show World allows you to load the default world when WorldView is loaded.

Show Status Bar will display a world loading statusbar when downloading a world from the Internet.

Show Information Center will show information on how WorldView is performing.

7.   In **Help** you can:

click on the **About** button that will show you version information about WorldView.

This version of WorldView does not come with a Help option.

The WorldView Toolbar in WorldView 0.9f for Windows 3.1

The toolbar's features are only applicable if you are on-line on the Internet. They do not apply if you are working off-line.

 This feature allows you to move back to a previous page you loaded on the Internet.

 This feature allows you to move forward to a page you loaded previously on the Internet.

 This feature allows you to reconnect to InterVista Software's Homepage (www.intervista.com).

 This feature allows you to reload (or refresh) the current page you are on. This is very helpful when a page stops loading in the middle; it helps to speed along the loading process.

 This feature allows you to input an Internet address of a homepage you want to load. This usually starts with `http://` input.address.here.

 This feature allows you to stop the loading of an Internet homepage (very helpful if you suddenly changed your mind and want to load a different page instead).

The WorldView 0.9f for Windows 3.1 Navigator Bar

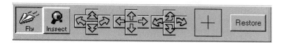

The Navigator Bar allows you to travel through your virtual world and manipulate the objects you have loaded. There are very helpful tools available, however, it might take some time to get used to the different features of each option. Following is a brief description of the navigational tools.

There are two different ways to navigate through your virtual world. One is in **Fly** mode and the other is in **Inspect** mode. The two different modes are listed next to each navigational tool.

 The **Fly** mode allows you to move around in the virtual world. That is, *you* move but the objects in the virtual world remain still.

 The **Inspect** mode allows you to manipulate, move, and tilt the virtual world and its objects. That is, you stand still and the objects in the virtual world move around.

The three sets of arrow buttons are a little more complex and operate as follows:

First set:

Move Forward

In Fly Mode this will move the virtual world and object closer to you.

In Inspect Mode this will move the virtual world and object further away from you.

Look Left      **Look Right**

Move Backward

In Fly Mode this will move the virtual world and object further away from you.

In Inspect Mode this will move the virtual world and object closer to you.

Second Set:

Look Up

In Fly Mode this will tilt the view angle up.

In Inspect Mode this will tilt the top of the virtual world or object toward you.

Tilt Left      **Tilt Right**

Look Down

In Fly Mode this will tilt the view angle down.

In Inspect Mode this will tilt the top of the virtual world or object away from you.

Third Set:

Move Up

In Fly Mode this will give the appearance of moving the virtual world or object down.

In Inspect Mode this will move the virtual world or object up.

Move Left      **Move Right**

Move Down

In Fly Mode this will give the appearance of moving the virtual world or object up.

In Inspect Mode this will move the virtual world or object down.

You can hold the Control or Alternate keys on your keyboard down while you are using the mouse to press the navigational buttons to accelerate the movement of the virtual world or object. This will simulate a spinning effect.

Next, the Cross Hair tool acts as a joystick to move around in your virtual world or manipulate an object freely in virtual space. By holding down the left mouse button and moving around in the Cross Hair space you will see that you can freely move the object in any way you desire. You can also hold down the Shift Key on your keyboard and the mouse to pan the image, or the Control and the mouse to pitch or roll the image.

 By pressing the Restore button your image will restore itself to the original setting when you first loaded the image. This is helpful when the image runs off the view screen and you are unable to get it back.

 The Ready bar at the bottom left side of the program will show the progress of a virtual world or object being loaded. It will show percentage-wise how much has been loaded, and it will show in bytes how much has to still be loaded. This is a helpful indicator when you are on-line to see if the virtual world has stopped loading or if there are errors in the parsing process.

WorldView comes pre-loaded with a few worlds that you can load and manipulate in order to become more familiar with the application. These worlds are loaded in the directory: **C:\WRLDVIEW\ WORLDS**. You can load these worlds by going to **File** and **Open File** and changing to the correct directory.

We recommend you load these worlds to become familiar with the WorldView Application and its navigational features.

The WorldView Toolbar in WorldView 1.0, Beta 3 for Windows 95

The WorldView 1.0, Beta 3 toolbar performs the same functions that you can find in the Menu bar. The toolbar serves as a shortcut menu to the Menu bar. A quick review of the buttons follows.

Most toolbar options will only work when you are actively connected to the Internet.

This button will open either an Internet address or a local
World file from your hard disk.

This is the print button to print the current world.

These are the **Go Back** and **Go Forward** buttons to navigate through Internet pages.

This is the **Stop** loading button. It will stop the loading of a
world.

This is the **Reload** button to reload a particular world.

If a particular world loads very slowly or has stopped loading, you
can sometimes click the Stop button and then click the Reload
button to reload the world. This usually solves 70 percent of the
slowly loaded world problem.

This is the **Home** button; clicking this will connect you to the
Intervista homepage on the Internet.

These two buttons will load the **Favorite Place** menu
and **Add to Favorite Place** menu.

This will display the **Information Center** for World-
View.

This will display WorldView Version information.

The WorldView 1.0B, Beta 3
for Windows 95 Navigator Bar

The Navigator Bar is the essential component in WorldView that allows you to navigate through the world. Many items in this version are similar to WorldView 0.9f, however, the 1.0Beta version allows more flexibility. Following is a brief description of the navigation tools.

 Navigate: Moves your world forward, back, left, and right.

 Pan Mode: Moves your world up, down, left, and right.

 Tilt Mode: Tilts your view of the world up, down, left, and right.

 Inspect Mode: Rotates the world or object in front of you up, down, left, and right.

 Go To: Zoom up to any object or world by choosing it with the crosshair cursor.

 Straighten Up: Fixes the view of the object or world so you are standing up straight.

 Restore View: Jumps back to the original viewpoint of the object or world.

Configuring WorldView for Use with Netscape

If you are already an avid user of the Internet and surfer of the World Wide Web, this information will be helpful for you. WorldView is a powerful VRML viewer. However, it lacks some of the powerful tools you may be needing when surfing on the World Wide Web. WorldView can be used as a helper application for use with Netscape. Typically, you might find it easier to use Netscape to surf from homepage to homepage on the Internet. Sadly, though, current versions of Netscape cannot automatically display files with the **.wrl** extension. However, Netscape can invoke WorldView at anytime you click on a file with .wrl extension, allowing you to see and explore the virtual world or object on the Internet.

In order to configure Netscape for use with WorldView and vice versa, you need to know which versions of Netscape you are using. An easy way to find this out is to click on the **Help** menu in Netscape and choose **About . . .** This will typically display the version number of the current application.

WorldView comes preconfigured for use with Netscape. However, WorldView assumes that you have Netscape saved in its default directory which is **c:\netscape\netscape.exe**. If Netscape is not stored in its default directory, you will have to edit the **wrldview.ini** file.

To edit the **wrldview.ini** file you should open Windows' Notepad (in the Accessories program group) and open the file: **C:\WINDOWS\WRLDVIEW.INI**. The following file will be displayed (see Figure 3-29).

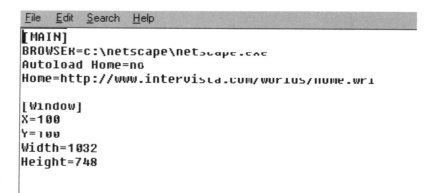

Figure 3-29
The WorldView.ini
File

In the **MAIN** section, edit the **BROWSER** section to point to the correct location of the Netscape Directory.

InterVista Software, the creators of WorldView, recommend using Netscape as your default browser.

WorldView 1.0, Beta 3 users do not have to edit the wrldview.ini file. You can make Netscape the WorldView helper application by going to *OPTIONS, PREFERENCES, NETWORKING,* and type in the location of your Netscape program in the HTML Browser command line.

If you plan on using Netscape as your primary browser, you will have to make sure that Netscape recognizes the **.wrl** file extension as one that needs to link to the WorldView helper application. There are two ways to do this. First, you can just access the **Options** menu bar item in Netscape. Under **General Preferences**, access the **Helpers** tag. Click on **Create New Type** and type in **x-world** as the Type and **x-vrml** as the Sub-type. Type in the **File Extensions** as **wrl,wrz,flr**. Finally, type in the location of the WorldView browser for the **Launch Application** field. If you used the default on installation of WorldView, this would be **C:\WRLDVIEW\WRLD-VIEW.EXE.** Otherwise, you can use the **Browse** button to locate WorldView. Finally, click on **OK** to finish.

Second, you can edit the **Netscape.ini** file. This file can be located in your Netscape directory.

To edit the **Netscape.ini** file, open Windows' Notepad in the Accessories program group and open the following file:

C:\NETSCAPE\NETSCAPE.INI (we assume you have installed Netscape in its default directory, if not, you will have to open the directory where you installed Netscape.). The following file will be displayed (see Figure 3-30).

```
 File   Edit   Search   Help

[Viewers]
HTML=
Tn3270=C:\NETMANAG\NETWARE\QWS3270.EXE
Telnet=C:\NETMANAG\FTP.EXE
audio/basic=C:\NETMANAG\NETSCAPE\NAPLAYER.EXE
audio/x-aiff=C:\NETMANAG\NETSCAPE\NAPLAYER.EXE
x-world/x-vrml=C:\WRLDVIEW\WRLDVIEW.EXE|
application/x-chat=C:\NETMANAG\GLOBLCHT.EXE
application/zip=
video/mpeg=
```

Figure 3-30
The Netscape.ini File

Locate the **VIEWERS** section and edit or add the following line:

```
X-WORLD/X-VRML=C:\WRLDVIEW\WRLDVIEW.EXE.
```

This will point Netscape to the correct Helper Application in case it needs to display WRL files.

Make sure that you are using the WorldView directory. If you did not install WorldView to the default WRLDVIEW directory, you need to enter the correct path to the WRLDVIEW.EXE file. Otherwise your application may not work.

Alternative VRML Browsers

The Internet serves a large community of computer enthusiasts in the business community, educational institutions, and government institutions worldwide. The Internet is therefore a perfect place for software developers to market their products. Many software companies offer free samples of their newest software developments—which are often perfectly working, full featured, software products.

If you are familiar with the Internet you might know about the multitude of products and software you can download at no charge. There is everything: virus-checkers, special editors, image utilities, sound utilities, and software utilities. Software related to the Internet for use on the Internet can be easily found by simply searching for a keyword with an Internet browser search program.

For example, a search on the keyword "VRML" with any popular Internet Search Engine (e.g., www.altavista.digital.com, www.yahoo.com. www.excite.com, etc.) can result in up to 500 different Internet sites that deal with VRML in one way or the other, and this number increases with the hour. Therefore, the Internet would be the perfect place to search for software that deals specifically with VRML browsers.

There are many different VRML browsers available on the Internet, all with their specific functions and features, running on many popular platforms. In this book we deal specifically with browsers that are used on the DOS/WINDOWS platform and the WINDOWS 95 platform. However, knowing the different platforms available we will not limit our search for VRML browsers to only these two platforms. You will find summaries of browsers that are native to the Apple Macintosh as well as to the UNIX platforms.

The following list is a summary of the different browsers available for each platform and where you can find them on the Internet.

VRML Browsers Summary

Program/Company	Platform	Where to Download
AmberGL VRML Browser (DIVE Laboratories, Inc.)	Windows NT	http://www.divelabs .com/vrml.html
Fountain (WorldSpace) (Galigari Corporation)	Windows 3.1 Windows 95	http://www.galigari. com/ws/fount.html
GLView (Holger Grahn)	Windows NT Windows 95	http://www.snafu.de/ ~hg/
i3D (CRS4)	SGI with IRIX	http://www.crs4.it/ ~3diadm/i3d-announce.html
Microsoft VRML Add-in Beta (Microsoft, Inc.)	Windows 95	http://www.microsoft. com/windows/ie/vrml
NAVFlyer Beta 2.2 (MicronGreen, Inc.)	Windows 3.1 Windows NT Windows 95	ftp.yoda.fdt.net/pub/ users/m/micgreen
Virtus Voyager (Virtus Corporation)	Macintosh Power Macintosh Windows 95	http://www.virtus.com/ voyager.html
VR Scout 1.1 (Chaco Communications, Inc.)	Windows 3.1 Windows NT Windows 95	http://www.chaco.com/ vrscout.html
Vrealm (Integrated Data Systems, Inc. & Portable Graphics, Inc.)	Windows 95 Windows NT	http://ids-net.com.ids/ vrealm.html

Program/Company	Platform	Where to Download
VRML Equinox	Power Macintosh	http://www.ipsystems. com/nps/EquiInfo.html
(North Plains Systems, Inc.)		
VRWeb	Windows 3.1	http://www.iicm.tu-graz. ac.at/Cvrweb
(IICM, NCSA)	Windows NT Windows 95 HP-UX SUN - OS SUN - Solaris SGI - IRIX DEC Alpha DEC Ultrix LINUX IBM AIX	
WebFX	Windows 3.1	http://www.paperinc. com/webfx.html
(Paper Software, Inc.)	Windows NT Windows 95	
WebOOGL 2.0	SGI	http://www.geom. umn.edu/software/ weboogl
(The Geometry Center)	SUN	
Webspace	SGI	http://www.sgi. com/Products/ webFORCE/
(Silicon Graphics Computer Systems, Inc. & Template Graphics Software)	Windows NT Windows 95 SUN - Solaris IBM AIX	WebSpace.html
WebView	SGI / UNIX	http://www.sdsc.edu/ EnablingTech/
(San Diego Supercomputer Center)		Visualization/vrml/ Webview.html

Program/Company	Platform	Where to Download
Whurlwind 3D	Macintosh	http://www.info.apple. com/qd3d/viewer.html
(Bill Enright & John Louch)		
WorldView	Windows 3.1	http://www.intervista. com
(InterVista Software, Inc.)	Windows NT Windows 95	

Internet sites change locations often. It is possible that the software may not be located at the sites where we found them at the time of publication. If you cannot find the software, we recommend you perform an Internet search on the company name instead.

Some Internet VRML Browsers are very large, even in their compressed format. You may want to download these programs at night in order to reduce cost on your phone bill.

A Brief Tour of Other VRML Browsers

AmberGL VRML Browser Version 1.0 (Dive Laboratories)

AmberGL is currently only supported on Windows NT (Intel). The software contains a built-in Web browser as well as a VRML viewer. The browser supports up to 65 thousand colors, multiple rendering modes, and multiple lights. Future releases of this software will include support for head mounted displays and cyber gloves. You can download AmberGL's alpha release at: http://www.divelabs.com/vrml.html.

Fountain (now known as worldSpace) (Galigari Corporation)

Fountain/worldSpace is a Windows 3.11 and Windows 95 VRML authoring package with the ability to read on-line VRML World files. The software includes 3D shape creation, 2D polygons, face editing, lathing, and sweeping. This is an excellent package if you plan to create your own worlds. It is especially suited for those who have experience with Computer Aided Design (CAD) software and Animation software. However, it's easy enough for even the most novice VRML user. Fountain/worldSpace includes a wide variety of tools that allow you to navigate through the world as well as manipulate the world. The package can be downloaded at the following location: http://www.galigari.com/ws/fount.html.

Figure 3-31 shows a view of the worldSpace version 0.9 main screen.

Figure 3-31
WorldSpace
Version 0.9 Main
Screen

GLView (Holger Grahn)

GLView is a Windows 95 and Windows NT Shareware written by Holger Grahn. GLView is a VRML browser as well as a 3D Object Viewer. The Shareware includes such functionality as Animation Extensions (e.g., Rotor, Blinker, Texture Rotor, Time Transform). It also includes support for the following Inline Texture Mappings: RGB, DIB, BMP, JPEG, GIF, and TARGA image files. Support is also provided for VRML version 1.0 files. GLView can be downloaded at the following location: http://www.snafu.de/~hg/.

i3D (CRS4)

i3D is a software package that combines the 3D input and high-performance rendering capabilities of high-end virtual reality systems with the simple abilities of a network browser. Unfortunately, i3D is not available for standard IBM x386, x486, x586 or Macintosh computer systems. Due to its high-performance rendering system and other high-performance three dimensional data animation, i3D is made for high performance RISC and/or UNIX machines. i3D is actively used at the European Laboratory for Particle Physics (CERN) for the exploration of the Large Hadron Collider (LHC). The project is called Virtual Environment Navigation in the Underground Sites (VENUS); and i3D is used as a detailed virtual prototype of the LHC premises where the engineer can "flythrough" the Collider. You can read more about i3D by going to the following location: http://www.crs4.it/~3diadm/i3d-announce.html.

Microsoft VRML Add-In Beta 1.1 (Microsoft, Inc.)

With the arrival of Microsoft's newest Operation System, Windows 95, Microsoft has announced its newest venture: The Microsoft Network (MSN). MSN comes with the Windows 95 Operating System and allows the user to be up and running on the Internet in just a few point and clicks. Microsoft has also made available their new Internet Explorer version 2.0, an Internet Web Browser. If you are already connected to the MSN, you can download the Web Explorer at: http://www.microsoft.com/windows/ie/vrml.htm. If you have a local Internet provider, you can still download the Explorer; however, it's configuration to your local provider's server might be complicated and time consuming. Microsoft also provides a high-performance VRML Add-In for the Explorer.

The VRML Add-In Beta 1.1 will only work with the Internet Explorer.

VRML Add-In Beta 1.1 supports a wide variety of VRML tools and utilities. Among the features are joystick support, GIF, JPG and BMP texture support, collision detection, camera animation, and full integration with Internet Explorer and Windows 95.

NAVFlyer 2.2b (MicronGreen, Inc.)

NAVFlyer (Navigator Flyer) version 2.2b is a freely distributed VRML Viewer by MicronGreen, Inc. NAVFlyer has many features that allow the user to navigate through a VRML world as well as manipulate and animate them. One drawback of NAVFlyer is that the software uses an enormous amount of memory (RAM) while rendering the World file. It is not uncommon to receive an Out of Memory message from Windows while NAVFlyer is rendering a world. If you plan on using NAVFlyer, it is recommended that you do shut down all non-critical Windows programs. If you are on the Internet, you may want to download and save the World locally on your hard drive and then look at it with NAVFlyer. NAVFlyer can be downloaded by Anonymous FTP at: ftp.yoda.fdt.net. You can login as anonymous using your E-mail address as your password. The file NAVFLW.ZIP is located in the pub/usr/m/micgreen directory. NAVFlyer can be used on Windows 3.11, 95 and NT machines.

Virtus Voyager (Virtus Corporation)

Virtus Voyager is a VRML helper application for Netscape or Mosaic for Macintosh and PowerPC Macintosh computers. Virtus Corporation plans on having a Windows 95 version available sometime in February of 1996. Virtus Voyager can be downloaded at: http://www.virtus.com/voyager.html.

VR Scout version 1.1 (Chaco Communications, Inc.)

VR Scout is a VRML viewer plug-in for use with Netscape Navigator and Netmanage's WebSurfer in Windows 3.1, 95 and NT. VR Scout supports a wide variety of textures (GIF, JPG, BMP, SFImage), as well as HTML (Hyper Text Mark-up Language) and inline VRML images. VR Scout works with almost all VRML compliant worlds, even with the not-so-quite-compliant VRML worlds. However, please make sure you are using Netscape Navigator version 2.0b4; VR Scout will not work with any earlier versions of Netscape Navigator. VR Scout can be downloaded at: http://www.chaco.com/vrscout.html.

VRealm (Integrated Data Systems, Inc. & Portable Graphics, Inc.)

VRealm is a Windows 95 and Windows NT compatible VRML viewer and Internet navigator. VRealm is a very powerful and easy-to-use package. It can be used as a stand alone Internet navigator or as a plug-in viewer with Netscape Navigator. Some powerful features are advanced image, video, audio, animation, and virtual reality techniques. Rendering of VRML worlds is surprisingly fast, both locally or on the Internet. VRealm's easy to use toolbar allows the user to quickly navigate from one side of the world to another. Some interesting features are the Auto-Navigate option that, upon activation, will allow VRealm to automatically navigate the world without the user's input; the Header Indicator allows the user to quickly change views and change direction in the world; and the View Position List allows the user to jump to pre-defined positions in the world. Altogether, VRealm is a must-have package for the avid VRML Internet user and can be downloaded at: http://www.ids-net.com/ids/vrealm.html. Be aware, the compressed VREALM1A.EXE file is 2.0 megabytes, downloading can take up to 30 to 40 minutes depending on the speed of your modem.

Figure 3-32 shows a view of the included IDS office.wrl using VRealm navigator.

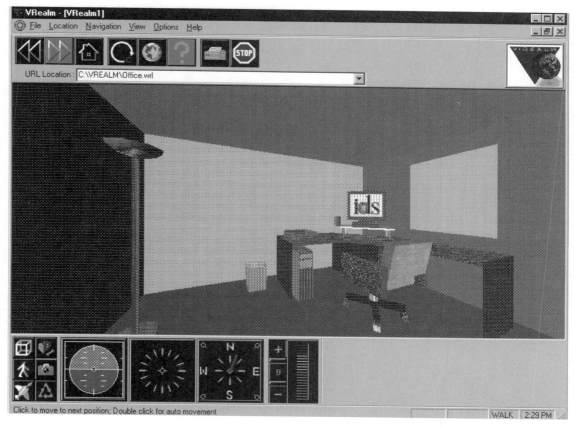

Figure 3-32
IDS Office.wrl using VRealm Navigator

VRML Equinox, Alpha Release (North Plains Systems, Inc.)

VRML Equinox is a VRML viewer for PowerPC Macintosh and supports the full set of VRML 1.0 specifications. VRML Equinox works as a plug-in for Netscape Navigator's Macintosh version and will display world files whenever Netscape points to one. VRML Equinox supported features are Shape Nodes (Cone, Cube, Cylinder, Sphere, etc.), Geometry/Material Nodes, Transformation Nodes, Lighting Nodes, and Group Nodes. VRML Equinox uses Apple's QuickDraw 3D technology that should be installed on the computer prior to using VRML Equinox. VRML Equinox can be downloaded at: http://www.ipsystems.com/nps/EquiInfo.html.

VRweb (IICM, NCSA, & Gopher Team)

VRweb is a powerful VRML viewer for Netscape Navigator and Mosaic and will run on a wide variety of hardware/software platforms (e.g., Windows 3.11, 95, NT, UNIX, SUN, DEC, AIX, and LINUX). VRweb's supported features are Group Nodes, Separators, Coordinates, Camera Angles, Texturing, Light Sources, and so on. Several navigational modes are also included, such as Flip Around, Walk Through, Fly-by Mode, and Head's-Up Mode. The VRweb team has also made available the source code for both UNIX and Windows versions of the program. VRweb can be downloaded at: http://www.iicm.tu-graz.ac.at/Cvrweb.

WebFX (Paper Software, Inc.)

WebFX is both a VRML viewer as well as a powerful Internet Explorer. It includes a wide variety of VRML tools as well as Internet navigational tools. Another feature that is included with WebFX is the 3D Internet Relay Chat (IRC-3D). VRML features included are VRML Authoring, Collision Detection, background rendering and parsing, GIF, BMP, RAS, RGB, and JPG Texture support, Multiple World Viewing, Lighting, Camera, Object Manipulation, and Multiple Nested Inlines Support. WebFX is available for Windows 3.1, 95, and NT. A Macintosh version will be available soon. WebFX can be downloaded at: http://www.paperinc.com/webfx.html.

WebFX is available as a Netscape add-in, taking most of the hassle out of installation. You just download WebFX, point it at your Netscape directory at installation, and sit back and relax. A *very* nice feature.

WebOOGL 2.0 (The Geometry Center)

WebOOGL (Web Object Oriented Graphics Language), is a quasi-compliant (according to the Geometry Center) VRML viewer. WebOOGL works on the Silicon Graphics and SUN platforms and will never be available for Windows and Macintosh based platforms. WebOOGL uses its own graphics libraries and not necessarily VRML libraries (for example, WebOOGL does not do textures, ASCII Text, or spotlight). WebOOGL can be downloaded at:

http://www.geom.umn.edu/software/weboogl.html.

WebSpace Navigator 1.1 (Silicon Graphics Computer Systems & Template Graphics Software)

WebSpace can be run as a stand-alone VRML browser, or as plug-in for Netscape Navigator. WebSpace is available for a wide variety of platforms, including SGI, Windows NT and 95, SUN Solaris and IBM AIX. WebSpace offers all conventional VRML specifications as well as some additional features. A new feature that is not seen in any other VRML browser is the rendering of the most important VRML object first, thus achieving a near constant frame update. You can already start navigating the world while it is still rendering. WebSpace offers Trackball and Joystick support, as well as detailed toolbar navigation support. WebSpace supports JPG, GIF, and RGB textures, and standard Internet browsing tools such as Open Location, Stop Loading, Reload, Goto Home Scene, Back, Forward, History, and View Source. Overall, WebSpace is a very powerful package and we recommend you add it to your VRML Browsing Programs library. You can download WebSpace Navigator at: http://www.sgi.com/Products/Web-FORCE/Webspace.html.

Figure 3-33 shows a view of SGI & TGS's WebSpace main screen, the image loaded is door.wrl.

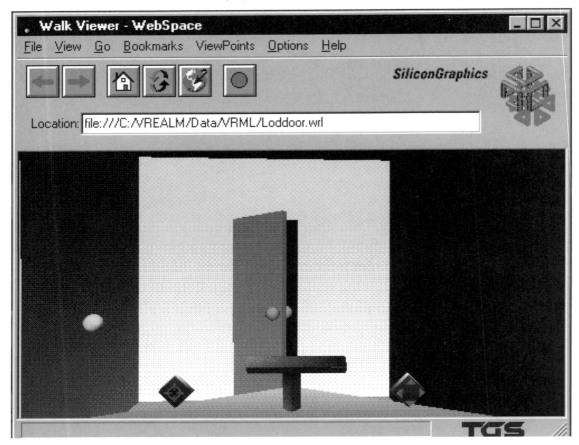

Figure 3-33
WebSace Main
Screen

WebView (San Diego Supercomputer Center)

WebView is a VRML browser for use with UNIX based computers.
WebView includes an integrated scene editor, multiple windows
viewing the same world and separate worlds at the same time, four
viewer styles (e.g., Examiner, Fly, Plane, Walk), and full source code.
WebView has been created as a public platform for the development
and testing of experimental additions to VRML. You can download
WebView at: http://www.sdsc.edu/EnablingTech/Visualization/
vrml/Webview.html

Whurlwind 3D Browser and Web Surfer (Bill Enright & John Louch)

Whurlwind 3D is a VRML browser and websurfer for use with PowerPC Macintosh computers using QuickDraw 3D. Whurlwind is still in its early days of development. Right now the application can view VRML scenes, change camera angles, and jump to other web sites. Future releases of the software will allow scene navigation as well as moving through and flying over 3-dimensional worlds.

At this time you are able to identify the minimum hardware and software components to successfully install Win32S (if necessary) and WorldView; and editing the files needed to run WorldView as a Netscape Navigator helper application. You will also be familiar with the common components implemented in the WorldView program and the features implemented with the program. You are also familiar with locating other VRML browsers on the Internet.

In the next chapter you will be putting this knowledge to active use on the Internet. You will learn how to locate world files and navigate through them using the Internet as your transport medium.

Chapter

4

Exploring
Virtual Worlds

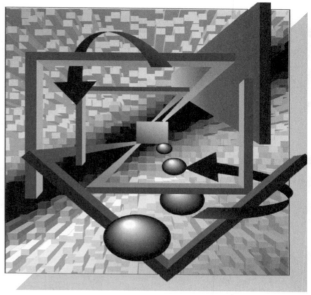

This chapter will introduce you to exploring virtual worlds on the Internet using a VRML browser. There are some important things to keep in mind when using a Web browser such as Netscape to explore these virtual worlds. This chapter will detail how you can more effectively locate VRML sites and resources on the Internet and navigate through them easily. The chapter will start with some simple VRML worlds and then explore some of the most complex VRML worlds on the Internet. Next, the practice of linking between virtual worlds is discussed, along with the possibility of *chatting* in real-time with other *virtual people* on the Internet. Finally, a list of great VRML sites on the Internet is included.

Introduction

In this chapter you will learn how to explore the World Wide Web and virtual worlds. You will be invited to visit sites that show and display virtual worlds, you will learn how to access virtual worlds and how to manipulate them. WorldView will be your tool for this excursion. However, you are not only limited to World-View. You may, of course, use different VRML browsers that have been discussed in the previous chapter. In this chapter you will notice many references to the words "cyberspace" and "Virtual Worlds". These words have been used before, without much of a definition or explanation. The following is a quick explanation of how these two words will be used in this chapter.

Cyberspace: is a virtual environment of the Internet. Cyberspace is the chaotic computer network that is called the Internet, thousands of computer servers and clients all interlinked by telephone lines and wide area networks. Most Internet users refer to the Internet as an actual environment or place where they can explore different areas and even manipulate them. Although these Internet sites are only a graphical representation of computer codes, HTML code (Hyper Text Mark-up Language), and, of course, VRML code sitting on a wide variety of computer servers around the world, they do give the Internet user the impression or feeling that they are actually visiting a place. Thus the word cyberspace is used to mean a world or place that exists out of the natural environment of everyday reality.

Virtual Worlds: are the actual VRML World representation in cyberspace. Virtual Worlds can actually be manipulated, moved through, flown over, and walked around. They are the actual graphical representation of something we could call a *cyberplace*. If we could write up the VRML code that would represent our computer laboratory, put it on one of our servers, and invite you to come by and visit us; you could (with a few clicks of a button) be standing in our computer laboratory. You would be able to see the computer we used to write this book. You could see our VRML server, and you might be lucky enough to catch the authors walking through the room. This is what we call a Virtual World.

Before Entering Cyberspace

Before entering cyberspace, you should be aware that the Internet contains a tremendous amount of information and sites you can access free of charge and on a unlimited basis. You can quickly jump from one site to another, unhindered and almost invisible. You might accidentally access sites that are inappropriate or offensive to some surfers. Our recommendation is: leave. The Internet is a world outside the world. It has all the advantages and disadvantages of our modern society in the physical world. A simple search on the Web for the term *VRML* can net up to a thousand or more entries all around the world. Practically all VRML sites you find with a search are legitimate VRML sites explaining everything from the VRML code to standards for Virtual Worlds. However, there are some people who will use a legitimate VRML site to lure you into areas where you might not want to be. If you feel that the site you are accessing is not what it is supposed to be, you should make a quick U-turn and go somewhere else. Unfortunately, there is nothing that can protect us from such sites except the user's discretion to leave.

Netscape Notes

The Netscape Communications Corporation's Netscape Browser will be the World Wide Web Browser we will use to start our exploration of cyberspace. However, you can use any World Wide Web browser you feel comfortable using. Netscape's Search Homepage offers a wide variety of search engines useful in locating great VRML sites. Netscape's newer versions will offer built-in VRML support for most VRML browsers and add-ins (Figure 4-1). For more information on locating, installing, and using Netscape, refer to Appendix A: Internet Browser Fundamentals.

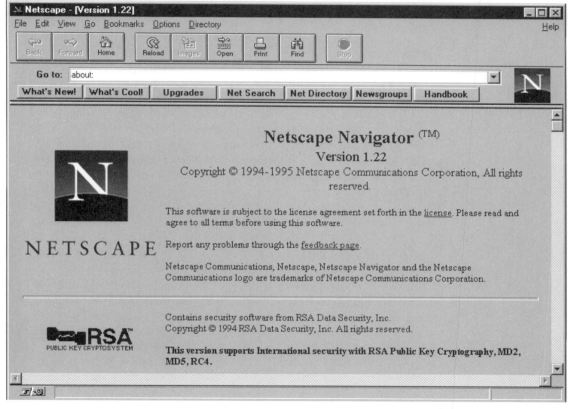

Figure 4-1
The Netscape "About" page

Netscape is a very powerful browser. It will allow you to find and see almost everything that you can find on the Internet. Many Internet sites are *Netscape enhanced,* which will give you the graphical interface appropriate for the site. You can find Netscape's homepage at: *http://home.netscape.com.* This will also be a site to download the newer versions of Netscape.

In the previous chapter you learned how to add-in the WorldView browser as a Netscape helper application. If you have not already done so, please refer to this chapter to find out how to do this. If you have not installed WorldView properly, WorldView might not work when you try to view Virtual Worlds on the Internet.

Exploring Cyberspace and Virtual Worlds

Now we are ready to enter the world of VRML in cyberspace. Double click on your TCP/IP (Transmission Control Protocol / Internet Protocol) dialer application and initiate a connection with your Internet Access Provider. Do not forget to fasten your seatbelt!

1. Entering Cyberspace

Once you have established a SLIP (Serial Link Interface Protocol) or PPP (Point to Point Protocol) connection with your Internet Service Provider, you can double-click on the Netscape Navigator icon and access Netscape Communications Corporation on the Internet (Figure 4-2).

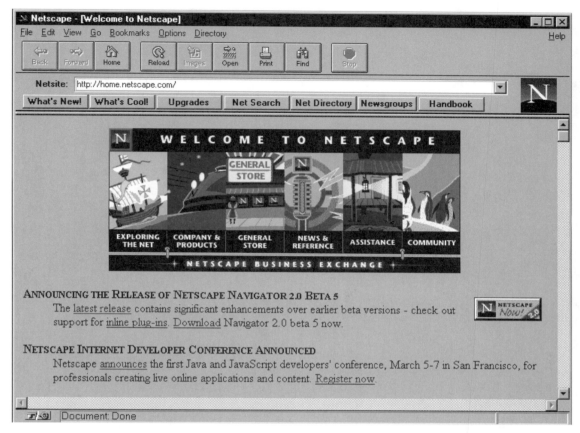

Figure 4-2
The Netscape
Navigator
Homepage

2. Finding VRML Resources on the Internet

The Netscape Explorer homepage allows you to perform several Internet functions to search the Internet for resources. In this case we will perform an Internet search for VRML resources on the Internet. Move your cursor to the *Net Search* button on the top middle of the browser and click it once (Figure 4-3). You will be able to perform a search by simply entering a keyword. In this case, we will use a wide search on the acronym VRML. Once you have entered the acronym in the provided space, press Search. You will find a wide variety of resources on VRML.

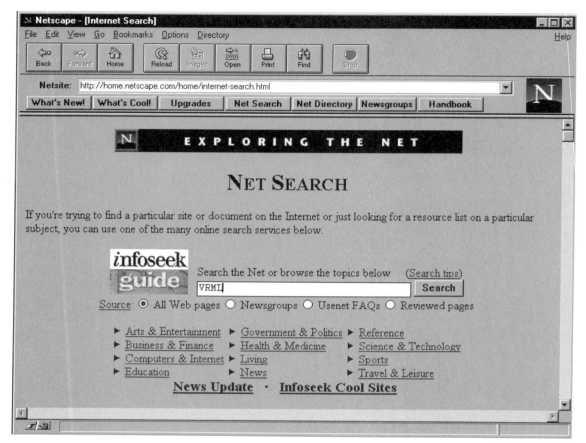

Figure 4-3
Netscape's search
page

You will notice that the Netscape will return with a *query result page* listing some hundred or so VRML resources on the Internet. All the sites are accessible by clicking on the blue hypertext words (Figure 4-4).

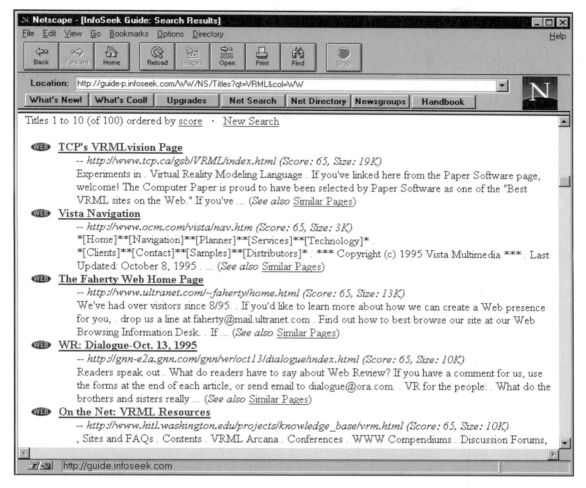

From here on, you can enter the world of VRML resources in cyberspace. By clicking on any of the hypertext words or sentences you will
automatically jump to the given VRML site. Nothing could be easier.

Figure 4-4
Sample Netscape
Search Results

Some Internet sites may take a long time loading up. If this happens, the site might have reached the maximum number of users,
or the server providing this site may not be active. You should
make note of the Internet address of this site and try it at a later
time or another day.

If you access a site that you find interesting and would like to explore
at a later date, you can add a *bookmark* to this site so you can access it

without noting down the Internet address. To do this you can click on "Bookmarks" on the top menu bar of Netscape and then click on Add Bookmark... You will see that the bookmark is added to the menu (Figure 4-5).

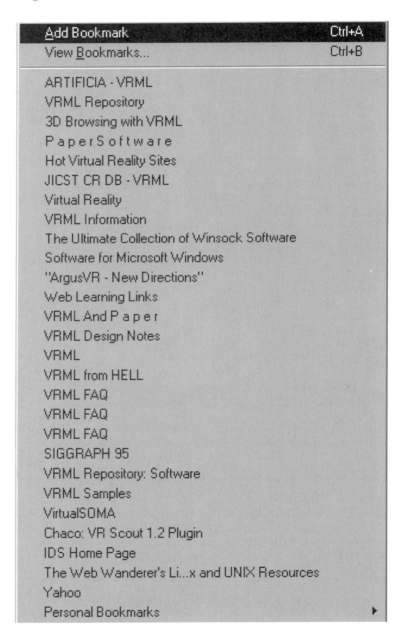

Figure 4-5
Netscape's
Bookmark Menu

When you add a bookmark, you should make sure that you add the actual main Web page of the site you are in, not a "sub-page" away from the homepage. Having the actual main page as a bookmark will leave you more pages to explore at a later time.

You can identify many professionally produced VRML pages by the official VRML logo (see Figure 4-6).

Figure 4-6
The Official VRML
Logo and Mark

Once you have located a Web page you think would be interesting for exploration, you can click on the hypertext link and be transported directly to the page you want. Many pages will have an index of resources offered at that Web site. For example, some of these resources might include VRML specifications, VRML software applications, repositories (where you can find world files to view), and so on. In the following figure, the browser has jumped to the http://www.sdsc.edu/vrml/ Web page, a major VRML site that offers a wide variety of resources (Figure 4-7).

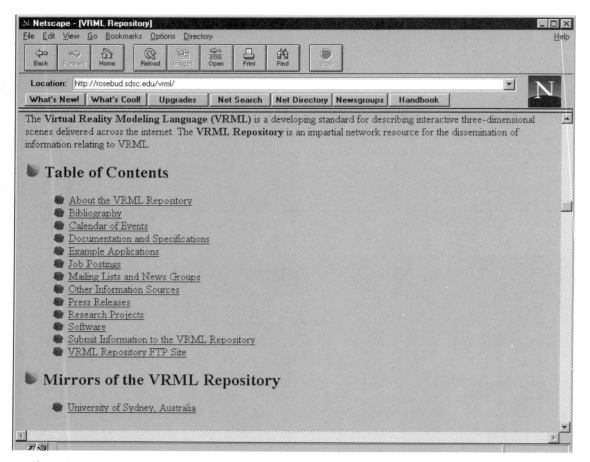

Figure 4-7
A VRML
Homepage on
the Internet

This particular site will allow you to jump to other VRML sites around
the world. It also is updated regularly with special events notifica-
tions, jobs in the VRML world, software sites, and so on. A neat feature is that you can actually submit your very own VRML worlds for
the rest of the world to see.

3. Exploring Virtual Worlds

Now we are ready to explore some virtual worlds on the Internet.
With your Netscape browser you can point to the following URL
(Universal Resource Locator): http://www.hitl.washington.edu/pro-
jects/knowledge_base/vrml.html (Figure 4-8).

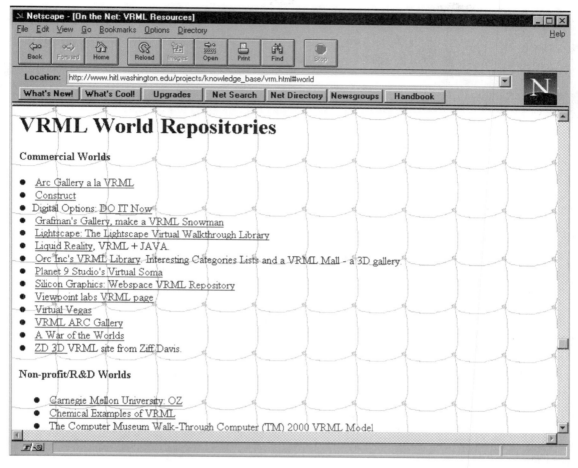

Figure 4-8
The On the Net:
VRML Resources
Homepage

This Internet page is one of the largest VRML site resource lists that you can find on the Internet. It has all links to hundreds of Internet sites worldwide for Virtual World exploration. And every page is merely a click of a mouse away. Just pick any page and click it once.

Commercial Internet sites may prompt you to become a member first before you can enter. This can sometimes involve money or a credit card number.

It is a good rule of thumb *never* to disclose your credit card numbers or for that matter *any* personal information over the Internet. Remember, the Internet is a very public place. It is easy for experienced computer hackers to eavesdrop on connections on the Internet. This rule generally does not apply to point-to-point dial-up links directly to the Internet service access provider, who often requires credit card information initially. But once on the Internet itself, be very careful.

Once you click on a site you will be transported through cyberspace to the designated VRML site. Once you have arrived at your destination you can click away freely to access Virtual Worlds (Figure 4-9).

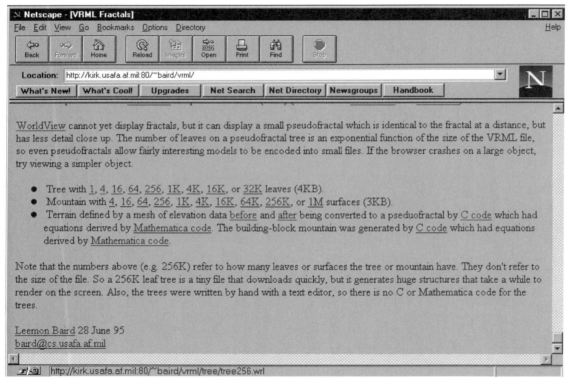

Figure 4-9
A Homepage with
Hypertext Links to
Virtual Worlds

For instance, at this site http://kirk.usafa.af.mil/~baird/vrml you can look at fractals (fractals are graphical representations derived from mathematical equations), with both the WorldView and WebSpace browsers.

Sometimes, once you have chosen the world you want to see you may notice this prompt (Figure 4-10):

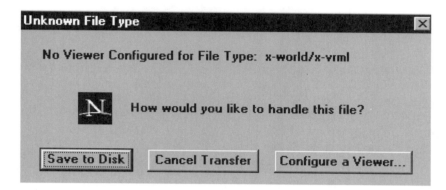

Figure 4-10
Netscape's Viewer
Configuration
Dialogue Box

This is a Netscape notification that the application (Netscape) is not properly configured for viewing of WRL files. Do not panic. At this point you can:

1. Save to Disk.

2. Cancel Transfer.

3. Configure a Viewer.

There are advantages to both 1 and/or 3. For example, if the file is large and will take a long time downloading, you may be better off saving the file to your hard disk and viewing it at your convenience. It will also decrease the amount of time you are on-line with your Internet provider and will decrease the access time cost. However, you may want to configure Netscape with the appropriate VRML browser/navigator application for future reference as well as actually walking through a Virtual World while you are *surfing* through cyberspace. Configuring a viewer will also allow you to view the world file before you save it to your hard disk.

Always check the files you have downloaded from the Internet for viruses. Even though World files cannot contain viruses, programs and files with the following extensions might: *.EXE, *.COM *.DLL. Some people find an incomprehensible pleasure in programming viruses that attach themselves to any program on the Internet that can destroy all the applications and data files of the unsuspecting Internet user. Make sure you have virus protection software on your computer, especially when accessing the Internet regularly.

To configure a VRML viewer at this point in Netscape, click on Configure a Viewer, and then click on Browse. Locate the VRML browser you want to view the WRL file with (it should be C:\WORLD-VIEW\WORLDVIEW.EXE if you installed it according to the directions in the previous chapter). Once you have located the VRML browser, just press OK (Figure 4-11).

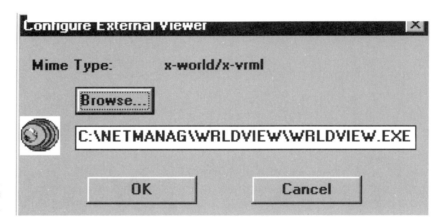

Figure 4-11
Simple
Configuration of
an External Viewer

As soon as you press OK the WRL file will load over the Internet connection. This may actually take from one minute to up to an hour depending on the complexity of the world you try to load (Figure 4-12).

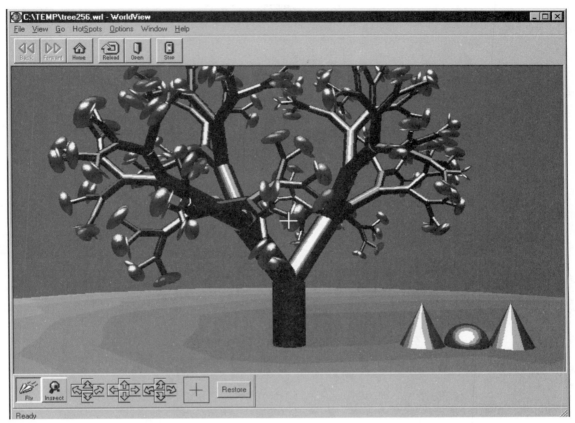

Manipulating Simple Objects in Cyberspace

Figure 4-12
A Fractral of a Tree
(Courtesy of Leemon
Baird's homepage)

There are many interesting and exciting objects you can manipulate and wonderful worlds you can navigate through on the Internet. However, you should be aware that the really great worlds are large and can take a tremendous amount of time parsing and rendering. (One world we downloaded, a virtual city, took our Pentium 100Mhz computer 4 hours to render—taking all Windows 95 processor resources into account). Be aware that your computer can lock-up and even *crash* on certain worlds.

It is therefore wise to start with simple worlds first. Many Web home-pages and sites that have VRML worlds for exploring also display the size of the world. Start with the smaller ones first to become familiar with navigation and fly modes of the WorldView program. Once you feel confident that you have mastered the WorldView program, you can venture to the more complicated worlds.

The following are some examples of simple worlds. These worlds will render quickly while you are connected to the Internet (see Figures 4-13 to 4-17).

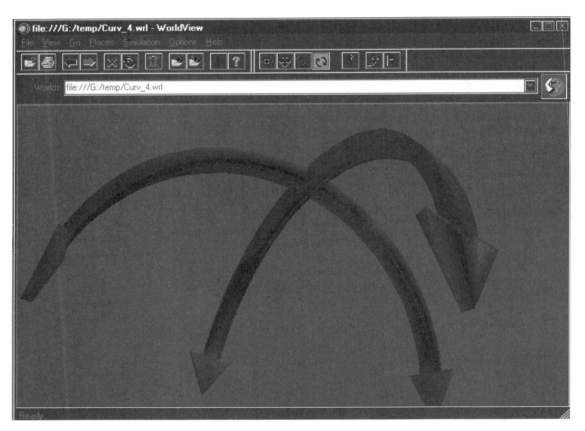

Figure 4-13
The Virtual Anchor

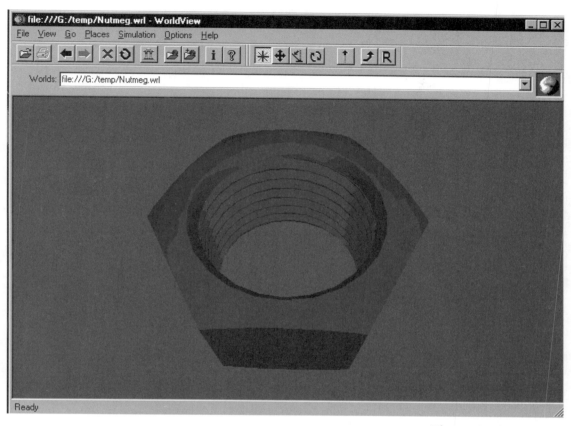

Figure 4-14
The Virtual Nutmeg

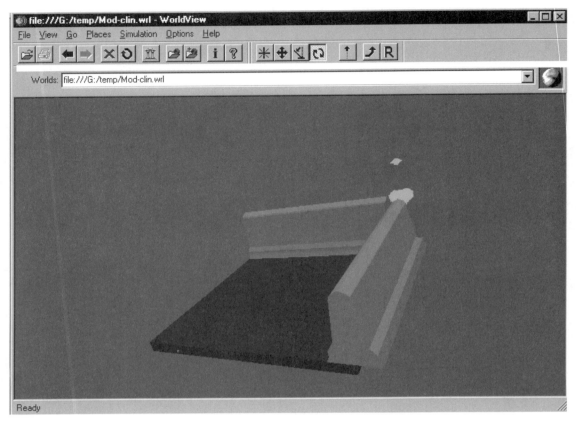

Figure 4-15
Another Virtual
Object

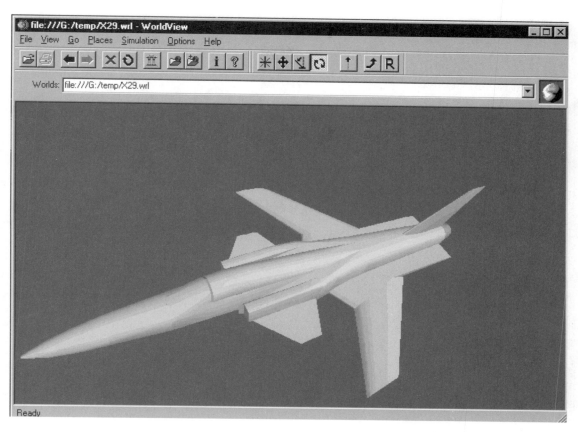

Figure 4-16
The Virtual X29 Fighter
Jet

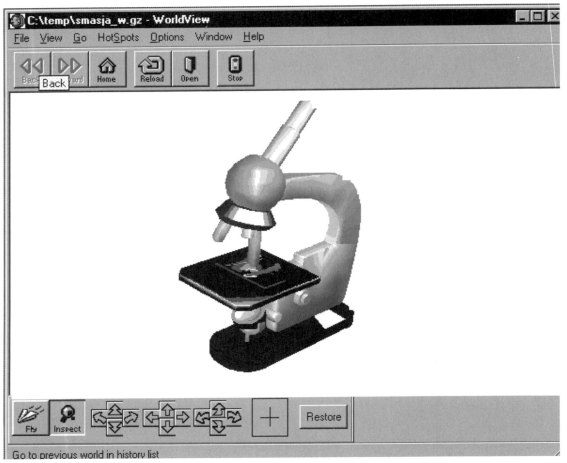

Figure 4-17
The Virtual
Microscope in
WorldView 0.9f

These example objects will allow you to become familiar with VRML quickly. They are simple yet sophisticated objects with many details to examine. When using WorldView to navigate through a world, it is recommended that you use the Inspect mode for navigation. This will allow you to approach the world from different angles and points-of-view. Even though WorldView defaults to Fly mode, you should use Inspect first.

Fly mode in any VRML browser can be tricky. If not used correctly, you can lose your world in the background. If that happens, quickly press Restore.

Once you are familiar with the inner workings of the WorldView program, you can venture out and navigate through Virtual Cities, Computers, Robots, and many more worlds in cyberspace.

Complicated Virtual Worlds

In the previous section you learned how to navigate through simple worlds. Now it is time to become familiar with the more sophisticated and complicated virtual worlds (see Figure 4-18).

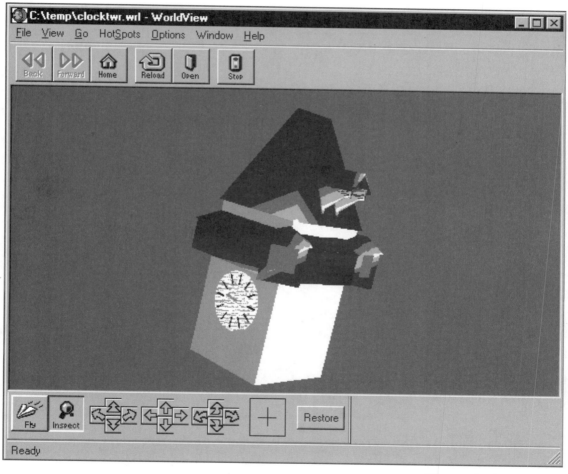

Figure 4-18
The Clock

Note

Some simple worlds can take a few minutes while they are down-loading to your computer. But it is not uncommon to have a wait-time of up to 30 minutes, or an hour, before the more complex worlds are fully downloaded and rendered.

By pressing the inspect button and navigating using the pointers and crosshair, you can look at this clock from many different angles (see Figure 4-19).

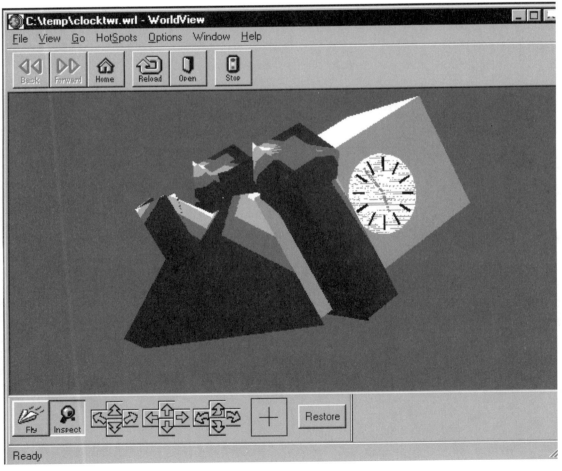

Figure 4-19
Manipulating the
Virtual Clock

You should also try to use the Special Effects features WorldView has to offer. Feel free to experiment with the world in any shape or form.

Here are some examples of the special effects. We are using a robot from the popular movie RoboCop as an example (see Figure 4-20).

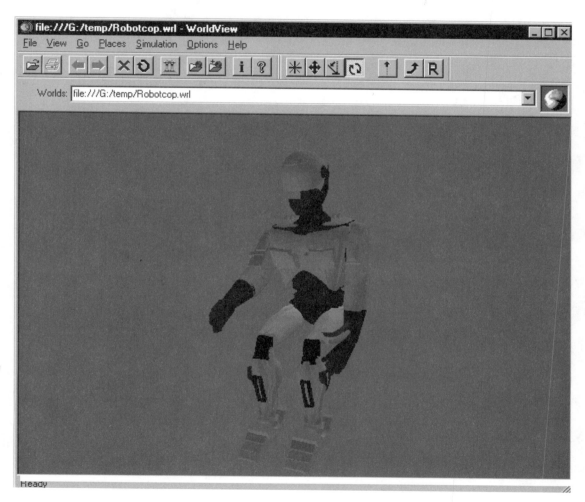

Figure 4-20
RoboCop

With Inspect mode you can move around the robot and view its many details (see Figure 4-21).

Figure 4-21
Manipulating the
Robot

You can also change the world by going to View on the main toolbar and click on WireFrame. You will now see how the robot was actually built in VRML (see Figure 4-22).

This is what the actual VRML code does: it interconnects many thousands of simple polygons to construct the World, or in this case, the skeleton of a robot.

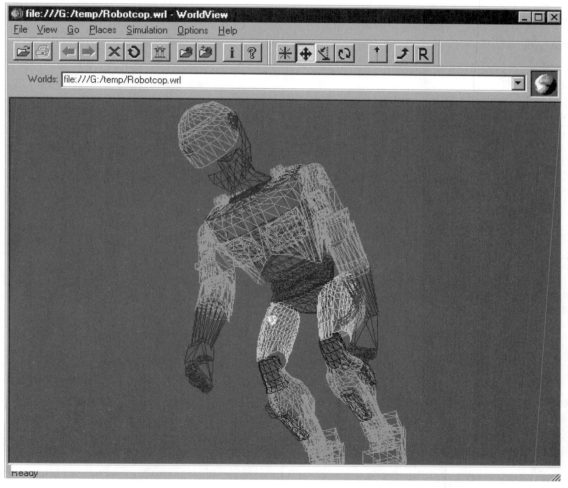

Figure 4-22
The Wireframe
Effect

By going to the toolbar again, you can now click on *Simulation,* and *Quality* and then *Good.* This will show the robot with less detail and fewer colors (see Figure 4-23).

There are two other special effects available in WorldView Version 0.9 for Windows 3.1 that are not available in the Windows 95 version. These are Gouraud and Phong shading. Gouraud is the WorldView default effect. Phong is very similar to Gouraud, the only difference is that it shines more than Gouraud does (Figure 4-24).

Figure 4-23
The Flat Effect

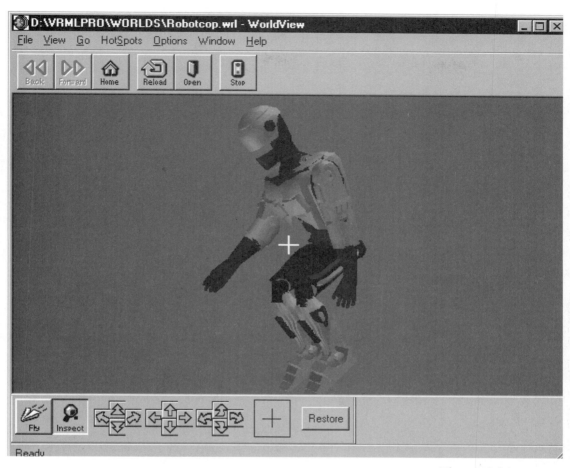

Figure 4-24
The Phong Effect

The potential of VRML is limitless. The code is fairly simple to write, and the world is only limited to what your imagination can do. The application of VRML has great potential. For example, imagine you want to go on vacation in a small city in the Netherlands called Wagenbos. However, having never been across the Atlantic you would want to find out what this city looks like. Imagine flying over the city right from the comfort of your own home or office (see Figure 4-25).

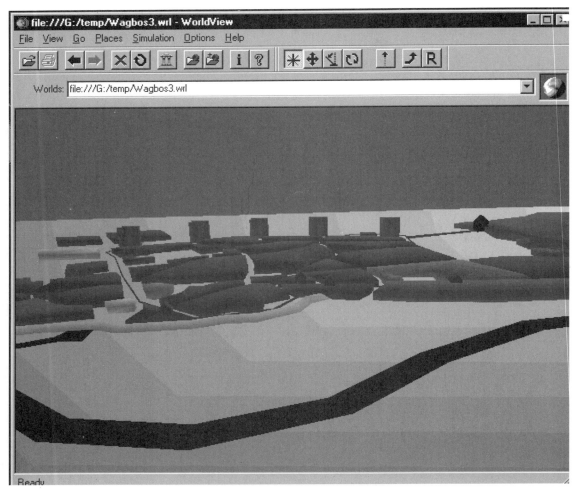

Figure 4-25
A Relaxed Fly-
over of the City
of Wagenbos

Currently, details in VRML are very hard to reproduce exactly. As
you can see (Figure 4-26), Wagenbos has no details concerning buildings, streets, or shopping centers. There are no people in the street.
However, VRML is only in its infancy; and just like any other computer application, VRML will grow to include these details and more.

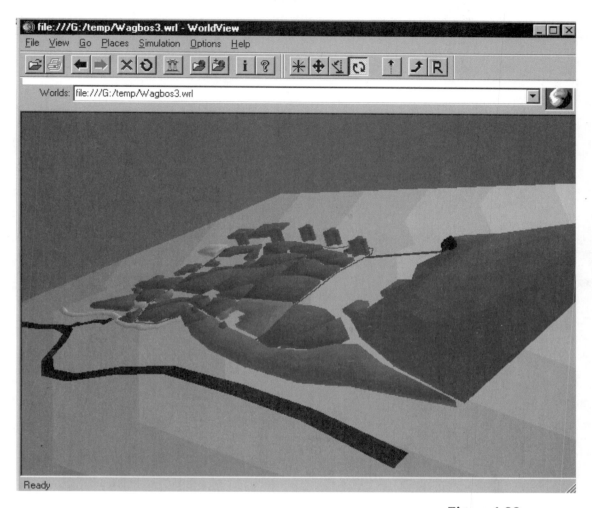

Figure 4-26
More Wagenbos
Sights

VRML will be used for many other real-life applications: medicine,
physics, sports, robotics, and many other applications. For example,
Real Estate! Visiting a house without leaving your own home (Figures 4-27 and 4-28).

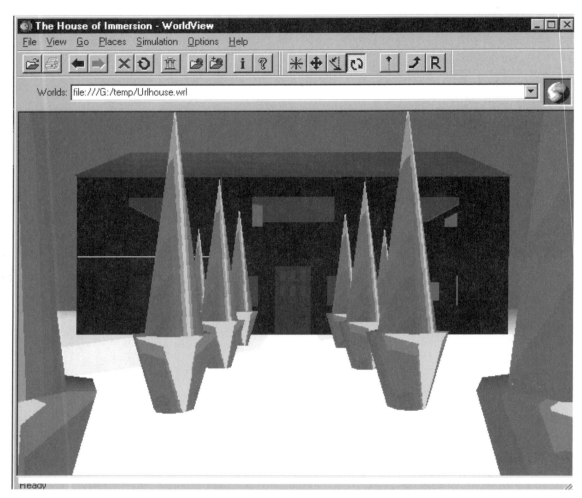

Figure 4-27
The Front Entrance
. . . The House
of Immersion

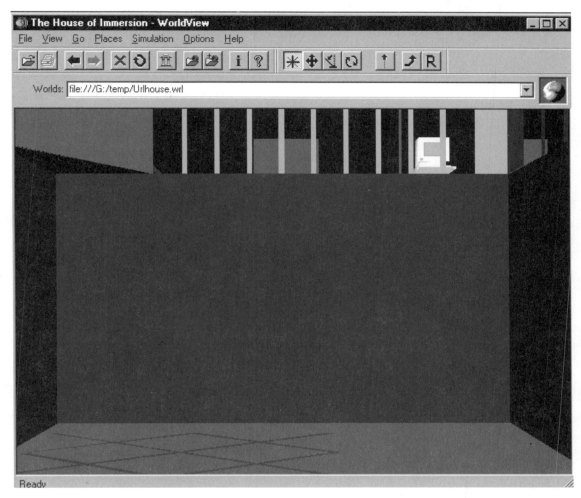

Figure 4-28
The House
of Immersion

We'll leave the rest of the exploration up to you.

VRML appears relatively simple when you read about it and see the pictures in this book. However, you should be aware that you may fail the first few attempts at downloading and looking at virtual worlds. Downloading is the most time-consuming area in VRML exploration. You may think that your computer is *hanging* or *crashing* while you attempt to download a world. However, most of the time, this is not the case. The WorldView software may just take a long time at rendering a complex world. One suggestion: don't give up! Cyberspace exploration is fun and exciting. If you give up easily, you will miss out on a whole *virtual* world of fun.

VRML resources on the Internet are growing tremendously. Day by day, hour by hour, more VRML sites are added to the Net. Great worlds can be downloaded and viewed. And many VRML sites have special projects involving VRML. For example, Intel Corporation has recently launched an "Interactive VRML adventure." Arm yourself with Netscape Navigator and your WorldView browser and check out the URL: http://www.intel.com/procs/homepc/vrml.html (see Figure 4-29).

Figure 4-29
Intel's VRML
Project

At the Intel site, click on *Review Episode 1*.

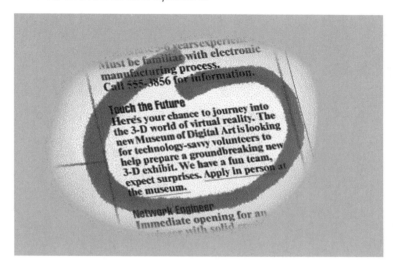

Figure 4-30
Follow the Add to
the World

To continue this adventure and proceed to the Museum of Digital Art, click on the newspaper (see Figure 4-31).

Figure 4-31
Entrance to the
Museum

To enter the Museum, click on *Welcome Volunteers* on the Information Booth. You are now asked if you have the tools for the job. These include a copy of Netscape Navigator, a VRML viewer, and a sound utility. Two of these you already have, and you can also download and install the sound utility. The Maintenance Engineer will now ask you to get the blueprints in the Museum (see Figure 4-32).

Figure 4-32
The Maintenance
Engineer

Click on the picture and prepare to enter into the Museum. But be aware, good navigation is the goal. Be prepared to fall over some items. Life is like that (see Figure 4-33).

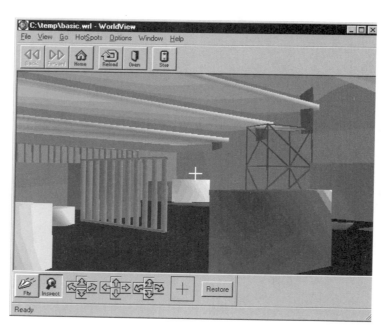

Figure 4-33
Inside the Museum

Enjoy the rest of the Adventure.

Linking to Other Worlds

One of the most interesting VRML features is that you can link to another world from within a world. You can see this, for example, when you launch WorldView. If you point to the turning globe with your mouse you will see that the **Intervista** Internet appears on the bottom left side of the program window (see Figure 4-34).

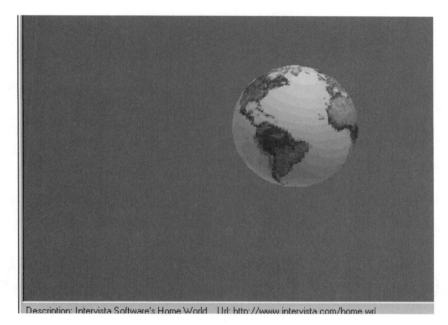

Description: Intervista Software's Home World Url: http://www.intervista.com/home.wrl

Figure 4-34
Linking Worlds

With this feature, VRML programmers can link dozens of Virtual worlds together over the Internet. In fact, the potential is so limitless that one could create an entire city with links to shops, hospitals, schools, libraries, movie theaters, and so on. Instead of calling the theater, you could jump into cyberspace and visit the theater and see what will be featured tonight.

There are already some linked worlds (virtual communities) on the Internet. One such project is "The Cave". The Cave can be found at the following URL:

> http://www.ncsa.uiuc.edu/General/VRML/ncsaApps.wrl, or
> at http://jaka.eecs.uic.edu/dav/vrml/cave.nongz

The Cave is a circle of doors where one can visit different locations. This is the view of the Cave.

Each door represents a link to another URL (Internet Address) or
VRML site/repository. However, instead of linking to a homepage,
the door links to another world. You will notice these links when you
move around within The Cave and touch the different portals (see
Figure 4-35).

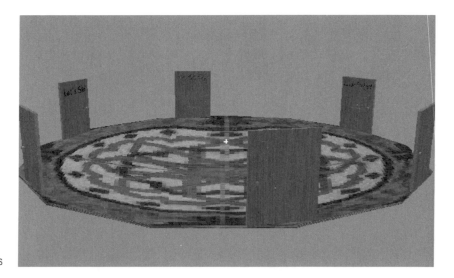

Figure 4-35
The Cave Doors

Figure 4-36
The Skiing Door

When you move the mouse over the door you will notice that the mouse arrow will change into a little hand, which means that you can push the left mouse button to go to the other side of the door. You will also notice that when you move the mouse over the door, the Internet address of the other world appears in the lower left corner of the WorldView program.

`Go to http://jaka.eecs.uic.edu/~pape/vrml/CAVE.nongz/ski_t.wrl`

Once you click on the door you will be transported to a ski resort.

Figure 4-37
Virtual Skiing

There are many linked virtual worlds on the Internet. However, some of them are a little difficult to access because they use a lot of memory and cache disk space. It is certain that with time and improvements to the VRML standard itself and efficiency techniques, the newer worlds will be lean in code and fast to load.

Another very interesting virtual world to visit is *Virtual Soma*. *Virtual Soma* is an entire city that links various sites together. Here is a preview . . . (see Figure 4-38)

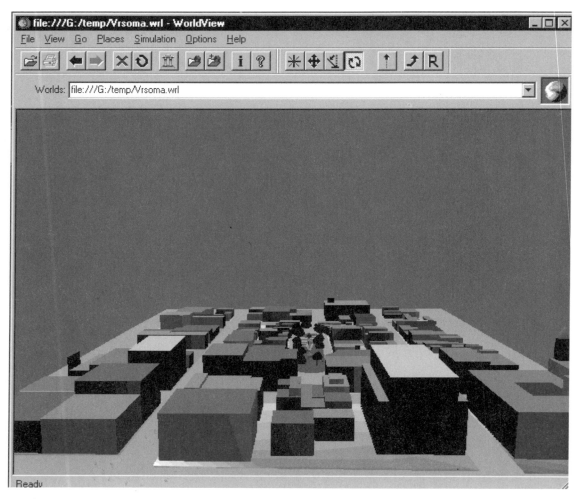

Figure 4-38
The Virtual Soma
City

Virtual Soma is a very interesting and complex world to navigate through. To access Virtual Soma on the Internet and explore the streets of soma, point your Netscape browser to the following URL: http://www.planet9.com.

Enjoy the excursion!

Figure 4-39
More Virtual Soma

Real-time Chatting with Virtual People on the Internet

This is all part of the moving illustration drawn by his computer according to specifications coming down the fiber-optic cable. The people are pieces of software called avatars. They are the audiovisual bodies that people use to communicate with each other in the Metaverse...Your avatar can look any way you want it to, up to the limitations of your equipment. If you're ugly, you can make your avatar beautiful. If you've just gotten out of bed, your avatar can still be wearing beautiful clothes and professionally applied makeup.

(Excerpt from Neal Stephenson's *Snow Crash*)

In the excerpt above, you can imagine a futuristic world where people create their own bodies, or avatars, to communicate with others in this place called the Metaverse. However, the notion is not at all futuristic. In fact, you can already communicate with people on the Internet, in real-time. This is called IRC, or Internet Relay Chat. But wouldn't it be kind of fun to see the person you are talking to, or just a personification of a body with a head that talks? This, in fact, exists. The Metaverse is the Internet. And you can find an avatar with an Internet software called Worlds Chat.

Worlds Chat is an IRC program in which you can pick out a virtual body to represent you on the Internet. Once you have chosen a body, or avatar, you can connect to the Worlds Chat IRC server and move through Virtual Worlds and talk to Virtual People. You can download Worlds Chat at the following URL: http://www.worlds.net.

The site *www.worlds.net* also has great VRML worlds to download; you should visit their main homepage.

Worlds Chat can perform very slowly on certain machines. Make sure you have adequate system resources and a fast modem.

This is the Worlds Chat main Avatar Gallery (see Figure 4-40). When you start Worlds Chat, you will automatically come here to pick out your avatar. You can choose between man, woman, child, object, or cartoon character.

Figure 4-40
World's Chat Avatar
Gallery

Take your time, there are enough avatars (see Figure 4-41). Make a good selection, this will be the avatar that will represent you in Cyberspace.

Figure 4-41
Browsing for a Body

Once you have chosen an avatar, you can click on *Embody Me!* and Worlds Chat will ask you to make up a *username* (this can be any name you choose) (see Figure 4-42).

Figure 4-42
Picking a Body

Once you have entered your username, you can click on *Enter Worlds Chat* and the program will connect to the Worlds Chat IRC server (see Figure 4-43).

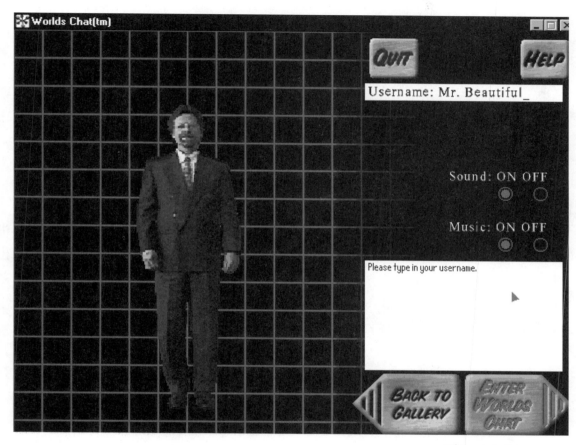

Figure 4-43
Assigning a Name to Your Body

Make sure you have an active Internet connection when you click on *Embody Me!* Worlds Chat will not run if you do not have an active connection.

This is the Worlds Chat main reception hall (see Figure 4-44). You can see there are already some people present. On the bottom right, you can see the actual representation of the building you are in. There are various chat rooms where you can go. Each sphere represents a chat room. The main square is the room we are currently located in.

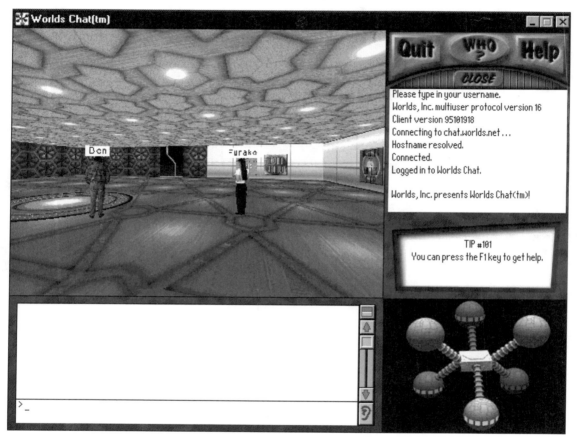

Figure 4-44
Inside World Chat

The Virtual World (or building) you are navigating through is very realistic. The walls are actually walls (see Figure 4-45). This means that you cannot go through them, such as in the conventional VRML worlds.

Figure 4-45
Navigating Through Worlds Chat's Chatrooms

Once you have met an avatar you want to talk with, you can simply point at them with the mouse and type your message in the space provided (see Figure 4-46).

Figure 4-46
Chatting with
Another Avatar

You should never, ever, give out private information. The same goes for insulting, obscene, or harassing messages. The messages you type can be seen by everybody. Beware the Telecommunications Act!

You will see that many avatars are the same as yours. If you want to be different, you can write your own avatar. Check out the Worlds Chat homepage for that information.

Great VRML Sites on the Internet

There are literally thousands of sites worldwide with information on VRML. You can find everything, from source code, to VRML specifications, software, worlds, and more links to other homepages. Here are some of the best VRML sites on the net.

http://www.intel.com/procs/homepc/vrml/2module

http://www.sdsc.edu/vrml

http://www.construct.net/worlds

http://www.chaco.com/vrml

http://www.zdnet.com/~zdi/vrml

http://www.ocnus.com/models

ftp://ftp.vrml.org/pub

http://www.geom.umn.edu/~daeron/objects

http://www.gwha.com/~jym

http://www-dsed.llnl.gov/documents

http://hyperreal.com/~mpesce/samhain/wrl

http://www.vrml.org/vrml/solids

http://jaka.eecs.uic.edu/dave/vrml/CAVE

http://andante.iss.uw.edu.pl/viso/vrml

http://www-ci.u-aizu.ac.jp/VRML

http://www.geom.umn.edu/~daeron/objects

http://bellatrix.pcl.ox.ac.uk/people/alan/WebSpace/builder

http://vrml.arc.org/gallery95

http://www.everyday.se/hem/zcentral/vrml

http://amber.rc.arizona.edu/vrml

http://reality.sgi.com/employees/robinh/Models

http://amber.rc.arizona.edu/vrml

http://www.next.com.au/vrml

http://www.us.paragraph.com/3Dsite/vrml

http://www.eye.com/event

http://dirac.bcm.tmc.edu

http://www.demon.co.uk/presence/vrml

http://www.hookup.net/~dave

http://www.mcp.com/people/mhughes/vrml

http://www.transend.com.tw/~rmm/vrml

http://vbn.com/~midinet/vrml

http://www.mcp.com/people/mhughes/vrml

http://w3.one.net/~willb/tricks

http://www.slip.net/~rhenry

http://coney.gsfc.nasa.gov/~mathews/Objects

http://www.virtpark.com/theme

http://www.well.com/user/spidaman/vrml

http://www.dgsys.com/~aihf

http://www.caligari.com/ftp/pub/fountain/contrib

http://www.nist.gov/itl/div878/ovrt/projects/vrml

http://www.eden.com/~etrigan/3d

http://expert.cc.purdue.edu/~gehowell/WRLDS

http://www.paperinc.com/vrml/models

http://www.swf3.de/nachtfieber/pics

http://www.bergen.gov/Statistics

http://tcc.iz.net

http://www.oz.nthu.edu.tw/~g843803

http://www3.ios.com/~rwcsj19

http://www.hyperion.com/planet9/worlds

http://speckle.ncsl.nist.gov/~gseidman/cybersaw

http://www.chemie.fu-berlin.de/~sunny

http://www.rust.net/~stanley/vrml

http://www.biba.uni-bremen.de/docs/users/bau

http://www.public.iastate.edu/~doctor42/

http://k12.colostate.edu/~jessed

http://www.penncen.com/yaz

http://w3.one.net/~willb/tricks

http://www.oz.is/OZ-Interactive

http://www.ch.ic.ac.uk/VRML

http://www.tcm.org/tcm/vrml

http://www.t0.or.at/escape.htm#vrml

http://www.nist.gov/itl/div878/ovrt/projects/vrml

http://www.neuro.sfc.keio.ac.jp/~aly/polygon/vrml/ika

http://kufacts.cc.ukans.edu/~mreaney

http://www.geom.umn.edu:80/software/weboogl

http://ws05.pc.chemie.th-darmstadt.de/vrml

http://nssdc.gsfc.nasa.gov/cohoweb/vrml

http://www.ar.utexas.edu/centrifuge

http://www.utirc.utoronto.ca/AdTech/rd

http://jaka.eecs.uic.edu/dave/vrml/CAVE

http://www.gsaup.ucla.edu:80/vrml

It is pretty much impossible to list all the VRML sites. The Internet is an ever-changing, ever-moving environment. By the time you read this book, some sites may have changed or moved to another location. Your best bet to find great VRML sites is to do an Internet search on the keyword VRML.

To get the maximum amount of information, you should use the powerful Digital Search Engine. You can use this search engine by going to the following URL: http://www.altavista.digital.com. But even a simple search on the word VRML can land up to 100,000 entries.

Some other powerful search engines on the Internet include:

http://www.excite.com

http://www.yahoo.com

http://www.lycos.com

You can try each one of these and see if they give you the desired results.

This chapter has given you a whirlwind, hands-on tour of some of the possibilities found in virtual worlds on the Internet. But just what is it that creates all this content in 3D rather than 2D? Perhaps the time has come to take a look at the VRML language itself.

Chapter

5

An Introduction to the VRML Language

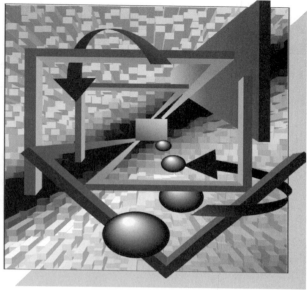

Computers have languages just as humans have languages. Humans use languages to communicate with each other, and so do computers. The information content that human languages express include things like greetings and salutations, complaints and compliments, and so on. The only human language requirement for conveying this information is that the speaker (source) and the listener (destination) understand the same language used for this information transfer. Any frustrated traveler knows that it is not easy to express themselves in a situation where the sender is capable of sending only English and the destination is capable of receiving only French.

Computer languages are much simpler in both form and content compared to their human counterparts. Computer languages are strictly formalized, meaning there is a written description of the language in a document somewhere that lets everyone who reads it know exactly what the computer language is for and how to express information content in the given language.

The information content expressed is much more modest in computer languages than in human languages. Computer languages are specialized in purpose. Some exist solely to describe mathematical formula (FORTRAN), others to be easy to learn and use (BASIC), and still others to enable page-formatting information to be passed from one computer to another over a network such as the Internet so that both graphics and text are presented uniformly to the user (HTML). Some of these languages require special compilers and are intended to produce executable code that can run directly on the computer. Other languages are intended to represent data in a standard way and do not need to be compiled or executed directly (VRML and HTML are examples of this type of language). All are characterized by the two aspects of formalization and specialization.

The VRML Language

VRML itself is a language created for the transfer of information about a virtual reality scene from a source computer (the server) to a destination computer (the client). Usually this transfer involves a network like the Internet, but other networks may be used, such as private corporate networks using Novell Netware or even IBM SNA networks. The network itself is not the essential element, but the source and destination computers are. In fact, a computer can use the VRML language internally, meaning that a VRML world can exist on the local PC hard drive (still the source) and the user may view the VRML world on the local PC monitor (still the destination) without a network at all. This is actually an advantage, and gives users the opportunity to build, test, and access virtual worlds without the constant availability and associated expense of a computer network. Of course, all of the example worlds in this book can be accessed without a computer network.

Think of VRML as a specialized and formalized language that allows the destination computer to build (*render* in VRML talk) a virtual world that is identical to the one that the virtual world developer envisioned when the world was designed on the source computer. The VRML language is a series of instructions sent over the network as a plain, ASCII text file to direct and guides the destination computer in this task. Like all computer languages, the source and destination computer programs must both understand what the instructions represent, and VRML is no exception. Exactly what is allowed and what is forbidden in VRML, and the format of VRML instructions, is described in the formal VRML specification.

The origins of the VRML language are interesting for several reasons, not least because the VRML specification was developed very rapidly and was quickly accepted as the desired standard for virtual worlds on the Internet. Computer language and network developers can be a contentious group, and quick agreement and specification writing can be a long, drawn out, and tedious process. The swiftness with which VRML has matured is a good measurement of the popularity of virtual worlds on the Internet.

VRML as an idea for a separate language was born in the spring of 1994, at the very first annual World Wide Web Conference held in

Geneva, Switzerland, birthplace of the World Wide Web itself. Right from the start, several participants expressed an interest in developing virtual reality interfaces to the World Wide Web. In fact, several projects along those lines were already underway, and a so-called "birds-of-a-feather" session was quickly organized within the conference itself to encourage the exchange of ideas among these participants.

The first thing agreed upon was the need for a common language for virtual reality on the Web, in the same way that HTML formed a common language for designing individual "home pages" on the Web. This way, no matter what the source computer platform, a UNIX-based workstation, an IBM-architected PC, or an Apple Macintosh, all destination computers would be able to render the virtual reality scene, as long as these server and user client computers all consistently used and understood the common language.

The original name proposed for this common language was *Virtual Reality Markup Language* (VRML) by direct extension from the *Hypertext Markup Language* (HTML) already in use for the Web. The term "markup" was soon changed to "modeling" to reflect both the complexity of VRML (much more than a simple editing red-line "markup" of a printed page) and the graphical nature of VRML (these worlds were a "model" of reality). The group left the conference determined to produce a Virtual Reality Modeling Language (VRML) specification as soon as possible.

Interest in the work of the VRML group was staggering. Within seven days, over one thousand people had expressed an interest in VRML by registering for an Internet electronic mail distribution list dedicated to the topic. The VRML mailing list enabled all interested parties to track the progress of individual members of the group and participate in discussions remotely via electronic mail.

The VRML group quickly decided that a preliminary VRML language specification should be ready for the next WWW conference in the Fall of 1994. While not impossible, the schedule essentially precluded any effort to come up with a virtual reality language from scratch. Accordingly, the group looked around for a virtual reality graphical description language that was stable, relatively bug-free, and (most importantly) worked well.

The VRML group eventually settled on the Open Inventor ASCII file format from Silicon Graphics Incorporated (SGI), an already respected graphics company made famous by the film *Jurassic Park* (all the computers in the movie were real, working SGI workstations) that was participating in the VRML group's activities. Open Inventor had many attractive features from a VRML standpoint. The file format included elements for specifying lighting, camera viewpoints, material textures, and other features that made for the rendering of extremely realistic scenes. There was an additional plus as well: SGI quickly put the Open Inventor file format into the public domain, meaning that anyone could freely use it without owing SGI any money or infringing on any SGI copyrights or intellectual property restrictions.

Silicon Graphics' Open Inventor ASCII File Format.

The SGI Open Inventor file format was first released in July 1992. It was designed to make the exchange of 3D modeling information between different software applications easier. With Open Inventor, two 3D modeling programs using different file formats to express modeling information could still inter-operate by exchanging the information with Open Inventor, the common format between them.

Open Inventor has been used by CAD, chemistry, financial data, scientific visualization, art history, presentation, architecture, animation, and other programs requiring 3D graphical representations of information. The very success of Open Inventor and its widespread acceptance was a point in favor of making Open Inventor the basis of VRML.

The original Open Inventor file format was created as part of the IRIS Inventor 3D Toolkit, an object-oriented 3D class library for the C and C++ languages, that enabled programmers to more easily write interactive programs with 3D graphics in them. Not only SGI products like Showcase and Explorer Scientific Visualization System use Open Inventor, but others like Industrial Light and Magic's animation system and Parametric Technology (among many others) use the Open Inventor File Format as well.

In a very real sense, VRML is a subset of the full Open Inventor ASCII File Format, with added networking elements and Web hypertext link extensions. The hypertext links are used to link documents together across the Web by specifying a URL for the Web browser to link to. These URLs may also be embedded into virtual worlds built with VRML to allow the same type of linking as on HTML Web pages.

The first version of VRML (VRML 1.0) was designed with three main goals. First, the VRML language had to be "platform independent." That is, VRML had to work on UNIX workstations, Windows PCs, and Apple Macintosh architectures equally well. Second, the VRML language had to be "extensible." This means that the VRML 1.0 language could be added to in the future without much of a problem. Since VRML was only a subset of the full Open Inventor language, this was definitely a good plan. Lastly, the VRML language had to work well on low-speed, dial-up connections, the type that most users have to access the Internet and use with their Web browsers.

This last design goal was essential. Many users consider their new 28.8 Kbps V.34 modems to be the state-of-the-art when it comes to speed. And this is true if the discussion is limited to equipment that works over dial-up, analog telephone lines that the vast majority of users have in their homes and offices. But modems that transfer data at 28,800 bits per second are considered to be "low-speed" in many business and academic environments, where for years the network speeds on digital links have started out at 64,000 bits per second (64 Kbps) and gone upwards into the megabit per second range (usually 1.544 Mbps), more than 50 times faster than a 28.8 Kbps analog modem.

Even with modestly sized VRML files, analog modems can be very slow to render scenes over the Internet. VRML will more than likely push the demand for bandwidth to the home PC to greater heights than ever before. Fortunately, an alternative to analog modems exists, known as ISDN (Integrated Services Digital Network). But ISDN may not be within the financial reach of many Web users today.

ISDN (Integrated Services Digital Network) and VRML

ISDN uses the same type of telephone wires as an analog modem but can deliver data 8 to 10 times faster. How? ISDN uses digital technology rather than analog to achieve transfer rates at 64,000 bits per second (64 Kbps) and above. Businesses have been using ISDN for years to build commercial data networks. Unfortunately, ISDN is not available in all areas (call your local telephone company), can be expensive (many telephone companies do not have low residential rates), and the regular serial port and modem on your PC will not work with ISDN. Special interface equipment, also rather expensive ($ 300-400), is needed for ISDN. But the end result, if affordable, is a very fast link for exploring virtual worlds.

Remember that VRML started out as an idea to extend the Web into virtual reality. The standard language of the World Wide Web, HTML, was already widely accepted and supported for formatting text-based information on the Web. The temptation was to start with HTML and just extend it for VRML capabilities, whether these extensions were based on SGI Open Inventor or not. This approach was rejected for a couple of reasons. First, HTML was "optimized for" (designed to work best with) textual information, not 3D graphics.

Second, the HTML language had its own group of specialists working on additions to this language independent of any VRML considerations. It was felt that adding VRML to HTML would only slow down the work of both groups. Lastly, the differences in the way that VRML sources would behave in serving up virtual worlds made the separation between HTML and VRML an important one, and not just a matter of philosophy.

How VRML Works

So the next generation of Web activity will not just involve the examination of simple text pages on the Internet. The next generation will involve not the creation and visiting of Home Pages on the Web, but the creation and exploration of *home spaces:* three-dimensional virtual reality-based *places* that can be walked around or flown through, rotated or approached, and still used for hypertext links and in-line images.

As mentioned above, the language of these new virtual worlds is not HTML but VRML (Virtual Reality Modeling Language). The purpose and use of these two languages are similar: they are both intended as ASCII-text descriptions of content that are sent between a Web site server and a browser (the client). In the case of HTML, the content described includes text formatting (<STRONG>) and layout (<IMG SRC=>) information.

In the case of VRML, the content described is almost entirely visual (the use of text in the virtual world of cyberspace is frowned upon given the international flavor of the Internet today). VRML concerns itself with things like initial point of view (PerspectiveCamera), lighting (DirectionalLight), and of course the actual objects in the scene (cube, sphere, etc.). The whole point is to describe the three-dimensional layout, look, and feel of the space to the VRML browser. Subtle changes in lighting and camera perspective can radically alter the mood of a place in VRML from warm, roomy, and inviting to cold, claustrophobic, and downright spooky.

However, such power is not granted without a price. While HTML, even in its most elaborate forms and extensions, remains fairly straightforward and easy to learn and use in an hour or so (much to the relief of more technically challenged Home Page builders), VRML remains much more complex and still more like a programming language than anything else.

For instance, the Web page shown in Figure 5-1 was produced entirely with the simple HTML file shown in Figure 5-2. Even relatively simple 3D scenes rendered with VRML must be represented with pages and pages of complex ASCII text commands formatted in VRML.

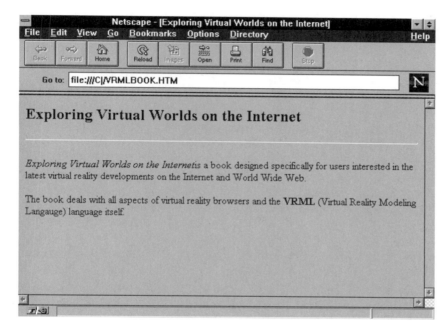

Figure 5-1
A Typical Web Page

```
<html>
<head>
<title>
Exploring Virtual Worlds on the Internet
</title>
</head>
<!- this is a comment ->
<body>
<h2>Exploring Virtual Worlds on the Internet</h2>
<hr>
<p><em>Exploring Virtual Worlds on the Internet</em> is a book designed
specifically for users interested in the latest virtual reality develop-
ments on the Internet and World Wide Web.</p>
<p>The book deals with all aspects of virtual reality browsers and the
<strong>VRML</strong> (Virtual Reality Modeling Langauge) language itself.
</p>
<address>

</address>
</body>
</html>
```

Figure 5-2
The HTML for
the VRML Book
Homepage

The size and complexity of VRML files is not necessarily a bad thing, but it means that VRML can be enormously cryptic to those ready to begin building Home Space add-ons to or replacements for their Home Pages. Almost anyone can be an HTML developer with a little patience. Developing spaces and whole virtual worlds with VRML will be much more of a challenge.

This means that there will be a vast market for VRML development tools, and indeed several exist already, such as Virtus WalkThrough and Caligari's worldSpace. But there are always those who will ask themselves, "just what are those tools doing when they create this perfectly incomprehensible ASCII-text VRML document?" This chapter is intended to answer this question briefly and simply.

The VRML language specification was developed by Tony Parisi of Intervista, Mark Pesce, and Gavin Bell of Silicon Graphics. VRML is based on a subset of the full Silicon Graphics Open Inventor graphics description language. Although the specification makes absolute sense to anyone with a graphics background or experience, reading the specification to learn VRML is about as useful an activity for those without the necessary skills as reading a foreign dictionary to learn a foreign language. The problem with specifications in general is that they are all-inclusive and usually lack any sense at all of what features are used all the time and that are hardly ever seen or used except in very special situations.

Here is an actual definition of a particular node type taken directly from the VRML specification:

Rotation

This node defines a 3D rotation about an arbitrary axis through the origin. The rotation is accumulated into the current transformation, which is applied to subsequent shapes:

```
FILE FORMAT/DEFAULTS

      Rotation {

                  rotation 0 0 1 0 # SFRotation

            }
```

(This is all quite clear to those with a 3D or graphics background, but not much help to anyone else.)

VRML in Action

It always helps to remember that VRML describes a three-dimensional space and not a two-dimensional page. So all VRML objects are laid out along an x, y, and z axis, just like in high school. This is known as the "Cartesian, right-handed, three-dimensional coordinate system" in VRML. "Cartesian" means (among other things) that there is both a plus and minus direction on an axis. "Right-handed" means that if your right index finger is pointing to the right (the positive x direction), your vertically held thumb points in the positive y direction (up) and your angled other fingers point in the positive z direction (into the screen). "Three-dimensional" just means there is an x, y, and z axis, and "coordinate" just means that any point in this space is fully described by three numbers (position along the x, y, and z axes).

The x, y, and z axes in VRML are related as shown in Figure 5-3.

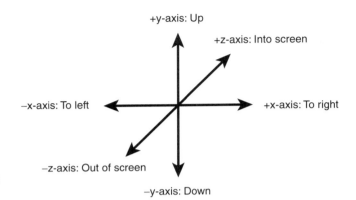

Figure 5-3
The VRML Axis
Orientations

All VRML objects are placed into this coordinate system by one of two major methods: pre-defined shapes and "point clouds." This chapter will consider the use of pre-defined shapes first. Point clouds will be considered later on in the chapter.

Building Virtual Worlds With Pre-defined Shapes

The VRML language itself contains a number of basic shapes that can be used in a VRML document to build up virtual spaces and worlds. For instance, there are cubes, spheres, and cones that can be easily inserted into a VRML document by basically just specifying a size and position (in x-y-z-space) for the object.

Figure 5-4 shows an example VRML document that defines a simple cube in the VRML space. The file is called "cube1.wrl". All VRML compliant documents must end with the .wrl (world) extension because all browsers do not have a clue about file contents or format aside from the file extension. The resulting cube ($2 \times 2 \times 2$) is centered on the 0,0,0 point and extends 1 unit along each axis.

```
#VRML V1.0 ascii


DEF myfirstthing Separator {
    Cube {                          # make a cube
            width 2
            height 2
            depth 2
    }
}
```

Figure 5-4
A Simple VRML
World

The .wrl file can be produced with any ASCII-based text editor, and even many regular word processing software application packages such as WordPerfect or Word for Windows. The cube produced by the VRML above can be viewed by any VRML browser. The cube is shown in Figure 5-5.

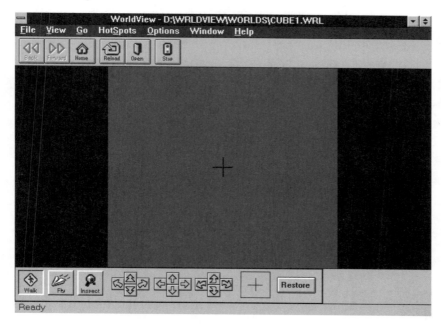

Figure 5-5
A Big Green Cube

Be very careful using word processing packages such as WordPerfect or Word for Windows to create or modify VRML documents, including the ones in this book. These packages regularly insert various control characters (such as "TAB" or "INDENT") into a document to produce the text formatting on the screen and printer. These are usually invisible to the user, but they are there nonetheless. Make sure the .wrl file contains *only* ASCII new line characters and no formatting control characters. All word processing packages allow users to save documents as plain, ASCII .txt files without formatting control characters. Make sure that you save your virtual world files in this format, even though the file extension is ".wrl".

Those familiar with HTML may notice that in VRML there are no < and > brackets. Instead, there are the VRML { and } (curly braces). Also, in VRML, the curly braces are "nested" one inside the other much more deeply than the brackets of HTML. And VRML world writers seldom worry about lining up nested braces in the same columns, as programmers have become accustomed to doing. This often makes it difficult to figure out exactly which { goes with which }.

One reason that knowing which braces belong together is important has to do with the way the most VRML browsers handle error conditions. Errors can arise in VRML documents in a number of ways, but the most common way when building VRML worlds by hand is simply by way of a typo. For instance, if a space is inadvertently inserted between the # (pound sign) and the VRML in the first line of a VRML document, then the browser will put an error message on the screen instead of a cube or other shape.

So far there is no problem. But VRML follows the lead of HTML when dealing with most other, and less obvious error conditions. That is, VRML, like HTML before it, simply ignores most statements that are in error. The VRML browser usually does not generate an error message for every error, like a programming language compiler, but renders a scene without the objects that contain the error. Sometimes the error results in a misshapen object that looks nothing like what was intended by the designer. The whole point is that VRML designers must be very careful of errors and test their worlds often as they are being built.

A valid VRML document must consist of at least one line: the initial "#VRML V1.0 ascii" string (there is no space between the # and VRML). In fact, this one line in a .wrl file is a completely valid VRML space that will launch a VRML browser to parse the file and fire up the rendering process to yield—nothing. The initial "#VRML V1.0 ascii" line has created the space, but there is nothing inside the space yet.

Tip

Think of the space created by the initial "#VRML V1.0 ascii" string as an empty stage. All the elements are there to put on a play, but the scenery is not in place yet. The rest of the VRML document, of course, will detail exactly what objects will appear and where these objects will be placed.

In subsequent lines, the # character is considered to initiate a comment, and all subsequent text is ignored by the browser until the beginning of the next line. In the above example "# make a cube" is a comment, not a VRML statement. The exception, of course, is the first line, which is not ignored and must appear as above.

To place a cube into cyberspace, more is needed beside the initial line, but not much. All VRML documents consist of none (as mentioned above) or more "nodes." Nodes are just the objects, but the term *object* has other meanings in computer science (as in object-oriented programming), so the term *node* is used. Nodes are collected into hierarchies called *scene graphs,* but the simple examples here consist of single objects only. In a very real sense, a VRML document is just a text description of the objects (or rather nodes) in a scene and the relationships between them.

All nodes in a VRML world have four main characteristics: a name, a type, a field, and children. *Children* are nodes themselves, and only "group nodes" are allowed to have *child* nodes. These are not considered further. Instead, the three remaining characteristics are examined more fully.

The relationship of these three characteristics, name, type, and field, is as follows:

```
DEF name type { fields }.
```

"DEF" is just the command used to designate the following word as the object (node) name. The use of DEF is optional, but encouraged in VRML. The type is the node type further described within the following braces. Some node types are the simple and intuitive shapes (cube, sphere, and so on), but other node types are things like lights, cameras, and the most important of all: the Separator node.

The Separator node is used to group things together in VRML. Actually, it is called a *separator* because it groups by excluding other VRML objects/nodes. There is also a Group node that groups by including objects/nodes, but these must be children of the parent node (is that clear?). So VRML documents are literally swarming with Separator *groups*, and the parade of curly braces can become bewildering.

In the cube example given above, the Separator node groups the Cube node inside it with the DEF name "myfirstthing". No other object/node in the scene will usually have this name associated with it. (Actually, it is legal to explicitly repeat a name, and occasions to do so, but this is another story.)

So much for names and types! The last major object/node characteristic is the field (or fields, if there are more than one). The fields following the node type form a parameter list for use in further describing the object/node. These fields are usually optional in the sense that they have a default value or values associated with the node type.

For instance, a Cube without further fields (parameters) is centered on 0,0,0 and extends exactly 1 unit in all six directions along the three axes. Units in VRML are by default meters, which gives the potential for real scale models in VRML worlds. However, early VRML developers have found that true scale model rooms and other human spaces look and feel very cramped in cyberspace. What this says about civilization is uncertain, but it surely means that cyberspace should leave plenty of elbow room.

The Cube node has three fields: width, height, and depth. In the previous example, all three are set to 2 units, yielding a geometric cube. But the following is also valid in VRML:

```
Cube {
    width 4
    height 6
    depth 1
}
```

The file cube2.wrl produces the shape illustrated in Figure 5-6. The result is still centered on 0,0,0, but forms a decidedly lopsided cube from a geometrical standpoint. But all is well: in VRML the Cube node is technically a "cuboid." In VRML, the Cube node is really an arbitrarily-shaped, six-faced *box* for all intents and purposes.

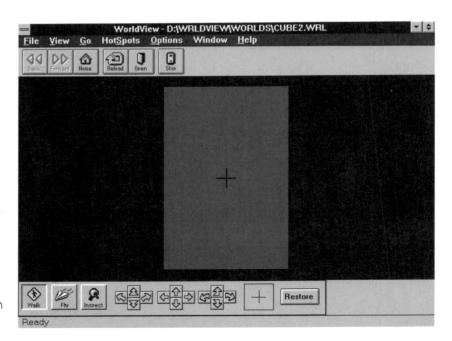

Figure 5-6
An Oblong Green
"Cube"

There is no compelling need to define a camera type and position or lighting scheme (just other nodes in VRML) because most browsers will provide a default camera and light that is suitable for most simple beginner worlds. One key thing that may not be provided adequately by default is color.

The Virtual World and Color

Adding colors to VRML nodes is only one aspect of the overall appearance of the node in the VRML world space. Real objects in the material world are made of substances that have a characteristic look (color, transparency) and feel (texture, smoothness). The Material node in VRML is used to set field parameters to more closely reflect this substantial aspect of the material world in the virtual world.

The Material node in VRML has many allowable fields, but not all are used, or even make sense to be used, in the same scene graph. For instance, real material objects either reflect light or emit light, but not both. The Material node has fields to enable a VRML designer to create shape nodes that also have one of these two properties.

To give a color to the cube in the example above, all that is needed is to specify a "diffuseColor" field in a Material node. The diffuseColor field has three parameters associated with it. These are just three numbers, ranging from 0.0 to 1.0 (with allowed 6 digit precision after the decimal point), that indicate the amount of red, green, and blue color saturation the designer requires in the node. This "RGB additive color scheme" is common in all computer graphics environments. The number 0.0 indicates no amount of a particular color, and 1.0 indicates the full color saturation amount.

For example, the three numbers "1 1 0" (decimals are not required for 0 or 1) will make a node object bright yellow. The additive color scheme in VRML adds full red to full green and gives full yellow. The string "0 0 1" makes objects blue, and "0 0 0" is black, while "1 1 1" is white. All three RGB values can be varied to give the VRML designer virtually any color imaginable.

So, the field "diffuseColor 1 1 0" will create bright yellow anythings. These anythings can be inside the nested node objects created in this Separator node. This can be confusing to newcomers, but the thing to remember is that setting a Material node with a color applies that color to any objects/nodes defined inside of a Separator (that is, inside the curly braces associated with this Separator node).

This is easier to understand with an example. The Material node added to the Cube node example from above is shown in Figure 5-7.

```
#VRML V1.0 ascii


DEF myfirstthing Separator {
    Material        {
            diffuseColor 1 1 0
            }
    Cube {          # make a cube
            width  2
            height 2
            depth  2
    }
}
```

Figure 5-7
A Simple VRML
World in Color

The braces show that there is a Material node set of braces and a Cube node set of braces. The VRML browser knows that this Material node must apply to the Cube node because (among other clues) the Separator node has isolated (grouping by exclusion) these two nodes, Material and Cube, from other parts of the VRML scene graph.

If there were another node defined immediately below the Cube node in the VRML document, a Sphere node perhaps, then that object would also be yellow. But in order for the yellow-making Material node to apply to the sphere, the sphere must be defined before the last brace of the VRML example that establishes the Separator node. Otherwise, the default color for the scene would be used by the browser to color the sphere.

The yellow cube produced by the file cube3.wrl is shown in Figure 5-8, but it appears as just a lighter shade of gray on the page.

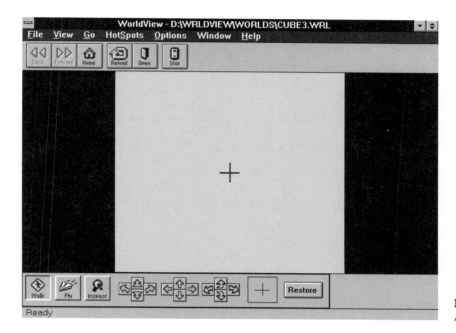

Figure 5-8
A Big Yellow Cube

The use of Separator nodes and the resulting flurry of nested braces is easily the most confusing and difficult aspect of VRML. Still, there are good reasons for including these constructions in the VRML specification. Figure 5-9 shows the cube3.wrl sample VRML document with all the ending braces labeled.

```
#VRML V1.0 ascii


    DEF cube3 Separator {
        Material       {
                diffuseColor 1 1 0
                }              # end material
          Cube {                      # make a cube
                width 2
                height 2
                depth 2
          }                    # end cube
}                              # end (only) separator
```

Figure 5-9
Cube3

Tip

Labeling the end braces when creating a virtual world with VRML by hand can save a lot of time when building up worlds object by object, as is usually done. The labels make is easy to find the exact point to add a node in a VRML file that goes on for several pages. Testing is made simpler and easier as well.

Creating a cube using the Cube node and associated fields is simple and straightforward, but there is a potential hazard that comes with this simplification.

3D World Rendering Considerations

The actual process that a VRML browser uses to interpret a VRML document and display the virtual space is known as *rendering*. This can be a processor-intensive and time-consuming process that is always "implementation dependent," meaning that the writer of the VRML browser software determines the actual step-by-step process of translating VRML directives into objects on the computer monitor. The most critical factor by far in determining the efficiency (and thus speed) of this practice is the polygon count in the virtual space. A polygon is just a "many-sided" figure from which VRML worlds are built.

The polygon count is the number of flat, two-dimensional polygons that must be assembled into three-dimensional objects to render the scene on the monitor. What looks like a sphere in the virtual world can usually be seen upon close inspection to look decidedly *fuzzy*. The fuzziness comes from the rendering software built into (or linked to from) the VRML browser that has decided that a sphere is composed of a tremendous number of joined, tiny triangles, the simplest and fastest polygon a computer can render. Even square or rectangular faces on walls may be split into two triangles for ease of rendering. The key is that this process is generally beyond the control of the VRML document designer, being implementation dependent.

The hazard of building virtual spaces and worlds with neatly packaged, understandable cubes and so forth is that polygon counts in excess of a few thousand or so can tax modestly equipped browsing computers (below 66 MHz). And an upper limit of 10,000 polygons or so seems to be suggested for even the fastest computers (up to about 133 MHz). So what appears to be an innocent little sphere floating in cyberspace can be an un-controllable 2,000 polygon render hog.

There are new plug-in graphics boards on the market today that are specifically designed to ease the rendering burden imposed by 3D objects, and not just those from VRML. Many PC and Macintosh games have elaborate 3D worlds as their basic game plan, and these games can suffer from rendering limitations also. These new hardware add-ons are still quite expensive ($300–400), but as 3D rendering becomes more of a requirement for new computers, the prices will drop, perhaps rapidly. Hardware-assisted rendering can speed up the whole rendering process 10 times over general software-only rendering computers.

Software accelerated rendering is possible also. A British company known as Rendermorphics was acquired by Microsoft in February 1995 in order to be able to bundle Rendermorphics' product, called "Reality Lab" into Windows 95. Microsoft's Reality Lab is a core component of Windows 95 and is also available for other platforms. The Worldview VRML browser uses Reality Lab as its rendering *engine.*

How can a VRML designer get some idea of just how many polygons a scene graph includes? With a design tool like worldSpace, the polygon count is built into the design tool software and the polygon counts can be determined with a few points and clicks. But designing virtual worlds from scratch means that the designer has no idea exactly how many polygons will be rendered when the VRML browser has to produce a sphere or cone on the monitor screen.

This can be a real problem. As mentioned above, scene graphs containing more than 10,000 polygons (and usually many less) can tax the rendering resources of even fast computers. The trouble is that a specific scene represented in VRML as a series of nodes with many spheres, cones, and even cubes, may contain 1,000, 5,000, or 10,000 polygons. There is no easy way to tell.

Even with software- and hardware-assisted rendering, the virtual world may contain so many polygons as to be useless, even though the VRML file may be relatively small. Designers like having a lot of control over their productions, whether the end product is automobiles or virtual worlds. How is this to be done in VRML? One answer is in the second way of representing scene graph node objects in VRML: the point cloud technique.

Building Virtual Worlds with Point Clouds

Polygon counts are not the only reason for using point clouds in VRML scene graphs. Only the simplest worlds can be represented using the pre-defined shapes that VRML includes. For more elaborate worlds, other techniques are needed.

The three pre-defined shapes in VRML are the sphere, the cone, and the cube. While a lot of interesting worlds can be built up quickly and easily using variously placed nodes containing these shapes, the real world displays infinite variety in shapes and forms. Even such basic shapes and forms as cylinders and pyramids are not present in VRML. To be truly eye-catching, a virtual world must contain more than simple, repetitive cubes and cones and the like.

The VRML specification includes the capability to define the most arbitrary shapes. VRML has defined several node types (remember, nodes are not just for shapes: the Material node above is an example) that must be used together to create these shapes. The two node types that must be used with point clouds are the Coordinate3 and IndexedFaceSet nodes. The "3" in Coordinate3 stands for "3-dimensions." IndexedFaceSet refers to the order in which a particular set of points is connected (by index number) to form the face of a polygon.

Before looking at point clouds in detail, a few more words of explanation are in order. All shapes in VRML are really made up of polygons, which are just many-sided plane (flat) figures. It is the joining of these flat shapes that makes an apparently solid 3D figure in the virtual world.

The simplest form of polygon is the triangle, a three-sided plane figure. In fact, many rendering software engines only render triangles, since any polygon of arbitrary shape can be broken up into a number of triangles. Figure 5-10 shows a seven-sided polygon broken up into triangles. In this case, the polygon is cut up into five triangles all starting at the left corner, but other ways to slice up the seven-sided polygon are possible. However, they all must include five triangles.

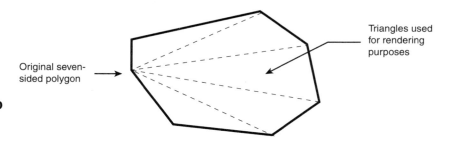

Figure 5-10
Triangles for
Rendering

All polygons, no matter how many sides they have, are made up of two things. First, this is a series of vertices, or corners, that form a series of points in space before they are connected. Second, the points are connected with edges, or lines, to form the entire polygon. The seven-sided figure above consists of seven vertices and seven edges

connecting them. Obviously, it matters how many points are connected, otherwise the resulting figure will not enclose a space. But it is
not so obvious that the *order* in which the points are connected is important also.

Many children still play with "connect-a-dot" puzzles where a child
uses a pencil to connect numbered dots until a final figure is revealed.
Polygons can be represented in much the same way. Figure 5-11 repeats the seven-sided polygon from above but numbers the vertices
from 0 to 6 (computers usually prefer to start numbering things with 0
rather than with 1). The lines (really the edges of the polygon) then
run from 0 to 1 to 2 to 3 and so on until the figure closes itself by connecting point 6 back to point 0.

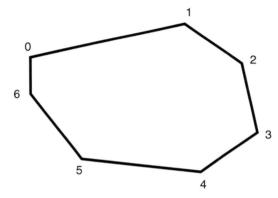

Figure 5-11
Vertex Numbering

But consider what would have happened if the points were not connected in 0-1-2-3-4-5-6-0 order. For instance, connecting the points in
the sequence 0-1-2-3-6-4-5-0 will not result in a single polygon at all,
even though all of the points only appear once in the list and the origin appears first and last, as before. The key is that the points are
listed out of sequence, going from 3 to 6 instead of the more logical
3 to 4. The result is shown in Figure 5-12.

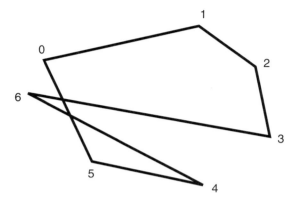

Figure 5-12
Another Possible
Numbering

Actually, the result in this case is two small triangles and one larger five-sided polygon. In this simple example, it is easy to see just what order the points must be connected in to produce the desired result. When designing actual virtual reality worlds, the correct order may not be so obvious. The whole problem is that the edges of a polygon in VRML are vectors. Vectors have a definite direction as well as a size in mathematics and computer graphics. So the order in which the vectors that connect the points are specified does indeed affect the resulting polygon.

These sets of points that are connected to make polygons are sometimes referred to as "directed graphs" to reflect the fact that the order is important, which is just another way of saying that the edges are vectors. In the above examples, the points must be connected from 0 to 6 to produce the seven-sided polygon. It is not necessary to include the "0" again, since the VRML browser will assume that the figure is meant to be closed after the last referenced point. The points in the example have numbers (0 to 6) that are the *index* numbers of the points in the example. The index numbers form the *face* of the object, since these flat polygons will eventually be used to assemble a solid, 3D object consisting of a number of connected flat polygons. This is, of course, why the second node is called the "IndexedFaceSet."

Renderers use the vertex order to determine if a polygon is facing toward or away from the viewer. If the order is consistently wrong, the renderer might only draw those faces of the object that face away from the viewer's current perspective. As a result, the object appears to be "inside out." So be consistent. Pick an order for vertices, and use the CLOCKWISE or COUNTERCLOCKWISE ShapeHint (not discussed further) to tell the browser which direction has been picked.

Figure 5-13 shows the "directed graph" nature of the IndexedFaceSet node that specifies just which points defined in the Coordinate3 node set are to be connected to form a polygon. Note that the direction could have easily gone in the opposite direction. It is only consistency that is important. When designing VRML objects by hand it is important to use a consistent direction when specifying points by index number.

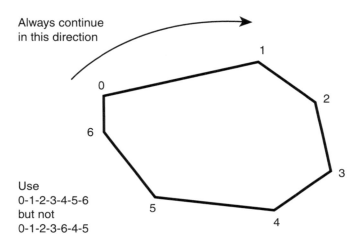

Figure 5-13
A Directed Graph

The use of the Coordinate3 and IndexedFaceSet VRML nodes to create point clouds and polygons is easier to understand after this preliminary look at polygons, directed graphs, edges, and faces. The following example will re-create the cube example without using the Cube VRML node at all.

The first thing needed is a set of points in 3D space to connect. The default VRML Cube node is a cube, centered on the origin at 0,0,0, and extending 1 unit along each axis, for a total size of 2 units on each face. The first "corner" of the cube will be located at -1,1,1. This is point "0" in the indexed set. Figure 5-14 shows how this point is located precisely in 3D VRML space by the three x,y,z coordinates.

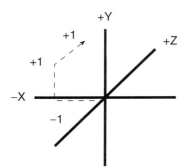

Figure 5-14

The figure shows that the coordinates -1,1,1 translate directly to units on the x,y,z axes. The set of -1,1,1 means "Go -1 unit on the x-axis (left), +1 unit on the y-axis (up), and +1 unit on the z-axis (into the screen). Put a point right there." Of course, to build a cube, a full set of eight points is needed. These points form the corners of the cube object. All eight points and their coordinates are illustrated in Figure 5-15.

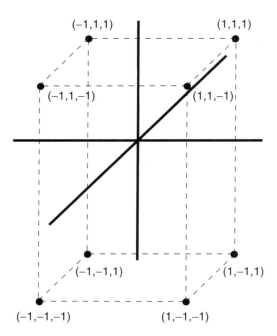

Figure 5-15

These eight points can be numbered, or indexed, from 0 to 7 and given their three x,y,z coordinate values to represent the point cloud for the VRML object. The points on the list can appear in any order. One possible point cloud from the cube example above would be:

Point 0: -1, 1, 1

Point 1: 1, 1, 1

Point 2: 1, 1, -1

Point 3: -1, 1, -1

Point 4: -1, -1, 1

Point 5: 1, -1, 1

Point 6: 1, -1, -1

Point 7: -1, -1, -1

The only problem with this point cloud is that it is not yet in a proper VRML format. To do so, it is necessary to group the points into a Coordinate3 node. The format of this node simply collects the x,y,z coordinates three at a time and separates the points by commas. The entire set is enclosed by brackets. The Coordinate3 node, with the point cloud from the cube above, looks like this:

```
Coordinate3 {
    point [
            -1   1   1,  # point zero
             1   1   1,  # point one
             1   1  -1,  # point two
            -1   1  -1,  # point three
            -1  -1   1,  # point four
             1  -1   1,  # point five
             1  -1  -1,  # point six
            -1  -1  -1.  # point seven
        ]
    } # end of Coordinate3 node
```

Note that the individual x,y,z coordinates in the Coordinate3 point cloud are *not* separated by commas, but each *point* is. Note also that the entire collection of points ends with a "." (dot or period). And just to make things interesting, x,y,z coordinates in VRML may be expressed with six-digit precision after the decimal point, if present. So, in the example, the numbers 1, +1, 1.0, and +1.000000 would all mean exactly the same thing: move one unit (meter) along the axis. And do not forget the square brackets!

The Coordinate3 node determines the point cloud for the VRML object, but does not connect the dots. This is the job of the IndexedFaceSet node. One of the reasons that comments were used in the example to number the points is that the IndexedFaceSet node uses these "index" numbers (not the comments, but the actual order of the points in the list) to tell the renderer exactly which points to connect, and in what order.

These collections of indexed points form the polygons that are rendered into the virtual object. Polygons can be of any arbitrary number of sides. A cube is composed of six four-sided polygons (squares) that form the faces of the cube (four sides, plus the top and bottom). So the eight points in the point cloud must be connected into six squares. Obviously, some of the points must appear as the corners of more than one square. That is all right, since the squares must attach to each other to form a cube anyway.

Again, the order in which the faces of the cube are specified is unimportant. What *is* important, however, is the order of the points within each polygon. Each polygon face must connect the points in a directed fashion, as mentioned above, or else the rendering software may not interpret the object description correctly.

The IndexedFaceSet node consists of a series of points from the point cloud created in the Coordinate3 node, referenced by index number (0,1,2, etc.). Each polygon is indicated by placing the number "-1" (since "-1" cannot be a valid index point) at the end of the list. A square is made up of four indexed points followed by a -1. A triangle would be made up of three indexed points followed by a -1. The individual polygons are listed in square brackets. The *order* of the faces listed is *not* important, but the order of the points *within* the face is.

The polygons specified in the IndexedFaceSet node are collected into a list known as the "coordIndex," since it is a list of the coordinates from the point cloud by index number. For the cube example, the six polygons that make up the cube faces could be specified as:

```
IndexedFaceSet {
    coordIndex [
            0, 1, 2, 3, -1, # the top of the cube
            4, 5, 6, 7, -1, # the bottom of the cube
            3, 2, 6, 7, -1, # the front of the cube
            2, 1, 5, 6, -1, # the left of the cube
            0, 3, 7, 4, -1, # the right of the cube
            0, 1, 5, 4, -1, # the back of the cube
            ]
    } # end of IndexedFaceSet node
```

Be aware of the small but important differences between the Co-ordinate3 and IndexedFaceSet node. Both contain a list enclosed by square brackets, but the differences within the brackets are summarized as follows:

	Coordinate3	**IndexedFaceSet**
Individual items:	Must be three	May be more than three
Separator:	None	Commas
End of list entry:	Comma	-1
End of list:	Period	None

Now all the pieces are in place to re-write the cube3.wrl example using a point cloud rather than the pre-defined cube node built into VRML. This was done to have more control over shapes in the scene graph virtual world and to acknowledge that even pre-defined VRML shapes are still rendered by software and hardware as a series of inter-connected polygons.

The point cloud cube4.wrl example is shown in Figure 5-16.

```
#VRML V1.0 ascii
DEF cube4 Separator {
     Material      {
             diffuseColor 1 1 0
             } # end of material node
     #
     # This node maps out the eight points forming the corners of a cube
     #
     Coordinate3 {
          point [
                     -1 1 1, # point zero
                      1 1 1, # point one
                      1 1 -1, # point two
                     -1 1 -1, # point three
                     -1 -1 1, # point four
                      1 -1 1, # point five
                      1 -1 -1, # point six
                     -1 -1 -1. # point seven
                 ]
             } # end of Coordinate3 node
     #
     # This node connects the points into six four-sided polygons
(squares)
     #
     IndexedFaceSet {
             coordIndex [
                     0, 1, 2, 3, -1, # the top of the cube
                     4, 5, 6, 7, -1, # the bottom of the cube
                     3, 2, 6, 7, -1, # the front of the cube
                     2, 1, 5, 6, -1, # the left of the cube
                     0, 3, 7, 4, -1, # the right of the cube
                     0, 1, 5, 4, -1 # the back of the cube
                     ]
             } # end of IndexedFaceSet node
} # end of separator node
```

Figure 5-16

More Points about Point Clouds

Point clouds are by far the more common way of specifying virtual world objects in VRML, especially when virtual world-building tools are used. Point clouds give the VRML designer much more control over the exact shape and size of an object. But point clouds are seldom used when designing VRML worlds by hand. This is because even a modest VRML world with only three or four objects may consist of literally hundreds of points and polygons. Many VRML .wrl files are mostly pages and pages of point lists and polygon sets. The truth is, no one creates complex virtual worlds by hand using point clouds.

One further point should be made about the polygons in the Indexed-FaceSet node used when making point cloud objects. The polygons used in the cube4.wrl example were squares. One of the main reasons that the point cloud method was introduced in this chapter was to provide a way of making the rendering process faster. However, the rendering process with the point cloud in cube4.wrl is not much faster than the pre-defined cube in cube3.wrl. Why?

Most VRML renderers do not render squares, pentagons (five-sided polygons), hexagons (six-sided polygons), or indeed any other higher-sided polygons directly. Even if these are specified in the Indexed-FaceSet list, a VRML renderer is likely to break everything up into a bunch of triangles.

Not only are triangles the quickest and easiest polygon to render, triangles have a further advantage over higher-sided polygons in VRML. Recall that each polygon in a VRML scene must be a *plane* figure. That is, the polygon must be completely flat, with no *kinks*. Think of it this way: the polygon must be able to lie flat on a floor, with no bumps or twists at all. This is sometimes hard to do by hand with higher-sided figures, even if they are only squares. But this is easy for triangles.

To see why, think of the plane that the polygon must lie in as being the floor of a house. A three-legged footstool cannot wobble. A four-legged table can, however, and many dining room tables frequently do. This is because, mathematically, three points are said to "determine the plane." The three points that are the ends of the three legs of the footstool determine the plane of the floor the footstool is placed on. No matter how long each leg is, each of the three must rest on the plane of the floor at the same time. This forms a triangle.

But a four-legged table has four points on the plane of the floor, one at the end of each leg. The table wobbles if all four points are not exactly in the same plane (exactly the same length). In this case, three of the points (legs) determine one plane and the fourth leg (along with the two adjacent legs) determines another plane entirely, causing the wobble. Anyone who has encountered a wobbly table and tried to get all four leg-points to determine the same plane knows how difficult this can be.

The same is true in virtual reality. Getting seven (or ten, or twelve) points to lie *exactly* in the same plane by hand is sometimes very difficult. And in scenes with hundreds or thousands of polygons, the task may be nearly impossible. What can be done to help?

If all polygons are rendered as a series of triangles, the problem disappears. If only three points are gathered into a triangle, no matter how complex the entire object, each of the triangles must determine its own plane. This eliminates the plane polygon problem entirely.

But what about the cube example in this chapter? How do the six faces of the cube translate to a number of triangles? Here is how.

Cubes as a Series of Triangles

Each face of any cube, or any 3D box-like solid object for that matter, has six faces that are four-sided plane polygons. For a cube, these faces are squares, but that is not important. The important thing is that any four-sided polygon can be split up into two (and *only* two) triangles. Figure 5-17 shows two four-sided polygons, a cube, and an irregular four-sided polygon, broken up into triangles.

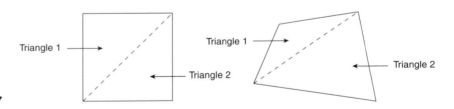

Figure 5-17

Remember that this breaking up of plane figures into triangles is done for a number of reasons by the VRML rendering software. These reasons include speed, simplicity, and ease of establishing a plane surface. The renderer will do all of this breaking up into triangles without the VRML designer even being aware of it, but this is the whole point.

The triangle rendering process removes control from the VRML designer entirely, which may be perfectly all right in the vast majority of cases. However, there may be instances where the VRML world designer wishes to gain complete control over the rendering process.

In order to accomplish this, the VRML designer must do two things. First, the designer must become familiar with the triangle rendering simplification process, which is one of the main points of this section. Second, the VRML designer must take control and break polygons up into triangles to begin with. Only by taking both of these steps can the VRML designer be absolutely sure that the rendering process is totally under the control of the world designer.

This triangle control is done in the IndexedFaceSet node. The Coordinate3 node remains completely unchanged. After all, cubes still consist of eight points in space. But instead of creating six four-sided polygons with the IndexedFaceSet node as above, the triangle rendering technique splits each of the six faces up into two triangles. This results in a total of twelve triangles that still share a number of edges, as did the squares before them.

Figure 5-18 shows the same cube VRML .wrl file with the IndexedFaceSet node re-written as a series of twelve triangles rather than six squares. The file is now cube5.wrl.

```
#VRML V1.0 ascii
DEF cube5 Separator {
    Material       {
            diffuseColor 1 1 0
            } # end of material node
    #
    # This node maps out the eight points forming the corners of a cube
    #
    Coordinate3 {
          point [
                  -1 1 1, # point zero
                   1 1 1, # point one
                   1 1 -1, # point two
                  -1 1 -1, # point three
                  -1 -1 1, # point four
                   1 -1 1, # point five
                   1 -1 -1, # point six
                  -1 -1 -1. # point seven
                  ]
          } # end of Coordinate3 node
    #
    # This node connects the points into six four-sided polygons (squares)
    #
    IndexedFaceSet {
         coordIndex [
                  0, 1, 3, -1, # the top of the cube - triangle 1
                  1, 2, 3, -1, # the top of the cube - triangle 2
                  4, 5, 7, -1, # the bottom of the cube - triangle 1
                  5, 6, 7, -1, # the bottom of the cube - triangle 2
                  3, 2, 7, -1, # the front of the cube - triangle 1
                  2, 6, 7, -1, # the front of the cube - triangle 2
                  2, 1, 6, -1, # the left of the cube - triangle 1
                  1, 5, 6, -1, # the left of the cube - triangle 2
                  0, 3, 4, -1, # the right of the cube - triangle 1
                  3, 7, 4, -1, # the right of the cube - triangle 2
                  0, 1, 4, -1, # the back of the cube - triangle 1
                  1, 5, 4, -1 # the back of the cube - triangle 2
                  ]
            } # end of IndexedFaceSet node
} # end of separator node
```

Figure 5-18

A quick look at the IndexedFaceSet node now shows that there are only three points per line for each polygon, exactly as expected for a triangle. The order of the points is no longer important, since all sets of three points determine one and only one triangle. And there are now twelve lines instead of six, reflecting the increase in the total number of polygons. This increase is actually okay, since many VRML tools that count polygons for the VRML designer will count triangles, not the many-sided polygons that the VRML file may actually specify.

Spheres and other curved surfaces like cones are composed of many tiny triangles. The VRML word for rendering curved surfaces as very small triangles is *polygon mesh*, or just *polymesh*.

Even the most innocent VRML world with a few spheres and cones may actually consist of thousands of triangular polygons. The more polygons that need to be rendered, of course, the slower the scene will unfold before the VRML browser. The key is to be aware of this behind-the-scenes process.

VRML Files: Big Coordinate3 and IndexedFaceSet Lists

The truth is that not many people, even experienced VRML designers, could handle scene graphs with more than a few tens of points. How would the designer even begin to represent them before composing the Coordinate# and IndexedFaceSet list? Any pencil and paper sketch would only be two-dimensional to begin with, and quickly become a maze of dots and coordinates as the designer struggled to "connect the dots" to form legal polygons. Coupled with the fact that VRML renderers prefer triangles, which of course maximizes the number of possible polygons in any scene, the net effect is to make it nearly impossible to design VRML worlds without computerized 3D tools.

This is just what everybody does in the real virtual world, if that phrase makes any sense. The result is that many VRML world .wrl files, if anyone looks at them with a text editor, consist of a few nodes to establish lighting and material, and then page after page of lines like "1.375549 -2.007421 4.176448", "678, 53, 922, -1" and so on. In other words, the point positions of the Coordinate3 node and the polygons (triangles) of the IndexedFaceSet node take over the VRML world (so to speak).

This complexity happens very quickly and with the simplest worlds. The VRML file a.wrl below is a very simple world indeed. The world consists solely of a large, red letter *A* floating in space. Not a very complex, or even exciting, world it would seem. Yet even the creation of this simple world would take a considerable amount of time to create by hand. In fact, this *A* world, like the vast majority of VRML worlds, was created with a tool designed specifically to simplify the creation of 3D letters in VRML.

The tool is called "WCVT2POV" and is freely available for use by anyone (freeware) wishing to convert almost any string of Windows True-Type fonts into 3D VRML solid letters floating in space. In this case, the letter *A* is from the Arial TrueType font. This process of adding a third dimension to normally flat letters is known as "extrusion." The process of extruding the letters is best left up to specialized tools like the one used in the example.

Figure 5-19 shows the resulting VRML file with its extensive Coordinate3 and IndexedFaceSet node lists.

(text continues on page 249)

```
#VRML V1.0 ascii
DEF a.wrl example Separator {
      DEF SceneInfo Info {
            string "Converted by wcvt2pov v2.6c"
      }
      PerspectiveCamera {
            position 0.000000 0.000000 -1.000597
            orientation 0 1 0 3.14
            focalDistance 5
            heightAngle 0.785398
      }
      PointLight {
            on      TRUE
            intensity        1.0
            color    1.0 1.0 1.0
            location 0.000000 0.250149 1.000597
      }
      PointLight {
            on      TRUE
            intensity        1.0
            color    1.0 1.0 1.0
            location 0.000000 0.250149 -1.000597
      }
```

Figure 5-19

```
PointLight {
      on      TRUE
      intensity        1.0
      color    1.0 1.0 1.0
      location 0.000000 2.501492 0.000000
}
PointLight {
      on      TRUE
      intensity        1.0
      color    1.0 1.0 1.0
      location 0.000000 -2.501492 0.000000
}
DEF TTFont Separator {
      Material {
            diffuseColor 1.000000 0.000000 0.000000
            ambientColor 0.100000 0.000000 0.000000
      }
      Coordinate3 {
            point [
                  0.060059 0.357910 0.100000,
                  0.334961 -0.357910 0.100000,
                  0.234375 -0.357910 0.100000,
                  -0.227051 -0.357910 0.100000,
                  -0.334961 -0.357910 0.100000,
                  -0.041992 0.357910 0.100000,
                  -0.143555 -0.141113 0.100000,
                  0.128418 -0.063965 0.100000,
                  0.155762 -0.141113 0.100000,
                  -0.114258 -0.063965 0.100000,
                  -0.039551 0.134277 0.100000,
                  -0.026582 0.169121 0.100000,
                  -0.015020 0.201387 0.100000,
                  -0.004863 0.231074 0.100000,
                  0.003887 0.258184 0.100000,
                  0.011230 0.282715 0.100000,
                  0.017148 0.255215 0.100000,
                  0.023965 0.227793 0.100000,
                  0.040293 0.173184 0.100000,
```

(continued)

```
                0.031680 0.200449 0.100000,
                0.049805 0.145996 0.100000,
                0.060059 0.357910 -0.100000,
                0.334961 -0.357910 -0.100000,
                0.234375 -0.357910 -0.100000,
                -0.227051 -0.357910 -0.100000,
                -0.334961 -0.357910 -0.100000,
                -0.041992 0.357910 -0.100000,
                -0.143555 -0.141113 -0.100000,
                0.128418 -0.063965 -0.100000,
                0.155762 -0.141113 -0.100000,
                -0.114258 -0.063965 -0.100000,
                -0.039551 0.134277 -0.100000,
                -0.026582 0.169121 -0.100000,
                -0.015020 0.201387 -0.100000,
                -0.004863 0.231074 -0.100000,
                0.003887 0.258184 -0.100000,
                0.011230 0.282715 -0.100000,
                0.017148 0.255215 -0.100000,
                0.023965 0.227793 -0.100000,
                0.040293 0.173184 -0.100000,
                0.031680 0.200449 -0.100000,
                0.049805 0.145996 -0.100000
            ]
    }
    IndexedFaceSet {
        coordIndex [
                2, 1, 0, -1,
                5, 4, 3, -1,
                5, 3, 6, -1,
                6, 8, 7, -1,
                6, 7, 9, -1,
                5, 6, 9, -1,
                5, 9, 10, -1,
                5, 10, 11, -1,
                5, 11, 12, -1,
                5, 12, 13, -1,
                5, 13, 14, -1,
```

(continued)

Figure 5-19
(continued)

```
5, 14, 15, -1,
0, 5, 15, -1,
2, 0, 15, -1,
2, 15, 16, -1,
2, 16, 17, -1,
17, 19, 18, -1,
17, 18, 20, -1,
17, 20, 7, -1,
2, 17, 7, -1,
7, 8, 2, -1,
23, 22, 21, -1,
26, 25, 24, -1,
26, 24, 27, -1,
27, 29, 28, -1,
27, 28, 30, -1,
26, 27, 30, -1,
26, 30, 31, -1,
26, 31, 32, -1,
26, 32, 33, -1,
26, 33, 34, -1,
26, 34, 35, -1,
26, 35, 36, -1,
21, 26, 36, -1,
23, 21, 36, -1,
23, 36, 37, -1,
23, 37, 38, -1,
38, 40, 39, -1,
38, 39, 41, -1,
38, 41, 28, -1,
23, 38, 28, -1,
28, 29, 23, -1,
1, 22, 21, -1,
1, 21, 0, -1,
0, 21, 26, -1,
0, 26, 5, -1,
5, 26, 25, -1,
5, 25, 4, -1,
4, 25, 24, -1,
4, 24, 3, -1,
```

(continued)

```
                        3,  24,  27,  -1,
                        3,  27,  6,   -1,
                        6,  27,  29,  -1,
                        6,  29,  8,   -1,
                        8,  29,  23,  -1,
                        8,  23,  2,   -1,
                        2,  23,  22,  -1,
                        2,  22,  1,   -1,
                        7,  28,  30,  -1,
                        7,  30,  9,   -1,
                        9,  30,  31,  -1,
                        9,  31,  10,  -1,
                       10,  31,  32,  -1,
                       10,  32,  11,  -1,
                       11,  32,  33,  -1,
                       11,  33,  12,  -1,
                       12,  33,  34,  -1,
                       12,  34,  13,  -1,
                       13,  34,  35,  -1,
                       13,  35,  14,  -1,
                       14,  35,  36,  -1,
                       14,  36,  15,  -1,
                       15,  36,  37,  -1,
                       15,  37,  16,  -1,
                       16,  37,  38,  -1,
                       16,  38,  17,  -1,
                       17,  38,  40,  -1,
                       17,  40,  19,  -1,
                       19,  40,  39,  -1,
                       19,  39,  18,  -1,
                       18,  39,  41,  -1,
                       18,  41,  20,  -1,
                       20,  41,  28,  -1,
                       20,  28,  7,   -1
                  ]
             }
         }
}
```

Figure 5-19
(continued)

Something very interesting has happened during the transition from building VRML worlds with pre-defined shapes like cubes and spheres to building worlds with point clouds, polygons, and triangles. Remember that most VRML worlds will be delivered to users over the World Wide Web. Naturally, in this environment, with many users having relatively low-speed, dial-up modem access to the Internet, smaller VRML files will download faster than larger VRML files. Yet the faster rendered point cloud VRML worlds will obviously download into the VRML browser much more slowly than the more compact VRML worlds made with pre-defined shapes! In fact, users may not see much of a difference between worlds made with either of the two methods at all.

There are several methods in common use to cut down on VRML file sizes. These methods may be applied by hand to any VRML file or used with a small utility program that automatically reads through a finished VRML file and removes the *fat*.

One common method is to remove the unnecessary precision in the point cloud specified by the Coordinate3 node. VRML tools are fond of producing points like 1.230000 or even 4.000000. Both involve the allowed VRML precision of six decimal places after the whole number portion of the point coordinate. Since VRML files are sent and received as plain ASCII text, each of the above points will require the transmission of eight characters of text, or fully 64 bits. Removing the trailing zeros from point clouds can make VRML files considerably smaller. In the examples above, zero removal will result in point coordinates of four characters (32 bits: a savings of 50%) in the case of "1.23" and in one character (8 bits: a savings of about 88%) in the case of "4."

Another method involves the reuse of previously defined nodes placed elsewhere in the scene graph with minor changes in size, material, texture, or color. This technique can save a considerable amount of space in the VRML file and is very useful in rendering structures such as buildings or houses, which usually contain a great number of repetitive elements in their design.

The entire field of VRML optimization is so new that it would be hazardous to mention more of these techniques. A good deal of plain old common sense will serve the new VRML world designer well until the whole process is better understood by the experts themselves.

Lights, Camera, Action!

There are a few other important concepts and node types that should be discussed as an introduction to VRML. In the big red *A* example world above, the VRML file began with more than just the simple Material node discussed already. The simple cube worlds built up until now have used the default browser lighting and camera position. All VRML browsers set a default lighting type and level, as well as a default camera position if these VRML parameters are not specified in the VRML file itself.

This use of default lighting and camera positions is not always a good idea. There is no guaranteed consistency between VRML browsers designed and written by different programmers with regard to choosing a default light level and type, or camera position. Some browsers may default to a barely lit world of shadows and dark corners, while others will blaze with blinding light. Some VRML browsers may produce shapes that loom large before the user, while others will leave the user seemingly miles from a distant form.

Obviously, the VRML world designer has methods to control these aspects of the VRML world's appearance. In fact, cameras and lighting are so important to VRML worlds that the VRML specification includes two types of cameras and three types of lighting.

Lighting is the more complex of the two concepts, so lighting will be discussed first. All lighting is established in a VRML world by means of special node types, of course. The three kinds of lighting that VRML defines are point lights, directional lights, and spot lights.

Point lights are like light bulbs. They radiate equally in all directions from wherever the point light is set in the virtual world. There is no shade on the virtual bulb, and the effects are different depending on whether the point light is placed close to or far from the object it illuminates. A *parallel* point light in VRML is so far away from the scene that it acts like the sun. That is, the rays from the remote point light do not diverge in all directions like the light rays from a light bulb, but fall on the scene like sunlight, equally across the entire virtual world.

The PointLight node has four parameters associated with it. The first is whether the point light is on or off initially (there are techniques planned for VRML to allow the changing of these initial values, but for now it makes little sense to create a light in VRML that is turned off!). The second is the intensity of the light, where "1" is the maximum and "0" is the minimum value. The next is the color of the light in the familiar R-G-B additive color pattern detailed previously. The last is the location of the light in x-y-z coordinates. A possible red point light shining on the cube from a few units away "out of the screen" (over the user's shoulder, so to speak) would appear as shown in Figure 5-20, which is now cube6.wrl.

```
#VRML V1.0 ascii
DEF cube6 Separator {
    PointLight {
            on          TRUE  # the light is on
            intensity 1     # at maximum intensity
            color       1 0 0 # the light is red
            location        0 0 -5 # five units out of the screen
            }             # end point light
    Material      {
            diffuseColor 1 1 0
            }             # end material
    Cube {                # make a cube
            width  2
            height 2
            depth  2
        }                 # end cube
}                         # end (only) separator
```

Figure 5-20

Be careful of creating colored lights shining on colored objects! In the simple cube world, a red light shining on a yellow object may yield unexpected results. Think of the colored lights in some restaurants making some dishes appear blue or other unappetizing colors.

Directional lights are like track lighting. While point lights are just created and shine with a given intensity, directional lights in a VRML world have both a location and a direction to shine in. The location is given in x,y,z coordinates and the direction is given in degrees of rotation of the x,y,z axis. These rotations are known as the yaw (rotation of the x-axis "side to side"), the pitch (rotation of the y-axis "up and down"), and the roll (rotation of the z-axis "ahead and back"). This may sound confusing to newcomers, but Figure 5-21 should help to illustrate the importance of orientation to directional lights in VRML worlds.

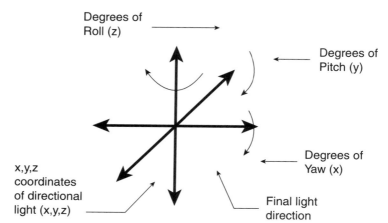

Figure 5-21
Pitch, Yaw, Roll

Directional lights add another parameter to the DirectionalLight node in addition to the four mentioned before in the PointLight node. The parameter is the direction, of course, and is measured by degrees of yaw, pitch, and roll.

Spot lights are a special kind of directional light in VRML. Along with both a location and direction, spot lights have a *focus* as well. The focus of a spot light is called the *umbra*. Outside of the spot light focus, or umbra, the spot light intensity falls off to nothing. The umbra can be very tight, like a thin laser beam, or less tightly focused, like automobile headlights. Figure 5-22 shows a spot light in VRML.

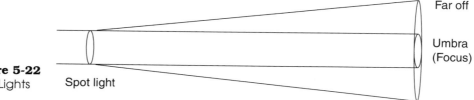

Figure 5-22
Spot Lights

Spot lights need more parameters in the SpotLight node, of course, in addition to on, intensity, color, location, and direction. Two additional parameters are needed to specify the amount of fall off and focus (umbra). These two parameters are the dropOffRate and cutOffAngle, each measured between 0 (minimum) and 1 (maximum).

The big red *A* world above contains not one, but three different VRML point lights. There is no real limit to how many, or even what kinds, of lights may be established in a VRML world. Generally, the more lights, the brighter and more inviting the world is for users.

Tip

Point lights are the easiest for beginners to use, especially when building simple worlds by hand. This is because a point light, no matter where it is placed in a VRML world, will illuminate the object(s). Directional lights and spot lights must be used carefully, since a light shining in the wrong direction may not illuminate the rendered objects at all!

Fortunately, cameras in VRML worlds are not as complicated as lights. All the VRML worlds built in this chapter had a camera, but it was the default browser camera type and position. The default position is two units from the origin toward the viewer (and so at the point (0,0,-2) and looks along the +z axis (into the screen). The default height of the *window* the scene is viewed through is two units high. Understanding this helps to explain why the cube worlds built so far tend to loom ominously close to the user on initial viewing. The camera is right on top of them.

There are only two kinds of cameras in VRML, but the difference between the two is significant. The difference is related to the concept of *perspective*. Perspective, invented by Renaissance artists, is the idea that objects that are distant not only appear smaller, but seem to be closer together. The objects in the distance appear to converge on something called the *vanishing point*. Railroad tracks seen head-on, lane markings on a highway, and even the streams of traffic on the highways, all seem to radiate outward close by and squeeze together to a point infinitely far away toward the horizon. The effect is so common that most people take it for granted.

In a VRML world, it is possible to establish a viewpoint with the PerspectiveCamera node. The viewpoint forms the default, initial camera position in the VRML world. All exploration begins there. If a person gets lost in a VRML world, there is usually a button on the browser screen to return the user to this initial location (real road systems should have this concept as well, but implementation is a problem).

The other type of camera defined in VRML is the OrthographicCamera. With an orthographic camera, the VRML world becomes an *orthographic projection*, a concept familiar to users of CAD (Computer Aided Design) programs. With an orthographic projection, objects will appear smaller as they recede into the distance, but will not converge onto a vanishing point.

At first this might seem odd. Why would anyone *not* want the convergence aspect of perspective in a VRML world? The answer is simple. Many VRML worlds are relatively small: rooms, houses, and so forth. The complications involved with calculating perspectives in these cramped quarters are formidable and the effect is slight. In these smaller arenas, perspective only serves to mildly warp the objects. Orthographic projections are better suited to these environments.

Usually, outdoor, roomy, campus settings benefit from perspective cameras in VRML. But the choice is strictly up to the VRML designer. It is easy to change back and forth between the two types of camera in VRML. They differ in only one parameter. Perspective cameras make a larger VRML world seem to have depth and make for a more realistic browsing experience.

VRML worlds with a single, large object may benefit from orthographic cameras. Worlds with a number of objects, especially outdoor scenes, will benefit more from perspective cameras. Experiment!

It is even possible in VRML to set up more than one camera in a VRML world. These are usually called "viewpoints" and most browsers will allow the user to rapidly move through a scene by jumping from viewpoint to viewpoint. There are of course more nodes for setting up viewpoints and switching between them. This concept is beyond the scope of this brief introduction.

Adding a perspective camera to a VRML is usually done at the very beginning of the scene graph. This sets up the camera position for the entire scene, no matter how many nodes are added to the scene later.

The four parameters for the PerspectiveCamera node are position, orientation, focalDistance, and height. Not all parameters need to be specified. Any parameters not included in the PerspectiveCamera node will be given their default values. The position parameter sets up the x, y, and z coordinates for the camera. The orientation parameter determines the direction that the camera is pointing, specified in the same way as light orientations. The default is along the negative z axis into the screen. The focalDistance parameter sets the distance at which objects will move out of focus. The default is 5 units. Finally, the heightAngle parameter determines exactly how much perspective the scene will have. The default value is 0.785398. The heightAngle is related to the user screen as shown in Figure 5-23. The whole idea of perspective means that the user screen "fans out" into the scene. The heightAngle parameter determines the amount of this perspective.

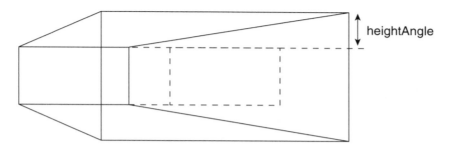

Figure 5-23
Perspective Camera

Here is how a perspective camera could be added to the cube worlds previously built. It makes the most sense to put the camera at the beginning of the scene graph. In this case, *beginning* means even before the Separator node creating the cube. Figure 5-24 shows the resulting cube7.wrl file.

```
#VRML V1.0 ascii
DEF openingshot PerspectiveCamera {
      position 0, 0, -5      # a little further than the default 0, 0, -2 position
      orientation 0, 0, 0    # this is the default, but specified for ease of changes
      focalDistance 10       # a little higher than the default of 5
      heightAngle 0.8        # a little more than the default of 0.78.5398
      }                      # end PerspectiveCamera node for whole world
DEF cube7 Separator {
   PointLight {
      on            TRUE     # the light is on
      intensity     1        # at maximum intensity
      color         1 0 0    # the light is red
      location            0 0 -5 # five units out of the screen
      }                # end point light
   Material    {
      diffuseColor 1 1 0
      }                # end material
   Cube {           # make a cube
      width 2
      height 2
      depth 2
   }                # end cube
}                # end (only) separator
```

Figure 5-24

Orthogonal cameras differ from perspective cameras only in the last parameter. The heightAngle parameter for perspective is not needed in orthogonal projections. Only the height of the viewer *window* need be given. The cube7.wrl can easily be changed to an orthogonal view by first changing the node name to "OrthogonalCamera" and changing the "heightAngle" parameter to "height" and giving it a value (2 units is the default).

Creating Objects Away From The Origin

So far, every cube in the cube-worlds has sat directly in front of the viewer. The simple worlds that result have seemed very claustrophobic and intimidating (imagine a packed elevator). Adjusting the cube size or perspective camera position would help, but there must be some way of just moving the cube to one side or up or down just to get it out of the user's face.

VRML provides a simple way to accomplish this goal of making objects anywhere in the virtual world. This does require some coordination of cameras and object position, though. It is not unusual for beginners to place objects away from the origin and cameras pointing off into space instead of at the object. The same thing happens frequently with the lights in a virtual world as well (except for the radiate-anywhere point lights).

The way to create objects away from the origin in VRML is basically to move the origin of the object somewhere else rather than saying "make a cube at (22, -16, -8)." There are a couple of benefits to this approach. First, with this method of origin-moving, all objects' nodes may be constructed as simply as possible whether they are at the (0,0,0) coordinate origin or really somewhere else. Second, the exact same node can be referenced anywhere in the world and *built* again. In other words, the building of two cubes could go something like this: Create a cube at the origin (which is 0,0,0). Move the origin to (0,5,0). Create a cube at the origin (which is now 0,5,0). The whole sequence is simple and efficient and uses exactly the same "create at cube at the origin" node in both cases.

The way to perform this origin moving in VRML is with the Transform node. The Transform node is usually used inside a group node (a gathering of object nodes most often grouped inside the Separator node). Moving the origin moves all of the object nodes inside the group.

The Transform node is a kind of *supernode* in VRML. Moving the origin is only one of its tricks. The Transform node can also be used to rotate, scale (change the size of), and perform even other changes on the objects within a particular node. Each of these operations basically has its own node in VRML. For instance, there is a Rotate, Scale, and Translate (move the origin) node that each perform one of the functions gathered into the Transform node. This introduction will only detail the use of the Transform node to move the origin. This process could also be done with the Translate node, but other fields can be added to the Transform node. This is not true of the Translate node, which only moves the origin.

Tip

It is usually better to use the Transform node instead of the Translate node, even just to move the origin. Other operations (rotate, scale, etc.) can easily be added to the Transform node, but adding these operations to an initial Translate node require other nodes entirely, or changing the name of the Translate node. Why bother?

To move the cube in the cube-world somewhere else, the Transform node needs only one parameter field. This is the "translate" parameter and specifies motion of the origin along the x, y, and z axes respectively. For example, a translate line of "translate 0 2 -4" would move the origin no units to the left or right, two units up (+y) and 4 units away from the viewer (+z into the screen). All objects created after this movement of the origin would be created at this point.

Figure 5-25 shows the cube8.wrl virtual world with the cube built a little off to the side and away from the viewer of the scene. Translation of the origin of objects created in a group node is simple task in VRML, but one that is done all the time.

```
#VRML V1.0 ascii
DEF openingshot PerspectiveCamera {
    position 0, 0, -5      # a little further than the default 0, 0, -2 position
    orientation 0, 0, 0    # this is the default, but specified for ease of changes
    focalDistance 10       # a little higher than the default of 5
    heightAngle 0.8        # a little more than the default of 0.78.5398
    }                              # end PerspectiveCamera node for whole world
  Transform {
    translate       -1 0 12     # move origin 1 unit left, 12 units away
    }                       # end of transform node
DEF cube8 Separator {
    PointLight {
    on                  TRUE     # the light is on
    intensity           1        # at maximum intensity
    color               1 0 0    # the light is red
    location            0 0 -5   # five units out of the screen
    }                       # end point light
  Material      {
    diffuseColor 1 1 0
    }                       # end material
  Cube {                    # make a cube
    width 2
    height 2
    depth 2
  }                         # end cube
}                           # end (only) separator
```

Figure 5-25
Camera in VRML

Linking to Other Places and Web Pages

The last essential element of any virtual world on the Internet is the ability to hyperlink anywhere on the World Wide Web. Without links in a VRML world, each world would be a dead-end with nowhere to go except back. This linking ability is, of course, the feature of the Web that users find the most essential. So VRML includes the ability to link to other places on the Web.

The most common use of these links at present is to create a virtual room or *neighborhood*. Each object can link to more information about a product in a showroom or a particular company represented by a storefront. The link is activated by a simple point-and-click, the same as following hypertext links with a traditional Web browser.

There is one major difference at present with virtual world links, however. Right now there is no consistent way to let the user know that a particular object contains a hypertext link. VRML has no obvious link "flag" like the blue underlined text of text-based Web pages. Instead, the user must essentially move the mouse cursor through the scene and wait for the cursor to change to the browser link indicator shape, such as a hand or some other form. This limitation may be addressed soon, but there is a considerable group of VRML developers that thinks such obvious flags will detract from the realistic feel of a world. However, the use of these flags would always be an option that the developer can choose to use or ignore.

A link is attached to an object in a VRML world with the WWWAnchor node. In its simplest form, the WWWAnchor node gives the name and description of the Web site or page linked to. A more advanced form can be used to pass the exact virtual world x,y, and z coordinates to the site, in the same manner as an image map on the Web. This introduction will be limited to simple links.

The only required parameter in the WWWAnchor node is the "name" field. This is a regular URL with no special form at all. The target of the link may be anywhere on the Web or Internet at all. The WWWAnchor node is a group node, meaning that the anchor can be associated not only with one object, but with an entire group of objects within the WWWAnchor node. This may sound confusing, but an example will help. The thing to remember is that the ending bracket for the WWWAnchor may be a page or so away from the beginning of the WWWAnchor node. Caution (and labels) are advisable.

The VRML world cube9.wrl in Figure 5-26 adds a link to the root URL of the World Wide Web to the scene. This means that a user clicking anywhere on the cube will link to Geneva, Switzerland, and bring up a traditional, text-based browser page. Notice how the link node encloses the cube node.

```
#VRML V1.0 ascii
DEF openingshot PerspectiveCamera {
    position 0, 0, -5        # a little further than the default 0, 0, -2 position
    orientation 0, 0, 0      # this is the default, but specified for ease of changes
    focalDistance 10         # a little higher than the default of 5
    heightAngle 0.8          # a little more than the default of 0.78.5398
    }                        # end PerspectiveCamera node for whole world
  Transform {
    translate  -1 0 12       # move origin 1 unit left, 12 units away
    }                        # end of transform node
DEF cube9 Separator {
    PointLight {
    on             TRUE      # the light is on
    intensity      1         # at maximum intensity
    color          1 0 0     # the light is red
    location       0 0 -5    # five units out of the screen
    }                        # end point light
  Material       {
    diffuseColor 1 1 0
    }        # end material
  #
  # The cube node MUST go inside the WWWAnchor for this to work
  #
  WWWAnchor{
    name "http://www.w3.org/"     # link to WWW root
    description "Link to WWW Root"
    Cube {                        # make a cube
    width 2
    height 2
    depth 2
    }                # end cube
  }                  # end WWWAnchor node
}                    # end (only) separator
```

Figure 5-26

The optional description field is used to let the user know in more friendly terms where the link leads. Otherwise, links like http://xyz.com/~sales/abc.html would appear at the bottom of the VRML browser screen when the mouse cursor is passed over the cube. In the example, the text "Link to WWW Root" appears, which is much more meaningful.

Building Virtual Worlds

This chapter has examined all of the VRML nodes needed to build a complete virtual world. Of course, a simple cube is not the most exciting world to visit, but it is a start. The next chapter will use all of the concepts and nodes explored here to build a more interesting, yet simple, virtual world with nothing more sophisticated than an ASCII text editor.

Chapter

6

Creating Simple Virtual Worlds

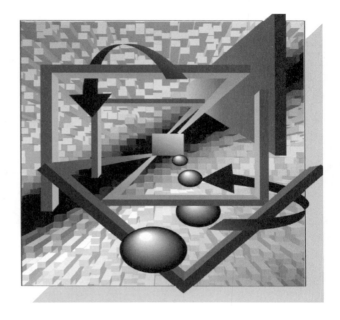

Pre-defined Shapes

Just like a six-year old child with his or her set of blocks building castles, houses, or cities, the basic pre-defined shapes that VRML supplies (the Cube, Sphere, Cylinder, and Cone) are the building blocks that a user will have to play with in cyberspace. Fortunately, unlike the six-year old, world builders have much more control with the blocks people can play with in cyberspace thanks to VRML. To begin with, the box of blocks will never run out; and, more importantly, there is control over the shape, size, and color of each and every block pulled from the box.

Not every child who played with blocks grew up to be an architect, but neither does that mean only architects know how to build things. Cyberspace grants anyone the opportunity to design, build, and modify a hut, a house, a castle, or even a world with very few resources and practically no cleanup when the builder is done. But to most users crossing the threshold into cyberspace is a brand new experience. No longer an adult in the *real* world, rather all users are like six-year olds in cyberspace just learning how to build with blocks. In this case, VRML is the toy box. So before anyone can hop into cyberspace and build a virtual Taj Mahal, *playing* with the basic building blocks is not only a necessity but will develop a better understanding of how to use them to build nearly everything and anything. As explained in the last chapter, VRML offers the ability to generate building blocks of any dimension with the use of point clouds. However, just by looking around at everyday objects it can be seen that many objects can be constructed with a combination of VRMLs four simple pre-defined shapes.

Fundamentals

Each node of the VRML pre-defined shapes have default values for their attributes as well as the ability to modify the shapes based on height, width, radius, and so on. As noted in the example of the cube in the previous chapter, the node name simply tells the VRML browser what shape to begin with. It is the fields, based on the attributes of each shape, that give the users the ability to modify each object to match their own desires. Each field within the nodes have a default value. If a user doesn't include a specific value for a field within a node, the VRML browser will always use the default value. When creating these objects it is important to remember that each object, when rendered, is centered upon the existing origin. This will be important later when multiple objects that need to be connected or separated using the Transform node are introduced.

Cube

Recall from the previous chapter that the cube node is not technically a cube at all, but rather an arbitrary shaped, six-faced "box" (see Figure 6-1). The VRML cube can be used for creating objects such as a skyscraper, cargo boxes, trailers for trains and trucks; or for the real cyberspace construction worker, a true 2 × 4.

Figure 6-1
Cube

Cube Node Format and Default Settings
```
Cube {
        width  2.0 # floating point value
        height 2.0 # floating point value
        depth  2.0 # floating point value
}
```

VRML browsers can be case sensitive! As a matter of fact the VRML specifications require it of browsers (even though many browsers in development do not always consistently do so, but that is why they are "in development"). So it is essential to make sure that your code matches the format, including the case of *all* letters, for each node definition.

The cubes **width** field is its length along the X-axis. The **height** field is the length along the Y-axis. And the **depth** field is the length along the Z-axis. As a default cube and centered at the origin (0, 0, 0) the cube therefore extends 1 unit in all six directions (+X, -X, +Y, -Y, +Z, -Z). This is why the default lengths are 2.0 units because each side extends 1 unit along each plane in both the positive and negative directions.

In creating a cube using the default values for the fields recall that it is not necessary to include the field names within the node. While the following two sets of VRML code produce the same result, it is usually considered good programming to include the values of a field even if the user wants to use the node with the default values.

```
#VRML V1.0 ascii

Cube {             # make a cube
}                  # end cube
```

```
#VRML V1.0 ascii

Cube {              # make a cube
    width  2.0
    height 2.0
    depth  2.0
}                   # end cube
```

Tip

To write VRML code nothing more is needed than a simple text editor. In a PC environment a user can use an aplication like Notepad, or in a UNIX environment the basic vi editor can be used. Simply save the file as a text file with the extension of ".wrl". All of the example files have been tested with the included World-View VRML browser. If, when attempting to view your VRML world with WorldView, the program does not render the object, an error in your code may exist. Hit the ALT key and WorldView will display the error and what it is expecting within your code. Copies of the example files reside on the CD-ROM in the d:\vrmlcode\ directory. A list of the file names corresponding to the figures in each example is contained within the appendix to this chapter.

A cube is a nice object but does not seem very practical for budding architects. Stretching the cube out in its **width** and **depth** fields can form one of the basic building blocks on all construction sites: the brick (see Figure 6-2).

```
#VRML V1.0 ascii


DEF brick Separator {
        Cube {                          # make a cube
                width   2.0
                height 1.0
                depth   4.0
        }                               # end cube
}                                       # end brick separator
```

Figure 6-2
Brick

Of course building anything brick by brick can be a tedious and time consuming operation either in the real world or a virtual one. Instead, taking the cube and stretching it in the **height** and **depth** fields makes it possible to form a nice straight wall that any accomplished mason would be proud of (see Figure 6-3). The **depth** and **height** fields are the length and height of the wall and the **width** field can be viewed as the thickness of the wall.

```
#VRML V1.0 ascii

DEF wall Separator {
        Cube {                    # make a cube
                width  1.0
                height 3.0
                depth  6.0
        }                         # end cube
}                                 # end wall separator
```

Figure 6-3
Wall

If anyone can build a brick and then a wall with the cube node, it should be no problem to build a building with it as well (see Figure 6-4). To build a skyscraper stretch the cube in the **height** field to give it a tall block look just like a modern commercial building in downtown Manhattan.

```
#VRML V1.0 ascii
DEF building Separator {
        Cube {                          # make a cube
                width  2.0
                height 8.0
                depth  2.0
        }                               # end cube
}                                       # end building separator
```

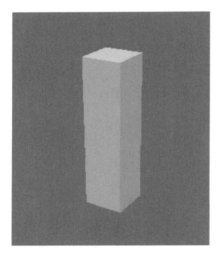

Figure 6-4
Building

These simple cube shapes can be combined in a number of ways to produce virtual cities with walls and towers. But there are other shapes that can be used as well.

Sphere

The sphere node is the simplest of all the pre-defined nodes, even simpler than the cube. It can be used to represent objects from such simple items as a beach ball to that of a planet (see Figure 6-5).

Sphere Node Format and Default Settings

```
Sphere {
        radius          1.0          # floating point value
}
```

Figure 6-5
Sphere

The **radius** field in the sphere node is allowed to contain a floating point value just like the fields in the other pre-defined shape nodes. This allows the user to enter in decimal values to better reflect the scalability of objects. The following code represents the rendering of a marble. Note that in this world we have defined that a unit is equivalent to an inch as opposed to the default value of a meter. This is not a parameter of the VRML language but is only a user-defined parameter. It is just like a key on the map that says 1 inch is equal to 10 miles. So if someone else comes along and says that 1 unit is equal to 1 mile, this will be a rather large marble.

```
#VRML V1.0 ascii
DEF marble Separator {          # 1 unit = 1 inch
        Sphere {                # make a sphere
                radius 0.75
        }                       # end sphere
}                               # end marble separator
```

With the sphere shape, simple features can be added to a VRML world. A tree, for example, can be represented as simply as a green sphere on top of a brown cubical tower. But a squarish tree trunk is not too appealing. Fortunately, there is another shape to use.

Cylinder

The cylinder node is a rather useful node with a lot of flexibility built into it. It can be used for tree trunks, barrels and cans, poles, wheels, columns, and plenty of other objects (see Figure 6-6). The node fields represent a capped cylinder centered upon the Y-axis and the **height** field is along the length of the Y-axis as well.

Cylinder Node Format and Default Settings

```
Cylinder {
          parts      ALL      # (ALL, SIDES, TOP, BOTTOM)
          radius     1.0      # floating point value
          height     2.0      # floating point value
}
```

Figure 6-6
Cylinder

The field that grants the cylinder its flexibility is the **parts** field. The cylinder node gives the user the ability to determine which pieces of the cylinder will be included when the browser renders the image of a cylinder. There are four values that the cylinder node will accept in the **parts** field; **ALL, SIDES, TOP,** and **BOTTOM.** To picture these parts imagine a regular soda can that represents a simple cylinder. The **SIDES** is its body, the actual cylindrical part of the can. The **TOP** would be the top circular face where the opening is and the **BOTTOM** is the bottom circular face; the bottom of the can. The **ALL** field, as the default field value, should be fairly obvious as indicating that all the pieces of the cylinder should be included when it is rendered.

The current WorldView browser included with this book is still in its development process. At the time of the writing of this book it was unable to render objects that were coded to render only parts of an object. Like HTML browsers there is a great difference in the design of VRML browsers. When designing worlds the best method is to test the worlds with different browsers and to include a statement that signifies which is the best browser to use when viewing (just like many Web documents claim to be 'best viewed using Netscape').

The **BOTTOM** or **TOP** field specification both will generate identical flat disks (see Figure 6-7). The key to choosing one over the other is to remember the importance of positioning. As noted before all objects are rendered centered upon the current origin. Therefore the **TOP** piece will be rendered in the XZ plane above the origin along the +Y-axis and the **BOTTOM** piece will be rendered in XZ plane below the origin along the -Y-axis. In the VRML example below notice that in choosing the **BOTTOM** piece the disk will be rendered at –0.25 units on the Y-axis.

```
#VRML V1.0 ascii

DEF disk Separator {
        Cylinder {                      # make a cylinder
                parts   BOTTOM
                height 0.5
                radius 2
        }                               # end cylinder
}                                       # end disk separator
```

Figure 6-7
Cylinder Bottom

When only the **SIDES** parameter is specified within the **parts** field a
user can create a ring or tube (see Figure 6-8).

```
#VRML V1.0 ascii


DEF ring Separator {
        Cylinder {                          # make a cylinder
                parts   SIDES
                height 0.5
                radius 2
        }                                   # end cylinder
}                                           # end ring separator
```

Figure 6-8
Cylinder Side

When specifying that the **parts** field will contain more than one part it
is necessary to separate the part names with a vertical bar "|" and
then enclose them within parenthesis (because that is the rule). The
following VRML code is an example of joining the pieces of the first
two examples, the disk and the ring, to form a cake dish (see Figure
6-9). The resulting dish is made from the joining of the **BOTTOM** and
SIDES of the cylinder.

```
#VRML V1.0 ascii

DEF cake-dish Separator {
     Cylinder {                    # make a cylinder
          parts (SIDES|BOTTOM)
          height 0.5
          radius 2
     }                            # end cylinder
}                                 # end cake dish separator
```

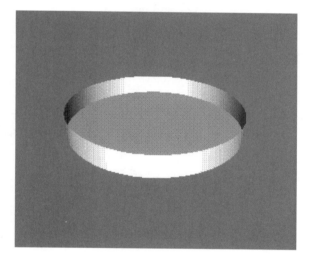

Figure 6-9
Cake Dish

Note that using the **TOP** piece as opposed to the **BOTTOM** would still have rendered the cake dish correctly, it just would have been up-side-down. The ability to pick and choose which pieces of the cylinder to render therefore does not limit the user to building only solid columns and posts. The cylinder node actually acknowledges that it is not a single object but rather one made up of three separate pieces, each with its own unique characteristics.

There is one more basic shape in VRML to add to the toybox.

Cone

Like the cylinder node, the cone is aligned along the Y-axis (see Figure 6-10). Its bottomRadius defines the radius size of the base of the cone which is located below the origin in the negative Y direction with the resulting apex ending above the origin in the positive Y direction.

Cone Node Format and Default Settings

```
Cone {
        parts           ALL       (ALL, SIDES, BOTTOM)
        bottomRadius    1.0       # floating point value
        height          2.0       # floating point value
}
```

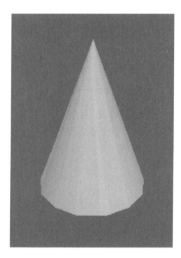

Figure 6-10
Cone

Also like the cylinder node, the cone node acknowledges that it is made up of parts. The cone is defined as having two parts, which it classifies as **BOTTOM** and **SIDES.** The **BOTTOM** is the circular base of the cone and the SIDES is considered to be the actual conical part of the cone. Additionally there is also an **ALL** classification, which is the default value in parts, that is just like the **ALL** classification in the cylinder node where the object will be rendered with all parts included.

With the cone node a user can create a variety of objects. From the hat on a fairy princess to the spire on her castle and even to her ice cream cone. The following VRML code creates a tall spire (see Figure 6-11) that might be found on the castle.

```
#VRML V1.0 ascii

DEF spire Separator {
        Cone {                          # make a cone
                parts         ALL
                bottomRadius  0.5
                height        7.0
        }                               # end cone
}                                       # end spire separator
```

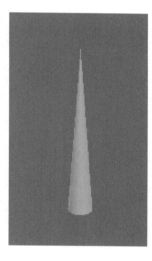

Figure 6-11
Spire

Overlapping

In looking at shapes and objects in the real world it is obvious that many of these items are really made of one or more of the basic pre-defined shapes that VRML supplies us with. Unlike these real-world building blocks, VRML allows a user to overlap shapes when trying to render complex objects. The skill in designing objects with VRML is to take the real world object and try to break it down into its basic parts and then build it back up with VRMLs primitive pre-defined shapes.

Take, for example, a rolling pin from a kitchen (see Figure 6-12). In essence it is made up of two cylinders. The handles are actually one long, thin cylinder that passes through the roller like a dowel rod so each end sticking out is one of the handles. The roller itself is just another fatter, yet shorter, cylinder. Figure 6-12 shows the resulting image from the following VRML code that defines the virtual rolling pin.

```
#VRML V1.0 ascii

DEF rolling-pin Separator {
      # Rolling pin handles
      Cylinder {                      # make a cylinder
            parts  ALL
            height 14
            radius 0.5
      }                               # end handles cylinder
      # Rolling pin roller
      Cylinder {                      # make a cylinder
            parts  ALL
            height 10
            radius 1.5
      }                               # end roller cylinder
}                                     # end rolling-pin separator
```

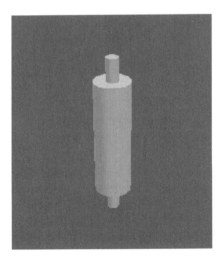

Figure 6-12
Rolling Pin

Translating

Once again in examining objects and shapes in the real world it becomes apparent that many of the shapes that make them up need to
be shifted around because the primitive shapes make up different
areas of the overall object. For example, a wine bottle is made up of
three basic shapes. The base is a fat cylinder, the top leading to the

neck is the top of a sphere and the neck is simply just a thin cylinder. Like the rolling pin, these shapes need to overlap, but unlike it, the center for each of these objects are at different areas of the bottle. Recall from the previous chapter that to create objects away from the origin, VRML basically allows the user to "move" the origin with a *translate* or *transform node*.

Translation Node Format and Default Settings

```
Translation {
#                         X Y Z
          translation 0 0 0       # floating point values
}

Within a Transform node:
Transform {
          translation 0 0 0       # floating point
}
```

> It is best to use the Transform node because there exist other transformation nodes such as *rotation* and *scaling* that can exist as separate nodes or can be inserted into the Transform node. The browser can interpret the single Transform node faster than a bunch of separate nodes. Therefore the Transform node offers advantages of both speed and as a container for all Transformations instead of being spread out over multiple nodes.

With the transform node, each piece of the bottle when created can be rendered in the area it should inhabit. Figures 6-13 through Figure 6-15 show the evolutionary steps in generating the wine bottle. The first step is to render the base of the wine bottle (see Figure 6-13). The base of the wine bottle is a simple cylinder centered upon the Y-axis with a height of 4 units.

```
# Wine bottle base
Cylinder {                   # make a cylinder
      parts  ALL
      height 4
      radius 1
}                            # end wine bottle base cylinder
```

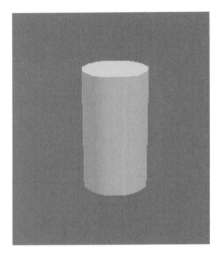

Figure 6-13
Wine Bottle Base

Next we need to move the origin up to the top of the cylinder to render the rounded top of the bottle. To be able to put the sphere evenly on the top of the cylinder it is important to remember that the base of the cylinder was drawn centered on the "true" origin. Therefore to move the sphere to the top of the 4 unit high cylinder, it need be translated only 2 units. Also, since the base was drawn along the Y-axis, the translation should only be in the Y (vertical) direction.

```
# Move to top of cylinder
Transform {
      translation 0 2 0     # move origin up Y-axis 2 units
}                            # end of transform node
```

Now a sphere can be created to reflect the rounded portion of the bottle. Because of the translation of 2 units only the top half of the sphere will be visible as the bottom half will be overlapped with the cylinder thus resulting in our rounded top (see Figure 6-14). Additionally the radius of the sphere should match the value of the radius of the cylinder so a smooth transition from the cylinder to the sphere will be made.

```
# Create top of bottle
Sphere {                          # make a sphere
     radius 1
}                                 # end bottle-top sphere
```

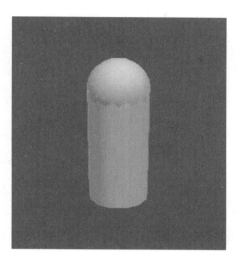

Figure 6-14
Wine Bottle Body

Now the neck of the wine bottle can be added. Once again the origin needs to be moved before rendering the neck of the wine bottle. This time though it must be placed above the top of the sphere so that when the neck cylinder is rendered it will extend up and also down just enough into the top of the sphere to create the image of a solid object.

```
# Move to top of bottle
Transform {
    translation 0 2 0       # move origin up Y-axis 2 units
}                           # end of transform node
```

The final step is to actually create the neck of the bottle. This is a slender cylinder. Notice that after moving the origin 2 units, the top of the sphere is only 1 unit away from the "new" origin. If the neck cylinder was rendered at 2 units in height it would extend the lower half of the cylinder 1 unit toward the sphere (while extending the other half 1 unit upwards) and would just touch the surface of the sphere (see Figure 6-15). This results in the flat end of the cylinder appearing to be precariously balanced on top of the sphere as opposed to being a part of the object. Not very realistic at all. Therefore when calculating the height of the cylinder it is important to remember that it needs to be large enough so that it extends into the sphere. This is why the cylinder height of the neck is set at 2.2 units.

```
# Create neck of bottle
Cylinder {                           # make a cylinder
    parts  ALL
    radius 0.25
    height 2.2
}                                    # end neck of bottle cylinder
```

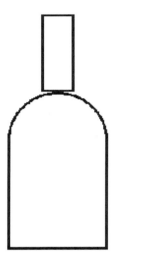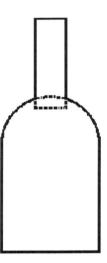

Figure 6-15
Connecting the
Bottle Neck

Listed below is the complete VRML code for the wine bottle. Figure
6-16 shows the completed and rendered virtual wine bottle.

Figure 6-16
Completed Wine
Bottle

```
#VRML V1.0 ascii

DEF wine-bottle Separator {
   # Wine bottle base
   Cylinder {                # make a cylinder
      parts   ALL
      height 4
      radius 1
   }                         # end wine bottle base cylinder

   # Move to top of cylinder
   Transform {
      translation 0 2 0    # move origin up Y-axis 2 units
   }                        # end of transform node

   # Create top of bottle
   Sphere {                 # make a sphere
      radius 1
   }                        # end bottle-top sphere

   # Move to top of bottle
   Transform {
      translation 0 2 0    # move origin up Y-axis 2 units
   }                        # end of transform node

   # Create neck of bottle
   Cylinder {               # make a cylinder
      parts   ALL
      radius 0.25
      height 2.2
   }                        # end neck of bottle cylinder
}                           # end wine-bottle separator
```

The wine bottle is a simple example of what can be done with overlapping shapes and some basic translations. But what may appear to be only basic steps can actually produce some interesting results. The following example takes the idea presented earlier of merely taking a cube and elongating it to create a generic skyscraper to instead, with a little imagination and utilizing the basics learned so far, transform it into the Empire State Building (see Figure 6-17). Try this on your own and perhaps use it as a model to design your own skyscrapers.

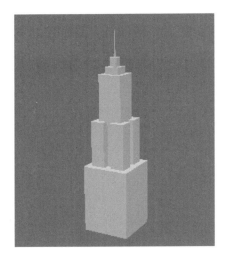

Figure 6-17
Empire State
Building

```
#VRML V1.0 ascii

DEF Empire Separator {

    # Base of building
    Cube {                              # make a cube
        width  10
        height 15
        depth  10
    }                                   # end base cube

    # Move above base
    Transform {
        translation 0 17.5 0
    }                                   # end of transform node

    # Main structure
    Cube {                              # make a cube
        width  5
        height 20
        depth  5
    }                                   # end main structure cube

    # Move to front right of building
    Transform {
        translation 2.25 -5 2.25
    }                                   # end of transform node
```

```
# Side edge of building
Cube {                         # make a cube
   width  3
   height 10
   depth  3
}                              # end side edge cube
# Move to front left of building
Transform {
   translation -4.5 0 0
}                              # end of transform node
# Side edge of building
Cube {                         # make a cube
   width  3
   height 10
   depth  3
}                              # end side edge cube
# Move to back left of building
Transform {
   translation 0 0 -4.5
}                              # end of transform node
# Side edge of building
Cube {                         # make a cube
   width  3
   height 10
   depth  3
}                              # end side edge cube
# Move to back right of building
Transform {
   translation 4.5 0 0
}                              # end of transform node
# Side edge of building
Cube {                         # make a cube
   width  3
   height 10
   depth  3
}                              # end side edge cube
```

```
# Move to top of building
Transform {
    translation -2.25 15.5 2.25
}                                   # end of transform node

# First cap on building
Cube {                              # make a cube
   width 3
   height 2
   depth 3
}                                   # end first cap cube

# Move to top of building
Transform {
   translation 0 2 0
}                                   # end of transform node

# Second cap on building
Cube {                              # make a cube
   width  1.5
   height 2
   depth  1.5
}                                   # end second cap cube

# Move to place antenna
Transform {
   translation 0 3.5 0
}                                   # end of transform node

# Place antenna
Cone {                              # make a cone
    parts        ALL
    bottomRadius 0.25
    height       9
}                                   # end of antenna cone
}                                   # end Empire separator
```

Rotating

In orientating the VRML shapes to create virtual world objects there is bound to come a time when there is a need to tilt or spin the shape for it to fit into the objects in the virtual world. An ice cream cone needs to be turned up to hold the ice cream and the Leaning Tower of Pisa needs to lean even in cyberspace. VRML supplies a **rotation** node that can be used individually or as a preferred approach of belonging within the **Transform** node. Like the **translation** node it is a method of moving the drawing origin to be able to render a shape in the exact area wanted. But while the translation node just moves the origin, the rotation node can manipulate the axis by tilting or spinning it in a new direction.

Rotation Node Format and Default Settings

```
Rotation {

#                       X Y Z angle

      rotation          0 0 1.0 0  # floating point values

}
```

Within a Transform node

```
Transform {

      translation       0 0 0      # floating point

      rotation          0 0 1.0 0  # floating point values

}
```

The first three values in the **rotation** node are values for the X, Y and Z coordinates. The VRML browser uses this as a reference point to create the axis which the object will be rotated around. To picture what the rotation command is defining for the VRML browser to do, imagine that a line is being drawn that connects and passes through both the origin (0, 0, 0) and the supplied X, Y, Z coordinates. This line is called the **axis of rotation.** The last value in the rotation node is the size of the angle of rotation that the user wants to rotate their object around this imaginary line. Unfortunately computers do not think in degrees when calculating angles, as people do. Instead computers need the values of the rotation angles in radians.

Tip

Radians is not the usual unit of measure used when calculating angles. It is therefore probably best if you keep a calculator handy when doing rotation nodes in VRML. Basically, radians are calculated on the principle that there are 360 degrees in a circle and the circumference of a circle is equal to 2π. Based on this, we can calculate that a 360-degree rotation is equal to 2π radians. Pi(π) is roughly equal to 3.142 and 2π is therefore equal to roughly 6.284. So to calculate the value of an angle in radians just divide the angle desired by 360 and multiply that by 6.284.

(angle in degrees $\div$ 360) $\times$ 6.284 = angle in radians

Items are rotated in a counter-clockwise fashion (to the left). If a user wanted to rotate in a clockwise fashion they could put in negative radian values for the angle. For example, a rotation of 270 degrees is equal to a *negative* rotation of 90 degrees. In radians, then, a rotation of 4.712 radians is equal to a rotation of −1.571 radians. The simple table below shows values for several of the common angles used for rotation.

Degrees(+)	Radians(+)	Radians(−)	Degrees(−)
0	0.000	−6.283	−360
10	0.175	−6.108	−350
30	0.524	−5.759	−330
45	0.785	−5.498	−315
90	1.571	−4.712	−270
180	3.142	−3.142	−180
270	4.712	−1.571	− 90
360	6.283	0.000	0

To demonstrate a simple implementation of the rotation node, a virtual world designer could take the previously mentioned ice cream cone (see Figure 6-18) and its desperate need for proper alignment, especially on hot summer days. To flip the cone upside-down, the designer needs to add a rotation of 180 degrees (3.142 radians). Conveniently the axis of rotation can actually be any line within the XZ plane since the rotation is 180 degrees.

```
#VRML V1.0 ascii
DEF ice-cream-cone Separator {
   # Spin 180 degrees
   Transform {
        #       X Y Z +180 degrees
      rotation 1 0 1 3.142
   }                        # end of transform node

   # Make wafer cone
   Cone {                   # make a cone
      parts       ALL
      bottomRadius 1.5
      height       4.5
   }                        # end wafer cone

   # Spin back 180 degrees
   Transform {
        #       X Y Z +180 degrees
      rotation 1 0 1 3.142
   }                        # end of transform node

   # Move to place ice cream scoop
   Transform {
      translation 0 3.58 0 # put scoop on top but slightly in cone
   }                        # end of transform node

   # Make first scoop
   Sphere {                 # make a sphere
         radius 2.0
   }                        # end first scoop sphere

   # Move to place second scoop
   Transform {
      translation 0 3 0     # second scoop pushed into first scoop
   }                        # end of transform node

   # Make second scoop
   Sphere {                 # make a sphere
      radius 2.0
   }                        # end second scoop sphere
}                           # end ice-cream-cone separator
```

Figure 6-18
Ice Cream Cone

Notice that in the code for the ice cream code there were two rotations. Once when the cone was spun to put it right side up, and then another to return the axis to its original orientation to place the scoops. A possible alternative method for placing the scoops was since the rotation caused the axis to flip exactly 180 degrees the positive and negative directions of the Y-axis have swapped, and thus to place the ice cream scoops the rotation could have been skipped and instead just a translation in the negative Y direction would have placed the scoops in the right place. But most rotations will not be simple 180 degree flips and trying to keep track of which way the axes are pointing can become very confusing. Therefore it is better to reset the origin as opposed to trying to do calculations based on the new axis generated by the rotation.

In this example it was a rather simple calculation to return the axis to its original setting because there was only a single rotation and by doing the rotation in reverse it easily reset the origin. The problem with this method used in the ice cream cone example is if more than one rotation, and/or with a combination of a translation or two occurs, it can become very difficult to keep track of where the rendering origin is in respect to the true origin. In complex worlds this could become a time consuming, frustrating, and error prone method. Instead VRML offers a special node called a **Separator** node.

Separator Node Format and Default Settings

```
Separator {
        # child nodes
}
```

This node allows the grouping together of any number of other nodes (such as Cube, Transform, Sphere, etc.) that are considered to be the children of the Separator. When the VRML browser comes upon a Separator node in the VRML code it first saves all the current properties such as the position and orientation of the axis, color, scaling, and so on. Some of these properties have yet to be discussed, such as color and scaling, but the central characteristic of the Separator node is the fact that it saves *all* of the current properties. Next the browser executes the child nodes within the Separator. When the VRML browser completes all of the child nodes and comes upon the Separator end bracket (}) the browser then restores all of the properties that it saved when it entered the Separator node.

Using the Separator node the ice cream cone example can be rewritten as in the example below. The Separator node, in addition to making it easier to calculate positions, from a good programming point of view breaks the code down into simple, manageable chunks of information that a user can identify and modify without effecting other parts of the VRML file.

```
#VRML V1.0 ascii


DEF ice-cream-cone Separator {
# Place the cone

Separator {                      # All current properties are saved such as
                                 # position and orientation of the axis

   # Spin 180 degrees
   Transform {
      #         X Y Z +180 degrees
      rotation 1 0 1 3.142
   }                       # end of transform node

   # Make wafer cone
   Cone {                  # make a cone
      parts          ALL
      bottomRadius 1.5
      height         4.5
   }                       # end wafer cone
```

```
}                                # end placing cone separator; all saved properties
                                 # are returned

# Notice that the Transform node with the rotation has been removed
    # Move to place ice cream scoop
    Transform {
        translation 0 3.58 0 # put scoop on top but slightly in cone
    }                        # end of transform node

    # Make first scoop
    Sphere {                     # make a sphere
        radius 2.0
    }                            # end first scoop sphere

    # Move to place second scoop
    Transform {
        translation 0 3 0    # second scoop pushed into first scoop
    }                        # end of transform node

    # Make second scoop
    Sphere {                     # make a sphere
        radius 2.0
    }                            # end second scoop sphere
}                                # end ice-cream-cone separator
```

It is important to emphasize the importance of trying to break down real world objects into their basic pieces and shapes when trying to render them in a virtual world. Looking at an object as a whole can be quite discouraging in its apparent complexity. To help show how to think things through, the next example will build a nice comfortable chair so that world builders can have a place to sit and contemplate how to break down real world objects.

Unlike the example of the wine bottle, with its simplicity, the Comfy Chair is more complex. When breaking down an object into manageable pieces do not jump immediately from object to primitive shape. Instead take the overall object, in this case the Comfy Chair, and break it into its basic pieces. The chair has a base, seat cushion, arms, and a back. Now take those pieces and break them down into *their* basic pieces.

For example: the arm of the chair is a tall, thin cube with a cylinder on top as the arm rest. Looking at the arm in its simplicity, it should be easy to write a small piece of code to render it. So now each piece of the chair is a small, simple piece of VRML code that can be contained within its own Separator node. All these Separator nodes are a piece of the overall Comfy Chair and therefore can be contained within the Comfy-Chair Separator node as Child Separators just like the primitive object nodes are children of each Separator. Going a step beyond just its own existence, the chair may only be a piece of furniture designed to exist in a larger program to render a complete room. So a world builder could bring the code for the Comfy-Chair Separator into the larger program and would then be a child of the Room Separator and so on and so forth. It all sounds confusing, but the example will clear this all up.

The Comfy Chair being rendered for this example is shown completely rendered in Figure 6-19. It may look complex but it is only a combination of primitive shapes with translations and simple rotations utilizing separators for each piece.

Figure 6-19
Comfy Chair

Here is the VRML code for rendering the Comfy Chair. As suggested before, the chair was broken down into its fundamental pieces. Then each piece of the chair is contained within its own separator node. Figures 6-20 through 6-23 show the rendering of the images produced by the separators of each piece.

```
#VRML V1.0 ascii

DEF comfy-chair Separator {
     # Base of chair
     Cube {                          # make a cube
          height 2.0
          width 5.0
          depth 4.0
     }                               # end base cube
```

Figure 6-20
Chair Base

```
# Right arm
Separator {
     # Move to place right arm
     Transform {
          translation 2.25 1 0
     }                               # end of transform node
     # Right arm side
     Cube {                          # make a cube
          height 4.0
          width  0.5
          depth  4.0
     }                               # end right arm side cube
```

```
      # Move to place right arm rest
      Transform {
            translation 0.25 2 0
            rotation 1 0 0 1.571    # rotate 90 degrees around the X-axis
      }                             # end of transform node

      # Right arm rest
      Cylinder {                    # make a cylinder
            height 4.0
            radius 0.5
      }                             # end right arm rest cylinder
}                                   # end right arm separator

# Left arm
Separator {
      # Move to place left arm
      Transform {
            translation -2.25 1 0
      }                             # end of transform node

      # Left arm side
      Cube {                        # make a cube
            height 4.0
            width  0.5
            depth  4.0
      }                             # end left arm side cube

      # Move to place left arm rest
      Transform {
            translation -0.25 2 0
            rotation 1 0 0 1.571    # rotate 90 degrees around the X-axis
      }                             # end of transform node

      # Left arm rest
      Cylinder {                    # make a cylinder
            height 4.0
            radius 0.5
      }                             # end left arm rest cylinder
}                                   # end left arm separator
```

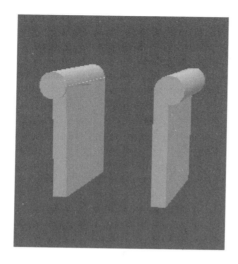

Figure 6-21
Chair Arms

```
# Back of chair
Separator {
      # Move to place back
      Transform {
            translation 0 3.5 -3.0
            rotation 1 0 0 -0.524 # add a 30 degree tilt to the back
      }                            # end of transform node

      # Back base
      Cube {                       # make a cube
            height 6.0
            width 5.0
            depth 1.0
      }                            # end back base cube

      # Move to place top of chair
      Transform {
            translation 0 2.5 0.5
            rotation 0 0 1 1.571  # rotate 90 degrees around the Z-axis
      }                            # end of transform node

      # Make top of chair
      Cylinder {
            height 5.0
            radius 0.5
      }                            # end top of chair cylinder
```

```
# Move to place back lump
Transform {
      translation -1 0 0
}                               # end of transform node

# Make back lump
Cylinder {
      height 5.0
      radius 0.5
}                               # end back lump sphere

# Move to back lump
Transform {
      translation -1 0 0
}                               # end of transform node

# Make back lump
Cylinder {
      height 5.0
      radius 0.5
}                               # end back lump sphere

# Move to back lump
Transform {
      translation -1 0 0
}                               # end of transform node

# Make back lump
Cylinder {
      height 5.0
      radius 0.5
}                               # end back lump sphere
}                               # end back of chair separator
```

Figure 6-22
Back of Chair

```
# Make pillow
Separator {
      # Move to pillow placement
      Transform {
            translation -1.5 1.5 0
            rotation 1 0 0 1.571   # rotate 90 degrees around the X-axis
      }                            # end of transform node

      # Make side
      Cylinder {                   # make a cylinder
            height 3.5
            radius 0.5
      }                            # end of side cylinder

      # Move
      Transform {
            translation 1.5 0 0
      }                            # end of transform node

      # Make pillow center
      Cube {                       # make a cube
            height 3.5
            width  3.0
            depth  1.0
      }                            # end center cube
```

```
# Move
Transform {
        translation 1.5 0 0
}                               # end of transform node

# Make side
Cylinder {                      # make a cylinder
        height 3.5
        radius 0.5
}                               # end of side cylinder

# Move & rotate to front of pillow
Transform {
        translation 0 1.75 0
        rotation 0 0 1 1.571    # rotate 90 degrees around the Z-axis
}                               # end of transform node

# Make corner
Sphere {                        # make a sphere
        radius 0.5
}                               # end corner sphere

# Move
Transform {
        translation 0 1.5 0
}                               # end of transform node

# Make front
Cylinder {                      # make a cylinder
        height 3.0
        radius 0.5
}                               # end of front cylinder

# Move
Transform {
        translation 0 1.5 0
}                               # end of transform node

# Make corner
Sphere {                        # make a sphere
        radius 0.5
}                               # end corner sphere
}                               # end pillow separator
}                               # end chair separator
```

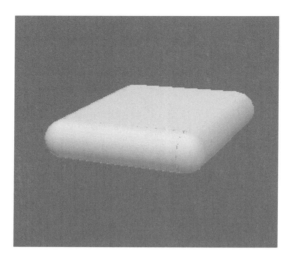

Figure 6-23
Chair Cushion

Scaling

In designing objects in VRML, everything is based upon a non-determinative unit of measure. For example a sphere has a radius of 2 units, a cube is 3 units by 2 units by 4 units. The VRML specifications state that 1 unit = 1 meter. But from a standpoint of modeling convience a VRML world author usually defines a unit to be whatever is the easiest for design, navigation, and perspective. Therefore a unit can equal an inch, a foot, a meter, or a mile. Recall from the beginning of the chapter in discussing the cube node that the same actions created both a brick and a building. As separate worlds these were fine, but bring them together and there either exists a really large brick or a very small building. Combining worlds within VRML is a very common function. As a designer of VRML worlds, a person can build a library of objects in which objects can be reused and inserted into any VRML world. But the units of measure may not necessarily match. To counter this, VRML offers another node called a **Scale** node. Like the Translation and Rotation nodes it can belongs to the Transform node as a child node.

Scale Node Format and Default Settings

```
Scale {
#                   X   Y   Z
    scaleFactor 1.0 1.0 1.0 # floating point values
}
```

Within a Transform node

```
Transform {
            translation 0 0 0        # floating point values
            rotation     0 0 1.0 0   # floating point values
            scaleFactor 1.0 1.0 1.0  # floating point values
}
```

The idea of the scale node is that it can either enlarge or shrink an object when it is being rendered. It does this by converting the entire units of measure on the axis by the new scale factor such that *all* attributes based on units has been modified. The scale factor is basically a multiplier. So if a scale factor is set to any value less than 1.0, such as 0.5, an object that is defined have an attribute 4.0 units would be shrunk to 2.0 units $(4.0 \times 0.5 = 2.0)$. This also means that a translation of 3.0 units would end up being only 1.5 units. Counter to this, any scale factor greater than 1.0, such as 2.0, would enlarge an object, so the 4.0 unit attribute would be 8.0 units $(4.0 \times 2.0 = 8.0)$.

The three values in the scaleFactor field in the Scale node are representative of the multipliers for the X, Y and Z values. To affect an object equally all the values of the X, Y, and Z multipliers should be set to the same value. For instance to shrink an object in half the Scale node should look like this:

```
Scale {
    scaleFactor 0.5 0.5 0.5
}                        # end scale transformation
```

Just like the Rotation node, each time a Scale node is encountered the VRML browser modifies its settings based on the current settings. So if a scale of 0.5 is followed later by another scale of 0.5 the resulting objects following the second Scale node will be rendered at a scale factor of 0.25. This is another case where the use of separator nodes are encouraged so that scaling will be contained to specific objects as opposed to effecting change on the entire environment.

The following example takes the wine bottle created earlier in the chapter and does a multiple Scale transformation to enlarge and shrink the bottle. Note Figure 6-24.

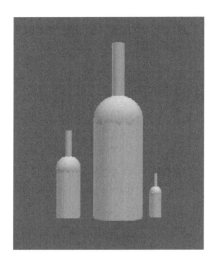

Figure 6-24
Scaling Bottles

```
#VRML V1.0 ascii


DEF wine-bottles Separator {

# Normal wine bottle
Separator {

        # Wine bottle base
        Cylinder {                      # make a cylinder
                parts ALL
                height 4
                radius 1
        }                               # end wine bottle base cylinder

        # Move to top of cylinder
        Transform {
                translation 0 2 0       # move origin up Y-axis 2 units
        }                               # end of transform node

        # Create top of bottle
        Sphere {                        # make a sphere
                radius 1
        }                               # end bottle-top sphere

        # Move to top of bottle
        Transform {
                translation 0 2 0       # move origin up Y-axis 2 units
        }                               # end of transform node
```

```
    # Create neck of bottle
    Cylinder {                        # make a cylinder
            parts  ALL
            radius 0.25
            height 2.2
    }                                 # end neck of bottle cylinder
}                                     # end normal wine bottle separator

    # Move
    Transform {
            translation 4.0 2.0 0
    }                                 # end of transform node
# Big wine bottle
Separator {
    # Scale double size
    Transform {
        scaleFactor 2.0 2.0 2.0
    }                                 # end of transform node

    # Wine bottle base
    Cylinder {                        # make a cylinder
            parts ALL
            height 4
            radius 1
    }                                 # end wine bottle base cylinder

    # Move to top of cylinder
    Transform {
            translation 0 2 0         # move origin up Y-axis 2 units
    }                                 # end of transform node

    # Create top of bottle
    Sphere {                          # make a sphere
            radius 1
    }                                 # end bottle-top sphere

    # Move to top of bottle
    Transform {
            translation 0 2 0         # move origin up Y-axis 2 units
    }                                 # end of transform node
```

```
        # Create neck of bottle
        Cylinder {                    # make a cylinder
              parts  ALL
              radius 0.25
              height 2.2
        }                             # end neck of bottle cylinder
}                                     # end big wine bottle separator

        # Move
        Transform {
              translation 3.0 -3.0 0
        }                             # end of transform node
# Small wine bottle
Separator {
        # Scale half size
        Transform {
              scaleFactor 0.5 0.5 0.5
        }                             # end of transform node

        # Wine bottle base
        Cylinder {                    # make a cylinder
              parts  ALL
              height 4
              radius 1
        }                             # end wine bottle base cylinder

        # Move to top of cylinder
        Transform {
              translation 0 2 0       # move origin up Y-axis 2 units
        }                             # end of transform node

        # Create top of bottle
        Sphere {                      # make a sphere
              radius 1
        }                             # end bottle-top sphere
        # Move to top of bottle
        Transform {
              translation 0 2 0       # move origin up Y-axis 2 units
        }                             # end of transform node
```

```
# Create neck of bottle
Cylinder {                              # make a cylinder
        parts   ALL
        radius  0.25
        height  2.2
    }                                   # end neck of bottle cylinder
}                                       # end small wine bottle separator

}                                       # end wine bottles separator
```

Let's USE It Again

In reviewing the previous example, the repetitive use of the code for the wine bottle shows how a VRML code file can get extremely large if it needs to include multiple copies of an object. It is a common situation in rendering worlds that a designer may wish to include copies of an object such as having identical chairs around a dining room table, or placing multiple trees in a yard. These copies of an object, referred to as *instances* in VRML, can be coded into the VRML file, with much more ease than retyping the code in, by using the **DEF** and **USE** commands.

DEF and USE Node Format and Default Settings

DEF node_name node

USE node_name

When coding in the first instance of an object, which VRML refers to as the *original*, the node should be preceded by the DEF command and a name to identify the node. The node is given a name so it can be referenced by this name later in the document with the use of the USE command. The named node can be any object node but is usually used with a Separator node so that an entire object contained within it can be identified as opposed to only a piece. All the examples rendered in this chapter have had the DEF statement used with the overall separator so that the entire object can be identified if ever these files were joined together for a single virtual world.

Once the original has been defined with the DEF command, it can be referenced repeatedly by name alone for each instance it needs to be re-rendered within the code. To do so, simply include the USE command with the name of the node given by the DEF command. The scaled three wine bottles VRML code could be rewritten as below.

```
#VRML V1.0 ascii

DEF wine-bottles Separator {

# Normal wine bottle
DEF Bottle Separator {
     # Wine bottle base
     Cylinder {                        # make a cylinder
          parts  ALL
          height 4
          radius 1
     }                                 # end wine bottle base cylinder

     # Move to top of cylinder
     Transform {
          translation 0 2 0           # move origin up Y-axis 2 units
     }                                 # end of transform node

     # Create top of bottle
     Sphere {                          # make a sphere
          radius 1
     }                                 # end bottle-top sphere

     # Move to top of bottle
     Transform {
          translation 0 2 0           # move origin up Y-axis 2 units
     }                                 # end of transform node

     # Create neck of bottle
     Cylinder {                        # make a cylinder
          parts  ALL
          radius 0.25
          height 2.2
     }                                 # end neck of bottle cylinder
}                                      # end normal wine bottle separator

     # Move
     Transform {
          translation 4.0 2.0 0
     }                                 # end of transform node

# Big wine bottle
Separator {
```

```
       # Scale double size
       Transform {
              scaleFactor 2.0 2.0 2.0
       }                              # end of transform node
       USE Bottle                     # call original rendering of bottle
       }                              # end big wine bottle separator

       # Move
       Transform {
              translation 3.0 -3.0 0
       }                              # end of transform node

# Small wine bottle
Separator {
       # Scale half size
       Transform {
              scaleFactor 0.5 0.5 0.5
       }                              # end of transform node
       USE Bottle                     # call original rendering of bottle
}                                     # end small wine bottle separator
}                                     # end wine bottles separator
```

Creating Funky Shapes

The Scale node is useful for more than just enlarging or shrinking objects. It can also be used to create some rather interesting shapes by warping the basic pre-defined shapes VRML supplies. In the previous example the scale factor values for X, Y, and Z are set to the same values so that each axis was affected identically. Instead, by using different values for the X, Y, and Z scale factors, normal objects can take on some rather interesting dimensions.

Using the Scale node to create warped objects only works with objects that have a radius field within their nodes. Squashing or enlarging an axis along the height of a cylinder or a cone is the same as just making the height smaller or greater for that object. Considering this fact, scaling a cube which has all linear measurements, in any direction, will not warp it, just change its dimensions.

Taking a sphere and stretching it in only one direction makes it first appear like an egg. Stretch it even more and it begins to look like a cigar. Figure 6-25 shows the sphere stretched double along the X-axis and Figure 6-26 shows the sphere stretched six times greater along the X-axis.

```
#VRML V1.0 ascii

DEF egg Separator {

     Transform {
          scaleFactor 2.0 1.0 1.0      # stretch double along the X-axis
     }                                 # end of transform node
          Sphere {                     # make a sphere
          radius 1.0
     }                                 # end sphere node

}                                      # end of egg separator
```

Figure 6-25
Egg

```
#VRML V1.0 ascii

DEF cigar Separator {

     Transform {
          scaleFactor 6.0 1.0 1.0      # stretch six times along the X-axis
     }                                 # end of transform node
     Sphere {                          # make a sphere
          radius 1.0
     }                                 # end sphere node

}                                      # end of cigar separator
```

Figure 6-26
Cigar

In addition to stretching objects, scaling can also produce squashing by using a scale factor less than 1.0. This is similar to shrinking an object, but by doing it in only one field, it too will warp an object. Scaling a cylinder by squashing it in half will end up looking like a flattened can (see Figure 6-27).

```
#VRML V1.0 ascii


DEF discus Separator {

        Transform {
                scaleFactor 0.25 1.0 1.0    # squash to 1/4 along the X-axis
        }                                   # end of transform node

        Cylinder {                          # make a cylinder
                parts  ALL
                height 2.0
                radius 1.0

        }                                   # end cylinder node

}                                           # end of discus separator
```

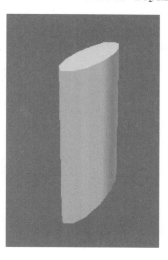

Figure 6-27
Crushed Can

Sample Examples

With a simple Scale node objects that have been created before and exist in a designer's library can be hauled out and become new objects. For example, instead of having to create a virtual casserole dish from scratch, just take the existing code for the cake dish created earlier in this chapter and scale it a bit. In comparing a cake dish to an oval casserole dish, it is longer and deeper. Therefore the cake dish can be scaled in two directions to raise its edges and stretch or squash the sides a bit to give it an oblong look. In this example both dishes will be rendered to compare them (see Figure 6-28).

```
#VRML V1.0 ascii


DEF dishes Separator {

# create a cake dish
Separator {
      Cylinder {                          # make a cylinder
             parts   (SIDES|BOTTOM)
             height 0.5
             radius 2
      }                                   # end cylinder
}                                         # end cake dish separator

# create a casserole dish
Separator {
      Transform {
             translation   4.0 0 0       # move over to place casserole dish
             scaleFactor   0.5 1.5 1.0    # squash sides and raise edges
      }                                   # end transform node

# Take existing cake dish code and render based on the new scale factor
      # create a cake dish
      Separator {
             Cylinder {                   # make a cylinder
                    parts   (SIDES|BOTTOM)
                    height 0.5
                    radius 2
             }                            # end cylinder
      }                                   # end cake dish separator
}                                         # end casserole dish separator

}                                         # end dishes separator
```

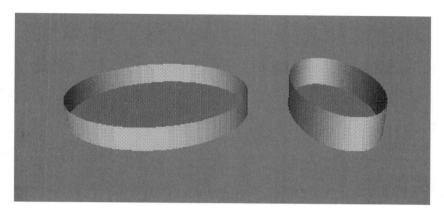

Figure 6-28
Dishes

Putting It All Together

The chapter up to this point has covered the basics for utilizing VRML to render objects in cyberspace. With the knowledge of the predefined shapes supplied by VRML and the ability to translate, rotate, and scale you should have a great foundation to start building in cyberspace. The following examples (see Figures 6-29 and 6-30) are intended to show what can be done by utilizing all of the specifications of VRML demonstrated so far.

Flying Saucer

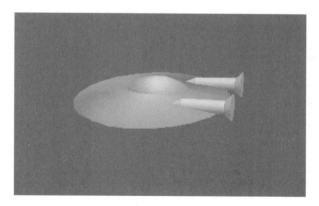

Figure 6-29
Flying Saucer

```
#VRML V1.0 ascii


DEF UFO Separator {
```

```
# Main Body
Separator {
      Transform {
            scaleFactor 2.0 0.25 2.0    # To flatten sphere into a disk
      }                                 # end of transformation
      # Body

      Sphere {                          # make a sphere
            radius 6.0
      }                                 # end of body sphere
}                                       # end of main body separator

# Cockpit
Separator {
      Transform {
            translation 1.0 1.0 0
            scaleFactor 1.0 0.5 0.5
      }                                 # end of transformation
      Sphere {                          # make a sphere
            radius 5.0
      }                                 # end sphere
}                                       # end cockpit separator

# Engines
      Transform {
            translation 5.0 1.0 5.0
            rotation    0 0 1.0 1.571
      }                                 # end of transformation

DEF Engine Separator {
      # front cap
      Cone {                            # make a cone
            parts         ALL
            bottomRadius 1.0
            height        2.0
      }                                 # end front cap cone

      Transform {
            translation 0 -4.0 0
      }                                 # end of transformation
```

```
# engine body
Cylinder {
    parts  ALL
    height 6.0
    radius 1.0
}

Transform {
    translation 0 -3.0 0
}                               # end of transformation
# exhaust funnel
Cone {                          # make a cone
    parts       ALL
    bottomRadius 2.0
    height      2.0
}                               # end exhaust funnel cone
}                               # end Engine separator

Transform {
    translation 0 0 -10.0
}                               # end of transformation
USE Engine                      # call original engine object

}                               # end of UFO separator
```

Cruise Ship

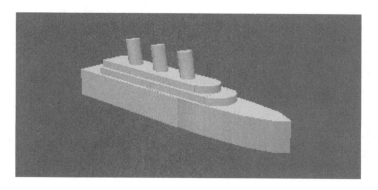

Figure 6-30
Cruise Ship

```
#VRML V1.0 ascii

DEF cruise-ship Separator {

# Hull
Separator {
      Cube {                              # make a cube
            width  10.0
            height 2.0
            depth  3.0
            }                             # end cube

      Transform {
            translation  5.0 0 0
            scaleFactor  5.0 1.0 1.0
      }                                   # end of transformation

      Cylinder {                          # make a cylinder
            radius 1.5
            height 2.0
            parts  ALL
      }                                   # end cylinder
}                                         # end hull separator

# First deck
      Transform {
            translation 2.0 1.25 0
      }                                   # end of transformation

      Cube {                              # make a cube
            width  10.0
            height 0.5
            depth  2.5
      }                                   # end cube

      Transform {
            translation 5.0 0 0
      }                                   # end of transformation
```

```
    Cylinder {                          # make a cylinder
        radius 1.25
        height 0.5
        parts  ALL
    }                                   # end cylinder

# Second deck
    Transform {
        translation -5.5 0.5 0
    }                                   # end of transformation

    Cube {                              # make a cube
        width  9.0
        height 0.5
        depth  2.0
    }                                   # end cube

    Transform {
        translation 4.5 0 0
    }                                   # end of transformation

    Cylinder {                          # make a cylinder
        radius 1.0
        height 0.5
        parts  ALL
    }                                   # end cylinder

# Smoke stack one
    Transform {
        translation -6.5 0 0
    }                                   # end of transformation

DEF Stack Separator {
    Transform {
        rotation 0 0 1 0.175            # give smoke stack a slight tilt
    }                                   # end of transformation node

    Cylinder {                          # make a cylinder
        radius 0.5
        height 4.0
        parts  ALL
    }                                   # end cylinder
```

```
}                                       # end of Stack one separator
# Smoke stack two
      Transform {
            translation 2.5 0 0
      }                                 # end of transformation
      USE Stack                         # call original Stack object
}                                       # end of smoke stack two separator

# Smoke stack three
      Transform {
            translation 2.5 0 0
      }                                 # end of transformation
      USE Stack                         # call original Stack object
}                                       # end smoke stack three separator

}                                       # end cruise ship separator
```

Color and Shading

So far the virtual world objects are shaped all right, but they all look
pretty bland. The shape of an object is only half the job in creating a
virtual image. People live in a world of color and texture and therefore the virtual objects need to have that same color and texture, too.
VRML goes to extended measures to provide methods for color, lighting, shading, and applying textures for all of its objects. The two fundamental nodes are the **Material** node and the **Texture2** node. The
Material node lets the user control the color, and the properties associated with that color, to an object.

Material Node Format and Default Settings

```
Material {
        ambientColor    0.2 0.2 0.2   # RGB color
        diffuseColor    0.8 0.8 0.8   # RGB color
        specularColor   0 0 0         # RGB color
        emissiveColor   0 0 0         # RGB color
        shininess       0.2           # floating point value
        transparency    0             # floating point value
}
```

In examining the Material node it becomes apparent that applying
color to an object can be as simple as "just color it red" to applying
more complicated properties like "tint the glass in the window a light
shade of blue." The values for the **ambientColor, diffuseColor, specu-**

larColor and **emissiveColor** fields are expressed by recording the RGB colors of the color desired. These values are derived from the property of light in which all color is made up of a combination of the three primary colors; **Red**, **Green**, and **Blue**.

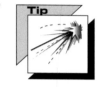
Tip

Do not confuse the properties in the mixing of light with those of mixing paint. While the idea is similar in that you mix different colors to produce a third, the properties of light and that of paint pigmentation are very different (the primary colors of light are red, green, and blue, while the primary colors for paint are red, blue, yellow, white, and black) For example, by mixing full red and full green light it will produce yellow light. If red and green paint were mixed it would be very far from yellow.

The best way to understand the difference is to picture light as bands of colored light. Pure white light is produced when all of the bands are present in that ray of light. The pigmentation in paint tries to absorb this white light. The bands of colored light it can not absorb reflect back. Therefore yellow paint looks yellow because it can not absorb the red light band and the green light band. It is this reflecting of the two lights in combination that produce the yellow color. So by mixing paint only the common bands of light that neither pigmentation can absorb will get reflected back. In mixing red and green paint, the reflected bands of light mix to produce brown. If you really compare yellow and brown light, notice that they do seem related (an old parchment 'yellows' or 'browns' with age). That's because brown is really just a set of bands of colored light that are a piece of what makes yellow!

The values of the RGB colors are expressed in three floating point values each representing an intensity of one of the primary colors. The value of 0.0 represents the absence of any of that color and the value of 1.0 represents full intensity of that color (values that are greater than 1.0 or less than 0.0 have no additional effect). By keeping the values of Red, Green, and Blue equivalent, the resulting color is simply a gray scale ranging from black at 0.0 to a mid-gray at 0.5 to pure white at 1.0. The table below gives some sample outcomes for the mixing of light. Many paint programs will give you a RGB value for a color in a 256x256x256 format. To translate these colors for use in VRML merely divide each value by 256 and enter it into the corresponding intensity value within the Material node.

RED	GREEN	BLUE	COLOR
0.0	0.0	0.0	BLACK
0.5	0.5	0.5	GRAY
1.0	1.0	1.0	WHITE
1.0	0.0	0.0	RED
0.5	0.0	0.0	DARK RED
0.0	1.0	0.0	GREEN
0.0	0.0	1.0	BLUE
1.0	1.0	0.0	YELLOW
1.0	0.0	1.0	MAGENTA
0.0	1.0	1.0	CYAN

The six fields of the Material node each has its own specific effect upon an object. The ambientColor field is an advanced setting that deals with lighting up the dark areas of an object that is not in direct lighting. For now the default settings for the browser use a headlight lighting system. Therefore this field is only used if the headlight is not used and an alternate lighting system, such as point lights, are used within the virtual world instead. The default settings are set for a dark gray, just like normal shadows. An example of the need to use the ambientColor field is to simply look under a desk. The lamp on the desk does not shine there but because of ambient light the dustballs are still visible.

The next field, diffuseColor, represents what most users would refer to simply as the color of the object. The specularColor field is another advanced setting for specifying what the color of the light will be that reflects off an object. For instance a red couch does not reflect a reddish color, but a copper kettle might reflect its color.

The emissiveColor field is used to set an object's glow color. Just like one of those glow in the dark key chains or the numbers on a digital clock, objects may need to be visible in the dark. While these objects do not actually give off light, they will be visible based on their color intensity even when no light source is present. The default setting for the emissiveColor field is set at black because most objects, of course, normally do not glow.

The final two fields are both floating point values measured only between 0.0 and 1.0. The **shininess** field controls how shiny an object is. After washing and waxing a car, it would have a high value in the shininess field, but drive it around during the winters in the Northeast and the resulting shininess drops as salt, dirt, and grime dull the finish. The last field in the Material node is **transparency.** A value of 1.0 renders an object completely transparent, like a piece of clean glass. As the transparency drops so does the field value such that a solid object would have a transparency of 0.0 (in other words, no transparency). The default setting for the transparency node is 0.0 as most objects are solid and light cannot pass through.

Unfortunately, with many VRML browsers transparency does not mean that objects can be seen through them as most VRML browsers are just not sophisticated enough. For now, a side effect of the PC VRML rendering engine architecture allows the passing of light as if an object were opaque. The transparency level does have an effect upon the intensity of the light passing through it, so if an object were behind another transparent object, it could be illuminated by a light source from outside, but it would be unseen unless the user went around the obstructing "transparent" object. Strange, but that is the way it currently works within the limitations of many browsers.

To add color to any of the previously rendered objects from earlier example virtual worlds, merely add the Material node with those properties that should belong to the object within that object's Separator node. The following example takes the previous completed comfy chair example and adds the following Material node to make the chair red. Many of the values are the default settings and do not have to be included in the code and are only included for this example.

```
#VRML V1.0 ascii


DEF comfy-chair Separator {

    Material {
        ambientColor 0.2 0 0   # parts of the chair in shadows are a DARK RED
        diffuseColor 1.0 0 0   # render in RED
        specularColor  0 0 0   # default - no reflective color
        emissiveColor  0 0. 0  # default - chair is not a glow in the dark model
        shininess 0.2          # default - chair is new
        transparency 0         # default - chair is very solid
    }

    # Base of chair
    Cube {                     # make a cube
        < . . . >
```

Texture and Image Maps

Using the Material node is not the only way to apply color or texture
to an object. For complicated images VRML allows the designer to
take a 2D image and map it onto an object. Many of the browsers have
a variety of support for image file formats. The most common among
them are GIF and JPEG, but it is always a good idea to test them with
different browsers. Fortunately for VRML the node format for pasting
these images into the documents and virtual worlds remain the same
no matter what the image file format is. Additionally, there are a multitude of easily attainable paint programs that can save the images
under multiple file formats and therefore converting files to GIF or
JPEG is a simple task.

Texture2 Node Format and Default Settings

```
Texture2 {
        filename   " "      # String value
        image      0 0 0    # Image pixel values
        wrapS      REPEAT   # wrap type: REPEAT, CLAMP
        wrapT      REPEAT   # wrap type: REPEAT, CLAMP
}
```

The **filename** field contains the name of the location and file to be
mapped upon the object. This name can even be a URL to a location
somewhere out on the Internet. The next three fields are for more advanced settings. The **image** field allows the user to map specific image
pixels instead of an image. In this case the filename field must be ex-
cluded otherwise a conflict will exist. This field is hardly ever used except by very advanced VRML programmers. The fields of **wrapS** and
wrapT are both enumerated fields with possible values of either RE-
PEAT or CLAMP. In the wrap fields the S represents the horizontal
coordinate of the image and the T represents the vertical coordinate.
When mapping an image onto an object the REPEAT command allows the browser to repeat the image in either the horizontal direction
(S) and/or the vertical direction(T). If CLAMP is used the image is
clamped in at one specific range on the object.

In the next example, the Texture2 node in a window frame world
made from wood will be used to establish a homey wood tone to the
image (see Figure 6-31).

Figure 6-31
Window Frame

```
#VRML V1.0 ascii

DEF window Separator {

# Make the frame
Separator {
      # Make it a wooden frame
      Texture2 {
            filename              "d:\vrmlcode\wood.gif"
      }

      Cube {                          # make a cube
            width  0.5
            height 15.0
            depth  0.5
      }                               # end cube

      Cube {                          # make a cube
            width  10.0
            height 0.5
            depth  0.5
      }                               # end cube
```

```
Transform {
      translation -6 0 0
}                                  # end of transformation

Cube {                             # make a cube
      width  2.0
      height 15.0
      depth  1.0
}                                  # end cube

Transform {
      translation 12 0 0
}                                  # end of transformation

Cube {                             # make a cube
      width  2.0
      height 15.0
      depth  1.0
}                                  # end cube

Transform {
      translation -6 -8.5 0
}                                  # end of transformation

Cube {                             # make a cube
      width  14.0
      height 2.0
      depth  1.0
}                                  # end cube

Transform {
      translation 0 17 0
}                                  # end of transformation

Cube {                             # make a cube
      width  14.0
      height 2.0
      depth  1.0
}                                  # end cube

}                                  # end of frame separator
}                                  # end of window separator
```

Textures are a great, simple way to give an object a natural look and to add a realistic edge to VRML worlds. Using any search engine on a Web browser you can find multiple sites that contain texture libraries. A few examples of good repositories for a library of texture images are located at both the VRML Repository: Software/Textures (http://sdsc.edu/SDSC/Partners/vrml/software/textures.html) and at Texture Land! (http://www.meat.com/textures.html). Even with a paint program and/or a scanner you can create many of your own images to be used in a world. Because building a good texture library is such an important part of advanced VRML world building, future browsers may come with standard texture libraries built right into them. One suggestion is to create a standard VRML texture library on a CD-ROM. This would not only greatly increase rendering speeds since textures would be located locally, it would allow designers to easily incorporate a huge volume of standard textures into VRML worlds.

Linking

In the previous chapter, the ability to set up Internet links within VRML documents was described as being one of the vital elements of a virtual world. It would be impossible to create one file that could contain an entire world (or if done it would be a VERY large file and take a VERY long time to render). Just like the World Wide Web that uses HTML, it is because of the near impossibility for one page to contain all of the information that linking documents together is so appealing. Besides, why do work twice and retype in redundant information when someone else has already compiled all the information on another page? The VRML concept works exactly the same way.

WWWAnchor Node Format and Default Settings

```
WWWAnchor {
     name            " "    # String value
     description     " "    # String value
     map             NONE   # Mapping type : NONE, POINT
}
```

The **WWWAnchor** node is actually just like a separator node. All of the other nodes contained within are child nodes. What the WWWAnchor node offers is that all of the object nodes contained within it have become a hyperlink. By clicking on the object, like clicking on a hypertext line in HTML, the browser then accesses the URL or file link indicated in the **name** field. The **description** field contains an optional string value that will be displayed in replacement of the browser displaying the link to the URL or file. The **map** field is an advanced feature of the WWWAnchor node that will send the actual X, Y, and Z coordinates back to the server.

If the Web server is setup to interpret mapping coordinates, it can have links associated with where a user clicks. The default setting for the map field is set to NONE, which basically disables the map function as most Web servers are not set up to handle this feature. In the case of a system enabled with mapping, then the POINT value will cause the browser to return the X, Y, and Z coordinates when the mouse is clicked.

The other method of linking that VRML offers is **WWWInline.** It is perhaps one of its greatest attributes in relation to the Internet's concept of sharing resources. When creating a virtual environment, a world builder may have previously created many of the objects, or perhaps someone else has created an object, that the designer may wish to include in this new environment. Instead of having to cut, paste, copy, and retype in the code for an object, VRML allows the user to create an in-line link that can go out, retrieve a file, either locally or across the Internet with a URL, and render it within the current VRML document. In a sense it is like the USE command except that the piece of code exits in another file instead of as an original within the current file.

WWWInline Node Format and Default Settings

```
WWWInline {
     name         " "      # String value
     bboxSize    0 0 0    # Floating point values
     bboxCenter  0 0 0    # Floating point values
}
```

The WWWInline node acts just like a separator node when rendering an object. The VRML browser will save the current properties of all settings before entering, then when completed, it will reset the properties to their previous saved settings. The **name** field is exactly like the name field within the WWWAnchor node. It is the location and name of the file, and URL if necessary, to be included in the VRML document. The **bboxSize** and **bboxCenter** are optional fields that create an imaginary bounding box that the VRML browser can use to determine if the image is visible from the users perspective. If it is not visible, the browser will not render the image until it is necessary, therefore saving processing time.

Also, if a user wants to disable the loading of in-line images, a wire frame bounding box is rendered to signify that normally an object would exist in this place. The bboxSize field is for the width, height, and depth of the box and the bboxCenter is the X, Y, and Z coordinates (in relation to the current origin) of the center of the box. If a user does not enter in values for bboxSize and bboxCenter, then the VRML browser generates an estimation for the values for the box.

Some VRML browsers do not automatically load inline images. There is usually a setting within the browser to activate this option. In WorldView select the Options within the tool bar. Then select Load Inline Objects. A check mark should appear next to it when you view it again to signify it is active. If a browser does not have this activated it may only load the boundary box to indicate where an image will be located.

Some previous examples in this chapter have created a virtual Empire State building and a UFO. The code for these two objects exist on the CD-ROM in the **d:\vrmlcode** directory under the names of **empire.wrl** and **ufo.wrl.** The following code shows how simple it is to create a simple VRML document that will access the object library and create a world with a UFO flying around the Empire State building, like something out of Orson Wells' *War of the Worlds* or the *X-files* (see Figure 6-32).

```
#VRML V1.0 ascii


DEF war-of-the-worlds Separator {

# Render the Empire State building
WWWInline {
     name "d:\vrmlcode\empire.wrl"
}                                    # end WWWInline of Empire State Building

# Render UFO one
Separator {
     Transform {
          translation 20.0 10.0 3.0
          rotation    1.0 0 0 0.349
          scaleFactor 0.25 0.25 0.25
     }                                # end transformation
```

```
    WWWInline {
          name "d:\vrmlcode\ufo.wrl"
    }                                    # end WWWInline
}                                        # end UFO one separator

# Render UFO two
Separator {
    Transform {
          translation -30.0 40.0 0.0
          rotation    1.0 0 1.0 1.571
          scaleFactor 0.25 0.25 0.25
    }                                    # end of transformation

    WWWInline {
          name "d:\vrmlcode\ufo.wrl"
    }                                    # end WWWInline
}                                        # end UFO two separator

}                                        # end of war-of-the-worlds separator
```

Figure 6-32
Alien Sightseers

Summary

The information presented in this chapter is not a complete explanation of what can be done with VRML. For example, the chapter has elaborated very little on lighting and camera positioning. But most beginning world builders can pretty much leave those things alone. The default lights and cameras in VRML provide a roomy, well-lit world to play in.

Even as this book is currently being written, the VRML language is continually being improved and standardized by the Internet community. In many ways this chapter only scratches the surface of some of the possibilities that VRML offers as a construction company for cyberspace. What it is intended to show is the basic fundamentals of the language so that anyone can create their own virtual worlds and objects that can be accessed and explored with any VRML browser, or even made available to others on the Web itself. Appendix F lists the names of all the source files on the CD-ROM for all of the examples of this chapter.

Playing with the VRML building blocks in cyberspace hopefully has de-mystified the complexity of VRML. The simple rule to always remember is anything complex can always be broken down into smaller pieces. Then it is just a matter of pulling the right blocks out of our cyberspace toy chest to build a virtual Taj Mahal. It is time to move from being the six-year old with blocks and become cyberspace architects and virtual world builders, even if you still, sometimes, play with blocks.

Chapter

7

The Future
of VRML

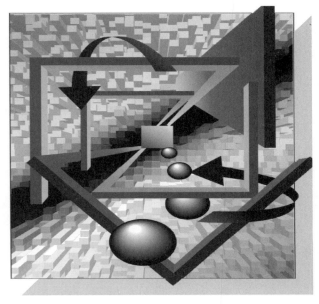

Imagine a virtual world as a soft, inviting meadow with a swift flowing brook running through it. The brook is fed by a splashing waterfall. Occasionally, birds fly by and perch on tree branches that bend under the added weight. The wind whistles through rustling leaves, the brook gurgles soothingly, and the birds chirp periodically. Like all other virtual worlds, the visitor can wander around and even fall into the brook if distracted.

There is no need to imagine this world. It exists today on the Internet at http://www.dnx.com/lr/. But it is not a VRML virtual world. This world includes motion and audio as well as 3D virtual objects. This Web site offers a glimpse at the possible future of VRML, a future that includes not only 3D objects but *behaviors* of objects in the virtual world. The site in question cannot be visited with a VRML browser. The site requires a special kind of multimedia 3D browser. The concept is called Liquid Reality, a commercial development from the Dimension X company. Liquid Reality is designed to run with Java-enabled browsers like Netscape 2.0 and extends VRML in a number of ways, especially with regard to behaviors.

This book has explored many aspects of VRML, from its roots and purposes through VRML browsers and even through the creation of virtual worlds. But it is important to remember that VRML is a moving target. VRML is an evolving standard. It is constantly changing to add new capabilities and features to improve the usefulness of VRML. There is, and will be, no *final* version of VRML.

This should come as no surprise to anyone. There is, and will be, no final version of a simple PC. Hardware evolves and PC platforms must evolve along with it. Software evolves even more quickly than hardware. There will be no final version of VRML just as there will be no final version of Novell Netware, Harvard Graphics, or even IBM's SNA. This sometimes makes life difficult for implementers and planners in the computer and networking fields and industries, but at the same time it makes this life quite interesting and never, ever boring.

That said, it is still true that the VRML world is eagerly awaiting the new VRML 2.0 specification, to be completed in late 1996. Since the process of moving from VRML 1.0 and VRML 1.1 to VRML 2.0 will be repeated numerous times in the future to VRML 3.0 and beyond, a little bit of what went on behind the scenes may be instructive. The call for ideas about just what VRML 2.0 should contain went out through the VRML Architecture Group (VAG) in early 1996. VAG is an organization that has as members anybody who is anybody in the VRML community. By February of 1996, which is a very fast timeframe for this type of activity, six proposals had been received. These proposals were:

1.   Active VRML from Microsoft.

2.   Dynamic Worlds from a group of companies.

3.   HoloWeb from Sun Microsystems (the Java folk).

4.   Moving Worlds from SGI.

5.   Out of this World from Apple.

6.   Reactive Virtual Environment from IBM Japan (a subsidiary of IBM itself).

Once these proposals were received and circulated among the VAG membership, a lively debate over the pros and cons, and strengths and weaknesses of each followed. There was even a vote taken in March 1996 as to which of the six proposals should form the basis for the working draft of VRML 2.0. This is not to say that the other proposals would be ignored or discarded. Rather, the best features of each would presumably be added to the VRML 2.0 working draft. The only question was where to start.

The voting allowed a range of five choices from "strongly in favor" to "strongly against." When all was said and done, the voting showed that the SGI proposal for Moving Worlds had both the highest support and least opposition. Considering VAG's stated "middle of the road" approach to VRML 2.0, both qualities were essential for any contender.

The timetable for the final VRML 2.0 specification is not set in stone. However, it appears that Moving Worlds will be merged with the best features of the other proposals by the end of 1996 to become the final VRML 2.0 specification. In fact, this is even an opportunity for people to actually watch VRML 2.0 unfold.

As VRML evolves beyond what the VRML 1.0 and even the VRML 2.0 standard says VRML must contain, some guideposts are clearly established. This final chapter will examine some of the issues involved in VRML development and future directions that VRML worlds and the browsers that cruise them will take.

What about Java?

Java has been mentioned several times in this work without much elaboration. Simply put, Java is a method of adding "interactive content" to Web pages in a standard, open, and multi-platform fashion. Java is even more than this, but a full description of Java would fill a book by itself. Several have already been written, and many more will come. This section will explore Java only to the extent that it is necessary for an understanding of how Java and VRML fit together, if at all.

Java was invented by Sun Microsystems and HotJava is the Sun Java-enabled browser. Introduced in May, 1995 at SunWorld 95, Java has been another hot topic on the Web and Internet. HotJava has been ported to several platforms, and Netscape 2.0 includes Java support.

Before Java, Web pages were strictly static entities. The Web page was loaded and examined, and that was that. The Web page content never shifted, never moved. Java changed all that. Java-enabled Web pages scroll banners, tell time, and play games interactively with users. The code that tells the Java-enabled Web browser how to do all this is loaded along with the Web pages, or when the user points and clicks at a certain page location.

Java effects need not be earthshaking or astonishing. The simplest motion on a Web page can be eye-catching and effective. One well-known Web page has a simple Java clock with a spinning red hand. It is difficult to convey this effect well in print. Nevertheless, here are two different "clock readings" from the page.

Figure 7-1
What Java Can Do

Java is more than wiggling Web pages. Java is an architecture. Java is an environment. Java is a programming language. As an architecture, Java is a standard way to implement features so that a Java-enabled Web page created with one software package can flawlessly interact with a Java-enabled Web browser written by someone else. As an environment, Java is a run-time system for interpreting Java "applets" to run on almost any hardware platform, from UNIX workstations to Intel-based Windows PCs. As a programming language, Java is an object-oriented, C-like, interpreted language for running distributed, multi-threaded applications (the applets).

Java is above all an object-oriented language. VRML, on the other hand, is not. Object-oriented languages stress breaking an application program down into a number of communicating, re-usable, dynamically linked and executed tasks. Older, procedural programming methods have been described as "the art of re-inventing the wheel." If a function or procedure that opened and read a file was needed in another program, the lines of code that performed this task was copied into the main program to be compiled and linked with the new program. In a suite of related programs, such as a word processor and spreadsheet package, each open-and-read-file mini-program had to be included in each main program. Every possible function of the programs must be added and packaged this way.

Object-oriented programming offers a way out. Let the word processing program and spreadsheet program share the open-and-read-the-file routine. Load the routine into memory, link to it, and run the routine only when either the word processing program or spreadsheet program needs it. The main program need only send a simple message to the routine: a message to open and read a specific file. The reply need only be the first record or an error message. The end result, of course, is very similar to Windows' *common dialog boxes* for performing these tasks. In fact, there are many ways to accomplish this result. Windows' OLE (Object Linking and Embedding), Novell's AppWare Data Bus (ADB), IBM's System Object Model (SOM), and NeXT's Portable Distributed Objects (PDO) are only the most well known.

The problem is that when system running all of these object packages linked to the Internet, how does a Sparc workstation in Colorado access an *object* residing on a Pentium PC in Vermont? They are not compatible at all. All programs written for multiple platforms must be re-compiled to be run on each individual architecture. Pulling up a common dialog box to open and read a file across the Internet in this scenario is pretty much impossible.

With Java, the problem goes away. Java is the same on a Sparc workstation as on a Pentium PC. Using Java to make Web pages jump and dance is only the most obvious application of this cross-platform capability. Java allows any machine attached to the Internet to run the same executable that includes the proper Java interpreter. The ultimate goal of Java is to make the only application that needs to be developed for an individual platform the Java application itself. This would create on each computer a Java Virtual Machine. Any Java application could then be loaded in exactly the same version across the Internet and executed properly on any platform at all.

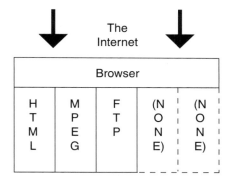

Figure 7-2
Traditional Browser
Architecture

On the Web, users are frequently frustrated that a site containing information desperately needed is in a format that cannot be read correctly by the Web browser. The "helper application" or viewer is not available. With Java, the necessary viewer can be present in one format (Java) at the site itself and downloaded as needed by any users whose browser requires the viewer. For example, a browser without a QuickTime (QT) movie viewer can download and operate a QT viewer on the spot and then view the movie file correctly. The same can be done with a VRML viewer.

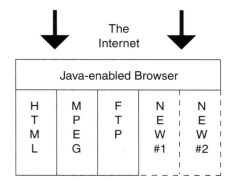

Figure 7-3
The Java Model
of a Web Browser

The Java Language

Java is designed to offer a number of features that make Java well-suited for developing applications for the Internet. Java is portable, robust, secure, and dynamic. Java also has several features used in newer programming languages, such as heavy object-orientation, high-performance techniques, and simplifications of complex C++ language constructs.

Java is portable because it is an interpreted language. This means that every computer running a Java applet must first translate the Java code into native machine language code. Interpreted languages used to be considered too slow to be used efficiently on PC platforms. But increased processor *horsepower* coupled with several high-performance features have made Java a respectable language in terms of raw speed. The nice thing about this approach is that Java code does not have to be separately compiled for different platforms. Such fundamental platform differences such as integer sizes (16 bit? 32 bit?) and byte order addressing schemes (*big endian* like RISC or Motorola? *little endian* like Intel?) never arise in the Java interpreted environment.

Java is robust because Java includes automatic features that give traditional programmers problems in writing solid code. Most errors in code occur from the mis-handling of pointers. No problem in Java: there are no pointers. No need to allocate and free memory either. Java manages memory automatically as well. Java also checks the bound of arrays or tables to prevent over-running these structures as well. While some programmers may miss the control they enjoyed with C++, most developers will appreciate the robustness of Java. Java bugs are much harder to generate.

Java is secure because distributed, connectionless network environments like the Internet need as much security as they can get to prevent the spread of computer viruses and thwart hacking attempts. The thought of loading code across the Internet automatically and running it immediately as Java does makes many local network administrators nervous, to say the least. To allay these justified fears, Java interpreters check the code for Java compliance, respect memory boundaries, and restrict local file system access.

Java is dynamic because Java allows for the loading of code objects on an as-needed basis. For example, if a file format is encountered with a Java-enabled browser that the browser cannot understand, the Java-enabled browser can download, link to, and run the required viewer of helper application for that format. In Java, this is "dynamically adding functionality by linking in new objects."

Java is said to be *heavily* object-oriented because there is just no possible way to circumvent the encapsulation methods that Java objects (known as classes) employ. Unfortunately, this also means that Java "applets" (a collection of Java classes) tend to look like a loose collection of code fragments that do not do much of anything on their own. It is very hard to *read* Java code to get an idea of what the applet is actually trying to do.

Java is said to include high-performance techniques because the Java developers have made every effort to make interpreted Java code as fast as possible. It is still unrealistic to expect interpreted code to run as quickly as compiled code, but Java is quick nonetheless. For instance, Java includes a built-in multi-threading capability. Multi-threading means that Java applets can perform more than one function at the same time. A multi-threaded word processor, for example, can spell check and grammar check a document at the same time.

Finally, Java is said to simplify many C++ language constructs because these constructs are just not allowed in Java. The lack of pointers has already been mentioned. In addition, Java banishes several other C++ features. (Non-C++ programmers need not read nor understand the following sentence.) In Java, there are no #defines, no structures or unions, no multiple inheritance, no individual functions, no operator overloading, no casting, and no goto. All of these C++ features were deemed to be unnecessary for the Java object-oriented approach.

Java and VRML

Java sounds like a wonderful Web tool, but what has all this to do with VRML and virtual worlds on the Internet? The simple fact is that the future of VRML may be in the arms of Java. To see why, it is important to realize that there are three major Internet activities that Java is particularly well-suited for. The three things are full applications, intelligent agents, and VRML world browsing.

Java is positioned to be *the* universal standard for the transfer of dynamic and executable Web content over the Internet. There are obvious benefits in having a single standard for Web developers, Internet site providers, and end users as well.

For the Web content developer, the Java environment provides a single development platform that can be used to construct applications that may be distributed both safely and efficiently to the whole Internet community. It will no longer be necessary to have a project team port an application to a dozen or more platforms in order to satisfy and reach every user on the Internet. For example, for the longest time, the most effective VRML browser, WebSpace, was not available on the most common Windows version. It could not be ported to that environment. Any Internet application developer can appreciate the large potential number of platforms that users are constantly agitating for applications to be ported to. But only major developers can afford the time and effort and resources needed to port programs to all possible environments. In this regard, Java will have the largest impact on smaller groups of developers, or even individuals, who have never had the resources to easily port applications before. Now application can be developed for exactly one platform—the Java Virtual Machine—and wind up with an application that can run anywhere.

For the Web site provider, the Java language can be implemented on any Web server. Java content can be served up on Web pages as easily as in-line images or audio files. But the nicest thing about Java is the end of the need for complicated and operating system-dependent CGI scripts for such simple Web site features as image maps or forms. All the image map and form functionality can be absorbed into the Java applet. The need for the browser to link back across the Internet to an executable module on the Web server just to figure out where the mouse was when the user clicked within an image is eliminated. The Java code can figure that out for itself. Web site administrators can just allocate some file space for the Web files and Java code and relax. The need for complicated path directives and CGI scripts are a thing of the past in the Java environment. The interactivity moves to where it properly belongs: to the client device.

For the end user, the Java environment means a more seamless and integrated Web browsing capability. Data, networking, and interactivity are all blended together. Users will no longer have to concern themselves that their Web browser includes the right viewer or helper application. The Java classes can provide for the encapsulation of all the data within objects that essentially take care of themselves. An intrepid Java Internet traveler can just load up a bare-bones browser, which is basically a Java interpreter with a minimum class structure for Internet access, and shove off. The Java browser will automatically load the data handlers needed from the visited Web sites and the user explores the Internet. And upgraded Java classes will be loaded automatically as they are released. This will make the need to download upgraded browsers, and the associated severe Web site congestion, a thing of the past.

Using Java for Applications

One of the most promising functions of Java is in the area of application development. As a full programming language, there is no reason that Java cannot be extended beyond simple applets into the realm of full-blooded application programs. Java programs can behave in a totally stand-alone manner. All of these stand-alone applications can work just like any other application and can be used to develop more traditional computer application programs like spreadsheets, word processors, and almost anything else. In fact, Java could be used to do things in application programs that are more difficult to do in other programming languages.

Java is being considered for use in so-called *metered use* applications. A lot of users would like to have a specialized program that could be used to produce a special report or lend a degree of sophistication to an otherwise bland production. For example, when writing this book, it would have been nice to have an application to generate eye-catching examples of mathematical visualization techniques for inclusion in the text. Unfortunately, the word processor program included no 3D surface generation tools, and buying a separate package for one-time use just to include pretty pictures would have been prohibitively expensive.

Some visualization programs could be downloaded as shareware over the Internet and used without cost for a trial period. But this is not a perfect solution in this case. The program would have been used, and productively, to produce pictures, not for simple evaluation and trial use. Again, the choice is between paying for the full product for one-time use, or feeling guilty about what was done for free (most users quickly get over such feelings). But Java offers hope for a third and more productive possibility.

With Java, the developers of the software would make a Java version available for downloading over the Internet. The user could download the program and use it once. When finished, the Java application would contact the source site, indicate how long it had been in use, and then delete itself from the user's system. The user would then be billed for using the program, perhaps at a rate as low as a few cents per minute. This would surely beat having to shell out hundreds of dollars for the full application, and then even more money to keep the application updated and current. The latest Java version would always be available at the Web site.

Even if a user had bought a shrink-wrapped version of the application program, periodic checks of the Web site would automatically download the latest updated versions with new and added features. Java could integrate the new classes seamlessly, independent of hardware platform.

Consider the possibilities if the application happens to be the latest VRML world authoring tool. Most people would use such a tool inter-mittently, or just once, to create a virtual world of their very own. The Java VRML world application would bill users equitably: less for sim-pler, quickly built worlds, and more for more elaborate and time-consuming places.

The big drawback of interpreted languages for larger applications used to be speed of execution. But the success of Microsoft's Visual Basic changed all that. The ease of use that Visual Basic gave to devel-opers and even end users for creating Windows applications offset any performance penalty. And the speed difference was only notice-able in the most demanding situations.

Using Java for Intelligent Agents

Another interesting possible use of Java is in the field of intelligent agents. Some software has already been developed that takes advan-tage of this concept. The most frequently cited example is MagicCap's Telescript software, but some would even include Microsoft's Bob in that category. The whole idea of intelligent agents is to place more and more of the decision-making process and task-handling features on the software and less and less of this burden on the user.

Without intelligent agents, a user seeking the lowest cost airfare to At-lanta from New York must access data on each airline flying that route, and sometimes each one repeatedly as fares change during the day. With an intelligent airline fare agent in action, the user simply in-structs the software to "book me the lowest NY-Atlanta fare, and let me know what you did at 5 o'clock" and then sits back. The agent software carries out the nitty-gritty work.

The Internet is the perfect place for the use of intelligent agents. The Internet abounds with all kinds of information, but even with special query and index sites, the information needed can be difficult to find. Intelligent agents can cruise un-assisted through the Internet and Web, gathering the needed data as requested. Intelligent agents can even graze sites periodically, just to see if anything has changed since the last visit.

Performing such an activity on the Internet would be impossible today. A program would have to essentially leave the user's computer and visit sites that had different platforms, file systems, and operating systems than the user's system. What application could feel equally at home on a Sparc workstation and a Windows PC? Only Java.

Java is the perfect language for intelligent agents. A Java agent could take advantage of its underlying dynamic and portable nature to move from system to system and access a database, collect data, and move on. And Java agents can do this on all hardware platforms. The secure nature of the Java language specification may help to alleviate fears of system administrators about letting programs come in from the Internet and execute on their systems. However, all of the best intentions of Java with regard to security may be undone due to the notoriously insecure nature of browser software and server hardware. Java may suffer because of this association.

A Java-implemented VRML *agent* could go out into the Web and seek out new virtual worlds on behalf of the user. The worlds might even match some user search criteria: new virtual cathedrals, for instance. As virtual worlds on the Internet become more popular, consider how long would it take to access 100 virtual reality sites by hand? How about 1000?

Using Java for VRML Browsing

Java is already influencing the development of VRML. All the talk of VRML *behaviors* is a direct result of the need to add more interactive content and animation to VRML worlds. Right now, VRML worlds are lonely places. Sixteen users can be exploring the same room, but to each one the place looks deserted. Where is everybody? To many observers, the addition of interaction between visitors to virtual worlds will finally let VRML cross over the boundary into *cyberspace*.

Java is being considered for adding that degree of interaction. With the addition of Java applets to a virtual world defined with VRML, the visitor's applets can all be coordinated to update each other's motions as they move about. Java-assisted VRML will eventually allow for the visitors to actually talk to each other and speak in their own words.

With Java, VRML worlds can come alive. Strangely, it is the Java developers that mention VRML much more frequently than the VRML developers and *gurus* mention Java. Instead, there are many references in VRML research documents and discussion groups about adding *behaviors* to VRML worlds, without so much as a word about the possibilities of Java.

JavaScript

Most of the potential of Java, especially when considered with regard to VRML, lies in the future. One of the problems is that the development of Java applets requires a working knowledge of the Java language. While Java is in many ways simpler to learn and use than C++, Java is not trivial.

Netscape and Sun have teamed up recently to introduce JavaScript. JavaScript is a more user-friendly scripting language that allows users to enhance and modify Java applets without having to learn the details of the C-like objects used by the full Java programming language. Just as users can create smart spreadsheets and customized word processing documents using a macro language, JavaScript can be used by HTML authors to build interactive features into any Web page.

JavaScript has strong industry support. Macromedia, Silicon Graphics (an important company in the VRML arena), and Oracle have announced commitments to JavaScript.

Shockwave and Other Web Tools

Java is not the only tool that is capable of adding animation and multimedia content to Web pages. Microsoft has announced the Internet Studio for Windows 95 (developed under the code name of "blackbird") that will include a way to mix HTML, VRML, and much more at a Web site. Microsoft is exploring ways to make existing tools like Visual Basic extensible enough to provide similar features like Java.

IBM and Macromedia have developed Shockwave for Director. Shockwave grew out of the Macromedia Director Multimedia Studio product. Director is a very capable multimedia authoring tool. It combines four widely used applications for multimedia authoring, 3D modeling, sound editing, and digital video development. Brought together under the Macromedia Director umbrella, these tools give a wide degree of freedom in creating multimedia content that is pretty much state-of-the art stuff.

The Director Multimedia Studio features a quite powerful and complete set of tools for creating very sophisticated multimedia productions. The Studio package includes Director, a powerful tool for multimedia production; Extreme 3D, a package for 3D modeling, animation, and post production work; SoundEdit 16, (for the Macintosh version) or Sound Forge (for the Windows version) for producing very clean and rich sound; and finally Fractal Painter, a very good paint and image-editing tool. These tools are combined to enable users to create corporate presentations, sales and marketing demonstrations, information kiosks, and interactive multimedia titles that can be delivered to Windows 95 or 3.1, Macintosh, and 3DO systems, as well as over the Internet using Shockwave.

Director is also a cross-platform player and viewer for multimedia including animation and audio. Shockwave is a method for extended Director authoring and browsing capabilities across the Internet.

Shockwave for Director is a full set of technologies that allows complete and standard Director movies to be played from Web pages on the Internet. Because Shockwave can use the standard Director movie format, the features of Director for creating interactive multimedia content are immediately familiar to all of the multimedia professionals who are currently using the Director product.

Both Director and Shockwave for Director are intended for creative non-programmers. Any and all graphic artists, writers, animators, imaging professionals, and many others can now use their multimedia skills to create Web pages that include or are even based on interactive multimedia content.

Shockwave is made up of two major components; afterburner, which is a program for compressing standard Director movies for use on the Web, and the Shockwave player, which is a Director player that has been extended to include security, caching and streaming features better optimized for playback over a network.

Director for Shockwave is optimized for Web multimedia content. Web page developers can easily produce such content as interactive advertising games, both for single and multiple users, presentations for communicating marketing and product messages, training and tutorial materials, information kiosks for both communication purposes and user input, and small "flying logo" type animations for adding interest to existing Web pages.

Macromedia has licensed Java for future versions of Director and Authorware. Java was chosen by Macromedia because it is a good language to use as a basis for network-based multimedia tools and applications. Shockwave will initially use Java to support the Internet and Web user community by providing playback in future versions of Director and Authorware with Java applets. At the same time, Macromedia will be looking at combining its own technology with Java as a system software development language to create a new "continuous publishing" tool for the high-bandwidth Internet and Web applications of the near future. The new Java-based tool will be intended for use at Web sites that need constantly updated multimedia and typographically rich content for their Web pages.

Shockwave and Java are really targeted at two very different user communities. Director itself and Shockwave for Director are easy to use for creative professionals with little or no programming experience. These users would include graphic artists, writers, animators, videographers, sound specialists, imaging professionals, trainers, educators, and so on (including 3D developers of animated VRML worlds).

On the other hand, Java is really best used by experienced programmers who want to create secure, multi-platform, distributed applications and systems. The C++ root of Java makes it familiar ground for
these users.

Shockwave uses Director to prepare content for the Web site pages
that need multimedia. A Director multimedia *author* prepares a movie
or set of movies using Director. The movie is then simply dragged
onto the Afterburner application that compresses it for optimal playback. The author then integrates the movie into a Web page by using
the HTML Embed tag in order to specify the movie name, height,
width, and position on the page. When the page is viewed using a
Shockwave-capable Web browser such as Netscape 2.0, the movie
plays and looks exactly as it did in Director.

Macromedia likes to call Web pages with ShockWave for Director
"shocked" pages. If a non-Shockwave capable browser is used to view
a shocked Web page, the familiar broken image graphic for that
browser will appear when attempting to view Director movies. The
same graphic will appear if the Shockwave extension is not installed
when using an otherwise Shockwave-capable browser. Shockwave installation is easy, and as automatic as possible.

Shockwave is being used already by both major corporations and
multimedia developers to add high-impact multimedia content to a
number of sites. These sites include Turner Home Entertainment, Via-
com, Intel, ad hoc Interactive, Xronos Inc, Time, Yahoo, and CNN.

A good rule of thumb for Internet delivery of Shockwave Director
movies is that a 100K file will take about a minute to download
over a 14.4KB line. A 100K file can include a small but complete
Director title, complete with interactivity, fast-moving animation,
and small sounds. In general, a small Director piece can be produced to fit in the space taken up by a GIF image in an HTML
page. So almost any GIF image currently in a Web page can potentially be replaced by an animated, fully interactive Director
piece.

While Microsoft's Internet Studio has yet to be generally released,
Shockwave is available as an add-on to browsers such as Netscape 2.0.
A sample of what Shockwave can do is available at Web sites such as
Intel's at http://www.intel.com/. A circuit board appears at the top
of the page. Before the user's eyes, the chip sends out paths to other
board components, while an audio "click-click" plays at the same
time. The whole thing lasts only about 10 seconds. But the impact is

lasting. Many users linger and play it over and over, which is, of course, the goal of any Web site.

Shockwave is much more closely related to Java than VRML, especially since both Java and Shockwave support behaviors and multimedia content already, while VRML does not. However, the current directions of VRML research will only lead to a convergence of Java, Shockwave, and VRML capabilities in the future.

Selected VRML Research Projects and Proposals

As the evolution of VRML continues, there are a number of sources of information that can be used to follow the planned developments more closely. Rather than rehash and re-interpret the latest research efforts and directions, at this point it is probably better to let the researchers speak for themselves. Also, much of the information is in the form of HTML Web pages, that do not lend themselves easily to sequential textual access and presentation. Here then is a list of selected VRML research projects and proposals. Most sites also include at least some traditional text material as well as hyper-linked information.

The best place to go on the Internet to gather information is the VRML Repository at the San Diego Supercomputing Center. The VRML Repository is a kind of clearing house for VRML information, software, browsers, and sample virtual worlds. The VRML Repository is located at http://www.sdsc.edu/VRML (Figure 7-4). The home page features the "official" VRML logo.

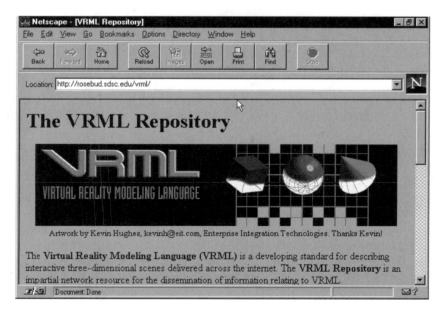

Figure 7-4
VRML Repository
Web Page

A little exploring of the VRML Repository will yield a large amount of information on the future plans for VRML and several other interesting VRML concepts. For example, Mark Pesce, one of the key people behind VRML, has created the *zero circle*. The zero circle is intended to become the starting point for all VRML world exploration. Links to all reachable places in virtual reality can be placed at the various *signposts* and give a real sense of orientation to an otherwise chaotic experience.

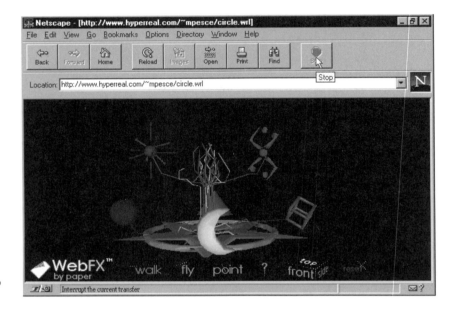

Figure 7-5
The VRML Zero
Circle

Some of the information on the future of VRML available at the VRML Repository includes the following items.

- The VRML Architecture Group: This site was started by the VRML gang at *Wired* magazine. *Wired* was and remains an early and great backer of VRML. The VRML Architecture Group (VAG) is looking at extending VRML to the ultimate level: a fully interactive, scaleable cyberspace, just like in the science fiction novels. VAG features notes, the new and improved VRML 1.0c, and (sometimes) the VRML 1.1 draft specification. This is where to go to monitor the development of the VRML 2.0 specification and check on implementation progress. There is even a mission statement: "The VRML Architecture Group mission is to establish VRML as the world's most reliable, useful, and widely used open specification for interactive 3D on the Internet and the World Wide Web, and to chart a course for the future versions of

VRML." All of the VRML founders and gurus hang out here, including Gavin Bell, Tony Parisi, and Mark Pesce. Check up on VAG at: http://vag.vrml.org/.

White Papers available at VAG:

Brian Blau's *VRML 1.X and Beyond—Proposal Mania*
http://www.bluerock.com/vrml/proposal.html

Jan Hardenbergh's *The VRML of Babel*
http://vrml.wired.com/future/jch.txt
and
Proposal for ElevationGrid node
http://www.oki.com/vrml/ElevationGrid.html

William Martens' *Audio in VRML*
http://hyperreal.com/~wim/vrsl.html

Tom Meyer's *Adding Behavior to VRML*
http://www.cs.brown.edu/research/graphics/research/papers/vrmlbehaviors.html

Mitra's *VRML+*
http://www.worlds.net/products/vrmlplus/technical
and
VRML Behaviors
http://earth.path.net/mitra/papers/behaviors/Behaviors.html
and
VRML Behaviors—an API
http://earth.path.net/mitra/papers/behaviors/Api.html
and
URNs and VRML
http://earth.path.net/mitra/papers/vrml-urn.html">

Tony Parisi's *VRML 1.1 Proposal*
http://www.hyperion.com/intervista/vrml/vrml11.htm

Mark Pesce's *Scale*
http://vrml.wired.com/future/scale.html

- Sony's extensions to VRML 1.0:   While many talk about extending VRML, some just do it. Sony has extended the VRML 1.0 standard in a number of ways, including scripting, object attributes, and audio features. Some things will undoubtedly find their way into VRML 2.0. The extensions are detailed at: http://www.csl.sony.co.jp/project/VS/evrml1.htm.

- VRML extensions and their implementations: A nice list of all VRML extensions and which browsers currently support them. The list is located at: http://earth.path.net/mitra.

- Adding behavior to VRML: This describes a general method allowing both for the specification of new types of VRML nodes and their associated behavior. Again, the intent is to make future versions of VRML more *Java-like*. A copy of the proposal is available at: http://www.cs.brown.edu/research/graphics/research/papers/vrmlbehaviors.html.

- Adding more behaviors to VRML: This is a model that has been presented at the ACM SIVE95 conference in Iowa City. The approach was not originally intended for VRML, but was adapted from a general model. More information is availlable at: http://wintermute.gmd.de:8000/vrml/behaviorSpec.html.

- Adding multi-user support to VRML: Some plans and ideas on how to add multi-user support to existing HTTP Web servers. Information is available at: http://wintermute.gmd.de:8000/vrml/VRML95.html.

- Database visualization and VRML: An application of VRML to more traditional data representation. Emphasizes "on the fly" world building and a more intuitive representation for complex data. A paper is available at: http://reality.sgi.com/employees/clay_corp/article/article.html.

- Behavior format for VRML: This paper outlines proposed extensions to VRML to allow for behaviors. The new format, called "BEF" (Behavior Format) by the authors, is envisioned for use in VRML 2.0. In BEF, the descriptions of behavior are included as just a new kind of data. The paper is found at: http://www.besoft.com/bef/.

- Simple behaviors for VRML: These proposed extensions to VRML are important in that they originate with one of the key figures in VRML 1.0 development: Gavin Bell. Bell would include the ability for users to interact with intelligent objects, the ability to create animated 3D objects, the addition of audio in virtual worlds, and so on; an important contribution to VRML 2.0.

The proposal may be found at: http://reality.sgi.com/employ-ees/gavin/vrml/Behaviors.html.

- A simple proposal for extending VRML: This is an effort to make VRML more object-oriented and adding behaviors, a good discussion of some un-resolved issues. The proposal may be found at: http://sunee.uwaterloo.ca/~broehl/vrml/simple_prop.html.

- Virtual Environment Systems: A proposal for a new Virtual Environment Systems (VES) protocol, the VES protocol would handle multiple TCP/IP streams and sockets. VRML would be integrated into the protocol very tightly. The proposal also in-cludes a plan for "virtual HTML," a modification to standard HTML to make it more like VRML, a thought provoking concept. The proposal may be found at: http://www.declab.usu.edu:8080/VES-VRML/.

- VRML Browser API: This is a proposal for an API through which external applications can drive VRML browsers. The whole idea of the API is to enable insertion and manipulation of objects into VRML worlds and scenes. The proposal can be found at: http://www.ubique.com/.

- VRML behaviors: An on-going and very technical discussion on possible behavior scripting for VRML scenes, this is an impor-tant contribution because it includes several proposals from the San Diego Supercomputer Center (SDSC), a pioneer in all Virtual Reality research activities, not only VRML research. The discus-sions may be found at: http://www.sdsc.edu/EnablingTech/Visualization/Behaviors.

Not Exactly VRML but of Related Interest

- Meme (Multitasking Extensible Messaging Environment):   Not all research is focused on VRML itself. Meme is a software pack-age for the development of virtual world applications. But vir-tual worlds built with Meme can be inhabited by multiple users who are connected to a computer network (like the Internet, of course). Meme virtual worlds are distinguished by providing rich object behavior, unlike many menu-driven systems that offer a fixed set of choices. More on Meme may be found at: http://www.immersive.com/.

- The Minimal-Reality Toolkit (MR Toolkit):   MR is also like VRML, but different. MR is a set of software tools for the pro-duction of virtual reality systems and other forms of 3D interfaces. MR consists of a set of subroutine libraries, device drivers, support programs, and a language for describing geometry and behavior. More information may be found at: http://web.cs.ualberta.ca:80/~graphics/MRToolkit.html.

- MSDL: (Manchester Scene Description Language</a>): MSDL was one of the languages seriously considered for the basis of VRML. This site describes the basics of MSDL and includes some sample pictures, generated at the University of Manchester from MSDL files. MSDL itself is available by anonymous ftp, together with some scenes and documentation. What VRML might have been. MSDL information is located at: http://info.mcc.ac.uk/CGU/MSDL/MSDL-intro.html.

- NPSNET: The military continues research into VRML also. NPSNET is currently capable of simulating moving humans and also ground and air vehicles in a distributed networked virtual environment. NPSNET can support about 250–300 *players* using currently available networking and workstation technology. NPSNET is the first 3D virtual environment that is capable of playing and being played across the multi-cast backbone (MBONE) of the Internet. Information on NPSNET is available at: http://www.cs.nps.navy.mil/research/npsnet.

- OOGL (Object-Oriented Graphics Language): Visualization will be an important part of VRML virtual world content of the Internet. OOGL is a geometric visualization format developed by The Geometry Center of the University of Minnesota. It is a non-proprietary, mature language with support for sophisticated graphics and support for hyperbolic geometry. Stop by and see what VRML can be. Check out OOGL at: http://www.geom.umn.edu/software/geomview/docs/oogltour.html.

- OVRT (Open Virtual Reality Testbed</a>): Hey, it's a big virtual world! Somebody's gotta test it! OVRT's mission is to facilitate the development of standard interfaces and testing methodologies to the many novel types of human interface devices: gloves, headgear, and so on, an important aspect of any Virtual Reality system. See how things are going at: http://www.nist.gov/itl/div878/ovrt/OVRThome.html.

- SDML (Spatial Data Modeling Language): Another look at visualization applications for 3D virtual worlds, SDML is a published format for the description of spatial data, particularly CAD and GIS sources. SDML supports geometric and attribute encoding for rich, interactive exploration and query environments. Information on getting data into SDML and WWW-based viewer technology can also be found here. SDML information is available at: http://www.clr.utoronto.ca/CLRMOSAIC/ SDML.html.

- The Tecate Visualization System</a>: Another data visualization effort. Tecate is an exploratory visualization system being developed at The San Diego Supercomputer Center (SDSC) as part of the "Sequoia 2000" project. The original goal of Tecate was to provide an environment that scientists themselves could use to browse and visualize data in a complex data environment. This has broadened with the continued use of the system to providing tools for non-experts to browse and visualize data. Tecate information is located at: http://www.sdsc.edu/SDSC/ Research/Visualization/Tecate/tecate.html.

The above information was compiled from the San Diego Supercomputing Center VRML Repository at: http://www.sdsc.edu/ VRML/.

Appendix

Hardware/Software You Need

Configuring Netscape

Other Tips and Suggestions

Internet Browser Fundamentals

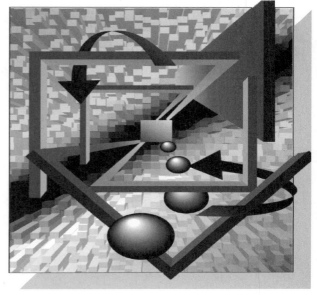

This appendix will explain the fundamentals of a World Wide Web Browser you should use while you are *surfing* on the Information Super Highway. A World Wide Web Browser is absolutely needed if you are planning to navigate through the millions of World Wide Web Homepages on the Internet. Down to the basics, the Internet is a largely unorganized network of information and resources. You can find EVERYTHING on the Internet. However, the tools you need to access this information is in the form of software.

Hardware/Software You Need

To access the Internet you need the following hardware/software configuration.

1. An 80486, 80586 or better computer system.

2. A 14,400Baud or 28,800Baud Modem or direct connection (ISDN, T-1).

3. TCP/IP Winsock.dll running on your computer system.

4. 256 color Graphics SVGA card.

5. A World Wide Web Browser!!!

The World Wide Web Browser is a fundamental tool you have to use to *surf* the Information Super Highway. The reasons are simple: they are easy to use, they are the best GUI (Graphical User Interface) for the Web, and they include ALL the tools you need to cruise through the Internet.

There are many World Wide Web Browsers available (for example: Netscape, Mosaic, NetShark, QMosaic, just to name a few). We recommend Netscape Communications Corporation's Netscape Navigator. The reasons for using this browser are that Netscape is easy to install and learn, and almost 80 percent of the Homepages on the Internet are *Netscape enhanced*. This means that the Homepage you will be viewing will probably look its best with Netscape.

There are some Netscape fundamentals you will need to know before continuing your journey on the World Wide Web. To obtain the Netscape Navigator you can download the compressed program from the Netscape homepage. The URL for this page is: http://home.netscape.com. However, this information is not helpful if you do not have access to a browser yet. You can also obtain the Netscape Navigator program by connecting to Netscape Communications Corporation's FTP (File Transfer Protocol) server.

FTP Sites for the Netscape Navigator Program

ftp1.netscape.com

ftp2.netscape.com

ftp3.netscape.com

ftp4.netscape.com

ftp5.netscape.com

ftp6.netscape.com

ftp7.netscape.com

Your login name will be: **anonymous**

Your password will be: **you@your.e-mail.address.here**

The first directories you will see are those for the various Beta releases of Netscape. You can download the files to your personal computer from here.

Of course, if you do not have Internet access yet, you can always just buy the Netscape Navigator software at almost any computer or software store.

To install Netscape, create a **C:\TEMP** directory on your hard drive and copy the Netscape self extracting **EXE** file to that directory. To execute the decompression of the program, just type its name. For example: If the file is called **N32E20B5.EXE,** at the DOS prompt, type **N32E20B5**.

You will see the file decompress itself into a multitude of smaller files. Once the decompression is completed, you can return to Windows and run the setup program.

In the Windows Program Manager, click on **File,** then on **Run . . .** In the dialogue box type: **C:\TEMP\SETUP.EXE.** (If you put Netscape in another directory, type the name of that directory instead).

You will be asked to designate a directory for the Netscape program. The default is **C:\NETSCAPE.** The program will then install itself in the designated directory and add the Netscape Icons to your Program Manager.

After the installation is complete, you can run the program. Netscape will automatically connect to the Netscape Communications Corporation's homepage on the Internet, assuming you have established Internet access through an Internet provider (see Figure A-1).

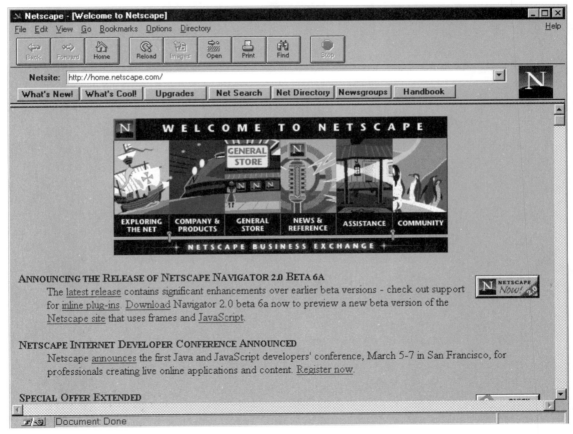

Figure A-1
The Netscape
Navigator Default
Homepage

From here you have the complete graphical user interface for the World Wide Web.

The toolbar below allows you to input the various addresses you want to visit. The HTTP stands for Hyper Text Transfer Protocol, and it is typically followed by a ":" (colon) and two "//" (forward slashes), and then the address of the Homepage you want to visit (see Figure A-2)

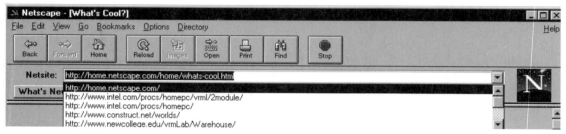

Figure A-2
Netscape Toolbar

An address can be both in alphabetical format or in numerical format, for example: http://www.the.address.here/ or http://199.199.199.166/.

The Netscape main homepage allows you to jump right into cyberspace with the various options already made available for you. The toolbar allows instant access to a multitude of Internet resources. For example, the "What's Cool" button will link you to numerous homepages that have been voted to be among the "coolest" on the Internet (see Figure A-3).

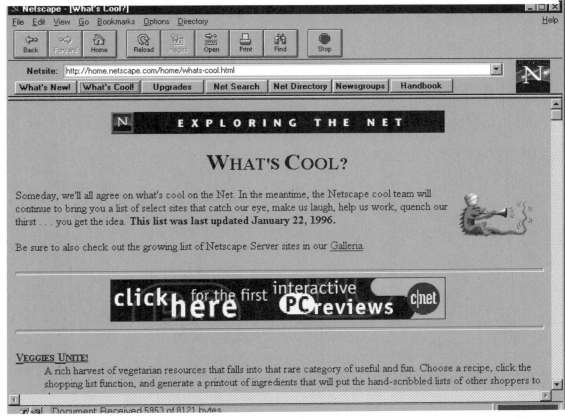

Figure A-3
Netscape's "What's
Cool" Homepage

The "What's Cool" homepage changes very often. If you find something on this homepage that you would like to explore further in the future, it is recommended that you add a bookmark for that homepage.

The "Net Search" page allows you to search the Internet for homepages, documents, software, and companies (see Figure A-4). Various search engines are linked to this page. The Netscape search engine is a nice, robust searching tool. However, do not feel limited by only that search tool. Netscape offers a wide variety of searching tools and you should try them all to find which one suits you best.

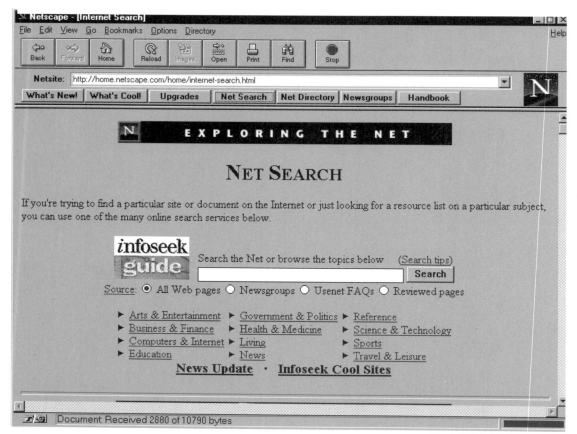

Figure A-4
Netscape's "Net
Search"
Homepage

World Wide Web search engines are very important applications for
Web *surfers*. Without the ability to search the Internet, cyberspace
would look like New York City without street signs. A search engine
is basically a pointer into the right direction, a sign to the resources
you are looking for. It may take you a few tries to get the right information, however, in the end, patience will pay off.

Configuring Netscape

Netscape has many built-in supports for other applications. For example, with the right tools you can play back video and audio files. You
can look at different graphics formats as well as walk through VRML

worlds. Most of this support is built into Netscape; and the configurations are made for you, however, you will have to check that Netscape has chosen the right application for the files you want to see, hear, or walk through.

From the Menu bar select **Options,** then click on **Preferences** (see Figure A-5).

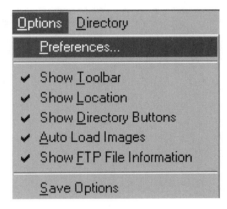

Figure A-5

At this point you will have a choice of various configuration options. Check **Helper Applications** to configure the right application associated with the files you want to be able to see, hear, and walk through (Figure A-6).

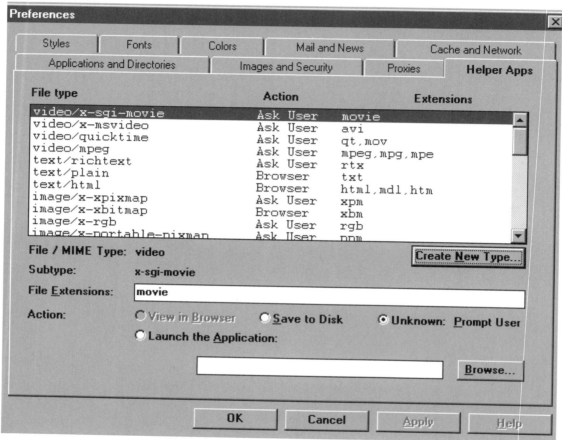

Figure A-6
Netscape
Preferences/
Configuration
Menu

The following file formats are used on the World Wide Web and Netscape offers configuration support for these files. Please make sure you have the right application configured for these files.

MOVIES	SOUND	TEXT	CONVERSION	GRAPHICS
MOVIE	WAV	RTX	RTF	XPM
AVI	AIF	TXT	AI	XBM
QT	AIFF	HTML	EPS	RGB
MOV	AIFC	HTM	PS	PPM
MPEG	AU	MDL	EXE	PGM
MPG	SND		BIN	PBM
MPE			SIT	PNM
			HQX	RAS
				TIFF
				TIF
				JPEG
				PG
				GIF

UNIX	COMPRESSION
TAR	ZIP
MAN	TAR
SH	GZ
LATEX	Z
CSH	

The **Helper Application** configuration menu will also allow you to configure files that Netscape does not support directly yet. For example, there is no listing for VRML files in this version of Netscape, so you can configure Netscape to use WorldView (or any other VRML Browser) as the default Helper Application.

To create a new file click on **Create New Type . . .** A Message box will appear (see Figure A-7).

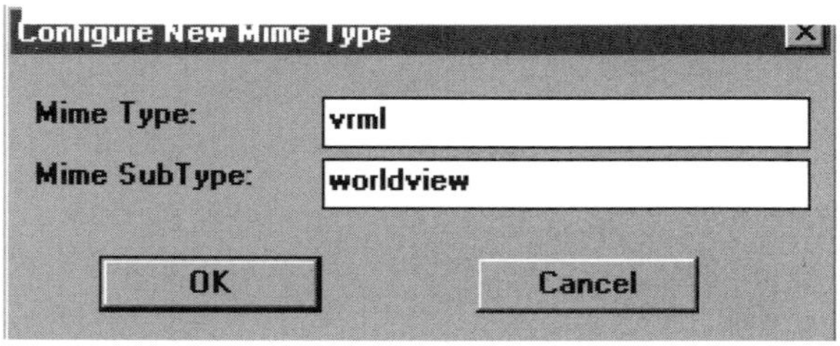

Figure A-7

Configure New Mime Type

Mime Type: vrml

Mime SubType: worldview

OK   Cancel

Mime Type: enter the application type, in this case **x-world**

Mime Subtype: enter another application type, in this case **x-vrml**

Next, in **File Extention** insert the file extention Netscape should look for before launching the helper application. In this case it would be **wrl, wrld, or wlz.**

Click on **Launch the Application** and then click on **Browse** to point to the VRML browser application you want to use (see Figure A-8).

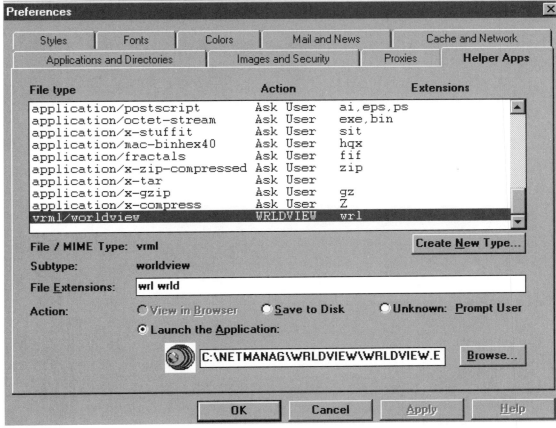

Figure A-8
Configuring Helper
Applications Menu

This type of configuration process is the same for all other VRML browser applications.

There are other applications you can configure Netscape to use for the Internet. Two of these are FTP (File Transfer Protocol) and Telnet 3270 (for IBM Mainframe access). To do this, go to **Preferences** and click on **Applications and Directories.** Locate the application you want to use with the **Browse** option and click on **OK** (see Figure A-9).

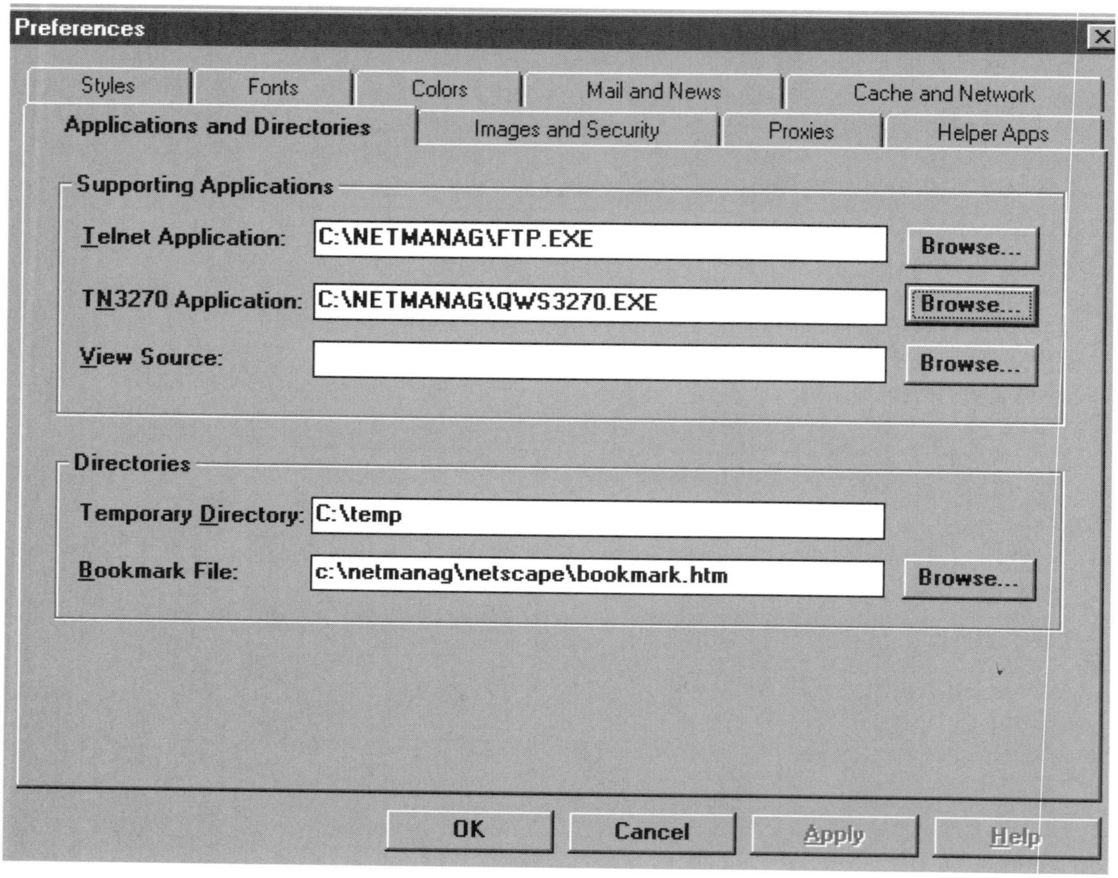

Figure A-9
Netscape's
Application
Configuration
Menu

Netscape is a resource-hungry application. It needs to have many computer resources available when it is connected to the Internet. In order not to tie up your Windows resources, Netscape uses something called **Cache.** This is similar to the Windows **Temp** directory. It's a directory where Netscape can put temporary (useless) files while it's downloading homepages from the Internet. However, you should be aware that unlike the Windows TEMP directory, the Netscape CACHE directory does not empty the files once you have finished using Netscape. To empty the Cache Directory, locate the **Cache and Network** Menu in **Preferences** (see Figure A-10).

Preferences

| Applications and Directories | Images and Security | Proxies | Helper Apps |

| Styles | Fonts | Colors | Mail and News | **Cache and Network** |

Cache

Memory Cache: `600` Kilobytes   **Clear Memory Cache Now**

Disk Cache: `5000` Kilobytes   **Clear Disk Cache Now**

Disk Cache Directory: `c:\netmanag\netscape\cache`

Verify Documents: ◉ Once per Session   ○ Every Time   ○ Never

Network Connections

Network Buffer Size: `6` Kilobytes

Connections: `4` **(Maximum number of simultaneous network connections)**

| OK | Cancel | Apply | Help |

Figure A-10
Cache and Network Menu

Click on **Clear Memory Cache Now ...** and on **Clear Disk Cache Now...**

This will erase the temp files from your hard drive.

Netscape will NOT erase any of your own Data files or program files, it will only clear the temp files in the C:\NETSCAPE\CACHE directory.

Clear the Disk Cache often (at least once a month). The Netscape cache can sometimes take up enormous amounts of disk space.

Netscape comes with a built in E-mail feature. This is very helpful when you need to send E-mail to a homepage embedded E-mail address. To configure E-mail, click on **Preferences** and click on the **Mail and News** menu (see Figure A-11).

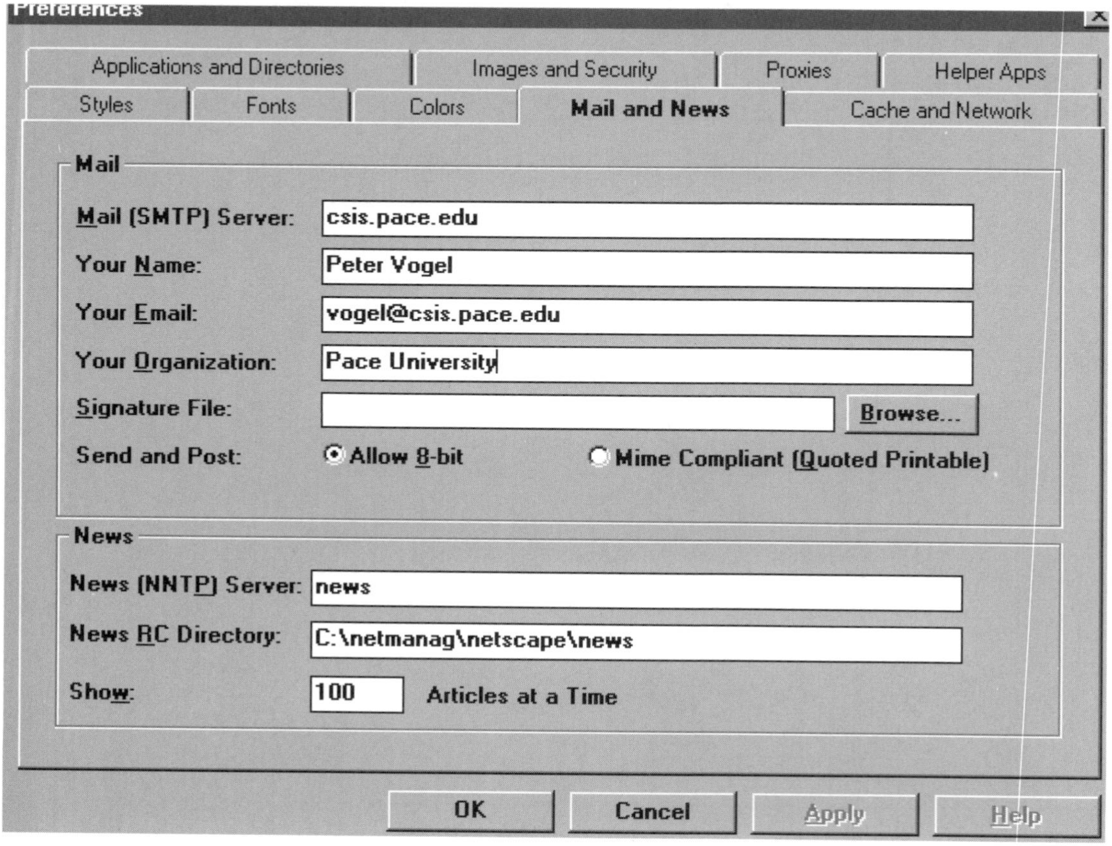

Figure A-11
E-mail Configuration Menu

Type your E-mail organization's address. This can be both an alphanumeric or a numeric address. Next, type in your full name, followed by your E-mail name and E-mail address; then your organization. The **Signature File** is if you have your actual Signature saved as an image on your computer.

All these configurations changes are saved in the **netscape.ini** file that is located in your Netscape directory. You can also edit this INI file.

Even though editing the netscape.ini file will give you more control over how Netscape behaves, it can also seriously foul things up. Make sure you make a backup copy of the netscape.ini file. Failure to do this can result in Netscape not working at all.

A sample **NETSCAPE.INI** file.

```
rem
rem This is the default initialization file for Netscape. Netscape
rem will look in win.ini in the [Netscape] section for the ini
rem entry and expect this file to be there. Failing that, Netscape
rem will look in the directory where it was launched for this file.
rem
rem If you install NetScape in a directory other than c:\netscape
rem you should make sure that you update the "History File"
rem and "File Location" (under "Bookmarks") to be pointers to
rem files in valid directories that NetScape can write to or
rem else you won't get global history or bookmarks across
rem sessions. In addition, you should make sure the directory
rem specified by "Cache Dir" exists and is writable.
rem
rem If you are having winsock problems you should try setting
rem
rem    [Network]
rem    Use Async DNS=no
rem
rem you might also need to set
rem
rem    [Network]
rem    Max Connections=1
rem
```

```
[Main]
Last Config Menu=8
Anchor Underline=yes
Fancy FTP=yes
Autoload Home Page=yes
Fancy News=no
Home Page=http://home.netscape.com/
Check Server=1
News RC=C:\NETMANAG\NETSCAPE\NEWS\NEWSRC
Temp Directory=C:\temp
Mozilla=Good-1.22


[Viewers]
HTML=
Tn3270=
Telnet=
audio/basic=C:\NETMANAG\NETSCAPE\NAPLAYER.EXE
audio/x-aiff=C:\NETMANAG\NETSCAPE\NAPLAYER.EXE
x-world/x-vrml=C:\NETMANAG\WRLDVIEW\WRLDVIEW.EXE
vrml/worldview=C:\NETMANAG\WRLDVIEW\WRLDVIEW.EXE
TYPE0=vrml/worldview


[Settings]
Background Image=
Users Colors Override=no
Custom Background=custom
Custom Text Color=no
Custom Followed Link Color=no
Custom Link Color=no
Background Color=192, 192, 192
Followed Link Color=85, 26, 139
Text Color=0, 0, 0
Link Color=0, 0, 238
Blinking=yes
```

```
[User]
Sig_File=
User_Organization=
User_Addr=
User_Name=

[Images]
Incremental Display=yes
Dither=yes

[Main Window]
y=83
x=193
height=470
width=629

[Bookmark List]
Start Menu With=Entire Listing
Add URLs Under=Top Level of Listing
File Location=c:\netmanag\netscape\bookmark.htm

[Tool Bar]
Button Styles=2

[Services]
SOCKS_ServerPort=1080
SOCKS_Server=
Socks Conf=c:\windows\socks.cnf
SMTP_Server=mail
NNTP_Server=news
Mapi=no
```

```
[Proxy Information]
Wais_ProxyPort=0
Ftp_ProxyPort=0
HTTPS_ProxyPort=0
News_ProxyPort=0
Gopher_ProxyPort=0
Http_ProxyPort=0
No_Proxy=
Wais_Proxy=
HTTPS_Proxy=
News_Proxy=
Gopher_Proxy=
FTP_Proxy=
HTTP_Proxy=

[Fonts]
Fixed Base Size=10
Fixed Family=Courier New
Proportional Base Size=12
Proportional Family=Times New Roman

[History]
History File=c:\netmanag\netscape\netscape.hst
Expiration=30

[Cache]
Cache Dir=c:\netmanag\netscape\cache
Disk Cache Size=5000
Memory Cache Size=600

[Network]
Use Async DNS=yes
Max Connections=4
```

```
Speed Over UI=No
TCP Buffer Size=6144

[Cookies]
Cookie File=c:\netmanag\netscape\cookies.txt

[Security]
Warn Entering=yes
Warn Leaving=yes
Warn Mixed=yes
Warn Insecure Forms=yes

[News]
News Directory=C:\netmanag\netscape\news
News Chunk Size=100
MIME Posting=no

[Suffixes]
audio/basic=au,snd
audio/x-aiff=aif,aiff,aifc
vrml/worldview=wrl

[URL History]
URL_1=http://home.netscape.com/
URL_2=http://www.ncsa.uiuc.edu/
URL_3=http://www.hitl.washington.edu/projects/knowledge_base/vrm.html
URL_4=http://kirk.usafa.af.mil/~bard
URL_5=http://kirk.usafa.af.mil/
URL_6=http://www.altavista.digital.com/
URL_7=http://www.yahoo.com/
URL_8=http://home.netscape.com/
URL_9=http://www.ids-net.com/
```

```
[Page Setup]

left=720

right=720

top=720

bottom=720

Header=3

Footer=7

SolidLines=0

BlackText=0

BlackLines=0

Reverse=0
```

Other Tips and Suggestions

Errors and Problems

Netscape is a very powerful browser and gives its users a great amount of freedom in *surfing* the World Wide Web. However, you may experience some problems at loading certain pages. The reason why some pages may not load correctly may be because there are too many graphics on the page, or the server where the homepage resides may be too busy to grant your requests at this time. Typically, you may be able to get a partial homepage (mostly without the graphics) when you click on **Stop** on the Toolbar.

If a Homepage loads very slowly, you can speed up the process by clicking on **Reload** on the Toolbar. This will overwrite the homepage cache and load it more quickly.

If all else fails, we recommend that you write down the address (you can always see the address appear on the bottom left side of the Netscape screen when you move the mouse over the HyperText link) and try connecting to the homepage at a later time.

Cutting and Pasting

Netscape allows the user to cut and paste an entire homepage off the World Wide Web. This is particularly helpful if you need to copy just one piece of information and do not want to print the entire homepage (some homepages are very big and can take a long time to print).

To cut and paste, just move the mouse over the text and hold down the left mouse button, the text or image will highlight. With the text highlighted, move the mouse to the **Edit** menu on the menu bar and click on **Copy.** You can then open Windows Notepad and **Paste** the text right onto it.

Netscape will not scroll down if you need to copy a large amount of text or image(s). However, you can highlight the text and click the **Page Down** key on your computer keyboard, this will move to the next page while still highlighting the text.

View HTML Source Code

Almost all Internet Browsers allow the user to view the HTML (HyperText Markup Language) code. In Netscape you can view the HTML code by clicking on **View** and then **Source.** This is very helpful if you want to write your own HTML homepages and need to find out how a particular page is made. You cannot copy from **Source,** unfortunately.

However, if you want to study the HTML coding of a particular homepage, you can **Save** the homepage to your hard drive and look at it with a text editor or a HTML editor. Click on **File** on the **Menu Bar** and then click on **Save** or on **Save As . . .** to designate the directory you want to save it in.

Appendix

B

Requirements of VRML 2.0

VRML 2.0 and SGI's Moving Worlds

Version 1.1 Draft (from VAG, but intended to be part of VRML 2.0)

Acknowledgements

The Virtual Reality Modeling Language

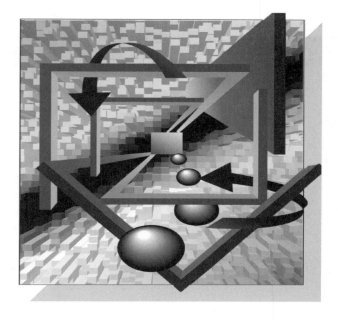

The VRML community is faced with the task of developing the full VRML 2.0 specification this year. Unfortunately, work on this new version of VRML is still in the early stages. Therefore, this Appendix can only point out the features and highlights of the VRML 2.0 specification, and then append the current draft of VRML 1.1. VRML 1.1 will be superseded by VRML 2.0 by the end of 1996.

Requirements of VRML 2.0

Performance—Speed is a key to a good interactive experience, so any proposed VRML syntax and technology must be able to be optimized. In particular, this means allowing for consistent, fast frame rates at the best possible image quality.

Scalability—VRML must allow the creation of very large virtual worlds. Any feature that limits scalability is unacceptable. In addition, any VRML technology must be portable to many different computer systems.

Composability—Related to scalability, one must be able to compose VRML worlds or objects to create larger worlds. Authors should be able to combine worlds that are created by different people simply by making a *meta-world* that refers to the other objects and VRML systems previously created and published.

Authoring—Sophisticated VRML authoring tools must be able to be created, and it should be possible to perform most of the tasks necessary to create an interesting, interactive VRML world using a graphical user interface. VRML will only be successful when artists, designers, and other non-programmers are able to create compelling and interactive VRML content.

Power—Programmers must be able to seamlessly extend VRML's functionality, by allowing them to create arbitrary scripts, applets, or VRML code that can then be easily reused by other non-programmers.

Inter-operability—VRML 2.0 must be able to inter-operate with and take advantage of other network, graphics, and language based standards. This could include but is not limited to VRML 1.0, HTTP, Java, Safe TCL, and JPEG.

Multiuser potential—VRML will evolve into a multiuser shared experience in the near future, allowing complete collaboration and communication in interactive 3D spaces. Any proposal must anticipate the needs of multiuser VRML in its design, considering the possibility that VRML browsers might eventually need to support synchronization of changes to the world, locking, persistent distributed worlds, event rollback, and dead reckoning.

Open Standard—VRML must be based in standards and technologies that are both open and available without any licensing. While a proposal may inter-operate with an owned technology, it must not be a requirement.

Backward Compatibility—As much as is possible (given the changes that will be required for interactivity) VRML 2.0 should be backward-compatible with VRML 1.0.

Completeness—The proposal should stand on its own, as a complete proposal, integrating each of the requirements. Works-in-progress are strongly discouraged. Any independent developer should be able to use the specification as the single source of documentation when implementing VRML technology. Ambiguities in concepts, syntax or wording definitions should be avoided.

VRML 2.0 and SGI's Moving Worlds

It seems clear that VRML 2.0 will depend heavily on SGI's Moving Worlds proposal, so this section will detail some of the highlights of this document.

Moving Worlds has grown out of the VRML 1.0 specification. It has been influenced by the VRBS work at SDSC as well as work at Silicon Graphics in the Inventor and Performer products. The initial proposal as it appears today is an integration of work done by Silicon Graphics, WorldMaker, and Sony. Every member of the VAG has had a hand in various pieces, and input from all over the VRML world has been incorporated. Gavin Bell has headed the effort at SGI to produce the final form of the proposal as it appears.

While VRML 1.0 provided a means of creating and viewing static 3D worlds; VRML 2.0 will provide much more. The overarching goal of the Moving Worlds proposal for VRML 2.0 is to provide a richer, more exciting, more interactive user experience than is possible within the static boundaries of VRML 1.0. The secondary goals of the proposal are to provide a solid foundation that future VRML expansion can grow out of, and to keep things as simple and as fast as possible—for everyone from browser developers to world designers to end users—given the other goals.

Moving Worlds provides these extensions and enhancements to VRML 1.0:

> Enhanced static worlds
>
> Interaction
>
> Animation
>
> Prototyping

Here are some details on each feature, all of which should be prominent in the VRML 2.0 specification.

- Enhanced Static Worlds: You can add realism to the static geometry of your world using new features of *Moving Worlds*. New nodes allow you to create ground-and-sky backdrops to scenes, add distant mountains and clouds, and dim distant objects with fog. Another new node lets you easily create irregular terrain instead of using flat planes for ground surfaces.

  Moving Worlds provides sound-generating nodes to further enhance realism—you can put crickets, breaking glass, ringing telephones, or any other sound into a scene.

  If you're writing a browser, you'll be happy to see that optimizing and parsing files are easier than in VRML 1.0, thanks to a new simplified scene graph structure.

- Interaction: No more moving like a ghost through cold, dead worlds: now you can directly interact with objects and creatures you encounter. New sensor nodes set off events when you move in certain areas of a world and when you click certain objects. They even let you drag objects or controls from one place to another. Another kind of sensor keeps track of the passage of time, providing a basis for everything from alarm clocks to repetitive animations.

And no more walking through walls! Collision detection ensures that solid objects react like solid objects; you bounce off them (or simply stop moving) when you run into them. Terrain following allows you to travel up and down steps or ramps.

- Animation: Moving Worlds wouldn't be able to move without the new Script nodes. Using Scripts, you can not only animate creatures and objects in a world, but give them a semblance of intelligence. Animated dogs can fetch newspapers or frisbees; clock hands can move; birds can fly; robots can juggle.

  These effects are achieved by means of events; a script takes input from sensors and generates events based on that input that can change other nodes in the world. Events are passed around among nodes by way of special statements called routes.

- Prototyping: Have an idea for a new kind of geometry node that you want everyone to be able to use? Got a nifty script that you want to turn into part of the next version of VRML? In Moving Worlds, you can encapsulate a group of nodes together as a new node type, a prototype, and then make that node type available to anyone who wants to use it. You can then create instances of the new type, each with different field values; for instance, you could create a Robot prototype with a robotColor field, and then create as many individual different-colored Robot nodes as you like.

Version 1.1 Draft (from VAG, but intended to be part of VRML 2.0)

VAG: This document is a draft. Don't rely on any part of it remaining stable. The VAG now follows the IETF guideline of "Rough Consensus and Working Code," this specification will only be officially finalized when two independent implementations on different platforms are available.

16-Dec-95

Gavin Bell, Silicon Graphics, Inc.

Anthony Parisi, Intervista Software

Mark Pesce, VRML List Moderator

Mitra, WorldMaker

YON - Jan C. Hardenbergh, OKI

Tom Meyer, Brown University

Bill Martin, Headspace

Rikk Carey, SGI

Jon Marbry, Microsoft

Brian Blau, Intervista Software

Revision History

- 1.0 first Draft—November 2, 1994
- 1.0 second Draft—May 8, 1995
- First 1.0 spec—May 26, 1995
- 1.0 clarifications—October 23, 1995
- 1.1 first draft—October 24, 1995
- 1.1 second draft—December 12, 1995

Table of Contents

Introduction

The Virtual Reality Modeling Language (VRML) is a language for describing multi-participant interactive simulations—virtual worlds networked via the global Internet and hyperlinked with the World Wide Web. All aspects of virtual world display, interaction, and internetworking can be specified using VRML. It is the intention of its designers that VRML become the standard language for interactive simulation within the World Wide Web.

The first version of VRML allows for the creation of virtual worlds with limited interactive behavior. These worlds can contain objects that have hyperlinks to other worlds, HTML documents, or other valid MIME types. When the user selects an object with a hyperlink, the appropriate MIME viewer is launched. When the user selects a link to a VRML document from within a correctly configured WWW browser, a VRML viewer is launched. Thus VRML viewers are the perfect companion applications to standard WWW browsers for navigating and visualizing the Web. Future versions of VRML will allow for richer behaviors, including animations, motion physics, and real-time multiuser interaction.

This document specifies the features and syntax of Version 1.1 of VRML.

VRML Mission Statement

The history of the development of the Internet has had three distinct phases; first, the development of the TCP/IP infrastructure that allowed documents and data to be stored in a proximally independent way; that is, Internet provided a layer of abstraction between data sets and the hosts that manipulated them. While this abstraction was useful, it was also confusing; without any clear sense of "what went where," access to Internet was restricted to the class of sysops/net surfers who could maintain internal cognitive maps of the data space.

Next, Tim Berners-Lee's work at CERN, where he developed the hypermedia system known as World Wide Web, added another layer of abstraction to the existing structure. This abstraction provided an *addressing* scheme, a unique identifier (the Universal Resource Locator) that could tell anyone "where to go and how to get there" for any piece of data within the Web. While useful, it lacked dimensionality; there's no there within the web, and the only type of navigation permissible (other than surfing) is by direct reference. In other words, I can only tell you how to get to the VRML Forum home page by saying, "http://www.wired.com/", which is not human-centered data. In fact, I need to make an effort to remember it at all. So, while the World Wide Web provides a retrieval mechanism to complement the existing storage mechanism, it leaves a lot to be desired, particularly for human beings.

Finally, we move to *perceptualized* Internetworks, where the data has been sensualized, that is, rendered sensually. If something is represented sensually, it is possible to make sense of it. VRML is an attempt (how successful, only time and effort will tell) to place humans at the center of the Internet, ordering its universe to our whims. In order to do that, the most important single element is a standard that defines the particularities of perception. Virtual Reality Modeling Language is that standard, designed to be a universal description language for multi-participant simulations.

These three phases, storage, retrieval, and perceptualization, are analogous to the human process of consciousness, as expressed in terms of semantics and cognitive science. Events occur and are recorded (memory); inferences are drawn from memory (associations) and from sets of related events; maps of the universe are created (cognitive perception). What is important to remember is that the map is not the territory, and we should avoid becoming trapped in any single representation or worldview. Although we need to design to avoid disorientation, we should always push the envelope in the kinds of experience we can bring into manifestation!

This document is the living proof of the success of a process that was committed to being open and flexible, responsive to the needs of a growing Web community. Rather than re-invent the wheel, we have adapted an existing specification (Open Inventor) as the basis from which our own work can grow, saving years of design work and perhaps many mistakes. Now our real work can begin; that of rendering our noospheric space.

History

VRML was conceived in the spring of 1994 at the first annual World Wide Web Conference in Geneva, Switzerland. Tim Berners-Lee and Dave Raggett organized a Birds-of-a-Feather (BOF) session to discuss Virtual Reality interfaces to the World Wide Web. Several BOF attendees described projects already underway to build three dimensional graphical visualization tools that inter-operate with the Web. Attendees agreed on the need for these tools to have a common language for specifying 3D scene description and WWW hyperlinks—an analog of HTML for virtual reality. The term Virtual Reality Markup Language (VRML) was coined, and the group resolved to begin specification work after the conference. The word "Markup" was later changed to Modeling to reflect the graphical nature of VRML.

Shortly after the Geneva BOF session, the www-vrml mailing list was created to discuss the development of a specification for the first version of VRML. The response to the list invitation was overwhelming;

within a week, there were over a thousand members. After an initial settling-in period, list moderator Mark Pesce of Labyrinth Group announced his intention to have a draft version of the specification ready by the WWW Fall 1994 conference, a mere five months away. There was general agreement on the list that, while this schedule was aggressive, it was achievable provided that the requirements for the first version were not too ambitious and that VRML could be adapted from an existing solution. The list quickly agreed upon a set of requirements for the first version, and began a search for technologies that could be adapted to fit the needs of VRML.

The search for existing technologies turned up a several worthwhile candidates. After much deliberation the group came to a consensus: the Open Inventor ASCII File Format from Silicon Graphics, Inc. The Inventor File Format supports complete descriptions of 3D scenes with polygonally rendered objects, lighting, materials, ambient properties, and realism effects. A subset of the Inventor File Format, with extensions to support networking, forms the basis of VRML. Gavin Bell of Silicon Graphics has adapted the Inventor File Format for VRML, with design input from the mailing list. SGI has publicly stated that the file format is available for use in the open market and has contributed a file format parser into the public domain to bootstrap VRML viewer development.

TODO: Gavin—History of clarifications etc to be added

Version 1.0 Requirements

VRML 1.0 is designed to meet the following requirements:

- Platform independence
- Extensibility
- Ability to work well over low-bandwidth connections

As with HTML, the previous are absolute requirements for a network language standard; they should need little explanation here.

Early on, the designers decided that VRML would not be an extension to HTML. HTML is designed for text, not graphics. Also, VRML requires even more finely tuned network optimizations than HTML; it is expected that a typical VRML scene will be composed of many more "in-line" objects and served up by many more servers than a typical HTML document. Moreover, HTML is an accepted standard, with existing implementations that depend on it. To impede the HTML design process with VRML issues and constrain the VRML design process with HTML compatibility concerns would be to do both languages a disservice. As a network language, VRML will succeed or fail independent of HTML.

It was also decided that, except for the hyperlinking feature, the first version of VRML would not support interactive behaviors. This was a practical decision intended to streamline design and implementation. Design of a language for describing interactive behaviors is a big job, especially when the language needs to express behaviors of objects communicating on a network. Such languages do exist; if we had chosen one of them, we would have risked getting into a "language war." People don't get excited about the syntax of a language for describing polygonal objects; people get very excited about the syntax of real languages for writing programs. *Religious* wars can extend the design process by months or years. In addition, networked inter-object operation requires brokering services such as those provided by CORBA or OLE, services that don't exist yet within WWW; we would have had to invent them. Finally, by keeping behaviors out of Version 1, we have made it a much smaller task to implement a viewer. We acknowledge that support for arbitrary interactive behaviors is critical to the long-term success of VRML; they will be included in Version 2.

What's New in Version 1.1

Changes from 1.0 to 1.1

- Near and Far clippng planes—PerspectiveCamera and OrthographicCamera now contain nearDistance and farDistance clipping plane specifications.

- ShapeHints—field defaults have changed

- input fields—Several 1.0 nodes have input fields. These fields are dynamic fields that can be modified by other nodes.

New Objects in 1.1

- Background—describes scene background

- Cameras—now have nearDistance and farDistance fields

- CollideStyle—describes collision information

- DirectedSound and PointSound—spatial sound objects

- ElevationGrid—describes a model as heights over a regular grid

- Environment—is from Inventor to do fog and ambient lighting

- GeneralCylinder—is a new node for describing numerous families of shapes

- NavigationInfo—contains view type, speed, and headlight state

- VolumeProximitySensor and PointProximitySensor—Sensors that detect viewer proximity

- WorldInfo—contains title and other document information

New Features in VRML 1.1

*   Prototyping—new node types can be defined in the VRML file

Language Specification

The language specification is divided into the following sections:

*   Language Basics
*   Coordinate System
*   Fields
*   Nodes
*   Instancing
*   Extensibility
*   An Example

Language Basics

At the highest level of abstraction, VRML is just a way for objects to read and write themselves. Theoretically, the objects can contain anything—3D geometry, MIDI data, JPEG images, anything. VRML defines a set of objects useful for doing 3D graphics. These objects are called Nodes.

Nodes are arranged in hierarchical structures called scene graphs. Scene graphs are more than just a collection of nodes; the scene graph defines an ordering for the nodes. The scene graph has a notion of state—nodes earlier in the scene can affect nodes that appear later in the scene. For example, a Rotation or Material node will affect the nodes after it in the scene. A mechanism is defined to limit the effects of properties (separator nodes), allowing parts of the scene graph to be functionally isolated from other parts.

Applications that interpret VRML files need not maintain the scene graph structure internally; the scene graph is merely a convenient way of describing objects.

A node has the following characteristics.

*   What kind of object it is. A node might be a cube, a sphere, a texture map, a transformation, and so on.
*   The parameters that distinguish this node from other nodes of the same type. For example, each Sphere node might have a different radius, and different texture maps nodes will certainly contain different images to use as the texture maps. These parameters are called Fields. A node can have zero or more fields.

- A name to identify this node. Being able to name nodes and refer to them elsewhere is very powerful; it allows a scene's author to give hints to applications using the scene about what is in the scene, and creates possibilities for very powerful scripting extensions. Nodes do not have to be named, but if they are named, they can have only one name. However, names do not have to be unique—several different nodes may be given the same name.

- Child nodes. Object hierarchy is implemented by allowing some types of nodes to contain other nodes. Parent nodes traverse their children in order during rendering. Nodes that may have children are referred to as group nodes. Group nodes can have zero or more children.

The syntax chosen to represent these pieces of information is straight-forward:

DEF objectname objecttype { fields children }

Only the object type and curly braces are required; nodes may or may not have a name, fields, and children.

Node names must not begin with a digit, and must not contain spaces or control characters, single or double quote characters, backslashes, curly braces, the plus character, or the period character.

For example, this file contains a simple scene defining a view of a red cone and a blue sphere, lit by a directional light:

```
#VRML V1.1 utf8
Separator {
    DirectionalLight {
    direction 0 0 -1 # Light shining from viewer into scene
    }
    PerspectiveCamera {
    position   -8.6 2.1 5.6
    orientation -0.1352 -0.9831 -0.1233 1.1417
    focalDistance    10.84
    }
    Separator {   # The red sphere
    Material {
    diffuseColor 1 0 0  # Red
    }
```

```
        Translation { translation 3 0 1 }
        Sphere { radius 2.3 }
    }
    Separator { # The blue cube
    Material {
    diffuseColor 0 0 1 # Blue
     }
    Transform {
    translation -2.4 .2 1
    rotation 0 1 1 .9
    }
  Cube {}
   }
}
```

General Syntax

For easy identification of VRML files, every VRML 1.1 file must begin with the characters:

```
#VRML V1.1 utf8
```

The identifier utf8 allows for international characters to be displayed in VRML using the UTF-8 encoding of the ISO 10646 standard. Unicode is an alternate encoding of ISO 10646. UTF-8 is explained under the Text node.

Any characters after these on the same line are ignored. The line is terminated by either the ASCII newline or carriage-return characters.

The # character begins a comment; all characters until the next newline or carriage return are ignored. The only exception to this is within double-quoted SFString and MFString fields, where the # character will be part of the string.

Comments and whitespace may not be preserved; in particular, a VRML document server may strip comments and extraneous whitespace from a VRML file before transmitting it. Info nodes should be used for persistent information like copyrights or author information. Info nodes could also be used for object descriptions. New uses of named info nodes for conveying syntactically meaningfull information are deprecated. Use the extension nodes mechanism instead.

Blanks, tabs, newlines, and carriage returns are whitespace characters wherever they appear outside of string fields. One or more whitespace characters separates the syntactical entities in VRML files, where necessary.

After the required header, a VRML file contains exactly one VRML node. That node may of course be a group node, containing any number of other nodes.

Field names start with lower case letters, node types start with upper case. The remainder of the characters may be any printable ascii (21H-7EH) except curly braces {}, square brackets [], single ' or double " quotes, sharp #, backslash \\, plus +, period . or ampersand &.

Node names must not begin with a digit but they may begin and contain any UTF-8 character except those below 21H (control characters and white space), and the characters {} [] ' " # \\ + . and &.

VRML is case-sensitive; Sphere is different from sphere.

Coordinate System

VRML uses a cartesian, right-handed, 3-dimensional coordinate system. By default, objects are projected onto a 2-dimensional device by projecting them in the direction of the positive Z-axis, with the positive X-axis to the right and the positive Y-axis up. A camera or modeling transformation may be used to alter this default projection.

The standard unit for lengths and distances specified is meters. The standard unit for angles is radians.

VRML scenes may contain an arbitrary number of local (or object-space) coordinate systems, defined by modelling transformations using Translate, Rotate, Scale, Transform, and MatrixTransform nodes. Given a vertex, V, and a series of transformations such as:

    Translation { translation T }

    Rotation { rotation R }

    Scale { scaleFactor S }

    Coordinate3 { point V } PointSet { numPoints 1 }

the vertex is transformed into world-space to get V' by applying the transformations in the following order:

$V' = T{\cdot}R{\cdot}S{\cdot}$

V (if you think of vertices as column vectors) OR

$V' = V{\cdot}S{\cdot}R{\cdot}T$ (if you think of vertices as row vectors).

Conceptually, VRML also has a "world" coordinate system as well as a viewing or "Camera" coordinate system. The various local coordinate transformations map objects into the world coordinate system. This is where the scene is assembled. The scene is then viewed through a camera, introducing another conceptual coordinate system. Nothing in VRML is specified using these coordinates. They are rarely found in optimized implementations where all of the steps are concatenated. However, having a clear model of the object, world, and camera spaces will help authors.

Fields

There are two general classes of fields; fields that contain a single value (where a value may be a single number, a vector, or even an image), and fields that contain multiple values. Single-valued fields all have names that begin with "SF", multiple-valued fields have names that begin with "MF". Each field type defines the format for the values it writes.

Multiple-valued fields are written as a series of values separated by commas, all enclosed in square brackets. If the field has zero values then only the square brackets ([]) are written. The last may optionally be followed by a comma. If the field has exactly one value, the brackets may be omitted and just the value written. For example, all of the following are valid for a multiple-valued field containing the single integer value 1:

    1
    [1,]
    [1]

TODO: Syntax/Rules for Input/Outputs Need to be Fleshed Out Here!

SFBitMask: A single-value field that contains a mask of bit flags. Nodes that use this field class define mnemonic names for the bit flags. SFBitMasks are written to file as one or more mnemonic enumerated type names, in this format:

(flag1 | flag2 | ...).

If only one flag is used in a mask, the parentheses are optional. These names differ among uses of this field in various node classes.

SFBool: A field containing a single boolean (true or false) value. SFBools may be written as 0 (representing FALSE), 1, TRUE, or FALSE.

SFColor/MFColor: Fields containing one (SFColor) or zero or more (MFColor) RGB colors. Each color is written to file as an RGB triple of floating point numbers in ANSI C floating point format, in the range 0.0 to 1.0. For example;

[1.0 0. 0.0, 0 1 0, 0 0 1]

is an MFColor field containing the three colors red, green, and blue.

SFEnum: A single-value field that contains an enumerated type value. Nodes that use this field class define mnemonic names for the values. SFEnums are written to file as a mnemonic enumerated type name. The name differs among uses of this field in various node classes.

SFFloat/MFFloat: Fields that contain one (SFFloat) or zero or more (MFFloat) single-precision floating point number. SFFloats are written to file in ANSI C floating point format. For example;

[3.1415926, 12.5e-3, .0001]

is an MFFloat field containing three values.

SFImage: A field that contains an uncompressed 2-dimensional color or greyscale image.

SFImages are written to file as three integers representing the width, height, and number of components in the image, followed by width*height hexadecimal values representing the pixels in the image, separated by whitespace. A one-component image will have one-byte hexadecimal values representing the intensity of the image. For example, 0xFF is full intensity, 0x00 is no intensity. A two-component image puts the intensity in the first (high) byte and the transparency in the second (low) byte. Pixels in a three-component image have the red component in the first (high) byte, followed by the green and blue components (so 0xFF0000 is red). Four-component images put the transparency byte after red/green/blue (so 0x0000FF80 is semi-transparent blue). A value of 1.0 is completely transparent, 0.0 is completely opaque. Note: each pixel is actually read as a single unsigned number, so a 3-component pixel with value "0x0000FF" can also be written as "0xFF" or "255" (decimal). Pixels are specified from left to right, bottom to top. The first hexadecimal value is the lower left pixel of the image, and the last value is the upper right pixel.

For example;

1 2 1 0xFF 0x00

is a 1 pixel wide by 2 pixel high greyscale image, with the bottom pixel white and the top pixel black. And

2 4 3 0xFF0000 0xFF00 0 0 0 0 0xFFFFFF 0xFFFF00

is a 2 pixel wide by 4 pixel high RGB image, with the bottom left pixel red, the bottom right pixel green, the two middle rows of pixels black, the top left pixel white, and the top right pixel yellow.

SFLong/MFLong: Fields containing one (SFLong) or zero or more (MFLong) 32-bit integers. SFLongs are written to file as an integer in decimal, hexadecimal (beginning with '0x'), or octal (beginning with '0') format. For example;

[17, -0xE20, -518820]

is an MFLong field containing three values.

SFMatrix: A field containing a transformation matrix. SFMatrices are written to file in row-major order as 16 floating point numbers separated by whitespace. For example, a matrix expressing a translation of 7.3 units along the X-axis is written as:

1 0 0 0 0 1 0 0 0 0 1 0 7.3 0 0 1

NEW in 1.1—SFNode/MFNode

... syntax is just node syntax, DEF/USE allowed, and so on.

SFRotation: A field containing an arbitrary rotation. SFRotations are written to file as four floating point values separated by whitespace. The 4 values represent an axis of rotation followed by the amount of right-handed rotation about that axis, in radians. For example, a 180 degree rotation about the Y-axis is:

0 1 0 3.14159265

SFString/MFString: Fields containing one (SFString) or zero or more (MFString) UTF-8 strings (sequence of characters). Strings are written to file as a sequence of UTF-8 octets in double quotes (optional if the string doesn't contain any whitespace). Any characters (including newlines and #) may appear within the quotes. To include a double quote character within the string, precede it with a backslash. For example;

Testing

"One, Two, Three"

"He said, \"Immel did it!\""

are all valid strings.

SFVec2f/MFVec2f: Field containing a two-dimensional vector. SFVec2fs are written to file as a pair of floating point values separated by whitespace.

SFVec3f/MFVec3f: Field containing a three-dimensional vector. SFVec3fs are written to file as three floating point values separated by whitespace.

NEW in 1.1—SFTime: Field containing a single time value. Each time value is written to file as a double-precision floating point number in ANSI C floating point format. A absolute SFTime is the number of seconds since Jan 1, 1970 GM.

NEW in 1.1—input fields

TODO: TBD

Nodes

VRML defines several different classes of nodes. Most of the nodes can be classified into one of three categories; shape, property, or group. Shape nodes define the geometry in the scene. Conceptually, they are the only nodes that draw anything. Property nodes affect the way shapes are drawn. And grouping nodes gather other nodes together, allowing collections of nodes to be treated as a single object. Some group nodes also control whether or not their children are drawn.

Nodes may contain zero or more fields. Each node type defines the type, name, and default value for each of its fields. The default value for the field is used if a value for the field is not specified in the VRML file. The order in which the fields of a node are read is not important; for example, Cube { width 2 height 4 depth 6 } and Cube { height 4 depth 6 width 2 } are equivalent.

Here are the nodes grouped by type. The first group are the shape nodes.

These specify geometry: Cone, Cube, Cylinder, ElevationGrid, IndexedFaceSet, IndexedLineSet, PointSet, Text, Sphere.

The second group are the properties. These can be further grouped into properties of the geometry and its appearance, matrix or transform properties, and cameras and lights: CollideStyle, Coordinate3, DocumentInfo, FontStyle, Info, LOD, Material, MaterialBinding, NavigationInfo, Normal, NormalBinding, TextLanguage, Texture2, Texture2Transform, TextureCoordinate2, ShapeHints MatrixTransform, Rotation, Scale, Transform, Translation DirectionalLight, PointLight, SpotLight.

These are the group nodes:

> Separator
>
> Switch
>
> WWWAnchor.

Finally, the camera, WWWInline, and Background nodes do not fit neatly into any category:

> OrthographicCamera, PerspectiveCamera
>
> Background, WWWInline.

Cone.   This node represents a simple cone whose central axis is aligned with the Y-axis. By default, the cone is centered at (0,0,0) and has a size of −1 to +1 in all three directions. The cone has a radius of

1 at the base and a height of 2, with its apex at 1 and its base at −1. The cone has two parts: the sides and the base.

The cone is transformed by the current cumulative transformation and is drawn with the current texture and material.

If the current material binding is PER_PART or PER_PART_INDEXED, the first current material is used for the sides of the cone, and the second is used for the base. Otherwise, the first material is used for the entire cone.

When a texture is applied to a cone, it is applied differently to the sides than to the base. On the sides, the texture wraps counterclockwise (from above) starting at the back of the cone. The texture has a vertical seam at the back, intersecting the YZ-plane. For the base, a circle is cut out of the texture square and applied to the cone's base circle. The texture appears right side up when the top of the cone is rotated towards the negative Z-axis.

PARTS

```
SIDES     The conical part
BOTTOM    The circular base
ALL       All parts
```

FILE FORMAT/DEFAULTS

```
Cone {
     parts         ALL    # SFBitMask
     bottomRadius 1      # SFFloat
     height      2       # SFFloat
}
```

MODIFIED 1.1—Coordinate3.   This node defines a set of 3D coordinates to be used by a subsequent IndexedFaceSet, IndexedLineSet, or PointSet node. This node does not produce a visible result during rendering; it simply replaces the current coordinates in the rendering state for subsequent nodes to use.

FILE FORMAT/DEFAULTS

```
Coordinate3 {
point 0 0 0 # input MFVec3f
}
```

Cube.   This node represents a cuboid aligned with the coordinate axes. By default, the cube is centered at (0,0,0) and measures 2 units in each dimension, from −1 to +1. The cube is transformed by the current cumulative transformation and is drawn with the current material and texture. A cube's width is its extent along its object-space X-axis, its height is its extent along the object-space Y-axis, and its depth is its extent along its object-space Z-axis.

If the current material binding is PER_PART, PER_PART_INDEXED, PER_FACE, or PER_FACE_INDEXED, materials will be bound to the faces of the cube in this order: front (+Z), back (−Z), left (−X), right (+X), top (+Y), and bottom (−Y).

Textures are applied individually to each face of the cube; the entire texture goes on each face. On the front, back, right, and left sides of the cube, the texture is applied right side up. On the top, the texture appears right side up when the top of the cube is tilted toward the camera. On the bottom, the texture appears right side up when the top of the cube is tilted towards the negative Z-axis.

FILE FORMAT/DEFAULTS

```
Cube {
    width   2    # SFFloat
    height  2    # SFFloat
    depth   2    # SFFloat
}
```

Cylinder.   This node represents a simple capped cylinder centered around the Y-axis. By default, the cylinder is centered at (0,0,0) and has a default size of −1 to +1 in all three dimensions. The cylinder has three parts: the sides, the top (y = +1) and the bottom (y = −1). You can use the radius and height fields to create a cylinder with a different size.

The cylinder is transformed by the current cumulative transformation and is drawn with the current material and texture.

If the current material binding is PER_PART or PER_PART_IN-DEXED, the first current material is used for the sides of the cylinder, the second is used for the top, and the third is used for the bottom. Otherwise, the first material is used for the entire cylinder.

When a texture is applied to a cylinder, it is applied differently to the sides, top, and bottom. On the sides, the texture wraps counterclockwise (from above) starting at the back of the cylinder. The texture has a vertical seam at the back, intersecting the YZ-plane. For the top and bottom, a circle is cut out of the texture square and applied to the top or bottom circle. The top texture appears right side up when the top of the cylinder is tilted toward the positive Z-axis, and the bottom texture appears right side up when the top of the cylinder is tilted toward the negative Z-axis.

PARTS

```
SIDES   The cylindrical part
TOP     The top circular face
BOTTOM  The bottom circular face
ALL     All parts
```

FILE FORMAT/DEFAULTS

```
Cylinder {
  parts  ALL  # SFBitMask
  radius 1    # SFFloat
  height 2    # SFFloat
}
```

DirectionalLight. This node defines a directional light source that illuminates along rays parallel to a given 3-dimensional vector.

A light node defines an illumination source that may affect subsequent shapes in the scene graph, depending on the current lighting style. Light sources are affected by the current transformation. A light node under a separator does not affect any objects outside that separator.

FILE FORMAT/DEFAULTS

```
DirectionalLight {
  on        TRUE       # SFBool
  intensity 1          # SFFloat
  color     1 1 1      # SFColor
  direction 0 0 -1     # SFVec3f
}
```

FontStyle. This node defines the current font style used for all subsequent AsciiText. Font attributes only are defined. It is up to the browser to assign specific fonts to the various attribute combinations. The size field specifies the height (in object space units) of glyphs rendered and determines the vertical spacing of adjacent lines of text.

FAMILY

```
SERIF      Serif style (such as TimesRoman)
SANS       Sans Serif Style (such as Helvetica)
TYPEWRITER Fixed pitch style (such as Courier)
```

STYLE

  NONE   No modifications to family

  BOLD   Embolden family

  ITALIC   Italicize or Slant family

FILE FORMAT/DEFAULTS

```
FontStyle {
    size   10   # SFFloat
    family SERIF  # SFEnum
    style NONE  # SFBitMask
}
```

IndexedFaceSet. This node represents a 3D shape formed by constructing faces (polygons) from vertices located at the current coordinates. IndexedFaceSet uses the indices in its coordIndex field to specify the polygonal faces. An index of -1 indicates that the current face has ended and the next one begins.

The vertices of the faces are transformed by the current transformation matrix.

Treatment of the current material and normal binding is as follows: The PER_PART and PER_FACE bindings specify a material or normal for each face. PER_VERTEX specifies a material or normal for each vertex. The corresponding _INDEXED bindings are the same, but use the materialIndex or normalIndex indices. The DEFAULT material binding is equal to OVERALL. The DEFAULT normal binding is equal to PER_VERTEX_INDEXED; if insufficient normals exist in the state, vertex normals will be generated automatically.

Explicit texture coordinates (as defined by TextureCoordinate2) may be bound to vertices of an indexed shape by using the indices in the textureCoordIndex field. As with all vertex-based shapes, if there is a current texture but no texture coordinates are specified, a default texture coordinate mapping is calculated using the bounding box of the shape. The longest dimension of the bounding box defines the S coordinates, and the next longest defines the T coordinates. The value of the S coordinate ranges from 0 to 1, from one end of the bounding box to the other. The T coordinate ranges between 0 and the ratio of the second greatest dimension of the bounding box to the greatest dimension.

Be sure that the indices contained in the coordIndex, materialIndex, normalIndex, and textureCoordIndex fields are valid with respect to the current state, or errors will occur.

FILE FORMAT/DEFAULTS

```
IndexedFaceSet {
   coordIndex       0 # MFLong
   materialIndex   -1 # MFLong
   normalIndex     -1 # MFLong
textureCoordIndex -1 # MFLong
}
```

IndexedLineSet.   This node represents a 3D shape formed by constructing polylines from vertices located at the current coordinates. IndexedLineSet uses the indices in its coordIndex field to specify the polylines. An index of -1 indicates that the current polyline has ended and the next one begins.

The coordinates of the line set are transformed by the current cumulative transformation.

Treatment of the current material and normal binding is as follows: The PER_PART binding specifies a material or normal for each segment of the line. The PER_FACE binding specifies a material or normal for each polyline. PER_VERTEX specifies a material or normal for each vertex. The corresponding _INDEXED bindings are the same, but use the materialIndex or normalIndex indices. The DEFAULT material binding is equal to OVERALL. The DEFAULT normal binding is equal to PER_VERTEX_INDEXED; if insufficient normals exist in the state, the lines will be drawn unlit. The same rules for texture coordinate generation as IndexedFaceSet are used.

FILE FORMAT/DEFAULTS

```
IndexedLineSet    {
   coordIndex       0  # MFLong
   materialIndex   -1  # MFLong
   normalIndex     -1  # MFLong
 textureCoordIndex -1 # MFLong
}
```

Info.   This class defines an information node in the scene graph. This node has no effect during traversal. It is used to store information in the scene graph, typically for browser-specific purposes, copyright messages, or other strings.

```
Info {
string "<Undefined info>"   # SFString
}
```

MODIFIED 1.1—LOD. This node is used to allow browsers to switch between various representations of objects automatically. The children of this node typically represent the same object or objects at varying levels of detail, from highest detail to lowest. LOD acts as a Separator, not allowing properties underneath it to affect nodes that come after it in the scene.

The distance from the viewpoint (transformed into the local coordinate space of the LOD node) to the specified center point of the LOD is calculated. If the distance is less than the first value in the ranges array, then the first child of the LOD is drawn. If between the first and second values in the ranges array, the second child is drawn, and so on. If there are N values in the ranges array, the LOD group should have N + 1 children. Specifying too few children will result in the last child being used repeatedly for the lowest levels of detail; if too many children are specified, the extra children will be ignored. Each value in the ranges array should be less than the previous value, otherwise results are undefined. Not specifying any values in the ranges array (the default) is a special case that indicates that the browser may decide which child to draw to optimize rendering performance.

Authors should set LOD ranges so that the transitions from one level of detail to the next are barely noticeable. Browsers may adjust which level of detail is displayed to maintain interactive frame rates, to display an already-fetched level of detail while a higher level of detail (contained in a WWWInline node) is fetched, or might disregard the author-specified ranges for any other implementation-dependent reason. Authors should not use LOD nodes to emulate simple behaviors because the results will be undefined. For example, using an LOD node to make a door appear to open when the user approaches probably will not work in all browsers.

For best results, specify ranges only where necessary, and nest LOD nodes with and without ranges. For example;

```
LOD {
  range [100, 1000]
LOD {
Separator { ... detailed version... }
  DEF LoRes Separator { ... less detailed version... }
  }
  USE LoRes
  Info { } # Display nothing
  }
```

In this example, nothing at all will be displayed if the viewer is farther than 1000 meters away from the object. A low-resolution version of the object will be displayed if the viewer is between 100 and 1000 meters away, and either a low-resolution or a high-resolution version of the object will be displayed when the viewer is closer than 100 meters to the object.

FILE FORMAT/DEFAULTS

```
LOD {

  range [ ]      # MFFloat

  center 0 0 0 # SFVec3f

  }
```

MODIFIED 1.1—Material.   This node defines the current surface material properties for all subsequent shapes. Material sets several components of the current material during traversal. Different shapes interpret materials with multiple values differently. To bind materials to shapes, use a MaterialBinding node.

The lighting parameters defined by the Material node are the same parameters defined by the OpenGL lighting model. For a rigorous mathematical description of how these parameters should be used to determine how surfaces are lit, see the description of lighting operations in the OpenGL Specification. Note that VRML 1.1 provides no mechanism for controlling the amount of ambient light in the scene, so use of the ambientColor field is browser dependent. Several other parameters (such as light attenuation factors) are also left as implementation details in VRML. Also note that OpenGL specifies the specular exponent as a non-normalized 0–128 value, which is specified as a normalized 0–1 value in VRML (simply multiplying the VRML value by 128 to translate to the OpenGL parameter).

For rendering systems that do not support the full OpenGL lighting model, the following simpler lighting model is recommended:

A transparency value of 0 is completely opaque, a value of 1 is completely transparent. Browsers need not support partial transparency, but should support at least fully transparent and fully opaque surfaces, treating transparency values >= 0.5 as fully transparent.

Specifying only emissiveColors and zero diffuse, specular, emissive, and ambient colors is the way to specify pre-computed lighting. It is expected that browsers will be able to recognize this as a special case and optimize their computations. For example;

```
Material {
  ambientColor [] diffuseColor [] specularColor []
  emissiveColor [ 0.1 0.1 0.2, 0.5 0.8 0.8 ]
}
```

Issues for Low-End Rendering Systems.   Many low-end PC rendering systems are not able to support the full range of the VRML material specification. For example, many systems do not render individual
red, green, and blue reflected values as specified in the specularColor
field. The following table describes which Material fields are typically
supported in popular low-end systems and suggests actions for
browser implementors to take when a field is not supported.

Field	Supported?	Suggested Action
ambientColor	No	Ignore
diffuseColor	Yes	Use
specularColor	No	Ignore
emissiveColor	No	Use in place of diffuseColor if != 0 0 0
shininess	Yes	Use
transparency	No	Ignore

It is also expected that simpler rendering systems will be unable to
support both lighted and unlighted objects in the same scene.

FILE FORMAT/DEFAULTS

```
Material {
    ambientColor  0.2 0.2 0.2  # input MFColor
    diffuseColor  0.8 0.8 0.8  # input MFColor
    specularColor 0 0 0        # input MFColor
    emissiveColor 0 0 0        # input MFColor
    shininess    0.2           # input MFFloat
    transparency  0            # input MFFloat
}
```

MaterialBinding.   Material nodes may contain more than one material. This node specifies how the current materials are bound to shapes
that follow in the scene graph. Each shape node may interpret bindings differently. For example, a Sphere node is always drawn using
the first material in the material node, no matter what the current MaterialBinding, while a Cube node may use six different materials to
draw each of its six faces, depending on the MaterialBinding.

The bindings for faces and vertices are meaningful only for shapes that are made from faces and vertices. Similarly, the indexed bindings are only used by the shapes that allow indexing.

When multiple material values are needed by a shape, the previous Material node should have at least as many materials as are needed, otherwise results are undefined.

Issues for low-end rendering systems. Some renderers do not support per-vertex materials, in which case the MaterialBinding values PER_VERTEX and PER_VERTEX_INDEXED will produce upredictable results in different browsers.

BINDINGS

DEFAULT	Use default binding
OVERALL	Whole object has same material
PER_PART	One material for each part of object
PER_PART_INDEXED	One material for each part, indexed
PER_FACE	One material for each face of object
PER_FACE_INDEXED	One material for each face, indexed
PER_VERTEX	One material for each vertex of object
PER_VERTEX_INDEXED	One material for each vertex, indexed

FILE FORMAT/DEFAULTS

```
MaterialBinding {
value OVERALL    # SFEnum
    }
```

MatrixTransform.   This node defines a geometric 3D transformation with a 4 by 4 matrix. Only matrices that are the result of rotations, translations, and non-zero (but possibly non-uniform) scales must be supported. Non-invertable matrices should be avoided.

Matrices are specified in row-major order, so; for example, a Matrix-Transform representing a translation of 6.2 units along the local Z-axis would be specified as:

MatrixTransform { matrix

```
 1 0 0 0
 0 1 0 0
 0 0 1 0
 0 0 6.2 1
 }
```

FILE FORMAT/DEFAULTS

```
MatrixTransform {
matrix 1 0 0 0    # SFMatrix
0  1  0  0
0  0  1  0
0  0  0  1
}
```

MODIFIED 1.1—Normal.   This node defines a set of 3D surface normal vectors to be used by vertex-based shape nodes (IndexedFaceSet, IndexedLineSet, PointSet) that follow it in the scene graph. This node does not produce a visible result during rendering; it simply replaces the current normals in the rendering state for subsequent nodes to use. This node contains one multiple-valued field that contains the normal vectors.

To save network bandwidth, it is expected that implementations will be able to automatically generate appropriate normals if none are given. However, the results will vary from implementation to implementation.

FILE FORMAT/DEFAULTS

```
Normal {
vector [ ] # input MFVec3f
   }
```

NormalBinding.   This node specifies how the current normals are bound to shapes that follow in the scene graph. Each shape node may interpret bindings differently.

The bindings for faces and vertices are meaningful only for shapes that are made from faces and vertices. Similarly, the indexed bindings are only used by the shapes that allow indexing. For bindings that require multiple normals, be sure to have at least as many normals defined as are necessary; otherwise, errors will occur.

BINDINGS

DEFAULT	Use default binding
OVERALL	Whole object has same normal
PER_PART	One normal for each part of object
PER_PART_INDEXED	One normal for each part, indexed
PER_FACE	One normal for each face of object

PER_FACE_INDEXED   One normal for each face, indexed

PER_VERTEX   One normal for each vertex of object

PER_VERTEX_INDEXED   One normal for each vertex, indexed

FILE FORMAT/DEFAULTS

```
NormalBinding {

value DEFAULT      # SFEnum

}
```

OrthographicCamera.   An orthographic camera defines a parallel projection from a viewpoint. This camera does not diminish objects with distance, as a PerspectiveCamera does. The viewing volume for an orthographic camera is a rectangular parallelepiped (a box).

By default, the camera is located at (0,0,1) and looks along the negative Z-axis; the position and orientation fields can be used to change these values. The height field defines the total height of the viewing volume.

A camera can be placed in a VRML world to specify the initial location of the viewer when that world is entered. VRML browsers will typically modify the camera to allow a user to move through the virtual world.

The results of traversing multiple cameras are undefined; to ensure consistent results, place multiple cameras underneath one or more Switch nodes, and set the Switch's whichChild fields so that only one is traversed. By convention, these non-traversed cameras may be used to define alternate entry points into the scene; these entry points may be named by simply giving the cameras a name (using DEF); see the specification of WWWAnchor for a conventional way of specifying an entry point in a URL.

Cameras are affected by the current transformation, so you can position a camera by placing a transformation node before it in the scene graph . The default position and orientation of a camera is at (0,0,1) looking along the negative Z-axis, with the positive Y-axis up.

The position and orientation fields of a camera are sufficient to place a camera anywhere in space with any orientation. The orientation field can be used to rotate the default view direction (looking down -Z-, with +Y up) so that it is looking in any direction, with any direction *up*.

The focalDistance field defines the point the viewer is looking at, and may be used by a browser as a navigational hint to determine how fast the viewer should travel, which objects in the scene are most important, and so on.

The nearDistance and farDistance are distances from the viewpoint (in the camera's coordinate system); objects closer to the viewpoint than nearDistance or farther from the viewpoint than farDistance should not be seen. Browsers may treat these values as hints, and may decide to adjust them as the viewer moves around the scene.

FILE FORMAT/DEFAULTS

```
OrthographicCamera {
    position        0 0 1        # SFVec3f
    orientation     0 0 1 0      # SFRotation
    focalDistance   5            # SFFloat
    height          2            # SFFloat
    nearDistance    1            # SFFloat
    farDistance     10           # SFFloat
}
```

Issues for low-end rendering systems: Most low-end rendering systems do not support the concept of focalDistance. Also, cameras are global to the scene; placing a camera beneath a particular Separator is equivalent to placing it at outermost scope. For broadest compatibility, cameras should only be placed at outermost scope.

MODIFIED 1.1—PerspectiveCamera. A perspective camera defines a perspective projection from a viewpoint. The viewing volume for a perspective camera is a truncated right pyramid.

By default, the camera is located at (0,0,1) and looks along the negative Z-axis; the position and orientation fields can be used to change these values. The heightAngle field defines the total vertical angle of the viewing volume.

See more on cameras in the OrthographicCamera description.

FILE FORMAT/DEFAULTS

```
PerspectiveCamera {
    position        0 0 1        # SFVec3f
    orientation     0 0 1 0      # SFRotation
    focalDistance   5            # SFFloat
    heightAngle     0.785398     # SFFloat
    nearDistance    1            # SFFloat
    farDistance     10           # SFFloat
}
```

PointLight.   This node defines a point light source at a fixed 3D location. A point source illuminates equally in all directions; that is, it is omnidirectional.

A light node defines an illumination source that may affect subsequent shapes in the scene graph, depending on the current lighting style. Light sources are affected by the current transformation. A light node under a separator should not affect any objects outside that separator (although some rendering systems do not currently support this).

FILE FORMAT/DEFAULTS

```
PointLight {
    on       TRUE      # SFBool
    intensity 1        # SFFloat
    color    1 1 1     # SFColor
    location  0 0 1    # SFVec3f
}
```

PointSet.   This node represents a set of points located at the current coordinates. PointSet uses the current coordinates in order, starting at the index specified by the startIndex field. The number of points in the set is specified by the numPoints field. A value of -1 for this field indicates that all remaining values in the current coordinates are to be used as points.

The coordinates of the point set are transformed by the current cumulative transformation. The points are drawn with the current material and texture.

Treatment of the current material and normal binding is as follows:

PER_PART, PER_FACE, and PER_VERTEX bindings bind one material or normal to each point. The DEFAULT material binding is equal to OVERALL. The DEFAULT normal binding is equal to PER_VERTEX. The startIndex is also used for materials or normals when the binding indicates that they should be used per vertex.

FILE FORMAT/DEFAULTS

```
PointSet {
startIndex  0    # SFLong
numPoints  -1    # SFLong
}
```

Issues for low-end rendering systems: Many low-end renderers do not support the concept of per-object lighting. This means that placing a light beneath a Separator, which implies lighting only the objects beneath the Separator with that light, is not supported in all systems. For the broadest compatibility, lights should only be placed at outermost scope.

MODIFIED 1.1—Rotation.   This node defines a 3D rotation about an arbitrary axis through the origin. The rotation is accumulated into the current transformation, which is applied to subsequent shapes.

FILE FORMAT/DEFAULTS

```
Rotation {
rotation 0 0 1 0  # input SFRotation
}
```

See rotation field description for more information.

MODIFIED 1.1—Scale.   This node defines a 3D scaling about the origin. If the components of the scaling vector are not all the same, this produces a non-uniform scale.

FILE FORMAT/DEFAULTS

```
Scale {
scaleFactor 1 1 1  # input SFVec3f
}
```

Separator.   A proposal to replace Separator's with Frames and Leafs is at

http://earth.path.net/mitra/papers/vrml-frames.html.

This group node performs a push (save) of the traversal state before traversing its children and a pop (restore) after traversing them. This isolates the separator's children from the rest of the scene graph. A separator can include lights, cameras, coordinates, normals, bindings, and all other properties.

Separators can also perform render culling. Render culling skips over traversal of the separator's children if they are not going to be rendered, based on the comparison of the separator's bounding box with the current view volume. Culling is controlled by the renderCulling field. These are set to AUTO by default, allowing the implementation to decide whether or not to cull.

CULLING ENUMS

ON   Always try to cull to the view volume

OFF   Never try to cull to the view volume

AUTO   Implementation-defined culling behavior

FILE FORMAT/DEFAULTS

```
Separator {
renderCulling     AUTO    # SFEnum
}
```

ShapeHints.   The ShapeHints node indicates that IndexedFaceSets are solid, contain ordered vertices, or contain convex faces.

These hints allow VRML implementations to optimize certain rendering features. Optimizations that may be performed include enabling back-face culling and disabling two-sided lighting. For example, if an object is solid and has ordered vertices, an implementation may turn on backface culling and turn off two-sided lighting. If the object is not solid but has ordered vertices, it may turn off backface culling and turn on two-sided lighting.

The ShapeHints node also affects how default normals are generated. When an IndexedFaceSet has to generate default normals, it uses the creaseAngle field to determine which edges should be smoothly shaded and which ones should have a sharp crease. The crease angle is the angle between surface normals on adjacent polygons. For example, a crease angle of .5 radians (the default value) means that an edge between two adjacent polygonal faces will be smooth shaded if the normals to the two faces form an angle that is less than .5 radians (about 30 degrees). Otherwise, it will be faceted.

Issues for low-end rendering systems: The shapeType and vertex-Ordering fields are used to determine whether or not to generate back faces for each polygon in a mesh. Most low-end rendering systems do not support built-in back face generation; browsers built on these systems need to create back faces explicitly.

VERTEX ORDERING ENUMS

UNKNOWN_ORDERING	Ordering of vertices is unknown
CLOCKWISE (from the outside)	Face vertices are ordered clockwise
COUNTERCLOCKWISE (from the outside)	Face vertices are ordered counter-clockwise

SHAPE TYPE ENUMS

UNKNOWN_SHAPE_TYPE	Nothing is known about the shape
SOLID	The shape encloses a volume

FACE TYPE ENUMS

UNKNOWN_FACE_TYPE	Nothing is known about faces
CONVEX	All faces are convex

FILE FORMAT/DEFAULTS

```
ShapeHints {
    vertexOrdering COUNTERCLOCKWISE    # SFEnum
    shapeType       SOLID             # SFEnum
    faceType        CONVEX            # SFEnum
    creaseAngle    0                  # SFFloat
}
```

Sphere.   This node represents a sphere. By default, the sphere is centered at the origin and has a radius of 1. The sphere is transformed by the current cumulative transformation and is drawn with the current material and texture.

A sphere does not have faces or parts. Therefore, the sphere ignores material and normal bindings, using the first material for the entire sphere and using its own normals. When a texture is applied to a sphere, the texture covers the entire surface, wrapping counterclockwise from the back of the sphere. The texture has a seam at the back on the YZ-plane.

FILE FORMAT/DEFAULTS

```
Sphere {
radius 1    # SFFloat
}
```

SpotLight.   This node defines a spotlight light source. A spotlight is placed at a fixed location in 3-dimensional space and illuminates in a cone along a particular direction. The intensity of the illumination drops off exponentially as a ray of light diverges from this direction toward the edges of the cone. The rate of drop-off and the angle of the cone are controlled by the dropOffRate and cutOffAngle fields.

A light node defines an illumination source that may affect subsequent shapes in the scene graph, depending on the current lighting style. Light sources are affected by the current transformation. A light node under a separator should not affect any objects outside that separator (although some rendering systems do not currently support this).

FILE FORMAT/DEFAULTS

```
SpotLight {
    on          TRUE       # SFBool
    intensity   1          # SFFloat
    color       1 1 1      # SFVec3f
    location    0 0 1      # SFVec3f
    direction   0 0 -1     # SFVec3f
    dropOffRate 0          # SFFloat
    cutOffAngle 0.785398   # SFFloat
}
```

Issues for low-end rendering systems: Many low-end renderers do not support the concept of per-object lighting. This means that placing a light beneath a Separator, which implies lighting only the objects beneath the Separator with that light, is not supported in all systems. For the broadest compatibility, lights should only be placed at outermost scope.

MODIFIED 1.1—Switch.　This group node traverses one or none of its children. One can use this node to switch on and off the effects of some properties or to switch between different properties.

The whichChild field specifies the index of the child to traverse, where the first child has index 0. This field is an input and thus can be modified by another node.

Open issue: It is expected that in a future version of VRML the Switch node will be defined to behave as a Separator node, not allowing its children to affect anything after it in the scene graph. To ensure future compatibility, it is recommended that all children of all Switch nodes be Separator nodes.

FILE FORMAT/DEFAULTS

```
Switch {
whichChild -1     # input SFLong
}
```

Text.　This node represents one or more text strings specified using the UTF-8 encoding of the ISO10646 character set. This is described below. An important note is that ASCII is a subset of UTF-8, so any ASCII strings are also UTF-8.

The text strings can be rendered in one of four directions: right to left (RL), left to right (LR), top to bottom (TB), or bottom to top (BT). The direction field governs this.

The justification field determines where the text will be positioned in relation to the origin (0,0,0) of the object coordinate system. The values for the justification field are BEGIN, END, CENTER. For a left to right (LR) direction, these would correspond to LEFT, RIGHT, CENTER.

For the directions RL and LR, the first line of text will be positioned with its baseline (bottom of capital letters) at y = 0. The text is positioned on the positive side of the X-axis for the direction LR and justification BEGIN; the same for RL END. The text is on the negative side of the X-axis for LR END and RL BEGIN. For CENTER justification and horizontal text (RL, LR), each string will be centered at x = 0.

For the directions TB and BT, the first line of text will be positioned with the left side of the glyphs along the Y-axis. For TB BEGIN and BT END, the text will be positioned with the top left corner at the origin; for TB END and BT BEGIN, the bottom left will be at the origin. For TB and BT CENTER, the text will be centered vertically at x = 0.

LR BEGIN	LR END	LR CENTER
VRML	VRML	VRML
adds a	adds a	adds a
dimension!	dimension!	dimension!

RL BEGIN	RL END	RL CENTER
LMRV	LMRV	LMRV
a sdda	a sdda	a sdda
!noisnemid	!noisnemid	!noisnemid

TB BEGIN	TB END	TB CENTER	BT BEGIN	BT END	BT CENTER
V a d	d	d	!	L a !	!
R d i	i	i	n	M n	n
M d m	m	a m	o	R s o	a o
L s e	e	V d e	i	V d i	L i
n	a n	R d n	a s	d s	M s s
a s	d s	M s s	n	a n	R d n
i	V d i	L i	L s e	e	V d e
•	R s o	a o	M d m	m	a m
n	M n	n	R d i	i	i
!	L a !	!	V a d	d	d

The spacing field determines the spacing between multiple text strings. All subsequent strings advance in either X or Y by $-($ size $*$ spacing). See FontStyle for a description of the size field. A value of 0 for the spacing will cause the string to be in the same position. A value of -1 will cause subsequent strings to advance in the opposite direction.

The extent field will limit and scale the text string if the natural length of the string is longer than the extent. If the text string is shorter than the extent, it will not be scaled. The extent is measured horizontally for RL and LR directions; vertically for TB and BT.

UTF-8 character encodings.   The 2 byte (UCS-2) encoding of ISO 10646 is identical to the Unicode standard. References for both ISO 10646 and Unicode are given in the references section at the end.

In order to avoid introducing binary data into VRML we have chosen to support the UTF-8 encoding of ISO 10646. This encoding allows ASCII text (0x0..0x7F) to appear without any changes and encodes all characters from 0x80..0x7FFFFFFF into a series of six or fewer bytes.

If the most significant bit of the first character is 0, then the remaining seven bits are interpreted as an ASCII character. Otherwise, the number of leading 1 bits will indicate the number of bytes following. There is always a 0 bit between the count bits and any data.

First byte could be one of the following. The X indicates bits available to encode the character.

0XXXXXXX	only one byte	0..0x7F (ASCII)
110XXXXX	two bytes	Maximum character value is 0x7FF
1110XXXX	three bytes	Maximum character value is 0xFFFF
11110XXX	four bytes	Maximum character value is 0x1FFFFF
111110XX	five bytes	Maximum character value is 0x3FFFFFF
1111110X	six bytes	Maximum character value is 0x7FFFFFFF

All following bytes have this format: 10XXXXXX

A two byte example: The symbol for a registered trade mark is "circled R registered sign" or 174 in both ISO/Latin-1 (8859/1) and ISO 10646. In hexadecimal it is 0xAE; In HTML®. In UTF-8 it is has the following two byte encoding 0xC2, 0xAE.

The text is transformed by the current cumulative transformation and is drawn with the current material and texture.

Textures are applied to 3D text as follows. The texture origin is at the origin of the first string, as determined by the justification. The texture is scaled equally in both S and T dimensions, with the font height representing 1 unit. S increases to the right, T increases up.

DIRECTION

LR   Characters are drawn from left to right

RL   Characters are drawn from right to left

TB   Characters are drawn from top to bottom

BT   Characters are drawn from bottom to top

JUSTIFICATION

BEGIN   Align beginning of text to origin

CENTER   Align center of text to origin

END   Align end of text to origin

FILE FORMAT/DEFAULTS

```
Text {
  string       ""  # MFString
  direction    LR  # SFEnum
justification BEGIN # SFEnum
  spacing      1   # SFFloat
  width        0   # MFFloat
}
```

TextLanguage.   There are many languages in which the proper rendering of the text requires more than just a sequence of glyphs. The TextLanguage node allows the author to specify which, if any, language specific rendering techniques to use. For simple languages, such as English, this node may be safely ignored.

The tag used to specify languages will follow RFC1766 - Tags for the Identification of Languages. ftp://ftp.isi.edu/in-notes/rfc1766.txt. This RFC specifies that a language tag may simply be a two letter ISO 639 tag, for example "en" for English, "ja" for Japanese, and "sv" for Swedish. This may be optionally followed by a two letter country code from ISO 3166. So, Americans would be absolutely safe with "en-US". ISO does not have documents on-line, yet. They can be ordered.

FILE FORMAT/DEFAULTS

```
TextLanguage {
textLanguage  ""  # SFString
}
```

Texture2.

TODO: Gavin—add sentence about grey scales to Texure2

This property node defines a texture map and parameters for that map. This map is used to apply texture to subsequent shapes as they are rendered.

The texture can be read from the URL specified by the filename field. To turn off texturing, set the filename field to an empty string (""). Implementations should support at least the JPEG image file format. Also supporting GIF and PNG formats is recommended.

If multiple URLs are presented, this expresses a descending order of preference, a browser may display a lower preference URL while the higher order file is not available. See the section on URNs.

Textures can also be specified in-line by setting the image field to contain the texture data. Supplying both image and filename fields will result in undefined behavior.

Texture images may be one component (greyscale), two component (greyscale plus transparency), three component (full RGB color), or four-component (full RGB color plus transparency). An ideal VRML implementation will use the texture image to modify the diffuse color and transparency of an object's material (specified in a Material node), then performing any lighting calculations using the rest of the object's material properties with the modified diffuse color to produce the final image. The texture image modifies the diffuse color and transparency, depending on how many components are in the image, as follows:

1. Diffuse color is multiplied by the greyscale values in the texture image.

2. Diffuse color is multiplied by the greyscale values in the texture image, material transparency is multiplied by transparency values in texture image.

3. RGB colors in the texture image replace the material's diffuse color.

4. RGB colors in the texture image replace the material's diffuse color, transparency values in the texture image replace the material's transparency.

Browsers may approximate this ideal behavior to increase performance. One common optimization is to calculate lighting only at each vertex and combining the texture image with the color computed from lighting (performing the texturing after lighting). Another common optimization is to perform no lighting calculations at all when texturing is enabled, displaying only the colors of the texture image.

WRAP ENUM

REPEAT   Repeats texture outside 0-1 texture coordinate range.

CLAMP   Clamps texture coordinates to lie within 0-1 range.

FILE FORMAT/DEFAULTS

```
Texture2 {
     filename   ""     # SFString
     image     0 0 0   # SFImage
     wrapS     REPEAT  # SFEnum
     wrapT     REPEAT  # SFEnum
}
```

Texture2Transform.   This node defines a 2D transformation applied to texture coordinates. This affects the way textures are applied to the surfaces of subsequent shapes. The transformation consists of (in order) a non-uniform scale about an arbitrary center point, a rotation about that same point, and a translation. This allows a user to change the size and position of the textures on shapes.

FILE FORMAT/DEFAULTS

```
Texture2Transform {
    translation 0 0    # SFVec2f
    rotation   0    # SFFloat
    scaleFactor 1 1    # SFVec2f
    center     0 0   # SFVec2f
}
```

TextureCoordinate2.   This node defines a set of 2D coordinates to be used to map textures to the vertices of subsequent PointSet, Indexed-LineSet, or IndexedFaceSet objects. It replaces the current texture coordinates in the rendering state for the shapes to use.

Texture coordinates range from 0 to 1 across the texture. The horizontal coordinate, called S, is specified first, followed by the vertical coordinate, T.

FILE FORMAT/DEFAULTS

```
TextureCoordinate2 {
point 0 0  # MFVec2f
}
```

MODIFIED 1.1—Transform.   This node defines a geometric 3D transformation consisting of (in order) a (possibly) non-uniform scale about an arbitrary point, a rotation about an arbitrary point and axis, and a translation. The transform node

```
Transform {
  translation T1
  rotation R1
  scaleFactor S
  scaleOrientation R2
  center T2
}
```

is equivalent to the sequence:

Translation { translation T1 }

Translation { translation T2 }

Rotation { rotation R1 }

Rotation { rotation R2 }

Scale { scaleFactor S }

Rotation { rotation -R2 }

Translation { translation -T2 }

FILE FORMAT/DEFAULTS

```
Transform {
   translation        0 0 0     # input SFVec3f
   rotation           0 0 1 0   # input SFRotation
   scaleFactor        1 1 1     # input SFVec3f
   scaleOrientation 0 0 1 0     # input SFRotation
   center             0 0 0     # input SFVec3f
}
```

MODIFIED 1.1—Translation.   This node defines a translation by a 3D vector.

FILE FORMAT/DEFAULTS

```
Translation {
translation 0 0 0  # input SFVec3f
}
```

WWWAnchor.   The WWWAnchor group node loads a new scene into a VRML browser when one of its children is chosen. Exactly how a user "chooses" a child of the WWWAnchor is up to the VRML browser; typically, clicking on one of its children with the mouse will result in the new scene replacing the current scene. A WWWAnchor with an empty ("") name does nothing when its children are chosen. The name is an arbitrary URL.

If multiple URLs are presented, this expresses a descending order of preference, a browser may display a lower preference URL if the higher order file is not available. See the section on URNs.

WWWAnchor behaves like a Separator, pushing the traversal state before traversing its children and popping it afterwards.

The description field in the WWWAnchor allows for a friendly prompt to be displayed as an alternative to the URL in the name field. Ideally, browsers will allow the user to choose the description, the URL or both to be displayed for a candidate WWWAnchor.

The WWWAnchor's map field is an enumerated value that can be either NONE (the default) or POINT. If it is POINT then the object-space coordinates of the point on the object the user chose will be added to the URL in the name field, with the syntax "?x,y,z".

A WWWAnchor may be used to take the viewer to a particular viewpoint in a virtual world by specifying a URL ending with "#cameraName", where "cameraName" is the name of a camera defined in the world. For example;

```
WWWAnchor {
  name "http://www.school.edu/vrml/someScene.wrl#OverView"
  Cube { }
}
```

specifies an anchor that puts the viewer in the "someScene" world looking from the camera named "OverView" when the Cube is chosen. If no world is specified, then the current scene is implied; for example;

```
WWWAnchor {
  name "#Doorway"
  Sphere { }
}
```

will take the viewer to the viewpoint defined by the "Doorway" camera in the current world when the sphere is chosen.

MAP ENUM

NONE   Do not add information to the URL

POINT   Add object-space coordinates to URL

FILE FORMAT/DEFAULTS

```
WWWAnchor {
name ""      # MFString
description "" # SFString
map NONE     # SFEnum
}
```

WWWInline.   The WWWInline node reads its children from anywhere in the World Wide Web. Exactly when its children are read is not defined; reading the children may be delayed until the WWWInline is actually displayed. A WWWInline with an empty name does nothing. The name is an arbitrary URL.

The effect of referring to a non-VRML URL in a WWWInline node is undefined.

If multiple URL's are specified, then this expresses a descending order of preference. A browser may display a URL for a lower preference file while it is obtaining, or if it is unable to obtain, the higher preference file. See also the section on URNs.

If the WWWInline's bboxSize field specifies a non-empty bounding box (a bounding box is non-empty if at least one of its dimensions is greater than zero), then the WWWInline's object-space bounding box is specified by its bboxSize and bboxCenter fields. This allows an implementation to quickly determine whether or not the contents of the WWWInline might be visible. This is an optimization hint only; if the true bounding box of the contents of the WWWInline is different from the specified bounding box, results will be undefined.

FILE FORMAT/DEFAULTS

```
WWWInline {
   name ""          # MFString
   bboxSize 0 0 0    # SFVec3f
   bboxCenter 0 0 0  # SFVec3f
}
```

NEW—New Nodes for 1.1

Background.   By providing a shaded ground plane, sky and scenic, textures, this node can be used to add substance to the void surrounding the scene. Only the first background node encountered is used, and it must be specified in the main file.

If groundColors are specified, then a ground plane is added to the scenegraph at y = 0 in global coordinate space. If more than one color is specified, then the ground color is interpolated between colors from 0 degrees downward to 90 degrees at the horizon. Similarly, skyColors interpolate from the 90 degree mark to 180 degrees overhead.

A scene may describe a more precise atmosphere and include background scenery in the scenery field. This field is used to add a texture to the scene that is conceptually distant enough that it does not translate with respect to the eyepoint. The texture should be mapped wrapped around a cylinder so that it runs all the way around from y=0 in global coordinate space.

If multiple URL's are specified then this expresses a descending order of preference, a browser may display a URL for a lower preference file while it is obtaining, or if it is unable to obtain, the higher preference file. See also the section on URNs.

```
Background{
  groundColors [ ]     # MFColor
  skyColors [ 0 0 0 ] # MFColor
  scenery ""      # MFString
}
```

Pros

- Resolves issue that most current scenes hover in black space.

- Implementation should make ground plane less expensive than general case.

- Geometry will provide good depth queue as closer objects move relative to the user.

- Geometry assumes nothing of what environment the author wants to portray.

- Geometry being part of scenegraph supports behaviors.

- Global coordinate space optimizes rendering of scenery.

Issues

- Global coordinates speed up implementation. If arbitrary ground plane is absolutely needed, consider a rotation and elevation to orient the ground plane in world space.

- There has been discussion of supporting different mapping for the background texture—cylindrical, spherical, hemispherical. However current renderers do not support this functionality and simulating it would be an unacceptable performance hit.

CollideStyle.   This node specifies to a browser what objects in the scene should not be navigated through. It is useful to keep viewers from walking through walls in a building, for instance. Collision response is browser defined. For example, when the camera comes sufficiently close to an object to register as a collision, the browser may have the camera bounce off the object, or simply come to a stop.

Since collision with arbitrarily complex geometry is computationally expensive, one method of increasing efficiency is to be able to define an alternate geometry that could serve as a proxy for colliding against. This collision proxy could be as crude as a simple bounding box or bounding sphere, or could be more spohisticated (for example, the convex hull of a polyhedron). This proxy volume is used ONLY to calculate the collision with the viewer and is NOT used for trivial rejection during the computation process. Efficient trivial rejection can be done using hierarchical bounding boxes or some other technique, and its implementation is not specified in the language.

VRML represents collision proxy volumes for objects through the CollideStyle property node. A CollideStyle node sets the collision proxy volume for all the geometry in the scene graph that follows it up to the next CollideStyle node. Like all other properties, the current collision style would be saved and restored by Separators. Like all other shapes, the geometry is defined in object space and is transformed by the current modeling transformation.

CollideStyle contains two fields: collide (a boolean) and proxy (a node). If the value of the collide field is FALSE, then no collision is performed with the affected geometry. If the value of the collide field is TRUE, then the proxy field defines the geometry against which collision testing is done. If the proxy value is undefined or NULL, the actual geometry is collided against. If the proxy value is not NULL, then it contains the geometry that is used in collision computations.

FILE FORMAT/DEFAULTS

```
CollideStyle {
    collide    FALSE  # SFBool
    proxy      NULL   # SFNode
}
```

Notes/Issues

- Open issue—no consensus on what collides with object. The viewer must have some geometry to collide against objects in the scene. In the future, this would be an avatar geometry. For 1.1, the collisionRadius fields of the NavigationInfo node are used.

DirectedSound

TODO: Bill to write up minor changes; loop/start/pause probably gone

- Sound formats AU, AIFF, WAV.
- Note implication that transport system will tell you the type of the file.

This node defines a sound source that is located at a specific 3D location and that emits primarily along a given direction. It adds directionality to the PointSound node. Besides the direction vector, there are minAngle and maxAngle fields that specify how the intensity of the sound changes with direction. Within the cone whose apex is the sound location, whose axis is the direction vector, and whose angle is specified by minAngle, the DirectedSound behaves exactly like a

PointSound. Moving along a constant radius (from the source location) from the surface of this cone to the surface of the similar cone whose angle is maxAngle, the intensity falls off to zero.

See the PointSound node for a description of all other fields.

FILE FORMAT/DEFAULTS

```
DirectedSound {
        name            " "         # MFString
        description     " "         # SFString
        intensity       1           # SFFloat
        location        0 0 0       # SFVec3f
        direction       0 0 1       # SFVec3f
        minRange        10          # SFFloat
        maxRange        10          # SFFloat
        minAngle        0.785398    # SFFloat
        maxAngle        0.785398    # SFFloat
        loop            FALSE       # SFBool
        start           0           # input SFTime
        pause           0           # input SFTime
}
```

ElevationGrid

VAG: Accepted—no changes

This node creates a rectangular grid with varying heights, especially useful in modeling terrain and other space creating surfaces. The model is specified primarily by a scalar array of height values that describe the height of the surface above each point of the grid.

The verticesPerRow and verticesPerColumn fields define the number of grid points in the Z and X directions, respectively, defining a surface that contains (verticesPerRow-1) x (verticesPerColumn-1) rectangles.

The vertex locations for the rectangles are defined by the height field and the gridStep field. The vertex corresponding to the ith row and jth column is placed at (gridStep[0] * j, heights[i*verticesPerColumn+j], gridStep[1] * i) in object space, where 0<=i<=verticesPerRow, 0<=j<=verticesPerColumn.

The height field is an array of scalar values representing the height above the grid for each vertex. The height values are stored so that row 0 is first, followed by rows 1, 2, ..., verticesPerRow. Within each row, the height values are stored so that column 0 is first, followed by columns 1, 2, ..., verticesPerColumn. The rows have fixed Z values, with row 0 having the smallest Z value. The columns have fixed X values, with column 0 having the smallest X value.

The default texture coordinates will range from [0,0] at the first vertex to [1,1] at the far side of the diagonal. The S texture coordinate will be aligned with X and the T texture coordinate with Z.

Treatment of the current material and normal binding is as follows: The PER_PART binding specifies a material or normal for each row of the mesh. The PER_FACE binding specifies a material or normal for each quadrilateral. The _INDEXED bindings are equivalent to their non-indexed counterparts. The default material binding is OVERALL. The default normal binding is PER_VERTEX.

If any normals (or materials) are specified, it is assumed you provide the correct number of them, as indicated by the binding. You will see unexpected results if you specify fewer normals (or materials) than the shape requires. If no normals are specified, they will be generated automatically.

By default, the rectangles are defined with a counterclockwise ordering, so the Y component of the normal is positive. Setting the vertex-Ordering field of the current ShapeHints node to CLOCKWISE reverses the normal direction. Backface culling can be turned on as for all shapes, by defining a ShapeHints node prior to the ElevationGrid node with the vertexOrdering field set to CLOCKWISE or COUNTER-CLOCKWISE and the shapeType field set to SOLID.

FILE FORMAT/DEFAULTS

```
ElevationGrid {
verticesPerRow 0       # SFLong
verticesPerColumn 0 # SFLong
    gridStep []        # SFVec2f
    height []          # MFFloat
}
```

Pros

- This is an extremely compact way to represent geometry (key for transmission times).

- There is a lot of data available that can be easily converted into this form (USGS Digital Elevation Models come to mind)

- Easy for browsers to do automatic LOD degradation to keep performance up.

Environment.   This node describes global environmental attributes such as ambient lighting, light attenuation, and fog.

Ambient lighting is the amount of extra light impinging on each surface point. It is specified as an ambientColor and ambientIntensity. Light attenuation affects all subsequent lights in a scene. It is a quadratic function of distance from a light source to a surface point. The three coefficients are specified in the attenuation field. Attenuation works only for light sources with a fixed location, such as point and spot lights. The ambient lighting and attenuation calculations are defined in the OpenGL lighting model. For a description of these and other lighting calculations, see the description of lighting operations in the OpenGL Specification.

Fog has one of four types, each of which blends each surface point with the specified fog color. Each type interprets the visibility field to be the distance at which fog totally obscures objects. A visibility value of 0 (the default) causes the Environment node to set up fog so that the visibility is the distance to the far clipping plane of the current camera. For more details on the fog calculations, see the description of fog in the OpenGL Specification.

FOGTYPE

NONE	No fog.
HAZE	Linear increase in opacity with distance.
FOG	Exponential increase in opacity.
SMOKE	Exponential squared increase in opacity.

FILE FORMAT/DEFAULTS

```
Environment {
    ambientIntensity 0.2     # SFFloat
    ambientColor    1 1 1    # SFColor
    attenuation     0 0 1    # SFVec3f
    fogType        NONE     # SFEnum
    fogColor       1 1 1    # SFColor
    fogVisibility   0        # SFFloat
}
```

GeneralCylinder

TODO: Gavin to edit, minor changes

This is a node for parametrically describing numerous families of shapes: extrusions (along an axis or an arbitrary path), surfaces of revolution, and bend/twist/taper objects.

General Cylinders are defined by four piecewise linear curves: cross-Section, profile, spine and twist. Shapes are constructed as follows. The crossSection is a 2D curve that is scaled, extruded through space, and twisted by the other curves. First, the crossSection is extruded and scaled along the path of the profile curve. Second, the shape is bent and stretched so that its central axis aligns with the spine curve. Finally, the shape is twisted about the spine by angles (in radians) given by the twist curve. The twist curve is a function of angle at given parametric distances along the spine.

Surfaces of Revolution: If the crossSection is a circle and the spine is straight, then the General Cylinder will be equivalent to a surface of revolution, where the General Cylinder profile curve maps directly to that of the surface of revolution.

Cookie-Cutter Extrusions: If both the profile and spine are straight, then the crossSection acts like a cookie-cutter, with the thickness of the cookie equal to the length of the spine.

Bend/Twist/Taper objects: Shapes like this are the result of utilizing all four curves. The spine curve bends the shape, the twist curve twists it, and the profile curve tapers it.

Planar TOP and BOTTOM surfaces will be generated when the crossSection is closed (i.e., when the first and last points of the crossSection are equal). However, if the profile is also closed, the TOP and BOTTOM are not generated; this is because a closed crossSection extruded along a closed profile creates a shape that is closed without the addition of TOP and BOTTOM parts.

The parts field determines which parts are rendered. The notion of BOTTOM versus TOP is determined by the profile curve. The end of the profile curve with a lesser y-value is the BOTTOM end.

The cone is transformed by the current cumulative transformation and is drawn with the current texture and material. The first material in the state is used for the entire GeneralCylinder, regardless of the current material binding.

GeneralCylinder automatically generates its own normals. Normal-Binding in the state is ignored. Orientation of the normals is determined by the vertex ordering of the triangles generated by General-Cylinder. The vertex ordering is in turn determined by the crossSection curve. If the crossSection is drawn counterclockwise, then the polygons will have counterclockwise ordering when viewed from the *outside* of the shape (and vice versa for clockwise ordered crossSections). The General Cylinder responds to the fields of the ShapeHints node the same way as IndexedFaceSet.

Texture coordinates are automatically generated by General Cylinders. These will map textures like the label on a soup can: the coordinates will range in the u direction from 0 to 1 along the crossSection curve and in the v direction from 0 to 1 along the spine. If the TOP and/or BOTTOM exist, textures map onto them in a planar fashion.

When a texture is applied to a General Cylinder, it is applied differently to the sides, top, and bottom. On the sides, the texture wraps [0,1] of the u-direction of the texture along the crossSection from first point to last; it wraps [0,1] of the v-direction of the texture along the direction of the spine, from first point to last. When the crossSection is closed, the texture has a seam that follows the line traced by the crossSection's start/end point as it travels along the spine. For the top and bottom, the crossSection is cut out of the texture square and applied to the top or bottom circle. The top and bottom textures' u and v directions correspond to the x and z directions in which the crossSection coordinates are defined.

PARTS

SIDES	The extruded surface part.
TOP	The top cross sectional face.
BOTTOM	The bottom cross sectional face.
ALL	All parts.

FILE FORMAT/DEFAULTS

```
GeneralCylinder {
spine [ 0 0 0, 0 1 0 ] # MFVec3f
crossSection [ -1 1, -1 -1, 1 -1, 1 1 ] # MFVec2f
profile [ 1 -1, 1 1 ] # MFVec2f
twist [ 0 -1, 0 1 ] # MFVec2f
parts  ALL  # SFBitMask
}
```

Pros

*   This is an extremely compact way to represent geometry (key for transmission times).

*   Easy for browsers to do automatic LOD degradation to keep performance up.

NavigationInfo.   This node contains information for the viewer through several fields: type, speed, collisionRadius, and headlight.

The type field specifies a navigation paradigm to use. The types that all VRML viewers should support are walk, examiner, fly, and none.

A "walk" viewer would constrain the user to a plane (X–Z), suitable for architectural walkthroughs. An "examiner" viewer would let the user tumble the entire scene, suitable for examining single objects. A "fly" viewer would provide six degree of freedom movement. The "none" choice removes all viewer controls, forcing the user to navigate using only WWWAnchors linked to viewpoints. The type field is multi-valued so that authors can specify fallbacks in case a browser does not understand a given type.

The speed is the rate at which the viewer travels through a scene in meters per second. Since viewers may provide mechanisms to travel faster or slower, this should be the default or average speed of the viewer. In an examiner viewer, this only makes sense for panning and dollying—it should have no affect on the rotation speed.

Open issue: no consensus on collisionRadius—see CollideStyle node.

The collisionRadius field specifies the smallest allowable distance between the camera position and any collision object (as specified by CollideStyle) before a collision is detected.

Open issue: no consensus on headlight field, relates to discussion on Avatars.

The headlight field specifies whether a browser should turn a headlight on. A headlight is a directional light that always points in the direction the camera is looking. This effect can be had by adding a DirectionalLight in front of a Camera in the scene. Instead, setting this field to TRUE allows the browser to provide a headlight, possibly with user interface controls to turn it on and off. Scenes that enlist precomputed lighting (e.g. radiosity solutions) can specify the headlight off here. The headlight should have intensity 1, color 1 1 1, and direction 0 0 -1. The effects of specifying headlight on in a NavigationInfo node are equivalent to an author adding a default DirectionalLight in front of a camera in the scene, except that using the NavigationInfo field allows a browser to provide user interface controlling the light.

FILE FORMAT/DEFAULTS

```
NavigationInfo {
    type            "walk"    # input MFString
    speed           1.0       # input SFFloat
    collisionRadius 1.0         # SFFloat
    headlight       TRUE      # SFBool
}
```

Notes/Issues

- The following fields may be dynamic: speed, height, collisionRadius, worldUp.

- How is the "knee cap" height specified? That is, at what height does the browser climb something (like stairs) as opposed to collide with it (like a table)? This is currently browser defined (probably as some percentage of the collisionRadius).

- What happens when the user navigates the viewer "off a cliff"? Does the browser hover, drop to terrain instantaneously, or fall at some rate? Forces and masses could come into play here, but then browsers would be doing simulations, which are beyond the scope of VRML 1.1.

- Currently, most browsers automatically turn a headlight on. WebSpace only turns a headlight on if there are no lights in the scene. This means scenes are rendered with different color saturations in different browsers. Adding a headlight field forces browsers to add headlights consistently.

PointSound

TODO: Bill to edit, minor edits

This node defines a sound source located at a specific 3D location. The name field specifies a URL from which the sound is read. Implementations should support at least the ??? ??? sound file formats. Streaming sound files may be supported by browsers; otherwise, sounds should be loaded when the sound node is loaded. Browsers may limit the maximum number of sounds that can be played simultaneously.

If multiple URLs are specified, then this expresses a descending order of preference, a browser may use a URL for a lower preference file while it is obtaining, or if it is unable to obtain, the higher preference file. See also the section on URNs.

The description field is a textual description of the sound, which may be displayed in addition to or in place of playing the sound.

The intensity field adjusts the volume of each sound source; an intensity of 0 is silence and an intensity of 1 is whatever intensity is contained in the sound file.

The sound source has a radius specified by the minRadius field. When the viewpoint is within this radius, the sound's intensity (volume) is constant, as indicated by the intensity field. Outside the minRadius, the intensity drops off to zero at a distance of maxRadius from the source location. If the two radii are equal, the drop-off is sharp and sudden. Otherwise, the drop-off should be proportional to the square of the distance of the viewpoint from the minRadius.

Browsers may also support spatial localizations of sound. However, within minRadius, localization should not occur, so intensity is constant in all channels. Between minRadius and maxRadius, the sound location should be the point on the minRadius sphere that is closest to the current viewpoint. This ensures a smooth change in location when the viewpoint leaves the minRadius sphere. Note also that an ambient sound can therefore be created by using a large minRadius value.

The loop field specifies whether or not the sound is constantly repeated.

By default, the sound is played only once.

The start input specifies the time at which the sound should start playing. The pause input may be used to make a sound stop playing some time after it has started. If the pause time is less than the start time then it is ignored. Changing the start input while the sound is playing will result in undefined behavior; however, changing the start input after the sound is paused is well-defined and useful. If the sound is not looped, the length of time the sound plays is determined by the sound file read, and is not specified in the VRML file.

A sound's location in the scene graph determines its spatial location (the sound's location is transformed by the current transformation) and whether or not it can be heard. A sound can only be heard while it is part of the traversed scene; sound nodes underneath LOD nodes or Switch nodes will not be audible unless they are traversed. If it is a later part of the traversal again, the sound picks up where it would have been had it been playing continuously.

FILE FORMAT/DEFAULTS

```
PointSound {
    name           " "         # MFString
    description    " "         # SFString
    intensity      1           # SFFloat
    location       0  0  0     # SFVec3f
    minRange       10          # SFFloat
    maxRange       10          # SFFloat
    loop           FALSE       # SFBool
    start          0           # input SFTime
    pause          0           # input SFTime
}
```

Issues

- What sound file formats do we want to support?

- Supporting real-time effects such as frequency modulation, re-verb, etc. requires too much CPU performance and is beyond the scope of this spec. Advanced browsers can always define more complicated sound sources and can use the IsA mechanism to maintain compatibility with less capable browsers.

- The scene graph semantics chosen allow sounds to be easily attached to objects; putting an object underneath a Switch node is the way to make it (temporarily) disappear from the world. If the sound is part of the object, the sound should also disappear when this happens.

WorldInfo.   Open issue: tied into pseudo node proposal, current proposal at http://earth.path.net/mitra/papers/vrml-pseudo.html, this is probably OK.

This node contains information about the world. The title of the world is stored in its own field, allowing browsers to display it, for instance, in their window border. Any other information about the world can be stored in the info field, for instance the scene author, copyright information, and public domain information.

FILE FORMAT/DEFAULTS

```
WorldInfo {
    title      " "     # SFString
    info       " "     # MFString
}
```

NEW for 1.1—Prototyping.   Prototyping is a mechanism that allows the set of node types to be extended from within a VRML file. It allows the encapsulation and parameterization of geometry, behaviors, or both.

PROTO.   A prototype is defined using the PROTO keyword, as follows:

```
PROTO typename [ eventIn fieldtypename name
IS nodename.eventInName nodename.eventInName ... ,
eventOut fieldtypename name
IS nodename.eventOutName nodename.eventOutName ...,
field fieldtypename name IS nodename.fieldName,
        ... ]
{ node { ... } Logic and/or ROUTES }
```

A prototype is NOT a node; it merely defines a prototype (named 'typename') that can be used later in the same file as if it were a built-in node. The implementation of the prototype is contained in the scene graph rooted by node. That node may be followed by Logic and/or ROUTE declarations, as necessary to implement the prototype.

The eventIn and eventOut declarations export events inside the scene graph given by node. Specifying the type of each event in the prototype is intended to prevent errors when the implementation of prototypes are changed, and to provide consistency with external prototypes. Specifying a name for each event allows several events with the same name to be exported with unique names.

Fields hold the persistent state of VRML objects. Allowing a prototype to export fields allows the initial state of a prototyped object to be specified by prototype instances.

The node names specified in the event and field declarations must be DEF'ed inside the prototype implementation. The first node DEF'ed in lexical (not traversal) order will be exported. It is an error (and results are undefined) if there is no node with the given name, or the first node found does not contain a field of the appropriate type with the given field name.

Prototype declarations have file scope, and prototype names must be unique in any given file.

Only nodes DEF'ed inside the prototype may be USE'ed inside the prototype, and nodes DEF'ed inside the prototype are not visible (may not be USE'ed) outside the prototype.

A prototype is instantiated as if typename were a built-in node. A prototype instance may be DEF'ed or USE'ed. For example, a simple chair with variable colors for the leg and seat might be prototyped as:

```
PROTO TwoColorChair [ field SFColor legColor IS leg.diffuseColor,
   field SFColor seatColor IS seat.diffuseColor ] {
   Separator {
   Separator {
     DEF seat Material { diffuseColor .6 .6 .1 }
     Cube { ... }
   }

Separator {
   Transform { ... }
   DEF leg Material { diffuseColor .8 .4 .7 }
```

```
Cylinder { ... }

}

} # End of root Separator } # End of prototype # Proto-
type is now defined. Can be used like:
```

DEF redGreenChair TwoColorChair { legColor 1 0 0 seat-
Color 0 1 0 }

USE redGreenChair # Regular DEF/USE rules apply. We're making distinctions between fields, which can be given an initial value but cannot be changed except by the node that they're contained in, and events, which (at least for the built-in nodes) are requests to change fields. So, if we want our TwoColorChair to have colors that can be changed, we'd need to expose the leg.setDiffuseColor 'eventIn' and seat.diffuseColor 'eventIn' events. All of which may make for confusing and wordy prototype declarations. Are there ever cases where you might want to ONLY allow initial values to be set, and NOT allow them to be changed later?

PROTO sort of gives people their non-instantiating DEF: PROTO foo [ ] Cube { } is roughly equal to DEF foo Cube { }, except that foo is now a type name instead of an instance name (and you say foo { } to get another cube instead of USE foo). Smart implementations will automatically share the unchanging stuff in prototype implementations, so the end result will be the same.

NodeReference. What if we wanted a prototype that could be instantiated with arbitrary geometry? For example, we might want to define a prototype chair that allowed the geometry for the legs to be defined, with the default (perhaps) being a simple cylinder.

VRML 1.1 will include the SFNode field type—a field that contains a pointer to a node. Using SFNode, it is easy to write the first part of the PROTO definition:

PROTO Chair [field SFNode legGeometry IS. ... but then we get stuck when we try to define the IS part of the prototype. We need some way of taking an SFNode field and inserting it into the scene. This can be accomplished with a new node, the NodeReference node:

```
NodeReference {
  node NULL # SFNode field (NULL is valid syntax for SFNode)
  # eventIn SFNode setNode
  # eventOut SFNode nodeChanged
}
```

Functionally, NodeReference is a "do-nothing" node—it just behaves exactly like whatever nodeToUse points to (unless nodeToUse is NULL, of course, in which case NodeReference does nothing). For example, this would be a verbose way to add a Sphere to the scene:

NodeReference { nodeToUse Sphere { } }

NodeReference is only interesting if its nodeToUse field is exposed in a prototype (or it receives a nodeToUse event). So, for example, our Chair with arbitrary leg geometry (with a Cylinder default if none is specified) can be filled out as:

```
PROTO Chair [ field SFNode legGeometry IS NR.nodeToUse ] {
  Separator {
  Separator {
  Transform { ... }
  DEF NR NodeReference { nodeToUse Cylinder { } }
  }
Separator {
  Transform { ... }
  USE NR
  }
  ... would reuse leg with a USE NR, would have
  geometry for seat/back/etc...
 }
}
```

Using the Chair prototype would look like:

```
Chair {
    legGeometry Separator { Coordinate3/IndexedFaceSet/etc }
}
```

It might also make sense to share the same geometry between several prototype instances; for example, you might do:

```
Chair {
    legGeometry DEF LEG Separator { Coordinate3/IndexedFaceSet/etc }
}
```

... somewhere later in scene...

```
Chair {
    legGeometry USE LEG
}
```

Note that SFNode fields follow the regular DEF/USE rules, and that SFNode fields contain a pointer to a node; using DEF/USE, an SFNode field may contain a pointer to a node that is also a child of some node in the scene graph, is pointed to by some other SFNode field, and so on.

The NodeReference node has nice, clean semantics, and allows a lot of flexibility and power for defining prototypes. It also has some nice implementation side effects:

Browsers that want to maintain a different internal representation for the scene graph can implement NodeReference so that nodeToUse is read and the different internal representation is generated. Optimizations might also be performed at the same time.

Browsers that optimize scene graphs can implement NodeReference such that, whenever nodeToUse changes, an optimized scene is created. When rendering, the optimized scene will be used instead of the un-optimized scene.

A really smart browser will figure out that nobody is using the un-optimized scene and may free it from memory.

Something else to think about: should a prototype be allowed to expose the fields or events of an SFNode that is passed in? For example:

```
PROTO Foo [ field SFNode transform   IS NR.nodeToUse,
    eventIn SFVec3f setPosition IS NR.nodeToUse.translation ]
Separator { DEF NR NodeReference { nodeToUse Transform {
} } Cube { } }
```

This could be pretty powerful, but might also be painful to implement, since the type-checking would have to be done at run-time when NR.nodeToUse changed.

EXTERNPROTO.   A second form of the prototype syntax allows prototypes to be defined in external files:

```
EXTERNPROTO typename [ eventIn fieldtypename name,
   eventOut fieldtypename name,
   field fieldtypename,
            ... ]
URL or [ URL, URL, ... ]
```

In this case, the implementation of the prototype is found in the given URL. The file pointed to by that URL must contain ONLY a single prototype implementation (using PROTO). That prototype is then given the name typename in this file's scope (allowing possible naming clashes to be avoided). It is an error if the eventIn/eventOut declaration in the EXTERNPROTO is not a subset of the eventIn/eventOut declaration specified in URL.

> The rules about allowing exporting only from files that contain a single PROTO declaration are consistent with the WWWInline rules; until we have VRML-aware protocols that can send just one object or prototype declaration across the wire, I don't think we should encourage people to put multiple objects or prototype declarations in a single file.

We need to think about scalability when using nested EXTERNPRO-TOs. EXTERNPROTOs don't have bounding boxes specified like WWWInlines, and they might need them. I'm starting to think that we might need to add bboxCenter/Size fields to Separator instead of having them only on WWWInline; with animations possible, pre-specifying maximum-possible bounding boxes could save a lot of work recalculating bounding boxes as things move.

MODIFIED 1.1—Extensibility

TODO: Jan to handle type_registry@vrml.org for new suffixes

Extensions to VRML are supported by supporting self-describing nodes. Nodes that are not part of standard VRML must write out a description of their fields first, so that all VRML implementations are able to parse and ignore the extensions.

This description is written just after the opening curly-brace for the node, and consists of the keyword "fields" followed by a list of the types and names of fields used by that node, all enclosed in square brackets and separated by commas. For example, if Cube was not a standard VRML node, it would be written like this:

```
Cube {
fields [ SFFloat width, SFFloat height, SFFloat depth ]
width 10 height 4 depth 3
}
```

Specifying the fields for nodes that ARE part of standard VRML is not an error; VRML parsers must silently ignore the field[] specification. However, incorrectly specifying the fields of a built-in node is an error.

The fields specification must be written out with every non-standard node, whether or not that node type was previously encountered during parsing. For each instance of a non-standard node, only the fields written as part of that instance need to be described in the fields[] specification; that is, fields that aren't written because they contain their default value may be omitted from the fields[] specification. It is expected that future versions of VRML will relax this requirement, requiring only that the first non-standard node of a given type be given the fields[] specification.

Just like standard nodes, instances of non-standard nodes do not automatically share anything besides the default values of their fields that are not specified in the VRML file but are considered part of the implementation of the non-standard nodes.

Is-a relationships.   A new node type may also be a super-set of an existing node, that is, part of the standard. In this case, if an implementation for the new node type cannot be found, the new node type can be safely treated as the existing node it is based on (with some loss of functionality, of course). To support this, new node types can define an MFString field called "isA" containing the names of the types of which it is a super-set. For example, a new type of Material called "ExtendedMaterial" that adds index of refraction as a material property can be written as:

```
ExtendedMaterial {
fields [ MFString isA, MFFloat indexOfRefraction,
  MFColor diffuseColor, MFFloat transparency ]
isA [ "Material" ]
indexOfRefraction .34
diffuseColor .8 .54 1
}
```

Multiple is-a relationships may be specified in order of preference; implementations are expected to use the first for which there is an implementation.

Note that IsA and PROTO are different ways to define new nodes, they should not be used together.

Nodes instantiated with isA should not copy default values or children from the first instantiation.

Alternate Representations.   To allow extension nodes to be handled gracefully by browsers that don't recognise them, an alternateRep field is supported. This is an SFNode field that specifies what to use if the extension node is not recognised. Typically it will be a WWWInline of a more complex representation, or of a CGI script that can generate the node dynamically; for example;

```
ColoredCube {
  isA Cube
  fields [ SFColor color ]
  color 2 0 0
    alternateRep {
    WWWInline {
    name "http://foo.com/cgi/ColoredCube/2/0/0"
        }
    }
}
```

Naming Conventions.   Check the General Syntax section of this standard for the rules on valid characters in names.

To avoid namespace collisions with nodes defined by other people, any of the following conventions should be followed.

1.   Anyone can pick names that include a suffix of an underscore followed by a domain name that you own with the periods changed into underscores. For example a company owning foo.com could create an extension node Cube_foo_com.

2.   If you are building a product, for example, an authoring tool, or a browser, or defining a lot of new nodes, then you can apply for a short prefix. E-mail type_registry@vrml.org to register for the prefix. This will normally be accepted if it is the most significant part of a .com, .org or .net address. In the above example foo.com could register the extension _foo and create nodes of the form Cube_foo.

3.   Extensions supported by several companies should be registered and use the _X extension.

This process may change as more experience is gained.

URN's.   VRML1.1 browsers are not required to support URNs although if they don't, then they should ignore URNs when they appear in MFString fields with URLs. URN support is specified in a separate document at http://earth.path.net/mitra/papers/vrml-urn.html, which may undergo minor revisions to keep it in-line with parallel work happening at the IETF.

An Example: This is a longer example of a VRML scene. It contains a simple model of a track-light consisting of primitive shapes, plus three walls (built out of polygons) and a reference to a shape defined elsewhere, both of which are illuminated by a spotlight. The shape acts as a hyperlink to some HTML text.

```
#VRML V1.1 utf8

Separator {
  Separator {      # Simple track-light geometry:
  Translation { translation 0 4 0 }
  Separator {
    Material { emissiveColor 0.1 0.3 0.3 }
    Cube {
      width  0.1
      height 0.1
      depth  4
    }
  }
  Rotation { rotation 0 1 0 1.57079 }
  Separator {
    Material { emissiveColor 0.3 0.1 0.3 }
    Cylinder {
      radius 0.1
      height .2
    }
  }
  Rotation { rotation -1 0 0 1.57079 }
  Separator {
```

```
    Material { emissiveColor 0.3 0.3 0.1 }
    Rotation { rotation 1 0 0 1.57079 }
    Translation { translation 0 -.2 0 }
    Cone {
      height .4
      bottomRadius .2
  }
    Translation { translation 0 .4 0 }
    Cylinder {
      radius 0.02
      height .4
      }
  }
}
 SpotLight {    # Light from above
 location 0 4 0
 direction 0 -1 0
 intensity    0.9
 cutOffAngle    0.7
}
 Separator {    # Wall geometry; just three flat polygons
 Coordinate3 {
 point [
 •  2 0 -2, -2 0 2, 2 0 2, 2 0 -2,
 •  2 4 -2, -2 4 2, 2 4 2, 2 4 -2]
 }
 IndexedFaceSet {
 coordIndex [ 0, 1, 2, 3, -1,
 0, 4, 5, 1, -1,
 0, 3, 7, 4, -1
            ]
  }
}
 WWWAnchor {   # A hyperlinked cow:
 name "http://www.foo.edu/CowProject/AboutCows.html"
```

```
Separator {
Translation { translation 0 1 0 }
WWWInline {  # Reference another object
name "http://www.foo.edu/3DObjects/cow.wrl"
    }
  }
 }
}
```

Browser Considerations

This section describes the file naming and MIME conventions to be used in building VRML browsers and configuring WWW browsers to work with them.

File Extensions.   The file extension for VMRL files is .wrl (for world).

MIME.   The MIME type for VRML files is defined as follows: x-world/x-vrml.

The MIME major type for 3D world descriptions is x-world. The MIME minor type for VRML documents is x-vrml. Other 3D world descriptions, such as oogl for The Geometry Center's Object-Oriented Geometry Language, or iv, for SGI's Open Inventor ASCII format, can be supported by using different MIME minor types.

It is anticipated that the official type will change to model/vrml"; at this time servers should present files as being of type x-world/x-vrml, browsers should recognise both x-world/x-vrml and model/vrml.

Acknowledgements

I want to thank three people who have been absolutely instrumental in the design process: Brian Behlendorf, whose drive (and disk space) made this process happen; and Tony Parisi and Gavin Bell, the final authors of this specification, who have put in a great deal of design work, ensuring that we have a satisfactory product. My hat goes off to all of them, and to all of you who have made this process a success.

Mark Pesce

I would like to add a personal note of thanks to Jan Hardenbergh of Oki Advanced Products for his diligent efforts to keep the specification process on track, and his invaluable editing assistance. I would also like to acknowledge Chris Marrin of Silicon Graphics for his timely contributions to the final design.

Tony Parisi

VRML 1.1 is a result of years of effort from the Inventor group at Silicon Graphics. All of the past and present members of the Inventor team deserve recognition and thanks for their excellent work over the last five years.

Gavin Bell

[—] 22-NOV-95

References.   The draft of the ISO UTF-8 proposal is online at:

http://www.stonehand.com/unicode/standard/wg2n1036.html.

The draft for making HTML internationalized is on-line. We are not as constrained as HTML, since VRML will rarely be primarily text. We can be a little less efficient.

ftp://ftp.alis.com/pub/ietf/html/draft-ietf-html-i18n-00.txt

ftp://ftp.isi.edu/in-notes/rfc1766.txt

OpenGL specification and man pages are on-line:

http://www.sgi.com/Technology/openGL/spec.html.

Addison Wesley's *The Inventor Mentor* and *Open Inventor C++ Reference Manual* are invaluable.

TODO

* URN

  Mark to write sample code

  Mitra to revise proposal in light of IETF meeting in early

December

* Gavin to spell check
* Rikk and Gavin—Input fields
* Gavin—add URL to this doc
* Gavin—deprecated features added to contents list
* Mark—specify conformance process
* VAG—check for other things which should be Input fields.
* VAG— revist NavigationInfo -
* VAG/Jan—which stings should be UTF-8, URLS? do we need a new type?

Appendix

C

Quick Reference to the WorldView VRML Browser for Windows 3.1 and Windows 95

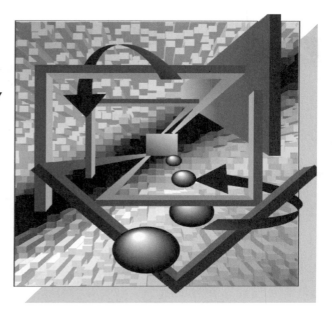

Introduction

This appendix serves as a quick reference to the WorldView VRML Browser for Windows 3.1 and Windows 95. Its commands, tools, and navigation methods are demonstrated in this appendix.

The Menubar In WorldView 0.9f for Windows 3.1

File View Go HotSpots Options Window Help

The File Menu

Open Location . . . The Open Location . . . Menu serves to open op remote URL (Uniform Resource Locator) pages on the Internet. Typically commands entered in the **Open Location** Dialogue box are: http://the.address.here/vrml. For example: http://www.intervista.com, http://www.vrml.com. (please note that you have to be connected to the Internet to use **Open Location**).

Open File . . . The **Open File . . .** dialogue box allows you to open world files (e.g., myworld.wrl) that are saved locally on your hard drive. For example: c:\vrml-file\myworld.wrl).

Save As . . . The **Save As . . .** option allows you to save remote files (e.g., remote *.wrl files stored at an Internet location) to your local hard drive.

Exit.   This will exit the WorldView program.

The View Menu

Reload.   Allows you to reload a previously loaded world, both locally and on the Internet. This allows you to refresh the screen and restart from the beginning of the world.

Save Viewpoint.   Allows you to save a viewpoint of an object in a world as well as an entire world.

Restore Viewpoint.   Allows you to restore a viewpoint that you saved with **Save Viewpoint.**

Look as Scene.   By clicking on this option the world will be shown with more details.

Stop.   The **Stop** option allows you to stop the current loading of a world and **Stop** the animation of a world.

Wireframe.   This is a special effect that allows you to view the world as a wireframe (please see Chapter Four for more details).

Flat.   This is a special effect that allows you to view the world's colors with a flat surface (please see Chapter Four for more details).

Gouraud.   This is the default special effect for WorldView (please see Chapter Four for more details).

Phong.   This is a special effect that gives your world colors more shine (please see Chapter Four for more details).

Dither.   This special effect will Dither your world, slightly distort it (please see to Chapter Four for more details).

Go Menu

Go Forward ...   This options allows you to move forward from one world to another. This option is especially helpful if you are accessing linked worlds.

Go Backward ...   This option allows you to go back to a world that you have previously accessed. This option is especially helpful if you are accessing linked worlds.

Home. This option will transport you back to the InterVista Web page (you have to be connected to the Internet to use this option).

View History . . . This will show all the VRML pages you have accessed during this WorldView session.

HotSpots

Add HotSpot. The **HotSpot** option allows you to add an Internet address as a bookmark so you can visit the site at a later date.

View HotSpot . . . Allows you to view and go to the **HotSpots** you have already saved.

Options

Preferences . . . This allows you to set optional parameters for more functionality in WorldView. You can set options such as **Rendering** parameters, **Viewpoint** specifications, and **Network Options.**

Load Inline Objects. If this option is checked, you will be able to load imbedded pictures (bitmaps or gif files) that are loaded into the world while you are looking at it. This also allows you to jump from one world to another.

Load Texture Maps. When checked, will load all detailed textures of the world you are looking at.

Show/Hide Crosshair. This will show or hide the crosshair on the middle of the scene screen.

Collision Detection. Collision Detection is very helpful when you are navigating through complex worlds. With this option checked, you will not be able to walk through walls and objects in the world. If the Collision Detection is not checked you can walk through all the objects and obstacles in the world, which makes navigation that more difficult.

Windows

Navigator. If this option is checked, you are using WorldView as the prime navigator. If this option is not checked, you are using World-View as an add-in helper application for another browser.

Parser Warnings.   This option will warn you if there is an error in the VRML code.

Help

Help is not available in this version of WorldView.

The WorldView 1.0B for Windows 95 Menu Bar

File   View   Go   Places   Simulation   Options   Help

1.   In **File** you can:

Open an Internet location by use of an internet address, or you can open local WRL files that are stored on your hard drive.

Save As ... allows you to save files you have retrieved from the Internet as well as files you have built yourself.

Print allows you to print a world on your printer.

Edit Source allows you to edit the source code of a particular world. Please refer to chapters 5 and 6 on how to build and edit worlds.

Exit will terminate WorldView.

2.   In **View** you can:

Reload a world that you recently loaded from the Internet as well as a world that you have saved locally on your hard drive. This allows the image to refresh itself.

Zoom Out or **Zoom In** a particular world for closer observation and analysis.

Add Camera will allow you to add different viewpoints to your world so you can look at it from different angles.

Default Camera will reset WorldView to use the default camera not the cameras added with **Add Camera**.

3.   In **Go** you can:

Go **Back** to a previously viewed Web page or world that you loaded from the Internet.

Go **Forward** will jump you to the next Web page or world that you loaded from the Internet.

Go to the **Home World** will connect you to InterVista Software's Internet Web page at **http://www.intervista.com** .

Stop Loading will interrupt the loading of a Web page or world from the Internet. This is especially helpful when the loading process becomes slow or has stopped loading.

View History of Web pages or worlds that you recently visited.

4. In **Places** you can:

Add favorite place this feature allows you to save a particular Web page or world that you have found on the Internet and wish to revisit at a later time.

View favorite place this feature allows you to retrieve the Web pages and/or worlds that you have saved with the **Add favorite place** feature.

5. In **Simulation** you can:

Animation: Animation allows you to animate your world to perform certain functions that you can then replay later. The following features are combined with animation:

A. **Start All** will start the animation recording process.

B. **Stop All** will stop the animation recording process.

C. **Reset** will reset the animation to its original settings

D. **Next** will jump you to the next animation.

E. **Previous** will jump you back to the previous animation

Quality: In Quality you can adjust the quality of your world. This is helpful if your world is rendering very slowly or if you need to see specific details of a world. The following quality controls are available:

A. **Best (smooth shading)** Most detailed display of the world (slow rendering)

B. **Good (flat shading)** Less detail, but still pretty good (fast rendering)

C. **Poor (WireFrame)** Wire frame details of your world, allows you to see how the world was made (very fast rendering).

Speed: In speed you can set the rendering speeds of your world. Typically this is set at **Very Fast** although sometimes you may need to decrease the speed because of loading and/or downloading problems. **Speed** has 5 different speed settings: **Very Slow, Slow, Medium, Fast,** and **Very Fast.**

Load Textures when checked will load all detailed textures of the world you are viewing. When not checked, the world will display in less detail.

Prevent Collisions: This feature, when checked, will allow you to navigate through a world without walking straight through objects in that world. It prevents you from colliding with a specific object (e.g., a wall, door, floor, etc.).

6. In **Options** you can:

Preferences: Set preferences on how you want worldview to behave and operate. Preferences has four major features that we will discuss at this point in detail. It is important to know what these features are because they direct how WorldView operates.

A.   **Imaging** (Figure C-1)

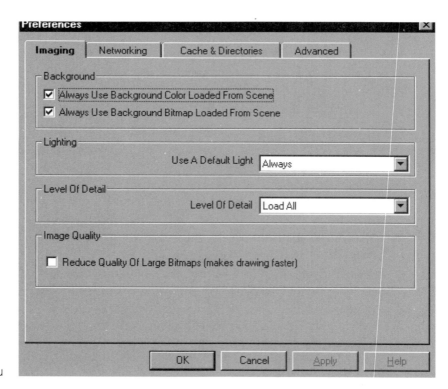

Figure C-1
WorldView
Imaging Menu

Imaging allows you to set the way WorldView will load **background** colors and images, which type of **lighting** it will use, what type of **details** you want displayed, and what type of image **quality** you want to use for all worlds you are going to load. The keyword for selecting these features is *speed*. If you have a slow machine with 8Mbyte of RAM and/or a slow Internet connection, it is recommended that you *not* load all details at once or *not* load specific backgrounds. Not checking these features will increase your speed, but will take away from the image quality.

B.   **Networking** (Figure C-2)

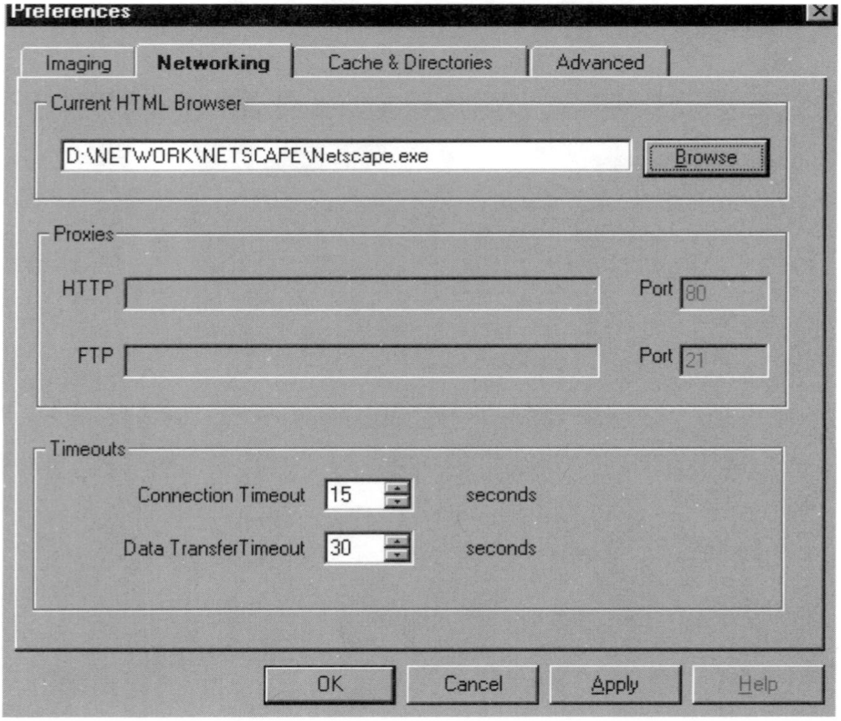

Figure C-2
WorldView
Networking Menu

Networking allows you to set Internet preferences. You can set the default **HTML browser** to view HTML pages on the World Wide Web. We have selected Netscape in this section, however, you can use whichever browser you are comfortable with (e.g., Spry Mosaic, Netmanage's Web-Surfer, Webcrawler, etc.). **Proxies** allows you to set helper applications that WorldView will invoke when neccesary. **Timeouts** allows you to set up the timeout delay in seconds before WorldView will stop trying to retrieve a world or Web page. For slower machines or slower modem users, the higher the timeout rate the better the chance of retrieving the world from the internet. Users with fast machines and fast modems or direct Internet connections do not need to change these options.

C.   **Cache and Directories** (Figure C-3)

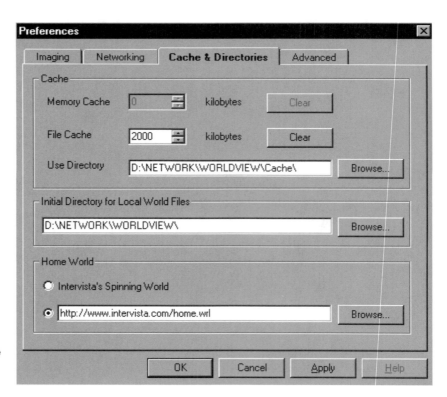

Figure C-3
WorldView Cache and Directories Menu

In **Cache and Directories** you can set the **Memory Cache** and **File Cache** sizes as well as the directory in which to load the cache files. Cache memory and files use a portion of your hard drive to temporarily store temporary files in order to increase the performance of WorldView—this is especially important for users who have slow computers. The temporary cache files are stored in the directory specified below. The default directory is a subdirectory below WorldView called cache.

When you install WorldView, the program installs a view sample world files on your computer to play with. The default directory is x:\worldview\worlds, where X:\ is the drive you installed WorldView on.

Home World is the default page you can specify for WorldView to load when loading WorldView.

Intervista's Spinning World is the Globe that loads automatically when WorldView is loaded.

Http://www.intervista.com/home.wrl is the world that is loaded automatically from the internet.

D.   Advanced (Figure C-4)

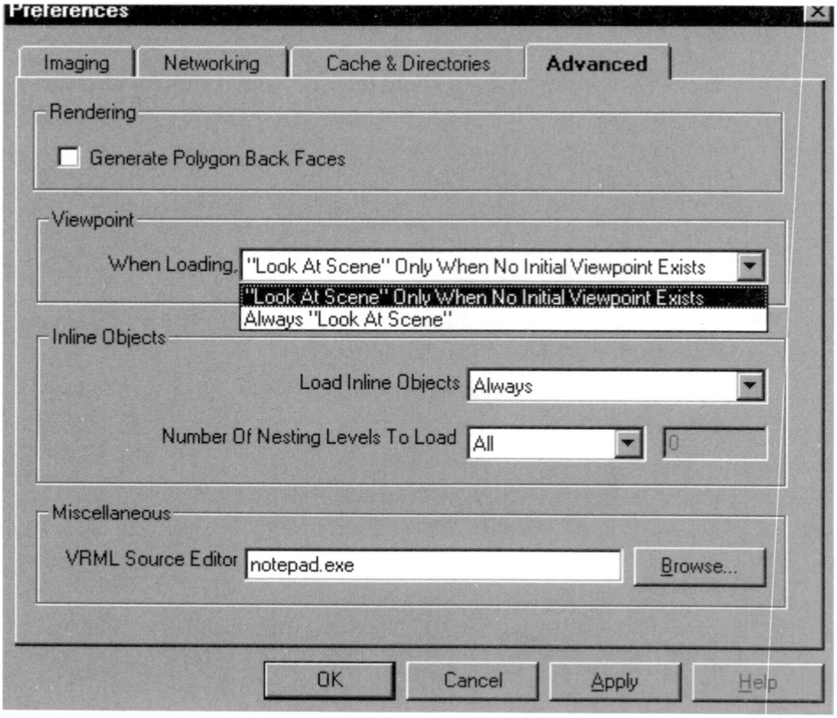

Figure C-4
WorldView's
Advanced Menu

The **Advanced** options allow you to specify the rendering
of a loading world. Depending on how you chose the following options, your speed will be either optimized or decreased. If you have a slow machine, do not mark **Generate
Polygon Back Faces**. The **Viewpoint** option allows you to
either load one object in the world at a time, or load all objects at once. **Inline Objects** allows you to load objects that
are not automatically loaded when a VRML world is first
accessed. The **VRML Source Editor** allows you to set an
external program that will be used to edit VRML code.
(please note that a VRML Editor must be a *text* editor, *not* a
Word Processor).

Show Navigator Tools allows you to load the Navigator toolbar when WorldView is loaded.

Show Toolbar allows you to load the Toolbar when WorldView is loaded.

Show World allows you to load the default world when World-View is loaded.

Show Status Bar will display a world loading status bar when downloading a world from the Internet.

Show Information Center will show information on how WorldView is performing.

7. In **Help** you can:
click on the **About** button that will show you version information about WorldView.

This version of WorldView does not come with a Help option.

The Toolbar in WorldView version 0.9f for Windows 3.1

To use the Toolbar you must be connected to the Internet and have TCP/IP running on your computer.

Back. The **Back** button allows you to go back to a previously accessed world.

Forward. The **Forward** button allows you to move forward to another world or Web page on the Internet.

Home. The **Home** button will reconnect you to the Intervista Web page (http://www.intervista.com).

Reload. The **Reload** button will reload a currently loaded world. This is especially helpful if a world file is loading slowly and/or is not loading correctly. This will also refresh your WorldView screen.

Open.   The **Open** button allows you to open up another location on the Internet. These are typically Internet addresses in alphanumerical format. (for example; http://this.is.my.address or http://999.999.888.123).

Stop.   The **Stop** button will stop the loading of a world.

The WorldView Toolbar in WorldView 1.0 Beta for Windows 95

The WorldView 1.0 Beta toolbar performs the same functions that you can find in the Menu bar. The toolbar serves as a shortcut menu to the Menu bar. One quick review of the buttons follows.

   This button will open either an Internet address or a local World file from your hard disk.

   This is the print button to print the current world.

   [These are the **Go Back** and **Go Forward** buttons to navigate through Internet pages.

   This isthe **Stop** loading button. It will stop the loading of a world.

   This is the **Reload** button to reload a particular world.

   This is the **Home** button, clicking this will connect you to the **Intervista** Web page on the Internet.

   These two buttons will load the **Favorite Place** menu and **Add to favorite Place** menu.

   This will display the **Information Center** for WorldView.

   This will display WorldView Version information.

The Navigation Bar in WorldView 0.9f for Windows 3.1

The Navigational bar has two modes for navigation: **Fly** and **Inspect**.

Fly Mode. The **Fly** mode allows you to fly over (or beneath) your world using the navigational tools on the Navigation bar. The **Fly** mode is typically more complex and will easily get you lost inside a world.

Inspect Mode. The **Inspect** mode allows you to walk through and around the world. This is typically a better navigational tool for close examination of the world you are viewing.

Navigation Tools

Move Forward

In Fly Mode this will move the virtual world and object closer to you.

In Inspect Mode this will move the virtual world and object further away from you.

Look Left   **Look Right**

Move Backward

In Fly Mode this will move the virtual world and object further away from you.

In Inspect Mode this will move the virtual world and object closer to you.

Look Up

In Fly Mode this will tilt the view angle up.

In Inspect Mode this will tilt the top of the virtual world or object toward you.

Tilt Left   **Tilt Right**

Look Down

In Fly Mode this will tilt the view angle down.

In Inspect Mode this will tilt the top of the virtual world or object away from you.

Move Up

In Fly Mode this will give the appearance of moving the virtual world or object down

In Inspect Mode this will move the virtual world or object up

Move Left **Move Right**

Move Down

In Fly Mode this will give the appearance of moving the virtual world or object up.

In Inspect Mode this will move the virtual world or object down.

Crosshair Navigation.   The **Crosshair** navigation tool is helpful for moving through the world using the left mouse button. Instead of using the Navigation buttons mentioned earlier, this is one tool that will simulate almost all of the options that are performed with the arrow buttons. The Cross Hair tool acts as a joystick to move around in your virtual world or manipulate an object freely in virtual space. By holding down the left mouse button and moving around in the Cross Hair space you will see that you can freely move the object any which way you desire. You can also hold down the Shift Key on your keyboard and the mouse to pan the image or the Control and the mouse to pitch or roll the image.

Restore.   The **Restore** button will reset the world VRML image to its original settings (very helpful when you get lost).

The WorldView 1.0B for Windows 95 Navigator bar

The Navigator Bar is the essential component in WorldView that allows you to navigate through the world. Many items in this version are similar to WorldView 0.9F, however, the 1.0Beta version allows more flexibility. Following is a brief description of the navigation tools.

Navigate: Moves your world forward, back, left, and right.

 Pan Mode: Moves your world up, down, left, and right.

 Tilt Mode: Tilts your view of the world up, down, left, and right.

 Inspect Mode: Rotates the world or object in front of you up, down, left, and right.

 Go To: Zoom up to any object or world by choosing it with the crosshair cursor.

 Straighten Up: Fixes the view of the object or world so you're standing up straight.

 Restore View: Jumps back to the original viewpoint of the object or world.

Appendix

D

Internet Access Providers (National)

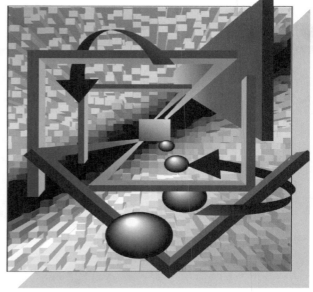

There is more to accessing the Internet than obtaining Netscape Navigator or some other browser. You need an *Internet Access Provider* to link up to. Software requirements, installation, and configuration details vary too widely to permit step-by-step instructions at this point. Contact the individual providers for prices and requirements.

22Solutions

Phone: (415) 431–9903

Fax: (415) 252–8600

URL: http://www.catch22.com/

A&W Internet Inc.

Phone: (604) 763–1176

Fax: (604) 860–1654

URL: http://www.awinc.com/

a2i communications

Phone: (408) 293–8078

Fax: (408) 263–0461

URL: http://www.rahul.net/

AbleCOM

Phone: (408) 441–6000

Fax: (408) 294–4646

URL: http://www.ablecom.net/

Access InfoSystems

Phone: (707) 422–1034

Fax: (707) 421–4683

URL: http://www.community.net/

Access Nevada, Inc

Phone: (702) 294–0480

Fax: (702) 293–3278

URL: http://www.accessnv.com/

AccessOne

Phone: (206) 827–5344

Fax: (206) 827–8792

URL: http://www.accessone.com/

Advanced Communications Exchange

Phone: (818) 787–9910

Fax: not available

URL: http://www.acex.com/

Aimnet Information Services

Phone: (408) 257–0900

Fax: (408) 257–5452

URL: http://www.aimnet.com/

Alternate Access, Inc

Phone: (206) 728–9585

Fax: not available

URL: http://www.aa.net/

American InfoMetrics

Phone: (209) 549–8333

Fax: (209) 549–8344

URL: http://ainet.com/

Annex Telecommunications

Phone: (818) 779–5646

Fax: (818) 779–5656

URL: http://www.annex.com/

ANS

Phone: (800) 456–8267

Fax: (703) 758–7717

URL: http://www.ans.net/

APlatform

Phone: (415) 941–2647

Fax: not available

URL: http://www.aplatform.com/

Arrownet

Phone: (517) 371–7100

Fax: (517) 371–2188

URL: http://www.arrownet.com/

AEnet

Phone: (408) 749–0501

Fax: not available

URL: http://www.arasmith.com/

auroraNET, Inc

Phone: (604) 294–4357

Fax: (604) 294–0107

URL: http://www.aurora.net/

Autobahn Internet

Phone: (503) 775–9523

Fax: not available

URL: http://www.northwest.com/

BaseNet

Phone: (618) 233–7625

Fax: (618) 244–9175

URL: http://www.basenet.net/

Bay Area Internet Solutions

Phone: (408) 447–8690

Fax: (408) 447–8691

URL: http://www.bayarea.net/

BBN Planet Corporation

Phone: (800) 472–4565

Fax: (617) 873–3599

URL: http://www.bbnplanet.com/

http://www.barnet.net/

Beckemeyer Development

Phone: (510) 530–9637

Fax: (510) 530–0451

URL: http://www.bdt.com/

Best Internet Communications

Phone: (415) 964–2378

Fax: (415) 691–4195

URL: http://www.best.com/

The Black Box

Phone: (713) 480–2684

Fax: not available

URL: http://www.blkbox.com/

Blue Sky

Phone: (800) 6–BLUSKY

Fax: (617) 270–4754

URL: http://www.bluesky.net/

Brainstorm Networks

Phone: (415) 988–2900

Fax: (415) 988–2906

URL: http://www.brainstorm.net/

California Internet

Phone: (510) 658–2177

Fax: (510) 652–3440

URL: not available

Caprica Internet Services

Phone: (213) 266–0822

Fax: not available

URL: http://www.caprica.com/

Carroll–Net

Phone: (201) 488–1332

Fax: not available

URL: http://www.carroll.com/

CASTLES Information Network

Phone: (707) 422–7311

Fax: (707) 422–5265

URL: http://www.castles.com/

CCINet

Phone: (403) 450–6787

Fax: (403) 450–9143

URL: http://www.ccinet.ab.ca/

CCnet Communications

Phone: (510) 988–0680

Fax: (510) 988–0689

URL: http://www.ccnet.com/

Central Connection

Phone: (818) 735–3000

Fax: (818) 879–9997

URL: http://centcon.com/

CERFnet

Phone: (800) 876–2373

Fax: (619) 455–3990

URL: http://www.cerf.net/

CICNet

Phone: (800) 947–4754

Fax: (313) 998–6105

URL: http://www.cic.net/

CineNet Communications

Phone: (310) 301–4500

Fax: (310) 301–4511

URL: http://www.cinenet.net/

Cloverleaf Network Services

Phone: (714) 895–3075

Fax: (310) 420–7255

URL: http://www.cloverleaf.com/

Colorado Internet Cooperative Association

Phone: (303) 443–3786

Fax: (303) 443–9718

URL: http://www.coop.net/coop/

Community ConneXion

Phone: (510) 601–9777

Fax: not available

URL: http://www.c2.org/

Compumedia, Inc.

Phone: (206) 623–8065

Fax: (206) 623–0706

URL: http://www.compumedia.com/

CompuTech

Phone: (509) 624–6798

Fax: (509) 624–9903

URL: http://www.iea.com/

Computer Systems Design Company

Phone: (303) 665–8053

Fax: (303) 443–0808

URL: http://www.csd.net/

Concentric Research Corp.

Phone: (800) 745–2747

Fax: (517) 895–0529

URL: http://www.cris.com/

CONNECTnet

Phone: (619) 450–0254

Fax: (619) 450–3216

URL: http://www.connectnet.com/

Connectus, Inc.

Phone: (702) 323–2008

Fax: (702) 323–9088

URL: http://www.connectus.com/

Connex Communications

Phone: (415) 386–7734

Fax: not available

URL: http://www.connex.com/

Cortland Electronics

Phone: (206) 217–0158

Fax: not available

URL: http://www.cortland.com/

CRL Network Services

Phone: (415) 837–5300

Fax: (415) 392–9000

URL: http://www.crl.com/

Crossroads Communications

Phone: (800) 892–7040

Fax: (602) 545–7470

URL: http://www.xroads.com/

CTS Network Services

Phone: (619) 637–3637

Fax: (619) 637–3630

URL: http://www.cts.com/

Cyber Access Internet Communications

Phone: (617) 396–0491

Fax: not available

URL: http://www.cybercom.net/

CyberDyne Systems

Phone: (503) 465–4743

Fax: not available

URL: http://www.cyber–dyne.com/

Cyberg8t Internet Services

Phone: (909) 621–1010

Fax: (909) 398–4621

URL: http://www.cyberg8t.com/

CyberGate

Phone: (800) NET–GATE

Fax: (305) 428–7977

URL: http://www.gate.net/

Cybergate Information Services

Phone: (209) 486–GATE

Fax: (209) 268–GATE

URL: http://www.cybergate.com/

CyberNet Communications

Phone: (404) 518–5711

Fax: not available

URL: http://www.atlwin.com/

CyberSpace

Phone: (206) 505–5577

Fax: not available

URL: http://www.cyberspace.com/

The Cyberspace Station

Phone: (619) 634–2894

Fax: not available

URL: http://www.cyber.net/

Dana Point Communications

Phone: (714) 443–4172

Fax: (714) 443–9516

URL: not available

DASH

Phone: (800) 624–8597

Fax: not available

URL: http://www.dash.com/

Data Transfer Group

Phone: (619) 220–8601

Fax: (619) 220–8324

URL: http://www.thegroup.net/

Databank

Phone: (913) 842–6699

Fax: (913) 842–8518

URL: http://www.databank.com/

DataTamers

Phone: (415) 364–7919

Fax: (415) 364–7919

URL: http://www.datatamers.com/

The Dayton Network Access Company

Phone: (513) 237–6868

Fax: not available

URL: http://www.dnaco.net/

Delphi

Phone: (800) 695–4005

Fax: (617) 441–4903

URL: http://www.dash.com/

DeltaNet

Phone: (714) 778–0370

Fax: (714) 778–1064

URL: http://www.deltanet.com/

The Destek Group

Phone: (603) 635–3857

Fax: (603) 635–7314

URL: http://www.destek.net/

DFWNet

Phone: (800) 2DFWNet

Fax: (817) 870–1501

URL: http://www.dfw.net/

The Diamond Lane

Phone: (510) 293–0633

Fax: (510) 782–4738

URL: http://www.tdl.com/

DigiLink Network Services

Phone: (310) 542–7421

Fax: (310) 542–1702

URL: http://www.digilink.net/

Digital Express

Phone: (800) 969–9090

Fax: (301) 847–5215

URL: http://www.digex.net/

Digital Popcorn

Phone: (818) 398–8018

Fax: not available

URL: http://www.pop.com/

Digital Telemedia Inc.

Phone: (212) 255–0827

Fax: not available

URL: http://www.emedia.net/

Direct Network Access

Phone: (510) 649–6110

Fax: (510) 649–7130

URL: http://www.dnai.com/

DirecTell

Phone: (801) 647–5838

Fax: (801) 647–9868

URL: http://www.ditell.com/

DirectNet

Phone: (213) 383–3144

Fax: (213) 383–8038

URL: http://www.directnet.com/

E–Znet Inc.

Phone: (716) 262–2485

Fax: (716) 262–3677

URL: http://www.eznet.net/

Earthlink Network

Phone: (213) 644–9500

Fax: (213) 644–9510

URL: http://www.earthlink.net/

Earthnet

Phone: (303) 546–6362

Fax: not available

URL: http://www.earthnet.net/

Edge Internet Services

Phone: (615) 726–8700

Fax: (615) 726–0665

URL: http://www.edge.net/

ElectriCiti Incorporated

Phone: (619) 338–9000

Fax: (619) 687–3879

URL: http://www.electriciti.com/

Electronic Communications Corp

Phone: (503) 385–3331

Fax: not available

URL: http://www.bendnet.com/

Electrotex

Phone: (800) 460–1801

Fax: (713) 639–6400

URL: http://www.electrotex.com/

elroNet

Phone: (212) 935–3110

Fax: (212) 935–3882

URL: http://www.elron.net/

emf.net

Phone: (510) 704–2929

Fax: (510) 704–2910

URL: http://www.emf.net/

EmiNet Domain

Phone: (407) 731–0222

Fax: (407) 737–8527

URL: http://www.emi.net/

Empire.Net, Inc.

Phone: (603) 889–1220

Fax: (603) 889–0366

URL: http://www.empire.net/

EmpireNet

Phone: (909) 787–4969

Fax: (909) 787–4987

URL: http://www.empirenet.com

EntertainNet

Phone: (303) 730–6050

Fax: (303) 739–6823

URL: http://www.entertain.com/

Envisionet

Phone: (303) 770–2408

Fax: (303) 770–2239

URL: http://www.envisionet.net/

Escape

Phone: (212) 888–8780

Fax: (212) 832–0210

URL: http://www.escape.com/

Eskimo North

Phone: (206) 367–7457

Fax: not available

URL: http://www.eskimo.com/

Europa Communications

Phone: (503) 222–9508

Fax: (503) 796–9134

URL: http://www.europa.com/

Evansville

Phone: (812) 479–1700

Fax: (812) 479–3439

URL: http://www.evansville.net/

Evergreen Internet

Phone: (602) 926–4500

Fax: (602) 926–8939

URL: http://www.enet.net/

Exodus Communications

Phone: (800) 263–8872

Fax: (408) 736–6843

URL: http://www.exodus.net/

Fairview Technology Centre

Phone: (604) 498–4316

Fax: (604) 498–3214

URL: http://www.ftcnet.com

ForFood

Phone: (714) 436–0736

Fax: not available

URL: http://www.forfood.com/

free.org

Phone: (715) 743–1700

Fax: not available

URL: not available

GeoNet Communications, Inc.

Phone: (415) 812–9130

Fax: (415) 494–8660

URL: http://www.geo.net/

GetNet International

Phone: (602) 943–3119

Fax: (602) 944–1510

URL: http://www.getnet.com/

Global Connect, Inc.

Phone: (804) 229–4484

Fax: (804) 229–6557

URL: http://www.gc.net/

Global Enterprise Services, Inc.

Phone: (800) 358–4437 x7325

Fax: (609) 897–7310

URL: http://www.jvnc.net/

Greenlake Communications

Phone: (810) 540–9380

Fax: (810) 540–0509

URL: http://www.cris.com/~greenlak/

HoloNet

Phone: (510) 704–0160

Fax: (510) 704–8019

URL: http://www.holonet.net/

Hypercon

Phone: (800) 652–2590

Fax: (713) 995–9505

URL: http://www.hypercon.com/

IBM Global Network

Phone: (800) 775–5808

Fax: not available

URL: http://www.ibm.com/globalnetwork/

Imagine Communications Corporation

Phone: (800) 5–MAGIXX, (800) 542–4499

Fax: (304) 291–2577

URL: http://www.imagixx.net/

Institute for Global Communications

Phone: (415) 442–0220

Fax: (415) 546–1794

URL: http://www.igc.apc.org/

Internet Access Houston

Phone: (713) 526–3425

Fax: (713) 522–5115

URL: http://www.iah.com/

IPSnet

Phone: (407) 426–8782

Fax: (407) 426–8984

URL: http://www.ipsnet.net

Kallback

Phone: (206) 286–5200

Fax: (206) 282–6666

URL: http://www.kallback.com/worldnet/

LogicalNet Corporation

Phone: (518) 452–9090

Fax: (518) 452–0157

URL: http://www.logical.net/

Northwest Internet Services

Phone: (503) 342–8322

Fax: (503) 343–1699

URL: http://www.rio.com/

NovaLink Interactive Networks

Phone: (800) 274–2814

Fax: not available

URL: not available

NTC's Earthlink.net

Phone: (800) 359–8425

Fax: (213) 644–9500

URL: http://www.earthlink.net/

Portal Information Network

Phone: (800) 433–6444

Fax: (408) 725–1580

URL: http://www.portal.com/

Performance Systems International (PSI)

Phone: (800) 82PSI82

Fax: (800) FAXPSI1

URL: http://www.psi.com/

Questar Microsystems, Inc.

Phone: (800) 925–2140

Fax: (206) 487–9803

URL: http://www.questar.com/

Traders' Connection

Phone: (800) 753–4223

Fax: (317) 322–4310

URL: http://www.trader.com/

Unlearning Foundation

Phone: (408) 423–8580

Fax: not available

URL: http://www.netcenter.com/air/air.html

Zocalo Engineering

Phone: (510) 540–8000

Fax: (510) 548–1891

URL: http://www.zocalo,net/

ZONE One Network Exchange

Phone: (212) 824–4000

Fax: (212) 824–4009

URL: http://www.zone.net

Appendix

VRML Specifications

VRML Documentation

Some Related Specifications

Related Documentation

Other Sources of Information: Web Sites with VRML Links

Specific VR Sites

VRML Documentation and Specifications Available through the VRML Repository

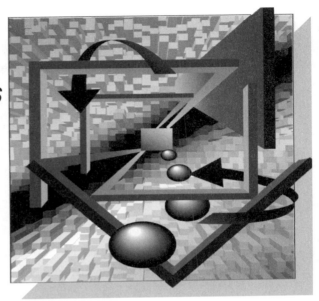

`(http://www.sdsc.edu/vrml/)`

VRML Specifications

VRML 1.0 Final Specification:

http://www.hyperreal.com/~mpesce/vrml/vrml.tech/vrml10-3.html

This is still the "official" specification for now.

The VRML 1.0 spec is available in other word-processing formats at:

http://www.fiu.edu/~jsosa01/vrml.html

A VRML-Enabled Version of VRML 1.0 Final Specification is available at:

http://www.virtpark.com/theme/vrml

This is a version of the VRML 1.0 Final Specification that includes links to VRML files with examples contained in the Spec and examples of VRML primitives.

VRML 1.1 Draft Specification:

http://vag.vrml.org/vrml-1.1.html

This is a draft version of the VRML 1.1 specification, the text of which appears as Appendix B. It will be officially finalized when two independent implementations on different platforms are available.

VRML Documentation

From Webspace to Cyberspace

http://www.eit.com/~kevinh/cspace/

Originally released as an internal white paper at EIT in December, 1994, it is now freely available. It is the sequel to "Entering the World Wide Web: A Guide to Cyberspace".

Mathematica To VRML—The Quick Way

http://www.rt66.com/buican/mathwww.htm

This quickly assembled page is meant to illustrate the simple approach to generating VRML files for 3D objects drawn by the Mathematica software package.

Stumbling into Cyberspace

http://www.sgi.com/ion/Spring_95/vrml.ezine.3.95.html

Notes on the history of the development of VRML.

VRML Design Notes

http://www.sgi.com/Technology/Inventor/VRML/

This is where the VRML 1.0 Final Specification came from. This document may still be useful since it provides more detailed information on the choices made during the design of the VRML 1.0 draft.

VRML Tutorial

http://honors.uhc.asu.edu:80/~joel/vrml

This is a quick VRML tutorial that teaches how to create VRML worlds by hand, without using an authoring tool.

VRML: Using 3D to Surf the Web

http://www.oki.com/vrml/VRML_S95.HTM

The VRML course notes from SIGGRAPH 95.

What is VRML?

http://livedv.com/Whitepapers/VRML.html

This gives an excellent overview of what VRML is, how it works, and what Web sites should look for in their VRML tools. Written by Konstantin Guericke, Executive Vice President of Caligari Corp.

Some Related Specifications

HTML 2.0 and 3.0 Specifications and Related Materials

http://www.w3.org/hypertext/WWW/MarkUp/MarkUp.html

HTML is the markup language for hypertext understood by all Web browsers. These pages discuss the HTML language, that is, its syntax and semantics, including information on the history of the language, status of the standard, and development issues.

The Java Language Specification

http://www.javasoft.com/1.0alpha3/doc/javaspec/javaspec_1.html

This document is a preliminary specification of the Java language. Both the specification and the language are subject to change.

PNG (Portable Network Graphics) Specification

http://www.w3.org/pub/WWW/TR/WD-png

The PNG format is intended to provide a portable, legally unencumbered, well-compressed, well-specified standard for lossless bit-mapped image files.

URI, URL, and URN Specifications and Discussion

http://www.w3.org/hypertext/WWW/Addressing/Addressing.html

The World Wide Web uses Uniform Resource Locators (URLs) to specify the location of files on other Web servers. A URL includes the type of resource being accessed (e.g., gopher, WAIS), the address of the server, the location of the file, and so on. Includes good information on URNs as well.

Related Documentation

3D Graphic Engines

http://www.cs.tu-berlin.de/~ki/engines.html

An overview of 3D engines, including RenderWare, QuickDraw 3D, Mesa, World

Toolkit, and VREAM.

Java Documentation

http://www.javasoft.com/documentation.html

This page provides links to all of the documentation for the Java language and the HotJava browser, in all of its various stages and formats.

Distributed Virtual Reality Resources

http://www.csh.rit.edu/~airwick/dist.html

Links to several sites with information on distributed virtual reality.

SGI Open Inventor

http://www.sgi.com/Technology/Inventor.html

Open Inventory is an object-oriented toolkit for developing interactive, 3D graphics applications. It also defines a standard file format for exchanging 3D data among applications. A subset of the Open Inventor file format forms the basis of the VRML 1.0 Specification.

Open Inventor FAQ

http://www.sgi.com/Technology/Inventor/FAQ.html

Open Inventor frequently asked questions.

Overview of the Open Inventor VRML Proposal

http://www.sgi.com/Technology/Inventor/VRML

The original proposal for a VRML design based on the Open Inventor file format.

Texture Mapping as a Fundamental Drawing Primitive

http://www.sgi.com/grafica/texmap/index.html

Many unusual uses for the important VRML concept of texture mapping are surveyed in this technical paper by Paul Haeberli and Mark Segal of Silicon Graphics.

Other Sources of Information: Web Sites with VRML Links

3DSite—a site dedicated to 3D computer graphics

http://www.lightside.com/3dsite/

An extensive collection of 3D computer graphics information, including VRML.

Construct

http://www.construct.net/

A VRML links page.

The Community Company (TCC) VRML Page
http://tcc.iz.net/tcc
A VRML links page.

Digest Links
http://www.well.com/www/caferace/vrml.html
A VRML links page.

Mesh Mart's VRML Library
http://cedar.cic.net/~rtilmann/mm/vrml.htm
More VRML worlds.

National Center for Supercomputing Applications (NCSA)
http://www.ncsa.uiuc.edu/General/VRML/VRMLHome.html
An excellent VRML links page.

Proteinman's Top Ten VRML Sites
http://www.virtpark.com/theme/proteinman/
A listing of VRML worlds, organized by size.

WebSpace VRML Sites
http://www.sgi.com/Products/WebFORCE/WebSpace/WebSpace-Sites.html
Some very nice VRML sites.

Spidaman's VRML-o-Rama
http://www.well.com/user/spidaman/vrml.html
An extensive VRML links page.

TGS Holodeck Home
http://www.sd.tgs.com/VRML/content.htm
TGS teamed with SGI in March of 1995 to develop the world's first VRML 1.0 browser, WebSpace(tm) Navigator. As a source licensee of Open Inventor, TGS is pushing VRML to new heights. TGS's Holodeck Home contains a collection of VRML 1.0 and future worlds showing next generation technology in Java, shared 3D, behaviors, and even more.

University of Toronto

http://www.utirc.utoronto.ca/AdTech/VRML/links.html

A VRML links page.

VResources, by Imaginative Entertainment

http://www.xmission.com/~gastown/imaginative/VResources.html

A well-organized catalog of VR-related information, including many VRML links.

The vrml.org

http://www.vrml.org/

Links to other VRML sites, plus a local VRML FTP site and test page.

VRML Forum at Wired.com

http://vrml.wired.com/

The original VRML forum, including information on the history of VRML, proto-VRML proposals, and archives of the WWW-VRML mailing list.

The VRML Foundry

http://www.mcp.com/general/foundry/

A web page dedicated to helping newcomers learn about and produce VRML worlds.

VRML Test Suite

http://www.chaco.com/vrml/test/

A repository of test files, designed to test browsers for compliance with the VRML specification. The intent is to create images of how various viewers display the files in the test suite, so writers of new viewers can see quickly what the more-compliant viewers do with various situations.

VRMLWorld

http://www.mecklerweb.com/netday/vrml.html

VRML World is a weekly on-line magazine that presents the latest news and information on VR-related, 3D interactive virtual worlds on the Internet. It covers not only VRML, but also other software such as Sun Microsystems's Hot Java, Apple's QuickTime VR, and more.

WWW Viewer Test Page

http://www-dsed.llnl.gov/documents/

A site for testing various Web viewers, including VRML browsers.

ZD Net's ZD3D

http://www.zdnet.com/~zdi/vrml/

Contains columns from VRML experts like Mark Pesce and Tony Parisi, in addition to Terminal Reality, ZD Net's own 3-D airport.

Specific VR Sites

Atlantis Cyberspace

http://vr-atlantis.com/

The concept of Atlantis Cyberspace is an innovative mix of entertainment, education, and retail, with the emphasis on entertainment.

Immersive Systems

http://www.immersive.com/

Immersive Systems develops and sells products based on Meme, a software technology for virtual reality. Unlike other VR systems, Meme has been designed from the ground up for multiuser networked virtual worlds.

Virtual Reality Association, Inc.

http://netspace.net.au./~splatt/vra/vra1.html

An Australian virtual reality users group.

VRASP—Virtual Reality Alliance of Students and Professionals

http://www.vrasp.org/vrasp/

The Virtual Reality Alliance of Students and Professionals is an international not-for-profit organization founded in March of 1992. The majority of members are professionals and include principals of most VR companies. All VRASPians benefit from our human resource support as well as the information disseminated in the magazine *PIX-Elation—Exploring Interactive Worlds*.

Appendix

F

VRML Browsers

Contents
of CD-Rom

Included on the CD-ROM supplied with this book are several VRML browsers as well as any examples and code used within the book. The contents are listed below.

VRML Browsers

WorldView Version 1.0, Beta 3: This is the popular VRML browser from Intervista Software used throughout the book.

VR Scout and **Pueblo**: Two propular VRML Applications from Chaco Communications Inc. **VR Scout** is a powerful VRML Browser and **Pueblo** is a 3D Graphical Interface for MUD (Multiuser Dimensions)

GLView: GLView is a VRML Browser and 3D File Viewer for Windows NT 3.51/4.0 and Windows 95 from EMD Enterprises.

Chapter 5 examples and code

Located on the CD-ROM in the **d:\Chap5** directory are all the files associated with Chater 5 : An Introduction to the VRML Language.

Chapter 6 examples and code

All of the examples in chapter 6 and their corresponding code is saved on the CD-ROM in the **d:\vrmlcode** directory. The figures that correspond with the example are matched also with the filenames of the VRML code files below.

FIGURE	FILENAME
Figure 6-1	cube.wrl
Figure 6-2	brick.wrl
Figure 6-3	wall.wrl
Figure 6-4	build.wrl
Figure 6-5	sphere.wrl
Figure 6-6	cylinder.wrl
Figure 6-7	cyl-disk.wrl
Figure 6-8	cyl-ring.wrl
Figure 6-9	cyl-dish.wrl
Figure 6-10	cone.wrl
Figure 6-11	spire.wrl
Figure 6-12	pin.wrl
Figure 6-13	wine_1.wrl
Figure 6-14	wine_2.wrl
Figure 6-16	wine_end.wrl
Figure 6-17	empire.wrl
Figure 6-18	icecream.wrl
	icecrm2.wrl
Figure 6-19	chair.wrl
Figure 6-20	base.wrl
Figure 6-21	arms.wrl
Figure 6-22	back.wrl
Figure 6-23	pillow.wrl
Figure 6-24	3bottles.wrl
	bottles3.wrl
Figure 6-25	egg.wrl
Figure 6-26	cigar.wrl
Figure 6-27	flatcan.wrl
Figure 6-28	dishes.wrl
Figure 6-29	ufo.wrl
Figure 6-30	ship.wrl
Figure 6-31	window.wrl
needs:	wood.gif
Figure 6-32	wow.wrl

Index

LICENSE AGREEMENT AND LIMITED WARRANTY

READ THE FOLLOWING TERMS AND CONDITIONS CAREFULLY BEFORE OPENING THIS DISK PACKAGE. THIS LEGAL DOCUMENT IS AN AGREEMENT BETWEEN YOU AND PRENTICE-HALL, INC. (THE "COMPANY"). BY OPENING THIS SEALED DISK PACKAGE, YOU ARE AGREEING TO BE BOUND BY THESE TERMS AND CONDITIONS. IF YOU DO NOT AGREE WITH THESE TERMS AND CONDITIONS, DO NOT OPEN THE DISK PACKAGE. PROMPTLY RETURN THE UNOPENED DISK PACKAGE AND ALL ACCOMPANYING ITEMS TO THE PLACE YOU OBTAINED THEM FOR A FULL REFUND OF ANY SUMS YOU HAVE PAID.

1. **GRANT OF LICENSE:** In consideration of your payment of the license fee, which is part of the price you paid for this product, and your agreement to abide by the terms and conditions of this Agreement, the Company grants to you a nonexclusive right to use and display the copy of the enclosed software program (hereinafter the "SOFTWARE") on a single computer (i.e., with a single CPU) at a single location so long as you comply with the terms of this Agreement. The Company reserves all rights not expressly granted to you under this Agreement.

2. **OWNERSHIP OF SOFTWARE:** You own only the magnetic or physical media (the enclosed disks) on which the SOFTWARE is recorded or fixed, but the Company retains all the rights, title, and ownership to the SOFTWARE recorded on the original disk copy(ies) and all subsequent copies of the SOFTWARE, regardless of the form or media on which the original or other copies may exist. This license is not a sale of the original SOFTWARE or any copy to you.

3. **COPY RESTRICTIONS:** This SOFTWARE and the accompanying printed materials and user manual (the "Documentation") are the subject of copyright. You may not copy the Documentation or the SOFTWARE, except that you may make a single copy of the SOFTWARE for backup or archival purposes only. You may be held legally responsible for any copying or copyright infringement which is caused or encouraged by your failure to abide by the terms of this restriction.

4. **USE RESTRICTIONS:** You may not network the SOFTWARE or otherwise use it on more than one computer or computer terminal at the same time. You may physically transfer the SOFTWARE from one computer to another provided that the SOFTWARE is used on only one computer at a time. You may not distribute copies of the SOFTWARE or Documentation to others. You may not reverse engineer, disassemble, decompile, modify, adapt, translate, or create derivative works based on the SOFTWARE or the Documentation without the prior written consent of the Company.

5. **TRANSFER RESTRICTIONS:** The enclosed SOFTWARE is licensed only to you and may not be transferred to any one else without the prior written consent of the Company. Any unauthorized transfer of the SOFTWARE shall result in the immediate termination of this Agreement.

6. **TERMINATION:** This license is effective until terminated. This license will terminate automatically without notice from the Company and become null and void if you fail to comply with any provisions or limitations of this license. Upon termination, you shall destroy the Documentation and all copies of the SOFTWARE. All provisions of this Agreement as to warranties, limitation of liability, remedies or damages, and our ownership rights shall survive termination.

7. **MISCELLANEOUS:** This Agreement shall be construed in accordance with the laws of the United States of America and the State of New York and shall benefit the Company, its affiliates, and assignees.

8. **LIMITED WARRANTY AND DISCLAIMER OF WARRANTY:** The Company warrants that the SOFTWARE, when properly used in accordance with the Documentation, will operate in substantial conformity with the description of the SOFTWARE set forth in the Documentation. The Company does not warrant that the SOFTWARE will meet your requirements or that the operation of the SOFTWARE will be uninterrupted or error-free. The Company warrants that the media on which the

SOFTWARE is delivered shall be free from defects in materials and workmanship under normal use for a period of thirty (30) days from the date of your purchase. Your only remedy and the Company's only obligation under these limited warranties is, at the Company's option, return of the warranted item for a refund of any amounts paid by you or replacement of the item. Any replacement of SOFTWARE or media under the warranties shall not extend the original warranty period. The limited warranty set forth above shall not apply to any SOFTWARE which the Company determines in good faith has been subject to misuse, neglect, improper installation, repair, alteration, or damage by you. EXCEPT FOR THE EXPRESSED WARRANTIES SET FORTH ABOVE, THE COMPANY DISCLAIMS ALL WARRANTIES, EXPRESS OR IMPLIED, INCLUDING WITHOUT LIMITATION, THE IMPLIED WARRANTIES OF MERCHANTABILITY AND FITNESS FOR A PARTICULAR PURPOSE. EXCEPT FOR THE EXPRESS WARRANTY SET FORTH ABOVE, THE COMPANY DOES NOT WARRANT, GUARANTEE, OR MAKE ANY REPRESENTATION REGARDING THE USE OR THE RESULTS OF THE USE OF THE SOFTWARE IN TERMS OF ITS CORRECTNESS, ACCURACY, RELIABILITY, CURRENTNESS, OR OTHERWISE.

IN NO EVENT, SHALL THE COMPANY OR ITS EMPLOYEES, AGENTS, SUPPLIERS, OR CONTRACTORS BE LIABLE FOR ANY INCIDENTAL, INDIRECT, SPECIAL, OR CONSEQUENTIAL DAMAGES ARISING OUT OF OR IN CONNECTION WITH THE LICENSE GRANTED UNDER THIS AGREEMENT, OR FOR LOSS OF USE, LOSS OF DATA, LOSS OF INCOME OR PROFIT, OR OTHER LOSSES, SUSTAINED AS A RESULT OF INJURY TO ANY PERSON, OR LOSS OF OR DAMAGE TO PROPERTY, OR CLAIMS OF THIRD PARTIES, EVEN IF THE COMPANY OR AN AUTHORIZED REPRESENTATIVE OF THE COMPANY HAS BEEN ADVISED OF THE POSSIBILITY OF SUCH DAMAGES. IN NO EVENT SHALL LIABILITY OF THE COMPANY FOR DAMAGES WITH RESPECT TO THE SOFTWARE EXCEED THE AMOUNTS ACTUALLY PAID BY YOU, IF ANY, FOR THE SOFTWARE.

SOME JURISDICTIONS DO NOT ALLOW THE LIMITATION OF IMPLIED WARRANTIES OR LIABILITY FOR INCIDENTAL, INDIRECT, SPECIAL, OR CONSEQUENTIAL DAMAGES, SO THE ABOVE LIMITATIONS MAY NOT ALWAYS APPLY. THE WARRANTIES IN THIS AGREEMENT GIVE YOU SPECIFIC LEGAL RIGHTS AND YOU MAY ALSO HAVE OTHER RIGHTS WHICH VARY IN ACCORDANCE WITH LOCAL LAW.

ACKNOWLEDGMENT

YOU ACKNOWLEDGE THAT YOU HAVE READ THIS AGREEMENT, UNDERSTAND IT, AND AGREE TO BE BOUND BY ITS TERMS AND CONDITIONS. YOU ALSO AGREE THAT THIS AGREEMENT IS THE COMPLETE AND EXCLUSIVE STATEMENT OF THE AGREEMENT BETWEEN YOU AND THE COMPANY AND SUPERSEDES ALL PROPOSALS OR PRIOR AGREEMENTS, ORAL, OR WRITTEN, AND ANY OTHER COMMUNICATIONS BETWEEN YOU AND THE COMPANY OR ANY REPRESENTATIVE OF THE COMPANY RELATING TO THE SUBJECT MATTER OF THIS AGREEMENT.

Should you have any questions concerning this Agreement or if you wish to contact the Company for any reason, please contact in writing at the address below or call the at the telephone number provided.

PTR Customer Service
Prentice Hall PTR
One Lake Street
Upper Saddle River, New Jersey 07458

Telephone: 201-236-7105